Marxist Archaeology Today

Historical Materialism Book Series

The Historical Materialism Book Series is a major publishing initiative of the radical left. The capitalist crisis of the twenty-first century has been met by a resurgence of interest in critical Marxist theory. At the same time, the publishing institutions committed to Marxism have contracted markedly since the high point of the 1970s. The Historical Materialism Book Series is dedicated to addressing this situation by making available important works of Marxist theory. The aim of the series is to publish important theoretical contributions as the basis for vigorous intellectual debate and exchange on the left.

The peer-reviewed series publishes original monographs, translated texts, and reprints of classics across the bounds of academic disciplinary agendas and across the divisions of the left. The series is particularly concerned to encourage the internationalization of Marxist debate and aims to translate significant studies from beyond the English-speaking world.

For a full list of titles in the Historical Materialism Book Series available in paperback from Haymarket Books, visit: www.haymarketbooks.org/series_collections/1-historical-materialism.

Marxist Archaeology Today

Historical Materialist Perspectives in Archaeology from America, Europe and the Near East in the 21st Century

Edited by
Ianir Milevski

Haymarket Books
Chicago, IL

First published in 2023 by Brill Academic Publishers, The Netherlands
© 2023 Koninklijke Brill NV, Leiden, The Netherlands

Published in paperback in 2024 by
Haymarket Books
P.O. Box 180165
Chicago, IL 60618
773-583-7884
www.haymarketbooks.org

ISBN: 979-8-88890-327-8

Distributed to the trade in the US through Consortium Book Sales and Distribution (www.cbsd.com) and internationally through Ingram Publisher Services International (www.ingramcontent.com).

This book was published with the generous support of Lannan Foundation, Wallace Action Fund, and the Marguerite Casey Foundation.

Special discounts are available for bulk purchases by organizations and institutions. Please call 773-583-7884 or email info@haymarketbooks.org for more information.

Cover art and design by David Mabb. Cover art is a detail of *A pattern of life 1, plan of Letchworth Garden City on William Morris Strawberry Thief fabric*, limited edition of 19 unique linocut prints on fabric (2019).

Printed in the United States.

Library of Congress Cataloging-in-Publication data is available.

Contents

List of Figures   VII
List of Tables   IX
Notes on Contributors   X

PART 1
Introduction

1   Marxist Archaeology Today: Observations on Dialectical Materialism in Archaeology, Its Sources and Tendencies   3
   Ianir Milevski

PART 2
Case Studies

2   Work and Subsistence in Preceramic Groups in Southeastern Mexico   39
   Patricia Pérez Martínez and Guillermo Acosta Ochoa

3   The Mode of Production of the Chalcolithic Period in Palestine   76
   Ianir Milevski, Bernardo Gandulla and Pablo Jaruf

4   An Exceptional Case of the Urban Revolution? A Marxist Perspective on the Preclassical Maya   107
   Marcus Bajema

5   Violence in the Prehispanic Andes: Materialities, Social Practices and the Moche Case   137
   Alex Gonzales-Panta and Henry Tantaleán

6   Marx, Marxism and Classical Antiquity   172
   Steve Roskams

7   Marxism, Historical Archaeology and Capitalism's 'Laws of Motion'   201
   LouAnn Wurst

PART 3
Balances and Perspectives

8   Marxism, Production, Society and Archaeology   231
      Vicente Lull

9   Politics and Social Ontology in Prehistory   261
      Vicente Lull, Rafael Micó, Cristina Rihuete Herrada and Roberto Risch

10 Vere Gordon Childe and Latin American Social Archaeology   270
      Marcelo Vitores

11 Transitions: from Archaeology to Historical Materialism   293
      Savas Michael-Matsas

    Index   325

Figures

2.1 Study Area. 52
2.2 Santa Marta: activity areas, Layer XVI, level 1. 56
2.3 Santa Marta: activity areas, Layer XVI, level 2. 57
2.4 Santa Marta: activity areas, Layer XVI, level 3. 58
2.5 Santa Marta: activity areas, Layer XVI, level 4. 59
2.6 Santa Marta: activity areas, Layer XVI, level 5. 60
2.7 Santa Marta: activity areas, Layer XVI, level 6. 61
2.8 Santa Marta: activity areas, Layer XVI, level 7. 62
2.9 Santa Marta: activity areas, Layer XVII, level 1. 63
2.10 Spoke shavers recovered from Santa Marta. 63
2.11 Pleistocene lithics from Santa Marta. 64
2.12 Faunal remains from Santa Marta. 65
2.13 Chemical analysis of occupation surfaces at Santa Marta, Layer XVI 65
2.14 Santa Marta: artefact SM 2472 with presence of wood cutting marks and artefact SM 2656 associated with the scraping work of plant tissue. 66
3.1 Map with the location of main sites and regions mentioned in the text. 78
3.2 Copper and other objects from Nahal Mishmar: 1. standard n° 21; 2. standard n° 41; 3. standard n° 50; 4. sceptre n° 126; 5. crown n° 7; 6. ivory tusk n° 2; 7. zoomorphic decorated mace-head n° 153. 89
3.3 Ossuaries: 1. ossuary from Peqi'in; 2. ossuary from Peqi'in; 3. ossuary from et-Taiyiba; 4. ossuary from Benei Beraq. 90
3.4 Figurines: 1. female figurine from Gilat; 2. zoomorphic figurine from En Gedi; 3. male figurine from Quleh. 91
3.5 Burial modes in the late prehistory of Palestine. 93
3.6 Model of socio-economic formations for the Chalcolithic and Early Bronze Age in the southern Levant. 95
5.1 Location of the main Moche sites mentioned in the text. 147
5.2 Map of Huaca de la Luna. 151
5.3 View of complete articulated individual, with their hands tied in back. 151
5.4 Modelled ceramic vessel, represents a prisoner tied to a tree and attacked by birds. 152
5.5 Modelled ceramic vessel and wooden mace recovered from Tomb 1 of the Platform II, in Huaca de la Luna. 153
5.6 Mural depicting prisoners in Huaca de la Luna. 156
7.1 The Niagara House. 211
7.2 Resettlement Administration poster. 213
7.3 The McNish barn, photograph from the 1936 Acquisition Plan for the Township of Hector, Schuyler County, New York. 215

7.4   Photo of the workers at Coalwood (c. 1901).   220
8.1   The constitution of society: socialisation and naturalisation.   249
8.2   The development of productive forces.   250
8.3   The unfolding of production.   254
8.4   The mediating role of distribution in the processes of production.   257
10.1   Vere Gordon Childe and workmen at Skara Brae, Britain (c. 1930).   271
10.2   Luis Guillermo Lumbreras at Lima, Peru.   278
10.3   Luis Felipe Bate at Ocozocoautla, Chiapas, México.   279

Tables

2.1 Types of hunter-gatherer societies.   48
2.2 Equivalences in the typology of hunter-gatherer sites.   50
2.3 Association of traces of use and identification of micro-remains.   68
3.1 Accepted chronology of the late prehistory of Palestine.   79
3.2 Parameters for the Chalcolithic period and the Early Bronze Age in Palestine, economics and social relations.   85
4.1 State and community in the preclassic period lowland Maya region.   118

Notes on Contributors

Guillermo Acosta Ochoa
is a full-time researcher at the Institute of Anthropological Research (UNAM) and co-head of the Laboratory of Prehistory and Human Evolution (IIA), and the director of various projects related to prehistory and American settlement, early agriculture and development of social complexity. He has developed applications of digital photogrammetry in the recording of archaeological heritage and in analysis of starch grains in archeology for the study of early agriculture. He recently directed the project 'El Desarrollo de las Sociedades Agrarias en la Cuenca de México', with the objective of evaluating the role played by the communities of the Playa (6000–4500 BC) and Zohapilco (3000–2200 BC) phases in the adoption of the patterns of residence, first settlers and agriculture-based subsistence system that characterises 'formative' societies.

Marcus Bajema
is an independent researcher based in the Netherlands. He gained his PhD in Archaeology from Leiden University in 2015, with a comparison of the earliest states of Mycenaean Greece and the lowland Maya area. His main research interests are comparative studies in history and archaeology, and current debates in Marxist theory. Currently, he is engaged in research for a book project on the implications of debates on aleatory materialism for Marxist understandings of history. The results of this study will engender different ideas for transcending capitalism from the perspective of aleatory materialism and the pluralist historical perspective derived from it.

Bernardo Gandulla
is a retired teacher of the University of Buenos Aires, the National University of Luján and Salvador's University. He received his PhD in History at the University of Buenos Aires, where he was researcher at the Ancient Oriental History Institute 'Dr. Abraham Rosenvasser'. His research focuses on the ancient history of the Levant, particularly cultural identities and population movements. Major publications include a book about the multicultural background of ancient Hebrew identity, titled *Los hebreos en el gran Canaán* (2005), and an edited volume titled *La etnicidad en la Mesopotamia Antigua* (1995).

Alex Gonzales-Panta
has a bachelor's degree in Social Sciences, with a specialisation on Archaeology, from Universidad Nacional Mayor de San Marcos in Peru and a master's in Pre-

history from Universidad Autónoma de Barcelona. He is a visiting professor at the Universidad Nacional San Antonio Abad in Cusco (UNSAAC). He has participated in different archaeological research projects on the Peruvian Andean coast and highlands. He is currently a PhD candidate at Universidad Autònoma de Barcelona, where he focuses on the history of violence in the Andes, particularly in societies from the north coast of Peru, during the last millennium before our era. His research includes the study of socioeconomic conditions, funerary practices and power relations. In addition, it aims to discuss how explanations of past violence influence present economic and social ideologies in the Andes.

Pablo Jaruf
is Academic Secretary at the Ancient Oriental History Institute 'Dr. Abraham Rosenvasser' at the University of Buenos Aires. He took his PhD in History at the same university and at present holds a postdoctoral fellowship at the National Scientific and Technical Research Council of Argentina. He teaches at the University of Buenos Aires, the National University of Luján and the Higher Institute 'Dr. Joaquín V. González'. His research focuses on the interrelation between socio-economic changes and burial and iconographic expressions during the Chalcolithic Period and Early Bronze Age I in the Southern Levant.

Vicente Lull
is Emeritus Professor in Prehistory at the Universitat Autònoma de Barcelona. He has worked with Cristina Rihuete Herrada, Rafael Micó and Roberto Risch since the 1980s on the development of a critical archaeological theory and method. His extensive scientific trajectory has focused on the Bronze Age societies of the western Mediterranean, in particular on El Argar in southeast Iberia, and on the later prehistory of the Balearic Islands. In terms of substantive theories, he has made remarkable contributions in the field of archaeological theory in general and the theory of the origin of the state in particular. His publications include *La "cultura" de El Argar* (1983), *Arqueología del origen del Estado: las teorías* (together with Rafael Micó, 2007), subsequently translated into English (2011), and *Los objetos distinguidos. La Arqueología como excusa* (2007).

Savas Michael-Matsas (Sabetai B. Matsas)
has been active in the international Marxist movement from the years of the military dictatorship in Greece up to now. He was born in Athens in 1947 and has an MD (Faculty of Medicine, University of Athens) and later studied

Philosophy, Political Economy and Cultural Studies in Paris. Michael-Matsas has taught postgraduate programmes in Philosophy and Cultural Studies (University of Athens, Panteion University of Athens and Aristotle University of Thessaloniki). He has lectured in universities all over the world, including New York University, London School of Economics, Glasgow University, Moscow State 'Lomonosov' University, Wuhan University, Universidade de São Paulo and Universidad de Buenos Aires. Michael-Matsas is a member of the editorial board of the theoretical journals *Critique* (editor Pr. Hillel Ticktin, University of Glasgow) and *Alternativi* (editor Pr. Alexander Buzghalin, Moscow State 'Lomonosov'). He is the author of many books and articles in Greek on cultural studies, politics and philosophy from a dialectical Marxist viewpoint. His essays and articles have been published in English, French, Spanish, Portuguese, Italian, Hungarian, Russian, Chinese, and Turkish.

Rafael Micó
is Professor in Prehistory at the Universitat Autònoma de Barcelona. He has worked with Cristina Rihuete Herrada, Vicente Lull and Roberto Risch since the 1980s on the development of a critical archaeological theory and method. His special contribution has been made in the field of the origins of the state theory and related archaeological research, leading to the publication *Arqueología del origen del Estado: las teorías* (together with Vicente Lull, 2007), subsequently translated into English (2011). His fieldwork has mainly been concerned with the archaeological knowledge of several late prehistory societies (third–first millennia cal BCE) in the Western Mediterranean. The main efforts have focused on the Early Bronze Age in Southeastern Iberia (El Argar society, c. 2200–1550 cal BCE) and the first millennium cal BCE in the Balearic Islands.

Ianir Milevski
is a researcher in the Multidisciplinary Institute of History and Humanities of the National Scientific and Technical Research Council, Argentina, and member of the programme 'Raíces', of the Ministry of Science and Technology of Argentina, and Visiting Professor in that country at different universities. He was previously a senior archaeologist in the Israel Antiquities Authority, fellow of the W.F. Albright Institute of Archaeological Research in Jerusalem, and also part of the TOPOI program at the German Institute of Archaeology in Berlin. Using Marxist theory, his research focuses on socio-economic issues of the late prehistory in the Levant. His current research projects include a long-term study of the social formations of the Neolithic, Chalcolithic and Early Bronze periods, a study of burial practices in those periods and a social history of art in the late prehistory of the Levant.

Patricia Pérez Martínez
is Laboratory Head (Laboratorio de Tecnología de Cazadores-Recolectores) at the Escuela Nacional de Antropología e Historia, where she also teaches classes on topics related to American prehistory and lithic technology. She has specialised in microscopic-based functional analysis and in the identification of micro-residues in lithic artefacts. A collaborator of various projects ('Cazadores del Trópico', 'Clovis Groups and the Initial Settlement of the Mexican Southeast', 'The Development of Agrarian Societies in the Basin of Mexico') under the direction of Dr. Guillermo Acosta Ochoa, she also co-directs the projects 'The first settlers of Sierra Gorda, Guanajuato' and 'Settlement, Initial Agriculture and Village Societies in the Basin of Mexico'.

Cristina Rihuete Herrada
is Professor in Prehistory at the Universitat Autònoma de Barcelona and Director of the Archaeological Museum of Son Fornés (Mallorca). She has worked with Vicente Lull, Rafael Micó and Roberto Risch since the 1980s on the development of a critical archaeological theory and method. Her main research interests include feminist theory, physical anthropology and the socioeconomic development of the western Mediterranean during later prehistory. Her research covers all aspects of the archeological activity, from the excavation of key sites (La Bastida, Tira del Lienzo, La Almoloya, Son Fornés) and investigation – including a wide array of interdisciplinary analyses – to dissemination and public presentation of archaeological sites. Her publications include *Bioarqueología de las prácticas funerarias* (2002) and *Ideología y Sociedad en la Prehistoria de Menorca* (1999, with Vicente Lull, Rafael Micó and Roberto Risch).

Roberto Risch
is Professor in Prehistory at the Universitat Autònoma de Barcelona and ICREA Acadèmia Research Fellow. He has worked with Cristina Rihuete Herrada, Vicente Lull and Rafael Micó since the 1980s on the development of a critical archaeological theory and method. His research is mainly concerned with economic theory, technology, social exploitation, ideology and ecology. He has participated in the investigation of several prehistoric sites in Spain, Germany and India, and conducted ethnoarchaeological fieldwork in Ghana and Mali. His publications include *Recursos naturales, medios de producción y explotación social* (2002), and since 2012 he is co-editor of the yearly international proceedings of the Museum of Prehistory of Halle (Germany), recently devoted to 'Surplus without the State: Political forms in Prehistory' (2018) and 'Ritual violence – Rituals of violence' (2020).

Steve Roskams
is Senior Lecturer at the Department of Archaeology, University of York. After spending ten years in rescue archaeology, directing excavations in Carthage and in London, he has recently worked in Algeria and Beirut and at a range of sites across the UK. He is interested in both theory and practice in archaeological fieldwork. The former involves the construction of Marxist perspectives on transitions within and beyond the Roman period, the latter includes the development of excavation methods and analytical techniques, and how commercial fieldwork can engage local communities. Recent publications include 'The Limitation of Water Flow and the Limitations of Postmodernism' (http://doi.org/10.16995/traj.371) and *Landscape and Settlement in the Vale of York* (https://library.oapen.org/handle/20.500.12657/39942).

Henry Tantaleán
studied Archaeology at San Marcos National University. He got his master's and PhD in Prehistoric Archaeology at the Universidad Autónoma de Barcelona. He has been Visiting Professor in different universities around the globe, including Universidad Autónoma de Barcelona, Escuela Superior Politénica del Litoral, Stanford University, Universidad de Sao Paulo, and Université de Rennes. Currently he is a full professor at San Marcos National University. His research focuses on the history of archaeology, theoretical archaeology and ancient Andean States. He led the Chincha Archaeological Program in the Peruvian Southern Coast and the Chicama Archaeological Program in the Peruvian Northern Coast. He has published several scientific articles and books. Recent publications include *Peruvian Archaeology: A Critical History* (Routledge, 2014) and *The Ancient Andean States: Political Landscapes of Pre-Hispanic Peru* (Routledge, 2020).

Marcelo Vitores
is an archaeologist researching and teaching at Universidad Nacional de Luján (UNLu). He graduated with honours from Universidad de Buenos Aires (UBA). Vitores is currently a research fellow and teaching assistant at UNLu, where he teaches undergraduate prehistory and anthropology courses. While his research focuses on hunter-gatherer pottery technology from late Holocene Patagonia, he has wider interests. He approaches some methodological aspects of archaeological enquiry, such as regional ethnohistory and the history of the discipline, and the impact of digital techniques in data acquisition and management. Other topics relevant to his research are public outreach, graphic communication and the impact of pseudo-archaeology. He serves as a member of the editorial board of the journal *Atek Na* and as editor of the Archaeology

section of *Cuadernos de Antropología*, both open access journals from UNLu. He is also a frequent collaborator of ArqueoLab-UBA, a cultural lab strongly oriented to science communication and archaeometry, where he assesses digitisation and photogrammetry aimed at cultural heritage.

LouAnn Wurst
is Professor in the Industrial Heritage and Archaeology programme in the Department of Social Sciences at Michigan Technological University. Her research focuses on Marxist theory and historical and industrial archaeology to study capitalism, labour, class struggle, gender and ideology in the United States during the nineteenth and twentieth centuries. Her current research projects include a long-term study of the transformations in capitalist agriculture based on excavations of 22 farms in Central New York's Finger Lakes National Forest; research on industrial labour in the lumber industry, emphasising the cordwood lumber camps operated by the Cleveland-Cliffs Iron Company in the Munising area of Michigan; and questions about unfree labour in the northern forest, focusing on the Civilian Conservation Corps and the German prisoner of war Camp Au Train in Michigan's Hiawatha National Forest.

PART 1

Introduction

∴

CHAPTER 1

Marxist Archaeology Today: Observations on Dialectical Materialism in Archaeology, Its Sources and Tendencies

Ianir Milevski

1 Introduction

The aims of this volume are to gather together papers written by a number of scholars utilising the methods of dialectical materialism, or historical materialism,[1] attesting not only to what Marxism has contributed to archaeology, but also to what archaeology has, and can, contribute to Marxism as a method for interpreting the history of humanity and for applying a historical perspective towards ending the exploitation of present-day capitalism.

This chapter is meant to highlight some aspects of dialectical materialism in the light of works of preceding scholars, synthesising their perspectives relating to archaeology, emphasising aspects of Marxism implicit in archaeology – specifically in its sources and some of its tendencies. Mainly, this chapter will address the sources and components of Marxism and their application to archaeology, the place of dialectical materialism in what was called 'alternative archaeologies', and the need to renew the application of this method based on the combination of theory and concrete archaeological studies. Also summarised here are the chapters presented in this volume, which comprise several case studies as well as papers that offer perspectives on how Marxist archaeology should be understood. In this chapter, I defend archaeology as praxis and provide some perspective on how Marxist archaeology should be performed. However, it is by no means my intention to present here the whole and complete picture of this subject, if such a thing could exist.

Some time ago, Matthew Spriggs asked what the value of a Marxist perspective in archaeology is, or, in other words, if Marxism can produce useful interpretations of the archaeological record.[2] Randal McGuire asked a similar

---

1 'Historical materialism' and 'dialectical materialism' will be used here as synonyms, although different authors prefer one of the two labels.
2 Spriggs 1984.

question in the second edition of his volume on Marxist archaeology.³ What was the meaning of these questions 40 and 20 years ago? Are they still relevant now? Are archaeologists still dubious of the kind of archaeological analysis we wish to present here?

In an article on Marxist archaeology by Francesco Iacono, published in one of the last handbooks on archaeological theory,⁴ the author noted that a complex relationship existed between Marxism and archaeology. This is true, but on condition that we point out the many 'ghosts', i.e. influences, the latter discipline has received from dialectical materialism, as suggested by Thomas Patterson,⁵ who showed that Marx's thought was deeply embedded in the interior of modern archaeology.⁶ From my viewpoint, Marxist interpretations have not only produced the most interesting and most utilised concepts in archaeology, such as the Neolithic and Urban revolutions as put forward by V. Gordon Childe,⁷ but have also created a corpus of methodological instruments to study human societies into the twenty-first century.

Karl Marx and Friedrich Engels were pioneers in interpreting the little available data at that time to study prehistoric and ancient societies,⁸ and their concept of social evolution regarding modes of production, technology and artefacts made in different (archaeological) periods was innovative and insightful. The following sentences synthesise the key concept that I wish to transmit:

> Relics of by-gone instruments of labour possess the same importance for the investigation of extinct economic forms of society, as do fossil bones for the determination of extinct species of animals. It is not the articles made, but how they are made, and by what instruments, that enables us to distinguish different economic epochs. Instruments of labour not only supply a standard of the degree of development to which human labour has attained, but they are also indicators of the social conditions under which labour is carried on.⁹

---

3 McGuire 2002.
4 Iacono 2018.
5 Patterson 2003.
6 And see also Wolff 1982.
7 Childe 1936, and 1942. And see Trigger 1980.
8 Patterson 2009.
9 Marx 1977, p. 286.

These sentences also show that the dialectical materialist method can explain these developments, not in a linear-evolutionary way but as a combination of uneven and combined processes that took place in different regions of the world.[10]

2   Marxist Archaeology and 'Alternative Archaeologies'

2.1   *Marxist Archaeological Trajectories*

With respect to early, comprehensive works on Marxist archaeology, we begin with Thomas Patterson, who in his volumes on Marx and archaeology had the goal to engage directly with Marx's works rather than those of the Marxist archaeological tradition.[11] As he wrote in one of these volumes, his research is Marxian rather than Marxist.[12] Of course, his were not the first volumes on the subject (as Patterson himself already recognised) and aside from Spriggs[13] and McGuire,[14] the volumes of Maurice Godelier,[15] Ángel Palerm[16] and others should be mentioned. Godelier and Maurice Bloch[17] actually made the association between the ancient world and Marxism, though not from an archaeological perspective but rather from an anthropological one.

Childe was no doubt the first Marxist-orientated archaeologist who elaborated dialectical materialist perspectives,[18] beginning with his adaptation of the interpretations of Lewis Morgan[19] and Engels.[20] Even if – as Nicolas Thomas concluded[21] – the positions of Childe have sometimes been obscured, dismissed and misread, it was under his influence in Latin America that a whole archaeological school, *Arqueología Social Latinoamericana* (Latin American Social Archaeology), developed after the Cuban revolution in 1959.[22] Luis Lum-

---

10 Letter from Marx to Zasulich, March 8, 1881; Marx and Engels 1964, nr. 164, p. 20; Novack 1974, and 2002, pp. 75–122; Plekhanov 1977, p. 635.
11 Patterson 2003.
12 Patterson 2008, p. ix.
13 Spriggs 1984.
14 McGuire 2002.
15 Godelier 1977.
16 Palerm 2008; Patterson 2008.
17 Bloch 1983.
18 Trigger 1980; McGuire 2006.
19 Morgan 1964.
20 Engels 1972.
21 Thomas 1982.
22 See Vitores, this volume.

breras[23] and Luis Bate[24] were some of the most representative archaeologists of this school. All the above-mentioned Marxist archaeologists were labelled as belonging to western Marxism. Marxist archaeology as created in the western capitalistic world, both in the imperialistic and the colonial and semi-colonial countries, was essentially a reflection of social struggle. However, archaeologists – mainly in the former Soviet Union and other so-called East Bloc countries – produced several works at the beginning of the twentieth century utilising different Marxist perspectives.[25]

Dialectical materialist perspectives in archaeology in countries that exhibited capitalist expropriation can be divided into two periods.[26] The first period occurred with the ascent of the revolutions, mainly the October Revolution, with new perspectives that tried to develop new terminologies for ancient societies. The second period was marked by the introduction, by force and 'from above', of supposedly Marxist categories in archaeology according to the agenda of the bureaucratic regimes, which also expropriated the revolutions and the working classes in favour of the parties and the functionaries of the state.[27] Archaeology in these countries had a 'distorted Marxist character', as it was inspired by the fact that it was supposedly of the 'official' Marxism. Archaeologists in many cases had to ally themselves with the bureaucratic leadership of those states under the aegis of Stalinism. Those who did not agree with Stalinist ideas suffered harsh repression and were removed from their positions, imprisoned or assassinated under false accusations.[28] The result of this situation is that today, after the restoration of capitalism in those countries, it is hard to find an archaeologist that claims he or she is a Marxist.

Many of the above-mentioned processes have been presented and described in the work of Leo S. Klejn.[29] Further, articles have been written in China to examine the history of archaeological thought there in an apparently critical way.[30] But, it seems that in many of these countries, the baby has been thrown out with the bathwater. Others simply present a backlash to Marxist theories and misunderstand the Stalinist phenomenon in Eastern European countries.[31]

---

23 Lumbreras 1974.
24 Bate 1984.
25 Trigger 1989, pp. 326–44; Klejn 2003, and 2012.
26 And see McGuire 1993, pp. 103–4.
27 On the character of the regime in the Soviet Union we follow Trotsky 1930.
28 Klejn 1993.
29 And see Marder et al. 2018, and Bajema 2019.
30 Olsenn 1987; Von Falkenhausen 1993; Wang 1997.
31 For example, see Lozny 2017, and particularly Milisauskas 2017.

For instance, in the Czech and Slovak republics, Marxism was introduced into archaeology 'from above' after 1948. According to Eduard Krekovič and Martin Bača, this influence changed as a result of the revolt against the bureaucratic regime and the ruling Soviet Union in 1968.[32] According to the same authors, few genuine efforts were made following this event to establish a scientific Marxist archaeology.

For China, the first years after the revolution of 1949 were important since the leadership of the state founded an organisational framework for archaeological fieldwork and research under the Chinese Bureau of Cultural Relics. During the first ten years of the Popular Republic of China, archaeologists were sent to the Soviet Union to learn fieldwork and research methods from their Russian colleagues. In the early years of the Popular Republic of China, archaeology followed the stadial Stalinist concept in which all societies underwent the same sequence of social formations in their history. Engels's *Origins of the Family*[33] and Stalin's *Dialectical and Historical Materialism*[34] were the main works in the curricula of its history and archaeology departments.[35] Some Chinese archaeologists, such as Su Bingqi (a founder of the Archaeology Program at Beijing [Peking] University),[36] rejected the Stalinist model of the transition from primitive society to slave society, and utilised an independent dialectical materialist method and successfully escaped the official doctrinaire archaeology of that country.[37]

After the revolution, the newly established leadership tolerated the freedom and privilege of intellectuals, including some Chinese archaeologists,[38] but only for a short period. Gradually the leadership imposed on scientific research what they considered 'Marxist ideology', requiring archaeologists to conduct their work according to the 'correct political line' and to eliminate 'bourgeois ideology' and ascribe to the 'proletarian ideology'.[39] Since 1968 and

---

32 Krekovič and Bača 2013.
33 Engels 1972.
34 Stalin 1940.
35 Liangren 2011, pp. 1052–3; Wang 1996, pp. 35–6. The same occurred in the Soviet Union, where all prehistorians working on the Palaeolithic period were obliged to recite Engels and Stalin. And see Klejn 1973, p. 697; Kriiska 2006, p. 65.
36 Su Bingqi 1987, and 1990; see also Su Bingqi, quoted by Wang 1997, p. 35.
37 Liangren 2013, pp. 897–900. But see Shelach 2004, and especially Shelach-Lavi 2019, pp. 24–5, in which Su Bingqi's paradigm is seen to have evolved into a structure supporting the linear continuity of Chinese history from the Neolithic period to present days, dovetailing the construction of a nationalist identity.
38 Wang 2011.
39 Cheng 1965; Chang 1977; Tong 1995; Wang 2011, p. 47.

after the Cultural Revolution, an 'archaeology of workers and farmers' has been pursued.[40] Since the 1980s, the Chinese government has adopted an 'open door' policy and ploughed ahead with capitalistic economic reforms. In this framework, according to Lotar von Falkenhausen,[41] the golden age of archaeology in China came to an end, returning to the large-scale looting of archaeological sites and to the practices of before the Chinese revolution of 1949.

A similar phenomenon happened in North Korean archaeology. From the beginning, it was nationalistic in orientation, mixing features from the programme of Soviet archaeology and the 'socialist patriotism' of both the Soviet Union and Japan.[42] In contrast to others, the archaeologist Toh Yu-ho[43] did not support the official archaeology.[44] For instance, Toh refused to accept the historical particularism of prehistoric Korea. However, he was heavily influenced by the culture-historical approach, following Montelius.[45]

2.2   Marxism and 'Alternative Archaeologies'

In 1984, Bruce Trigger suggested there are three types of archaeologies – nationalist, colonialist and imperialist.[46] Trigger's basic typology was intended to explore variability in archaeology as it related to the position of countries within the modern capitalistic world, or as defined by Vladimir I. Lenin: imperialist, colonial and semi-colonial countries.[47]

This tripartite division was corrected and supplemented in 2008 by Trigger,[48] although, in my opinion, he wrongly included the archaeology of the Soviet Union from 1929 onwards in the imperialist type.[49] Furthermore, Trigger did not correctly address the archaeologies of China, which he dubbed simply as

---

40   This new tendency is evident in several works, such as the paper published in the journal *Wenwu* in 1976, under the title 'New things happening at the front line of archaeology and cultural relics. A story of the archaeology and cultural relics training class for those who are farmers and workers at Jinancheng'; see Wang 2011, pp. 70–1.
41   Von Falkhausen 1993, pp. 843–4.
42   Lee 2013; see also Kim 2008, p. 124.
43   For example, Toh 1962, quoted by Lee 2013.
44   Lee 2013, p. 406. And see also Trigger 2008, p. 189.
45   For example, Montelius 1899.
46   Trigger 1984a.
47   Lenin 1977b, pp. 222–30.
48   Trigger 2008. For instance, archaeology in Israel was dubbed as colonialist instead of nationalist. This was changed by Trigger following Abu el-Haj 2001. And see Milevski and Gandulla 2016.
49   Trigger 1984a, p. 365.

nationalist.[50] Although nationalism was indeed a component of the politics of the leadership of China, and nationalist elements were present in the country's archaeology after the revolution[51] – as in the Soviet Union after the 1930s – Chinese archaeology was not primarily nationalistic.[52]

Despite this criticism, Trigger's work demonstrates his broad knowledge of archaeology in the Soviet Union and in countries of the so-called Sino-Soviet bloc. For instance, he rightly points out that 'no previous government in history was so openly and energetically in favour of science' as the Soviet Union was in the first years of the revolution. This enthusiasm of course extended to archaeology, exemplified by the foundation of the Russian Academy of Material Culture.[53] Here, as in other aspects of the Soviet Union, archaeology became an important topic after the October Revolution, until a bureaucratic and antirevolutionary regime took power with Stalin, which deformed and destroyed the achievements of the revolution. Nonetheless, archaeology in the Soviet Union also produced highly critical and knowledgeable personalities such as Klejn, who opposed Stalinism.[54]

3 Sources and Components of Marxist Archaeology

If we return to the basis of Marxism and the history of the relationship between Marxism and archaeology, we will find that this dialogue – as Palerm, McGuire and Patterson[55] have called the process – involves a dialectic developed in diverse contexts and at many levels. Indeed, following Lenin's well-known text, the integral parts of Marx's thought were based on three basic disciplines: philosophy, economics, and socialist politics. For Lenin, the Marxist doctrine is the legitimate successor to 'the best that man produced in the nineteenth century', as represented by German philosophy, English political economy and French socialism.[56]

---

50 Trigger 1984a, p. 359. Moreover, Trigger did not refer to the archaeology of Eastern Europe or other countries where revolutions and capitalist expropriation had occurred during the twentieth century.
51 Trigger 1984a, p. 359. And see Trotsky 1976, on the nationalist tendencies already in the Communist Party of China.
52 Wang 2011. The 'official' archaeology of China changed several times since the Revolution in 1949.
53 Trigger 1984a, p. 365, and 1989, p. 212.
54 Klejn 1993, and 2012.
55 McGuire 2002; Palerm 2008; Patterson 2008.
56 Lenin 1977a, p. 20.

3.1 Political Economy and Politics

The critique of the political economy is one of the most interesting and debated subjects explored in both prehistoric and historic contexts, focusing on the subject of the modes of production of pre-capitalistic societies and its application to archaeological categories. The concepts developed by Gordon Childe[57] on the revolutions in past societies, including the Neolithic period and the Early Bronze Age, are a good example of the application of Marxist concepts to the study of the political economy.[58]

Marx observed that human beings do not own their history, since it is not chosen by them but directly encountered, given and transmitted from the past. Thus, he proposed that with a scientific, dialectical study of past societies, there is a need for a historical perspective in the struggle against exploitation and oppression.[59] This subject is fully developed in this volume in the papers by Pérez Martínez and Acosta Ochoa, Milevski and colleagues, Bajema, Roskams, and Lull.

While I will return later to the question of dialectics in archaeological thought, I would like to stress that the question of politics in archaeology has been developed by several authors. For instance, Trigger[60] has dealt with the archaeology of government, while Vicente Lull and Rafael Micó have researched intensively what they call 'the archaeology of the state'.[61] However, there are other colleagues, like Reinhard Jung,[62] who have developed and analysed social movements in prehistoric periods with archaeological methods, as recorded in the destruction of the Bronze Age palaces in the Mediterranean world. Other examples are papers presented in this volume by Gonzales-Panta and Tantaleán, as well as the articles by Micó[63] and Risch,[64] which deal with glorifications of violence and class exploitation.[65] After all, one of the fundamental concepts of Marx and Engels was that the 'history of all hitherto

---

57 Childe 1942, 1936.
58 Marx 1970, 1977, and 1993.
59 Marx 1937. And see Kohl 1981, p. 112, and Trigger 1989, p. 354.
60 Trigger 1974.
61 Lull and Micó 2011, and see Lull et al., this volume. On a processual point of view on the state in archaeology, see Earle 1991, and 2002. Furthermore, on this subject, see Bernbeck 2009, and also Earle and Spriggs 2015.
62 Jung 2016, and 2018.
63 Micó 2020.
64 Risch 2020.
65 Other perspectives on violence in archaeology exist, but they do not consider the component of class divisions or other Marxist perspectives. For example, see Bar-Yosef 2010.

existing society is the history of class struggles',[66] and this should be researched and documented in the archaeological record by Marxist archaeologists. Of course, we can ask ourselves if an archaeology of class consciousness can be accomplished, as Mark Leone did in his research on the manipulation of historical archaeology in the United States,[67] following György Lukács's concept of 'hegemonic ideology'.[68] Reinhard Bernbeck and Randall McGuire's volume has shown that ideology encompasses multiple domains of social practice, and they have pointed out that archaeological interpretations are invariably conditioned by the historical context in which they are formulated.[69] Furthermore, the global imperialist system today is also represented in the way several archaeological projects function. As Akira Matsuda and Katsuyuki Okamura have introduced in their volume on public archaeology,[70] most international excavation projects are conducted by archaeologists from imperialist (economically advantaged) countries and undertaken in colonial or semi-colonial (economically disadvantaged) countries, following the legacy of colonial archaeology of the nineteenth and twentieth centuries.

Here, we should certainly also consider the value of archaeology as political action and theory.[71] Marxist perspectives in archaeology offer a scientific critique of reactionary currents in the humanities, including resurgences of imperialist, colonialist and racist explanations of historical processes that have been concurrent with various crises of the twenty-first century. Marxist archaeology can be seen to defend working classes and exploited peoples throughout history by exploring the perspectives of the oppressed with archaeological methods.

For this reason, this volume offers a critical counterbalance to other archaeological schools of thought that utilise mechanical materialism, idealism or social functionalism and which, in my view, are unable to provide a robust interpretation of the archaeological record. These approaches do not consider labour processes, social contradictions or historical and geographical condi-

---

66   Marx and Engels 1937.
67   Leone 1995.
68   Lukács 1971. Some archaeologists (e.g. Urban and Schortman 2019, p. 4) returned to similar Gramsci concepts, stressing the fact that dominant classes (e.g. the bourgeoisie) do not maintain power through force alone. In fact, the statement that the ruling ideas were always just the ideas of the ruling class could be found in Marx's and Engels's *German Ideology* (1970). For me, Gramsci's ideas are today represented more by post-processualism than by Marxism. See Rosengarden 1984–5.
69   Bernbeck and McGuire 2011.
70   Matsuda and Okamura 2011, p. 9, with bibliography therein.
71   For example, McGuire et al. 2005; McGuire 2008.

tions – i.e. the concrete situations in which archaeological remains should be analysed. In the context of such perspectives, such as those offered by processual archaeology, the question of studying ecology to understand past human societies has been raised, as it relates to the defence of present ecological habitats,[72] while post-processual (interpretative) schools have broached the question of gender in archaeology in relation to feminism.[73] Other political issues, such as the question of 'agency',[74] have been addressed in archaeology by processualism and post-processualism, but in most cases are abstract and lack social context. A Marxist critique of these approaches has been presented by Dean Saitta.[75]

3.2 Anthropology

To the three fundamental components of Marxism, we can also add ethnography or anthropology. In this, we support Patterson's idea that Karl Marx can in a general manner be labelled as an anthropologist and in another way as an archaeologist of the origins of capitalism.[76] According to Patterson,[77] during 1837, Marx took an anthropology course taught by Henrik Steffens at the University of Berlin, and he attended lectures by the anthropologist-geographer Carl Ritter.[78] Of course, when Marx and Engels lived, knowledge had not yet been divided into the academic disciplines as we know them today, and knowledge on archaeology and epigraphy was almost non-existent.[79] Anthropology as a scientific discipline was incorporated into Marxism from the beginning, as a fourth source. Notably, in the case of Engels, the work of the American anthropologist Lewis Morgan[80] provided the basis for *Origins of the Family, Private Property and the State*.[81] Furthermore, Marx also perceived that the dialectics of natural history could be compared to his and Engels's works, as on the occasion of the publication of the works of Charles Darwin.[82] In a letter addressed to Engels, Marx states that Darwin's book contains 'the basis in natural history

---

72 Trigger 1984a, p. 367.
73 For example, Moore 1988. And see on this subject McGuire 2008, pp. 73–7.
74 See Friedman and Rowlands 1978; Earle and Preucel 1987; Shanks and Tilley 1987; and Hodder 1991.
75 Saitta 1994.
76 Patterson 2009.
77 Patterson 2009, pp. 1–3.
78 Kelley 1984; Ryding 1975, p. 7.
79 Hobsbawm 1965.
80 Morgan 1964.
81 Engels 1972.
82 Darwin 1861.

for our view'.[83] In a different letter to Ferdinand Lasalle, Marx wrote that 'Darwin's book is very important and serves me as a basis in natural science for the class struggle in history'.[84]

In a scientific world that only a few years before discovered the remains of Neanderthals, Engels's work on the role played by labour in human evolution,[85] which utilises dialectical materialist methods, does not stand up to modern criticism, given present-day knowledge of human evolution. However, Engels felt the great value of Darwin's work when he stated at Marx's funeral in 1883: 'Just as Darwin discovered the law of the development of nature, Marx discovered the law of the development of human history'.[86] Of course, here natural history and human history should be seen as dialectically connected, as Gilman suggests in his paper on the Palaeolithic Revolution.[87]

It is not by chance that anthropologists and ethnographers like Godelier, Meillassoux and Bloch applied Marxism to anthropology.[88] Godelier combined this approach with one of the main schools in anthropology, i.e. Structuralism,[89] which was derived directly from linguistics.[90] Structuralism is criticised by Marxists because of its formal, apparently anti-dialectical way of analysing not only languages but also past and present societies.[91] Here, it is suggested that we consider anthropology as a scientific discipline which analyses, among other things, kinship structures in past societies,[92] as another contribution not only to Marxist archaeology, in particular, but also to Marxism in general.

3.3 *Dialectical Thought*

It should be borne in mind that the historical process is not a sum of independent factors but is a developing totality. A century and a half ago, Giorgi Plekhanov[93] and Antonio Labriola[94] disputed that dialectical materialism consisted solely or predominantly of the 'economic factor'. They contested the

---

83 Letter from Marx to Engels, December 19, 1860.
84 Letter from Marx to Lasalle January 16, 1861. See also Ruiz Rejón 2020 on the critics of Marx to Darwin; also see Marx and Engels 1964, pp. 260–76.
85 Engels 1975. And see Patterson 2008, pp. 67–76.
86 Darmangeat 2012, p. 7.
87 Gilman 1984.
88 Meillassoux 1975; Godelier 1977; Bloch 1983.
89 Lévi-Strauss 1966.
90 de Saussure 1916.
91 Sève 2016.
92 As did the pioneer Lewis Morgan, despite the modern critique of this work. See Darmangeat 2012.
93 Plekhanov 1977.
94 Labriola 2005.

theory of factors – political, cultural, ideological – since, for them, Marxism was a given totality, which developed according to its contradictions, with equivalent consequences for all its aspects. Plekhanov[95] explained how Hegel's dialectical view of social life[96] was intended to refer to the historical and social process in its totality, including all those aspects and manifestations relating to the activity of social beings. The same can be pointed out with regard to archaeology and the processes of material culture it describes. Periods are sometimes described as rigid structures, stadially changing, but a Marxist perspective analyses them as part of a dialectic mode in which contradictions of social, economic, technological, ideological and other factors are present. Furthermore, as 'pure' – i.e. impartial – definitions of a political situation do not exist, there are no 'pure' historical or archaeological categories, whether they are chronological periods, cultures, defined entities or socio-economic formations as expressed by their modes of production. While analysing the situation in France in the 1930s, Trotsky pointed out that Marxist thought is dialectical and considers all phenomena in their development as they pass from one phase to another.[97] For instance, Trotsky said that there is not an absolute opposition between a revolutionary situation and a non-revolutionary one. The metaphysical question, according to the formula 'what is, is; what is not, is not' does not exist. Dialectics, however, can distinguish between two phases, when a transformation of quantity into quality occurs (and vice versa), as suggested by Hegel in his *Science of Logic*,[98] and it is in this spirit that archaeological phases should be viewed.

A dialectical perspective in archaeology considers all concrete situations as actually transitional ones.[99] They are a combination of cultural settings, economic and social relations within a region, and of the internal and external relations of communities between a region and others, at a specific geographic, historical and technological stage of development. Thus, Marxist archaeology does not only consider the economic (or technological) aspects of material culture. As Engels wrote to Joseph Bloch:

> According to the materialist conception of history, the ultimately determining element in history is the production and reproduction of real life. Neither Marx nor I ever asserted more than this. Therefore, if somebody

---

95 Plekhanov 1977.
96 Hegel 1975.
97 Trotsky 1936, p. 24.
98 Hegel 2010, pp. 288 ff.; and see also Engels 1954.
99 And see Michael-Matsas, this volume.

twists this into saying the economic factor is the only determining one, he is transforming that proposition into a meaningless, abstract, absurd phrase.[100]

4 This Volume

This volume is committed to the presentation of rigorous intellectual work produced by many acknowledged archaeologists throughout the world who work within the Marxist tradition. The colleagues who have contributed to this volume represent the second or third generation following the Marxist scholars noted at the beginning of this chapter. Although only perspectives from discrete areas of the world are presented in this book – i.e. from the Americas, Europe and the Near East – we hope this volume will be of help in the interpretation of social and historical processes worldwide.

The present volume is divided into three parts, the first one being this Introduction. The second consists of several case studies – arranged following a certain chronological order – in which historical materialist methods are applied. The third part consists of articles that present different perspectives on Marxist thought in archaeology.

4.1 Case Studies

Patricia Pérez Martínez and Guillermo Acosta Ochoa present a case study focused on preceramic groups of Southeast Mexico (c. 12,000 years ago). The authors offer a study of lithic artefacts as an important element through which to approach labour processes, which include both the organisational strategies directed to subsistence as well as the relations of production and reproduction. To determine the functionality of the lithic assemblages and the activities carried out in the settlements, and to assess the role that these activities had in the economic organisation of preceramic groups, the different ways in which the productive process is fulfilled is presented. The paper portrays how labour modes are configured from the Marxist theory of value in order to define the specific relationship between a set of instruments of production, a particular organisation of labour, and the ideology that unifies and justifies these processes. Defining the spectrum of resources used by hunter-gatherer groups that inhabited southeastern Mexico towards the end of the Pleistocene and the beginning of the Holocene from a dialectical perspective of production-

---

100 Marx and Engels 1977, p. 75, quoted in McGuire 2002, p. 124. And see Gonzales-Panta and Tantaleán, this volume.

consumption allows us to characterise the diverse geographic and climatic environments in the area and to deduce the range of subsistence activities and patterns of settlement and social organisation over time.

A second article by Milevski, Gandulla and Jaruf aims at defining the socio-economic formations in Palestine during the Chalcolithic period (c. 4,500–3,700 BC) and possible socio-political formations. This is one of the most discussed periods in the late prehistory of the Levant. The authors consider the different modes of production suggested by both Marxist and non-Marxist scholars working in the Near East. They then analyse all aspects of the archaeological record of this period utilising the method of dialectical materialism. This involves taking into account not only the settlement distribution, architecture and material finds, but also the ideological aspects of the Chalcolithic communities, including burial practices and iconography. The paper concludes that the social formation of Palestine at that time was 'communal', a later variant of the so-called 'primitive mode of production' known from the preceding Neolithic Revolution. The 'communal form' includes an advanced phase of the 'secondary products revolution'. It shows that there was not one but a series of property forms and modes of production that characterised these late prehistoric communities.

In the third case study, Marcus Bajema explores the model of the Urban Revolution in Pre-Classic Mayan societies. The author first discusses the long-term history of the lowland Maya area and the terms currently used that are derived from a Eurocentric perspective resulting from Winckelmann's periodisation of Greece.[101] From the main divisions of Mesoamerican history (Pre-Classic, Classic, and Post-Classic periods), the focus of this paper is on the Pre-Classic period (c. 2,000 BC – 250 AD), itself divided into different phases. At the end of this period, called Terminal Pre-classic, there is a decline of the first generation of states. Bajema traces the developmental histories at both local-level (village) communities and (city) states, making them, and especially the interaction between them, the mainstay of his analysis. Mayan archaeologists have long recognised two distinct kinds of economy, a social one focused on communities and a political economy derived from state actors. By utilising Gordon Childe's model of the Urban Revolution,[102] the author stresses that behind the abstraction of the archaeological record there lies a creative Marxist perspective that can be applied to Pre-Classical Mayan archaeology. The models proposed by Althusser are also recalled by Bajema,[103]

---

101 Winckelmann 2013, pp. 81–114.
102 Childe 1950.
103 Althusser 2006.

mainly the theory of the encounter, i.e. that a plural temporality exists in the historical changes. For Bajema, to commence with the forces of production does not imply that they have a determining role in everything that follows.

In their contribution on violence in the Prehispanic Andes of Perú, Alex Gonzales-Panta and Henry Tantaleán analyse social conflicts and practices, utilising the cultural material record. According to the authors, investigations of violence in the Central Andes have attempted to explain the evidence of the past using political, sociological and anthropological models constructed from ethnohistoric and ethnographic records. However, these investigations, often contain ideological, economic and political premises that originate in liberal philosophy and economics. These archaeological explanations place the practice of violence in an ahistorical framework. Their paper presents a historical materialist synthesis of the main pre-colonial archaeological periods and 'cultures' (e.g. Moche from the third century AD until 1532 AD). It suggests that the existence of violent practices was based on historical and social conditions, and that it that functioned within the context of political institutions and structural violence.

Steve Roskams reviews Marxist perspectives on classical antiquity, mainly Greece and Rome. The author advocates, as did Trotsky[104] and subsequently McGuire,[105] that Marxism demands an integral relationship between political theory and practice. Roskams suggests that by utilising analytical techniques to understand past classical antiquity, it is possible to change the present world into something more fulfilling and sustainable in the future. After a brief consideration of the significance of the ancient world for modern society and the essentially descriptive accounts offered by conventional wisdom, the author discusses social dynamics based on more explicit historical materialist approaches suggested by previous authors. According to Roskams, the misconceptions of previous authors concerning the notion of the 'mode of production' limits its utility. He further argues that the more incisive and vibrant work of G.E.M. de Ste. Croix characterises antiquity in a way that archaeology can test, explore and elaborate to good effect.[106]

LouAnn Wurst presents an interesting case of a Marxist archaeological interpretation of the capitalist 'laws of motion'. The author stresses that the work of Marx was dedicated to understanding the inner workings of the capitalist

---

104   Trotsky 1906.
105   McGuire 2002.
106   de Ste. Croix 1983.

system.[107] Thus, she argues that in the United States, it is logical that Marxist researchers work in historical archaeology more than other archaeological specialities. Wurst argues that Marxism – as a philosophy of internal relations emphasising dialectics, social totality and analytical abstraction – provides powerful tools to confront capitalism as a social formation. Historical archaeological case studies help to flesh out how capitalism unfolded and humanised these processes. They also help us to see the sensual implications of these large-scale abstract processes. This requires us to focus our attention on questions of class, labour, property and alienation – that is, issues relating to the control of production. Considering individual archaeological case studies from the perspective of capitalism's laws of motion forces us to confront their commonalities and the world that capitalism has wrought, a consciousness needed to end the exploitation of modern capitalism.

4.2 Balances and Perspectives

The current volume also presents studies that demonstrate how Marxism could be applied to archaeology. The paper by Vicente Lull is a synthesis of extensive research on Marxism and several aspects of archaeology. This paper offers a comprehensive study of the Marxist concepts of production, and of tangible objects as productive objects, as they may be applied in archaeology. The object is a starting and end point. It is the ground on which archaeology develops. It is medium and vehicle, motive and objective. In archaeology, we work with tangible objects that make up the concrete synthesis of social relations. They have been produced by the relations between humans, and between them and the rest of nature. Material remains are perfect indicators of such relations and their development. They establish our environment, reorder space and cancel or reshape pre-existing material relations. They build the silent surroundings that show us the limits of reason and the intensity of each archaeological period. They establish the rules of contrast and geometry. Wherever language is absent, the resulting object is the wholeness, the link capable of recording experience and passing it on. To understand the object (as a whole) we must appeal to its history, which is at the same time inside and outside of it. The object's external history, of universal composition, seeks its presence and provides it with a material body; its internal history, which is its own history, enables it to be active. As pointed out by Lull in the paper: 'The object may not be in charge or the protagonist of its own history, but it will become the protagonist and responsible for everyone's history'.

---

107   Marx 1970, 1977, and 1993.

In the paper that follows – written by Lull and colleagues from the Barcelona research team Rafael Micó, Cristina Rihuete Herrera and Roberto Risch – the authors explore the concept of the political in the archaeological record and apply the Marxist notion of the state, as the instrument of oppression of one social class by another, in the sense used by Lenin.[108] This paper examines how an alternative understanding of political action can be derived from Marx's general economic thinking (e.g. in the *Grundrisse*),[109] where the fundamental contradiction existing in all human societies, including prehistoric ones, emerges between the moment of the production of goods, as a collective enterprise, and the moment of consumption, where each member of the community might have different needs, preferences, and desires. From the perspective of the archaeological research of politics, the authors propose a syntagmatic approach in which the meaning emerges by regarding archaeological objects in themselves and in their relations with others.

Marcelo Vitores presents a paper evaluating the influence of Vere Gordon Childe on the Latin American Social Archaeology (LASA). This school took Childe as a reference point and an inspiration with which to explore the archaeological and social processes in Latin America, a sort of connection between the past and the present. The pioneers of this school are Luis F. Bate and Luis Guillermo Lumbreras.[110] Rejecting dogmatic perspectives and the influence of French structuralism, LASA was deeply influenced by the Cuban Revolution and undertook several reformulations of historical materialism. Salient among the strictly archaeological antecedents is the *Prehistory of Cuba*, by Raul Tabío and Estrella Rey in the 1960s, which followed works of Soviet Union scholars that were influenced by Stalinist models.[111]

In his paper, Vitores explores the continuities, differences and convergencies between Childe's perspectives and those of the Latin American archaeologists as they relate to Marxist methods. Using examples, the author shows how the Australian archaeologist's legacy has influenced new world archaeology. This review suggests that a critical evaluation of Childe's work can be beneficial for the development of a social archaeology.

Finally, Savas Michael-Matsas presents a paper on the concept of transition in historical materialist thought and archaeology. Michael-Matsas suggests that in the post-2008, unresolved global capitalist crisis – itself exacerbated by the global pandemic shock – humanity lives a most dramatic inflection point in

---

108   Lenin 1964b.
109   Marx 1993.
110   Lumbreras 1974; Bate 2007.
111   Tabío and Rey 1966.

history. Consequently, historical materialism has to successfully revolutionise its own form. The break from a linear conception of history is more crucial than ever before. Michael-Matsas considers work recently published by David Graeber and David Wengrow[112] in a critical way, but indicates that their work cannot be ignored or overlooked. He stresses the importance of breaking with all misconceptions about a linear evolution of history, and the need to make the necessary 'conceptual shift' to open new horizons in history and archaeology. Furthermore, the author criticises the prehistory/history divide, noting the linearity of historical time as a main epistemological problem.

Michael-Matsas's chapter is a call for historical materialism to respond to the challenge of that conception. He considers Gordon Childe's groundbreaking work, the first to establish the relevance of historical materialism into archaeological research. Yet, he also considers this a reciprocal relationship: archaeology can, and should, open new horizons for historical materialist dialectics. The dialectical category of 'Transition in History' should integrate archaeological discoveries, the content of which is correspondingly enriched by historical materialism.

5 Marxist Archaeology in Present Perceptions

As Marxists, we are totally conscious that the present world's situation influences our writing and our research of past societies, while the uneven and combined developments of history still show us that some pre-capitalist forms of production exist on the globe. Thus, this volume does not 'stand on air' as merely an intellectual creation but reflects political and social struggles across the world, in which the working classes and oppressed peoples and social groups participate. Given the broad global reach of this volume, as can be seen in the different chapters presented here, there are differences in the ways the authors understand not only Marxist thought but also Marxist interpretations of the archaeological record.

I am convinced that this volume will make an important contribution to revitalise the application of Marxist methods to the interpretation of archaeology. Archaeology should not only be one of the tools to understand past societies and those that initiated the capitalistic mode of production but should also serve as a discipline through which to improve Marxist understandings of human evolution and revolutions over time. As Trotsky synthetised in his writ-

---

112 Graeber and Wengrow 2021.

ings on Marxist thought, the founder of dialectical materialism did not work in order to discover 'eternal laws' of economy, society and history, but to apply his methods to understand the development of human society.[113]

Modes of production, social and political relations and ideological forms change, but one era does not totally replace the other, and, along with the changes, elements of the past continue to exist. Most importantly, there should not be a static vision of social evolution; each stage must be analysed in motion, in a concrete way at each given moment, in comparison with that which went before and that which follows after. Of all the different perspectives in archaeology, the dialectical materialist method best facilitates the study of social evolution by regarding multiple factors. These cannot be considered as separate parts, but dynamically as a whole. It is not a question of continuing to repeat formulas. Dialectics recognises that all formulas are provisional; the same should be true for archaeology, and one should not seek to impose such formulas, as in textbooks.[114] We must strive to study specific archaeological cases, their conditions of emergence and their characteristics from the archaeological point of view. On the one hand, paraphrasing the words of Lenin,[115] we could say that 'without archaeological theory, there cannot be archaeology'. On the other hand, as that same revolutionary said,[116] quoting Goethe, 'Grey, my friend, is all theory, and green the golden tree of life'.[117]

It is evident that Marxist archaeology is not only a part of a social discipline, but is distinct from imperialistic, colonialist and nationalist archaeologies. For Marxist archaeology to succeed, it should be an instrument working against the oppression of workers and peoples on any basis, and it should not be used as an excuse for denying freedom to any group – social, national or religious.[118] Marxist archaeology is also distinct from the archaeology imposed by bureaucratic regimes (some of which are identified with socialism) which made of dialectical materialism a dogma. This approach is opposed not only to dialectics, but also to the study of the concrete social formations and archaeological cultures. Archaeology is certainly local or regional in essence, since the researched cultures and societies developed locally. But the contents of

---

113   Trotsky 1963, pp. 14–5.
114   And see Novack 1971, pp. 70–3.
115   Lenin 1961.
116   Lenin 1964a.
117   'Grau, theurer Freund, ist alle Theorie, und grün des Lebens goldner Baum', von Goethe 2003, lines 2038–9. We utilise here the English translation of Goethe. The English translation of Lenin is a little bit different: 'Theory, my friend, is grey, but green is the eternal tree of life'.
118   And see Milevski and Gandulla 2016.

archaeology are universal, as is humanity, and so the struggle for a future society without the exploited and exploiters should be universal. Moreover, as Marxism is internationalist and not nationalist, Marxist archaeology should not be based on the search for national identities or national exceptionalism. It should be founded on the study of concrete local material culture and its developments through the application of dialectical materialist methods and the elaboration of archaeological theories in the *long durée*.

Furthermore, archaeologists should be aware of the difficulties to be faced when local and regional cultures correspond with modern national boundaries. It is the task of a critical archaeology in general, and a Marxist archaeology in particular, to criticise the 'national frontiers' that archaeology too often supports. Such 'national' approaches tend to create factoids supporting nationalist narratives for the wider public, which often support the oppression of other peoples while not being supported by the archaeological evidence. Nationalism in archaeology is a form of false consciousness, inverting the reality, defending the rights of the 'old peoples' against the modern.[119]

6 In Defence of Archaeology[120]

Human civilisation today is challenged and menaced by the recent global COVID-19 pandemic, climate change and the international economic crisis.[121] Governments utilise the arsenal of modern technology for destruction but are incapable of defending the archeological sites that are testament to human heritage, revealing a lack of concern for heritage itself. Even in times of 'peace' the fields of archaeology, science and culture are endangered.

This is exactly the crisis that V. Gordon Childe pointed out years ago when he compared the evolution of natural and exact sciences versus the humanities.[122] Over the course of the last hundred years, modern societies have attained a remarkable dominance over nature. In contrast, control over the social environment – over the relationships between individuals, groups, nations and classes – has not achieved a comparable degree of success. In the span of the last decades, several world wars plus an endless series of regional wars and per-

---

119 And see Trigger 1989, pp. 148–55.
120 This section is inspired by the manifesto of a revolutionary independent art published by Breton and Rivera 2019.
121 Michael-Matsas 2020; IPCC 2021; and see Michael-Matsas, this volume.
122 Childe 1947, pp. 1–3.

manent conflicts have released destructive forces that threaten to sweep away everything that the productive forces have organised slowly, and so perhaps promote the extinction of humanity itself.

Furthermore, in several regions of the world, capitalist governments and contractors are destroying antiquities for the sake of the 'development of the country',[123] although in very few instances are the real needs or interests of local communities taken into account. The destruction of antiquities for economic reasons occurs equally in developed countries as in their colonies and semi-colonies. The difference is that while in some countries there are laws designated to 'defend' antiquities, in many of the so-called 'developing countries', e.g. South America, such laws do not exist or, where they do, they are not applied at all.[124] In others (e.g. Australia), private international companies show 'support' for archaeology but in fact endanger or even destroy archaeological sites following the dictates of their business interests.[125] Further testimony to this is the looting of antiquities and selling of them to museums and private collectors,[126] which has not been stopped even with the COVID pandemic. Some museums have even had to sell off part of their collections to survive, e.g. the Museum of Islam in Jerusalem.[127] Selling museum objects has taken on an entirely new dimension during the pandemic, even affecting institutions such as the Metropolitan Museum of Art in New York.[128] Looting of antiquities provides the private market with 'commodities' aimed at enriching the already rich. A further consequence is that entire civilisations are transferred to and owned by museums located in the capitals of first world countries. Most of these museums have not returned items that were looted, often under colonial rule, from Asia, Africa, America, Oceania and Mediterranean Europe.[129]

In the realm of academia, archaeological and human science institutes are the first to be closed by the university authorities or ministries of education or culture. Among those affected are the Department of Archaeology at the University of Sheffield, the Institute of Classical Archaeology at Leipzig Uni-

---

123 Yekutieli 2008; Marciniak 2011; Pellini 2017.
124 Milevski 2017.
125 Lilley 2017.
126 Kersel 2012; Lazrus and Barker 2012.
127 Riba 2020.
128 See: https://www.nbcnewyork.com/news/local/in-controversial-move-met-museum-may-sell-artwork-in-order-to-make-up-covid-losses/2934422/ and https://www.nytimes.com/2021/03/19/arts/design/deaccession-museum-directors.html.
129 For example, Hamilakis 1999. It should be stressed that I do not support the utilisation of nationalistic agendas of the local bourgeoisies to exploit 'national symbols' against the people of their countries.

versity,[130] the Faculty of Humanities at the University of Halle-Wittenberg, Saxony-Anhalt,[131] the Norwegian Institute at Athens,[132] and the Institute of Archaeology and Antiquity of the University of Birmingham.[133] Similar steps have been taken by dictatorial regimes, such as the junta ruling Argentina in 1976–83, which wanted to close the Department of Anthropology at Buenos Aires and other universities.[134] Some European 'democracies', such as Denmark, are attacking the freedom of research including in the humanities and archaeology, as resolutions passed through Parliament by the 'Social Democratic Party' has specifically targeted critical research and teaching, especially in the fields of race, gender, migration and post-colonial studies.[135] In other parts of the world, such as in Israel, archaeologists who are not in the mainstream are commonly not employed at universities and are forced to search for jobs elsewhere.[136]

The regimes of the former Soviet Union and others that termed themselves 'socialist' controlled archaeology as a 'state ideology' and dictated what Marxist archaeology should be. They were hostile to every sort of spiritual value and freedom of thought in our discipline. Gordon Childe was a critic of Stalinism – not only in 1956,[137] but long time before in the 1930s.[138] Even after the fall of most of these regimes, his observations are still accurate today – after the collapse of the Soviet Union and other Stalinist administrations – in countries dominated by the bureaucratic 'socialist' regimes.

It goes without saying that true socialism is not afraid of archaeology or any expression of the human sciences. It realises that the role of the archaeologist in a decadent capitalist society is determined by the conflict between the need to study past humanities and the governments that are hostile to such invest-

---

130 See: https://blogs.brown.edu/joukowsky/2014/02/17/petition-for-the-preservation-of-the-institute-of-classical-archaeology-and-the-collection-of-antiquities-of-leipzig-university germany/.
131 See: https://www.openpetition.de/petition/online/kahlschlag-an-der-mlu-verhindern-fa kultaeten-retten.
132 See: https://www.petitions.net/save_the_norwegian_institute_at_athens.
133 See: https://www.change.org/p/the-university-of-birmingham-extend-the-consultation-period-of-the-iaa-merger-review.
134 Politis and Curtoni 2011, p. 511.
135 And see: https://docs.google.com/forms/d/e/1FAIpQLSf-RmUIF6b6M8u1ZVPmRfkWAAD 1c9__HUKi2ErwIAPx6K1YJA/viewform.
136 Ussishkin 1982; Rosen 2003; Politis and Curtoni 2011.
137 Green 1981, p. 122; Faulkner 2007.
138 Trigger 1984b, pp. 2–10; Irving 2020, pp. 341–3. But see McVey (2020) who pointed that Childe's position vis-à-vis both the Soviet Union and Stalinism was inconsistent.

igation. Paraphrasing Marx,[139] his conception of the writer's function applies to the archaeologist. For Marx, the writer must make money in order to live and write, but he should not under any circumstances live and write in order to make money. The writer by no means looks at his work as a means, for it is an end in itself. If it is necessary, he sacrifices his existence to the existence of his work. The same can be said of archaeologists, mainly those working for government institutions or for contract companies. After all, archaeologists, working in different institutions, are part of the working class.[140]

Defending the freedom of thought should not be interpreted as a justification for political indifference. It is far from my wish to revive a so-called 'pure' archaeology which generally serves the extremely impure ends of reactionary forces, such as the intention to deny the right of the Palestinian people to biblical archaeological interpretations.[141] Our conception of the role of archaeology is not above negating its influence on the fate of humankind. In this regard, it is apt to quote from Michael Shanks and Christopher Tilley[142] to state that 'archaeological theory is as a practice which cannot be separated from the object of archaeology, itself indelibly social, and the present sociopolitical context of this practice, this mediation of past and present'. Tilley[143] and McGuire[144] have also emphasised that archaeology is a form of sociopolitical action in the present, and although it cannot end war, alleviate global poverty or transform capitalism, it constitutes part of modern culture and helps us to understand it.

Communal archaeology is one of these socio-political actions. For instance, American Marxist archaeologists have pointed out the necessity of establishing a connection between the archaeological discipline and indigenous communities in North America as a sort of praxis.[145] In Middle Eastern archaeology, Palestinian archaeologists in the territories of the Palestinian Authority have founded a Palestinian Association for Cultural Exchange (PACE) in order to protect archaeological sites.[146] Through the Emek Shaveh association in East

---

139   Marx 1974, pp. 40–1.
140   Independent of their social and political consciences; see Wurst, this volume.
141   Khalidi 1992; Abu al Haj 2001; Greenberg and Keinan 2007. Hamilakis and Yalouri (1996) have considered that 'political innocence' was broken with the advent of post-processual archaeology, but Marxist approaches have always understood epistemological principles in archaeology related to political issues. See also Trigger 1980.
142   Shanks and Tilley 1988, p. 27.
143   Tilley 1989.
144   McGuire 2008.
145   McGuire et al. 2005.
146   Yahya 2005. And see the volume of Kletter and colleagues (in press).

Jerusalem, a project is in place involving the participation of Israeli archaeologists with the local Palestinian population of the village of Silwan, in order to oppose the excavations promoted by Jewish settlers that have occupied houses in the village.[147]

I believe that the task of archaeology and of archaeologists is to take part actively and consciously in the preparation of a new socialist world. But the archaeologist cannot serve the struggle for freedom unless he/she subjectively assimilates its social content. Archaeology is not a national issue (even if it has national or local forms); it is a social issue concerning the whole of humanity and the progressive forces represented by the working classes.

Antiquities should not be commodities, but social values – not 'symbolic capitals', instruments of domination of one country over another, instruments of 'national identity', nor expressions of superiority of cultures or peoples (in the style of the Nazi Gustav Kossinna),[148] and nor should they serve as symbols of the national bourgeoisie in the colonies, semi-colonies or in non-imperialistic countries.[149]

While protecting antiquities, the archaeologist should fight capitalistic economic interests which threaten to destroy ancient remains. And on a more practical level, archaeologists worldwide should demand more resources from the state and governments.

We must find a common ground on which all independent and radical archaeologists may be united in defence of the liberty of archeological thought and practice. We believe that archaeological schools and tendencies of the most varied sort can find a common ground. Marxists and other independent and radical archaeologists can work together in rejecting the reactionary polices of recent history, defending archaeology as a free discipline. The aims of an independent Marxist archaeology should be the independence of archaeology for socialism, socialism for the complete liberation of archaeology.

Acknowledgments

I wish to thank all the contributors of this volume as well as the editors of the Historical Materialism and the colleagues and workers who did the layout and take care of the technical aspects of the volume. Special thanks to my friend

---

147   Greenberg and Mizrachi 2010.
148   Kossina 1911; and see Trigger 1989.
149   And see Hamilakis and Yalouri 1996.

Daniel Gaido, who pushed me into the enterprise of publishing this volume. I also want to thank Gideon Shelach for his help with the publications of Su Bingqi. Finally, I am indebted to Liora Kolska Horwitz and Ciara Patten, for the revision of the text and the editing of this and other papers in the present volume, and to an anonymous reader whose critical comments greatly contributed to the improvement of the papers. I remain solely responsible for this paper.

References

Abu el-Haj, Nadia 2001, *Facts on the Ground: Archaeological Practice and Territorial Self-Fashioning in Israeli Society*, Chicago, IL: University of Chicago Press.

Althusser, Louis 2006, *Philosophy of the Encounter: Later Writings, 1978–1987*, London: Verso.

Bajema, Marcus 2019, 'A Review of *Ancient Irrigation Systems of the Aral Sea: The History origin and Development of Irrigated Agriculture* by Boris V. Andrianov, and *Soviet Archaeology: Schools, Trend, and History* by Leo S. Klejn', available at: http://www.historicalmaterialism.org/book-review/soviet-archaeology-theory-and-practice.

Bar-Yosef, Ofer 2010, 'Warfare in Levantine Early Neolithic: A Hypothesis to be Considered', *Neo-Lithics*, 10, 1: 6–10.

Bate, Luis F. 1977, *Arqueología y materialismo histórico*, México D.F.: Ediciones de Cultura Popular.

Bate, Luis F. 2007, *Arqueología y marxismo. Contribuciones al pensamiento marxista en la reflexión arqueológica*, Santiago de Chile: Las Armas de la Crítica.

Bernbeck, Reinhard 2009, 'The Rise of the State', in *Handbook of Archaeological Theories*, edited by R. Alexander Bentely, Herbert D.G. Maschner and Christopher Chippindale, Lanham, MD: AltaMira Press.

Bernbeck, Reinhard and Randall McGuire, Randall H. (eds.) 2011, *Ideologies in Archaeology*, Tucson, AZ: University of Arizona Press.

Bloch, Maurice 1983, *Marxism and Anthropology: The History of a Relationship*, London and New York: Routledge.

Breton, André and Diego Rivera 2019 [1938], 'Manifesto: Towards a Free Revolutionary Art', in *Anthologie Kulturpolitik. Einführende Beiträge zu Geschichte, Funktionen und Diskursen der Kulturpolitikforschung*, Schriften zum Kultur- und Museumsmanagement, edited by Martin Tröndle and Claudia Steigerwald, Bielefeld: Transcript Verlag.

Childe, Vere Gordon 1936, *Man Makes Himself*, London: Watts & Co.

Childe, Vere Gordon 1946, *What Happened in History*, London: Penguin Books.

Childe, Vere Gordon 1947, *History*, London: Cobbet Press.
Childe, Vere Gordon 1950, 'The Urban Revolution', *The Town Planning Review*, 21,1: 3–17.
Darmangeat, Christophe 2012, *Le communism primitif n'est plus ce qu'il était: Aux origins de l'oppression des femmes & une historie de famille*, Toulouse: Smolny.
Darwin, Charles 1861, *On the Origin of Species by Means of Natural Selection: Or the Preservation of Favoured Races in the Struggle for Life*, 3rd ed., London: John Murray.
Earle, Timothy K. (ed.) 1991, *Chiefdoms: Power, Economy and Ideology*, Cambridge: Cambridge University Press.
Earle, Timothy K. 2002, *Bronze Age Economics: The Beginnings of Political Economies*, Boulder, CO: Westview Press.
Earle, Timothy and Robert Preucel 1987, 'Processual Archaeology and the Radical Critique', *Current Anthropology*, 28, 501–38.
Earle, Timothy and Matthew Spriggs 2015, 'Political Economy in Prehistory: A Marxist Approach to Pacific Sequences', *Current Anthropology*, 56, 4: 515–44.
Engels, Friedrich 1954 [1878], *Anti-Düring*, Moscow: Foreign Languages Publishers.
Engels, Friedrich 1972 [1884], *The Origins of the Family, Private Property and the State*, New York, NY: Pathfinder Press.
Engels, Friedrich 1975 [1876], *The Part Played by Labour in the Transition from Ape to Man*, Peking: Foreign Language Press.
von Falkenhausen, Lotar 1993, 'On the Historiographical Orientation of Chinese Archaeology', *Antiquity*, 67, 257: 839–49.
Faulkner, Neil 2007, 'Gordon Childe and Marxist Archaeology', *International Socialism: A Quarterly Review of Socialist Theory* 116, available at: http://isj.org.uk/gordon-childe-and-marxist-archaeology/.
Friedman, Jonathan and Michael Rowlands, 1978, 'Notes toward an Epigenetic Model of the Evolution of "Civilization"', in *The Evolution of Social Systems*, edited by Jonathan Friedman and Michael Rowlands, Pittsburgh, PA: University of Pittsburgh Press.
Gilman, Antonio 1984, 'Explaining the Upper Palaeolithic Revolution', in *Marxist Approaches in Archaeology*, edited by Matthew Spriggs, Cambridge: Cambridge University Press.
Godelier, Maurice 1977, *Perspectives in Marxist Anthropology*, Cambridge: Cambridge University Press.
von Goethe, Johann W. 2003 [1808], *Faust: Parts I & II*, translated by A.S. Kline, Yale: Yale University Press.
Graeber, David and David Wengrow 2021, *The Dawn of Everything*, London: Allen Lane.
Gramsci, Antonio 1971 [1929–35], *Selections from the Prison Notebooks*, translated and edited by Quintin Hoare and Geoffrey Nowel Smith, New York: International Publishers.

Green, Sally 1981, *Prehistorian: A Biography of V. Gordon Childe*, Bradford-on-Avon: Moonraker Press.

Greenberg, Raphael and Adi Keinan 2007, *The Present Past of the Israeli-Palestinian Conflict: Israeli Archaeology in the West Bank and East Jerusalem Since 1967*, Tel Aviv: Tel Aviv University.

Greenberg, Raphael and Yoni Mizrachi 2010, *From Shiloah to Silwan: Visitors Guide to Ancient Jerusalem (City of David) and the Village of Silwan*, available at: http://www.alt-arch.org/docs/Guide_English_Preview.pdf.

Hamilakis, Yannis 1999, 'Stories from Exile: Fragments from the Cultural Biography of the Parthenon (or "Elgin") Marbles', *World Archaeology*, 31, 2: 303–20.

Hamiliakis, Yannis and Eleana Yalouri 1996, 'Antiquities as Symbolic Capital in Modern Greek Society', *Antiquity*, 79: 117–29.

Hegel, Georg W.F. 1975 [1837], *Lectures on the Philosophy of World History*, translated by H.B. Nisbet, New York: Cambridge University Press.

Hegel, Georg W.F. 2010 [1813–16] *The Science of Logic*, edited and translated by G. di Giovanni, Cambridge: Cambridge University Press.

Hodder, Ian 1991, *Reading the Past*, Cambridge: Cambridge University Press.

Hobsbawm, Eric 1965, 'Introduction', in *Pre-Capitalist Economic Formations*, Karl Marx, New York: International Publishers.

Iacono, Francesco 2018, 'Marxist Archaeologies', in *The Oxford Handbook of Archaeological Theory*, edited by Andrew Gardner et al., Oxford: Oxford University Press.

Irving, Terry 2020, *The Fatal Lure of Politics: The Life and Thought of Vere Gordon Childe*, Melbourne: Monash University Publishing.

Jung, Reinhard 2016, '"Freide den Hütten, Krieg den Palästen!" – In the Bronze Age Aegean', in *Arm und Reich – Zur Ressourcenverteilung in prähistorischen Gesellschaften*, edited by Harald Meller et al., Halle (Saale): Landesmuseum für Vorgeschichte Halle.

Jung, Reinhard 2018, 'Inferno in der Bronzezeit: Das Ende der ostmediterranen Königreiche', in *Mykene: Die sagenhafte Welt des Agamemnon*, herausgegeben vom Badischen Landesmuseum Karlsruhe, Baden: Philipp von Zabern Verlag.

Kelley, Donald R. 1984, 'The Science of Anthropology: An Essay on the Very Old Marx', *Journal of the History of Ideas*, 45, 2: 245–62.

Kersel, Morag 2012, 'The Value of a Looted Object: Stakeholder Perceptions in the Antiquities Trade', in *The Oxford Handbook of Public Archaeology*, edited by Robin Skeates, Carol McDavid and John Carman, Oxford: Oxford University Press.

Khalidi, Walid 1992, *All that Remains: The Palestinain Villages Occupied and Depopulated by Israel in 1948*, Washington D.C.: Institute of Palestinian Studies.

Kim, Minkoo 2008, 'Multivocality, Multifaceted Voices, and Korean Archaeology', in *Evaluating Multiple Narratives: Beyond Nationalist, Colonialist, Imperialist Archaeologies*, edited by Junko Habu, Clare Fawcett and John M. Matsunaga, New York: Springer.

Kletter, Raz, Liora Kolska Horwitz and Emannuel Pfoh (eds.), in press, *Community Archaeology in Israel/Palestine*, Sheffield: Equinox.

Klejn, Leo S. 1973, 'Marxism, the Systemic Approach, and Archaeology', in *The Explanation of Culture Change: Models in Prehistory*, edited by Colin Renfrew, Liverpool: Duckworth.

Klejn, Leo 1993, *La arqueología soviética*, translated by Ignacio Clemente and Daniel Medina, Barcelona: Crítica.

Klejn. Leo S. 2012, *Soviet Archaeology: Trends, Schools, and History*, translated by R. Ireland and K. Windle, Oxford: Oxford University Press.

Kohl, Philip L. 1981, 'Materialist Approaches to Prehistory', *Annual Review of Anthropology*, 10, 89–118.

Kossinna, Gustav 1911, *Die Herkunft der Germanen*, Leipzig: Kabitzch.

Krekovič, Eduard and Martin Bača 2013, 'Marxism, Communism and Czechoslovak Archeology', *Anthropologie*, 51, 2: 261–70.

Kriiska, Avivar 2006, 'The Research of the Stone Age', in *Archaeological Research in Estonia 1865–2005*, edited by Valter Lang et al., Tartu: University of Tartu Press.

Labriola, Antonio 2005 [1896], *Essays on the Materialistic Conception of History*, New York: Cosimo Books.

Lazrus, Paula K. and Alex W. Barker (eds.), 2012, *All the King's Horses: Impact on the Looting and the Illicit Antiquities Trade on Our Knowledge of the Past*, Washington, D.C.: Society for American Archaeology.

Lee, Hyeong Woo 2013, 'The Politics of Archaeology in North Korea: Construction and Deterioration of Toh's Knowledge', *International Journal of Historical Archaeology*, 17, 2: 401–21.

Lenin, Vladimir I. 1961 [1902], 'What is to be Done?', in *Lenin Collected Works*, Volume 5, 347–530, Moscow: Foreign Languages Publishing House.

Lenin, Vladimir I. 1964a [1917], 'Letters on Tactics', in *Lenin Collected Works*, 42–54, Moscow: Progress Publishers.

Lenin, Vladimir I. 1964b [1917], 'The State and the Revolution', in *Lenin Collected Works*, 381–492, Moscow: Progress Publishers.

Lenin, Vladimir I. 1977a [1913], 'The Three Sources and the Three Component Parts of Marxism', in *Lenin Selected Works*, Volume 19, 21–8, Moscow: Progress Publishers.

Lenin, Vladimir I. 1977b [1917], 'Imperialism, the Highest Stage of Capitalism', in *Lenin Selected Works*, 169–262, Moscow: Progress Publishers.

Leone, Mark P. 1995, 'A Historical Archaeology of Capitalism', *American Anthropologist*, 97, 2, 251–268.

Lévi-Strauss, Claude 1966 [1962], *The Savage Mind*, London: Weidenfeld & Nicolson.

Liangren, Zhang 2011, 'Soviet Inspiration in Chinese Archaeology', *Antiquity*, 85, 1049–59.

Liangren, Zhang 2013, 'The Chinese School of Archaeology', *Antiquity*, 87, 896–904.

Lilley, Ian 2017, 'World Heritage and Cultural Diversity in Oceania', *Claroscuro*, 16, 1–28, available at: http://ppct.caicyt.gov.ar/index.php/claroscuro/issue/view/700.

Lozny, Ludomir R. (ed.) 2017, *Archaeology of the Communist Era. A Political History of Archaeology of the 20th Century*, New York: Springer.

Lull, Vicente and Rafael Micó, *Archaeology of the Origin of the State: The Theories*, Oxford: Oxford University Press.

Lukács, György 1971 [1928], *History and Class Consciousness*, Cambridge, MA: MIT Press.

Lumbreras, Luis G. 1974, *La Arqueología como ciencia social*, Lima: Histar.

Marciniak, Arkadiusz 2011, 'Contemporary Polish Archaeology in Global Context', in *Comparative Archaeologies: A Sociological View of the Science of the Past*, edited by Ludomir R. Lozny, New York: Springer.

Marder, Ofer et al. 2018, 'A Russian Before and After the Revolution: P.P. Efimenko, a Pioneer of Levantine Prehistoric Research', *Palestine Exploration Quarterly*, 150, 2: 90–109.

Marx, Karl 1861, *Correspondence Marx-Lasalle*, January 6, 1861, available at: https://www.marxists.org/archive/marx/works/1861/letters/61_01_16-abs.htm.

Marx, Karl 1881, *Correspondence Marx-Zasulich*, March 8, 1881, available at: https://www.marxists.org/archive/marx/works/1881/zasulich/reply.htm.

Marx, Karl 1937 [1869], *The Eighteenth Brumaire of Louis Napoleon*, Moscow: Progress Publishers.

Marx, Karl 1970 [1859], *A Contribution to the Critique of Political Economy*, edited with an introduction by Maurice Dobb, New York: International Publishers.

Marx, Karl 1974 [1842], 'Debates on Freedom of the Press and Publication', in *On Freedom of the Press and Censorship*, edited and translated by Saul Padover, New York: McGraw-Hill.

Marx, Karl 1977 [1867], *Capital: A Critique of Political Economy*, Volume I, introduced by E. Mandel, translated by B. Fowkes, New York: Vintage Books.

Marx, Karl 1993 [1857–1858], *Grundrisse: Foundations of Political Economy*, translated with a foreword by M. Nicolaus, London and New York: Penguin Classics.

Marx, Karl and Friedrich Engels 1937 [1848], *The Manifesto*, New York: International Publishers.

Marx, Karl and Friedrich Engels 1964 [1845–95], *Lettres sur le Capital*, translated by G. Badia, J. Chabbert and P. Meier, Paris: Editions Sociales.

Marx, Karl and Friedrich Engels 1970 [1832], *The German Ideology*, New York, NY: International Publishers.

Marx, Karl and Friedrich Engels 1977, *Selected Letters*, Peking: Foreign Language Press.

Matsuda, Akira and Katuyuki Okamura (eds.), *New Perspectives in Global Public Archaeology*, 1–18, New York: Springer.

McGuire, Randall H. 1993, 'Archaeology and Marxism', *Archaeological Method and Theory*, 5: 101–57.

McGuire, Randall H. 2002, *A Marxist Archaeology*, New York: Percheron Press.
McGuire, Randal H. 2006, 'Marx, Childe and Trigger', in *The Archaeology of Bruce Trigger: Theoretical Empiricism*, edited by Ronald F. Williamson and Michael S. Bisson, Montréal: McGill-Queens University Press.
McGuire, Randall H. 2008, *Archaeology as Political Action*, California: University of California Press.
McGuire, Randall H., María O'Donovan and LouAnn Wurst 2005, 'Probing Praxis in Archaeology: The Last Eighty Years', *Rethinking Marxism*, 17: 355–72.
McVey, Judy 2020, 'Vere Gordon Childe and Prehistory: A Way of Thinking, and Much More', *International Socialism: A Quarterly Review of Socialist Theory*, 169, available at: http://isj.org.uk/v-gordon-childe-prehistory/.
Meillassoux, Claude 1975, *Femmes, gréniers et capitaux*, Paris: Editions Maspéro.
Michael-Matsas, Savas 2020, 'Pandemic and Crisis: The Perfect Storm 1', *Política Obrera*, 26, available at: https://politicaobrera.com/internacionales/2613-pandemic-and-crisis-the-perfect-storm-1.
Micó, Rafael 2020, 'The Public Display of Physical Violence as a Key Factor in the Long Term Submission to Political Power in Class Societies', in *Rituelle Gewalt – Rituale der Gewalt. Ritual Violence – Rituals of Violence*, edited by Harald Meller et al., Halle (Saale): Landesmuseum für Vorgeschichte Halle.
Milevski, Ianir 2017, 'Diversidad cultural en la arqueología mundial', Claroscuro, 16, 1–8, available at: http://ppct.caicyt.gov.ar/index.php/claroscuro/issue/view/700.
Milevski, Ianir and Bernardo Gandulla 2016, 'Biblical Archaeology, Processualism, Postprocessualism, and Beyond: Politics and Archaeological Trends', in *Framing Archaeology in the Near East the Application of Social Theory to Fieldwork*, edited by Ianir Milevski and Thomas E. Levy, Sheffield and Bristol: Equinox.
Milisauskas, Sarunas 2017, 'Observations on Archaeology in the Polish People's Republic, 1945–1989', in *Archaeology of the Communist Era: A Political History of Archaeology of the 20th Century*, edited by Ludomir R. Lozny, New York: Springer.
Montelius, Oscar G. 1899, 'Prehistoric Chronology', *The Journal of the Anthropological Institute of Great Britain and Ireland*, 29, 3–4: 308–10.
Moore, Henrietta L. 1988, *Feminism and Anthropology*, Minneapolis: University of Minnesota Press.
Morgan, Lewis H. 1964 [1877], *Ancient Society*, edited by Leslie A. White, Cambridge, MA: Harvard University Press.
Novack, George E. 1971, *An Introduction to the Logic of Marxism*, New York: Pathfinder Press.
Novack, George E. 1974, *Understanding History: Marxist Essays*, New York: International Press.
Palerm, Ángel 2008, *Antropología y Marxismo*, México D.F.: Centro de Investigaciones y Estudios Superiores en Antropología Social, Universidad Autónoma Metropolitana.

Patterson, Thomas C. 1989, *Marx's Ghosts: Conversations with Archaeologists*, Oxford and New York: Berg.

Patterson, Thomas C. 2009, *Marx Anthropologist*, Oxford and New York: Berg.

Pellini, José Roberto (ed.) 2017, *Arqueología comercial: Dinero, Alienación y anestesia*, Madrid: Ediciones JAS.

Plekhanov, Georgi 1977 [1897], *Selected Philosophical Works*, Volume I, Moscow: Progress Publishers.

Politis, Gustavo G. and Rafael Pedro Curtoni 2011, 'Archaeology and Politics in Argentina During the Last 50 Years', in *Comparative Archaeologies: A Sociological View of the Science of the Past*, edited by Ludomir R. Lozny, New York: Springer.

Riba, Naama 2020, 'Inside the Battle Over Sell-off at Israel's Museum for Islamic Art', *Haaretz*, available at: https://www.haaretz.com/israel-news/.premium.MAGAZINE-from-a-tax-haven-to-sotheby-s-inside-the-battle-at-the-museum-of-islamic-art-1.9299701.

Risch, Roberto 2020, 'The Glorification of Violence at the Dawn of Class Exploitation', in *Rituelle Gewalt – Rituale der Gewalt. Ritual Violence – Rituals of Violence*, edited by Harald Meller et al., Halle (Saale): Landesmuseum für Vorgeschichte Halle.

Rosen, Steven 2003, 'Coming of Age: The Decline of Archaeology in Israeli Identity', available at: https://in.bgu.ac.il/en/heksherim/2005/Coming-of-Age.pdf.

Rosengarden, Frank 1984–85, 'The Gramsci-Trotsky Question (1922–1932)', *Social Text*, 11: 65–95.

Ruiz Rejón, Manuel 2020, 'Two Clashing Giants: Marxism and Darwinism', BBVA *Open Mind*, available at: https://www.bbvaopenmind.com/en/science/leading-figures/two-clashing-giants-marxism-and-darwinism/.

Ryding, James N. 1975, 'Alternatives in Nineteenth-Century German Ethnology: A Case Study in the Sociology of Science', *Sociologus*, 25, 1: 1–28.

Saitta, Dean 1994, 'Agency, Class, and Archaeological Interpretation', *Journal of Anthropological Archaeology*, 13, 3: 201–27.

de Saussure, Ferdinand 1916, *Cours de linguistique générale*, edited by Charles Bally and Alert Sechehaye with the assistance of Albert Riedlinger, Lausanne and Paris: Payot

Sève, Lucien 2016, 'The Structural Method and the Dialectical Method', *International Journal of Sociology*, 2, 2–3: 195–240.

Shanks, Michael and Christopher Tilley 1987, *Reconstructing Archaeology*, Cambridge: Cambridge University Press.

Shelach, Gideon 2004, 'Marxist and Post-Marxist Paradigms for the Neolithic', in *Gender and Chinese Archaeology*, edited by Katheryn M. Linduff and Yan Sun, Walnut, CA: AltaMira Press.

Shelach-Lavi, Gideon 2019, 'Archaeology and Politics in China: Historical Paradigm and Identity Construction in Museum Exhibitions', *China Information*, 33, 1: 23–45.

Su Bingqi 1987, 'A Few Words for the Young Generation', *Wenwu tiandi*, 4 [Chinese].

Su Bingqi 1990, 'Culture and Civilization', *Liahohai wenwu xuekan*, 1 [Chinese].

Spriggs, Matthew (ed.), *Marxist Approaches in Archaeology*, Cambridge: Cambridge University Press.

de Ste. Croix, Geoffrey 1983, *The Class Struggle in the Ancient Greek World*, London: Duckworth,

Stalin, Joseph 1940 [1938], *Dialectical and Historical Materialism*, New York: International Publishers.

Tabío, Ernesto E. and Estrella Rey 1966, *Prehistoria de Cuba*, La Habana: Departamento de Antropología, Academia de Ciencias de Cuba.

Thomas, Nicholas 1982, 'Childe, Marxism and Archaeology', *Dialectical Anthropology*, 6, 3: 245–52.

Tilley, Christopher 1989, 'Archaeology as Socio-political Action in the Present', in *Critical Traditions in Contemporary Archaeology: Essays in the Philosophy, History and Socio-politics of Archaeology*, edited by Valerie Pinsky and Alison Wylie, Cambridge: Cambridge University Press.

Toh, Yu-ho 1962, 'Lecture: What is the Paleolithic?', *Munhwayusan* [*Cultural Heritage*], 4: 48–55 (Korean).

Trigger, Bruce 1974, 'The Archaeology of Government', *World Archaeology*, 6, 1: 95–106.

Trigger, Bruce 1980, *Gordon Chile: Revolutions in Archaeology*, London: Thames and Hudson.

Trigger, Bruce 1984a 'Alternative Archaeologies: Nationalist, Colonialist, Imperialist', *Man*, 19: 355–70.

Trigger Bruce G. 1984b, 'Childe and Soviet Archaeology', *Australian Archaeology*, 18: 1–16.

Trigger, Bruce 1989, *A History of Archaeological Thought*, Cambridge: Cambridge University Press.

Trigger, Bruce 2008, '"Alternative Archaeologies" in Historical Perspective', in *Evaluating Multiple Narratives: Beyond Nationalist, Colonialist, Imperialist Archaeologies*, edited by Junko Habu, Clare Fawcett, and John M. Matsunaga, New York: Springer.

Trotsky, Leon D. 1931 [1930], *The Permanent Revolution*, translated by John G. Wright, available at: https://www.marxists.org/archive/trotsky/1931/tpr/rp-index.htm.

Trotsky, Leon D. 1935, *Écrits 1928–1940*, Paris: Publications Quatriéme Internationale.

Trotsky, Leon D. 1976 [1925–40], *Leon Trotsky on China*, introduction by Peng Shu-tse, New York: Monad Press.

Urban, Patricia A. and Edward Schortman 2019, *Archaeological Theory in Practice*, London: Routledge.

Ussishkin, David 1982 'Where Is Israeli Archaeology Going?', *The Biblical Archaeologist*, 45, 2: 93–5.

Wang, Tao, 1997, 'Establishing the Chinese Archaeological School: Su Bingqi and Contemporary Chinese Archaeology', *Antiquity*, 71: 31–9.

Wang, Tao 2011 "Public Archaeology" in China: A Preliminary Investigation, in *New Perspectives in Global Public Archaeology*, edited by Katuyuki Okamura and Akira Matsuda, New York: Springer.

Winckelmann, Johann Joachim 2013, *Winckelmann on Art, Architecture, and Archaeology*, translated with an introduction and notes by D. Carter, Rochester, NY: Boydell & Brewer.

Wolf, Eric 1982, *Europe and the People Without History*, Berkeley, CA: University of California Press.

Yekutieli, Yuval 2008, 'From the Field of Nationalism to the Field of Capital', in *Archaeology and Nationalism in Israel*, edited by Michael Feige and Zvi Shiloni, Jerusalem: The Ben-Gurion Research Institute for the Study of Israel and Zionism [Hebrew].

PART 2

Case Studies

∴

CHAPTER 2

Work and Subsistence in Preceramic Groups of Southeastern Mexico

Patricia Pérez Martínez and Guillermo Acosta Ochoa

1   Introduction: Marxism and Archaeology: a Latin American Perspective

Against the dominance of theoretical proposals developed in the Anglo-Saxon world, and as a theoretical alternative to the dominant processual archaeology in the United States and the historical particularism rooted in the academy in Latin American countries, a theoretical alternative was established during the last two decades of the twentieth century. This theoretical position has gone through various discussions of a theoretical-methodological nature, which have been developed between Latin American colleagues who share a historical materialist position. The places of these discussions have been Teotihuacán (1979), Cusco (1984), Caracas (1985) and Oaxtepec (1986), and has formed therein a group of academics that

> ... dealt mainly with the conceptual and theoretical problems involved in the categories of socio-economic formation, way of life and culture, as well as the characterization of the various sociohistorical formations and their processes of development and change; likewise, the category of ethnicity and the problems involved in ethnic-national situations have been discussed. That is, they have focused on the issues of the substantive theory of History.[1]

These first meetings were important, without doubt, to form the working group of what has since been called Latin American Social Archaeology (LASA),[2] and later Amero-Iberic Social Archaeology (AISA) after the incorporation of academics from Spain and Portugal, and although this initial stage can be defined as a period dominated by 'statements of principles', it was one of

---

1   Bate 1998, p. 20.
2   And see Vitores, this volume.

intense theoretical debate on the main concepts that underlie the substantive theory of the theoretical position.[3] Under this inertia, social archaeology in the eighties and nineties of the last century focused on defining its general concepts, although the empirical examples in which the proposals were evaluated remained scarce. In the last two decades, however, there has been a growing interest in confronting the theoretical proposal of Social Archaeology to specific cases of study. The study presented here is one of those examples, because of a fertile critical discussion of the ASAI, which has been strengthened in recent meetings held in Mexico City where several colleagues have emphasised the need to confront Marxist theory within archaeological practice.[4]

2   Labour and Society: a Marxist Approach to the Production and Activity-Area Analysis

One of the most relevant theoretical debates of our discipline has been the problem of explaining the formation and transformation of the archaeological context, as well as the link between the materials and contexts to broader social theories. This debate resulted in two polarised groups with opposing archaeological propositions. The first claimed that the past does not exist and that all archaeological knowledge is constructed from the present (post-processual archaeology). The second claims that the link between the past and the archaeological context should be defined by the construction of a mid-range theory, explaining how context is formed and transformed, aiming towards establishing, in some uncertain future, 'big theory' that explains the fundamental aspects of past societies. From a historical-materialist perspective, both proposals are wrong. The first because it eliminates the history and memory of past societies, denying the links of archaeological contexts with the societies that produced them; the second because it refuses to use a general theory as a starting point, which has led, in the words of Kent V. Flannery, to the construction of 'Mickey Mouse Laws' or theoretical proposals of very low explanatory scope.[5]

---

3 See Veloz Maggiolo 1984; Vargas-Arenas 1985, and 1990; Sanoja 1983; Bate 1977, 1978, and 1998; Gándara 1990, 1992, and 1994.
4 For example, see Tantaleán and Aguilar 2012.
5 Flannery 1973.

2.1 The Work as Origin of Value

According to Marx, 'work is the source of all wealth and all culture'.[6] Under this principle, we start from the idea that archaeological materials and contexts are the result of past human work (or objectified work in the form of 'material culture'). Under this perspective, and based on the Marxist definition, work is the condition of all human activity in society and is distinguished from animal work by being a conscious activity aimed at the creation of satisfiers. In the most general sense, 'it is the deployment of the pure and simple workforce that possesses on average all ordinary men and that is inherent on their physical organism without the need for special development'.[7] Undoubtedly, work to create use value and exchange value is a fundamental basis in the economic theory of Karl Marx, but it is also a solid basis to explain the history of archaeological contexts.[8] On this basis, we develop a theoretical proposal that allows for the linking of the phenomenological aspect of material culture to other more general processes that can be explained by historical materialism as a general social theory, for example characterising the intermediate aspects – such as activity areas, modes of work or ways of life – to the most general aspects of a human society – such as the mode of production or social formation. A more detailed version of this proposal is exposed in a previous work,[9] so only its basic outline is traced below.

2.2 The Archaeological Context as Result of Past Work

Marx investigates what determines the value of goods, concluding that it is 'the human labour embodied in them'.[10] The investment of work transforms the original raw material into objectified work. The objectified work in a product can even be the modification of the physical properties of the antecedent matter – since its appropriation and transport from its original source – using the means of work, which can involve human and animal work. The purpose of this objectified work is to solve a human need, or to satisfy the nature of this need. The anthropogenic processes of the transformation of matter into objectified work – objectivated in the form of products of labour – are work processes.

The objectified work is presented to experience as an object on which a certain amount of work has been invested and can manifest itself under the

---

6   Marx 1979.
7   Marx 1946, p. 11.
8   Bate 1999.
9   Acosta 1999.
10 Marx 1984, p. 47.

double aspect of use value and exchange value. The use value acquires reality only in the consumption process.[11] Use values are immediate livelihoods (bread for food, the hammer to hit). Conversely, these means of existence are products of social life, and are the result of the life force invested by humans and materialised in objectified work.[12] On the other hand, use values create the material content of wealth, whatever the social form of this.[13] Even when an object loses its use value, it still retains the quality of being a product of past work, but if it loses its use value, it also loses the material elements and the forms that convert them into such use value.[14]

The exchange value, on the other hand, appears first as a quantitative relation in which the values of use are interchangeable (one kilo of beans per two of corn).[15] Products that are both use values and exchange values are called goods or merchandise. To be merchandise, a product must pass into the hands of another – the consumer or the intermediary – through an act of exchange.[16] The relationship between the use value and the exchange value is a relation of production between work as an individual product and work as a social product.

The labour force is the primary condition for production, but so are the *means of work*.[17] With the means of work, the human being uses the mechanical, physical and chemical qualities of the materials to use them according to the purpose pursued. The means of work allow for the reduction of the time of work necessary in the production, or its optimisation.

The means of work, however, are not only the instruments of work (tools), but 'all those material conditions that must concur for the work process to be carried out'.[18] This includes all conditions that are not directly identified with this process, but without which it cannot be executed, such as the physical and social space of the work process. The *locus standi* to which Marx referred. In archaeological culture, these spatial conditions are included in the properties of the archaeological contexts, arranged in their surfaces and volumes, so they

---

11   Marx 1984, p. 45.
12   Marx 1984, p. 47.
13   Marx 1946, p. 4.
14   Marx 1946, p. 5.
15   Marx 1984, p. 46.
16   Marx 1946, p. 8.
17   The work means are that object or set of objects that the worker interposes between him and the object that works, and that serves to redirect his activity on this object (see Marx, 1946, p. 131).
18   Marx, 1946, p. 133.

have undergone the same processes of generation and transformation and are explained by the history of archaeological contexts.[19]

The objects of work can be natural elements, like all those things that the work does nothing to but detach from the earth (as happens with mining).[20] On the contrary, when the work object is the result of a previous work, it is called raw material. The raw materials can, on the one hand, constitute the main substance of a product, or simply serve as auxiliary materials for its manufacture; in the latter case, the auxiliary materials are absorbed by the instrument or the work object. These auxiliary materials are exemplified by the coal or wood consumed by the kiln to produce ceramics, or by the stove for cooking food. It may happen that the work process handles the product in ways that can only be used as raw material. In such cases, raw materials link work processes and are called intermediate articles – as they would be, for example, in the way of textile work, cotton, yarn or warp. Each of these products are the result of consecutive work processes that are related in a necessary way to generate a final product (a blanket, a dress, etc.). In these consecutive work processes, the original raw material goes through a certain gradation of different processes, where it functions successively as a raw material, under a different form each time, until it reaches the final work process, from which it ends up being a product ready for consumption.

Finally, in consumption, the values of use of these final products are absorbed into a profitable way for a specific purpose. As means of life are absorbed by individual consumption, as means of work are consumed in a new process of work, and as means of domination are superstructurally consumed. Thus understood, the cycle of productive activities keeps a defined order, where the chain of consecutive work processes is linked as precedent work processes and subsequent work processes (you cannot knit before yarn is woven, and you cannot weave before cotton is spun), involving a defined relationship between production and consumption.

The final products and waste are the result of the productive process insofar as they are the effects of the productive activity, without being elements of it, while the simple elements of the work process are the causal factors of production. Waste, because of the work process, does not constitute goods. This waste is the effect of two possible activities, first, as a direct result of the productive activity (production waste). Production waste never had functional quality and, therefore, no use value. Second, as effects of the consumption process

---

19   Bate 1998.
20   Marx 1946, p. 131.

(consumer waste). Consumer waste at some point had use value, which was extinguished in the consumption process. Waste can only recover a use value if new useful work is invested in them, as happens in the processes of recycling, reuse and, in a certain way, archaeological work.

In the archaeological context, objects have lost the use value or exchange value that they contained in a living society, since use value is extinguished with consumption, and they only retain the property of being products of work. This property allows us to infer that materials contained in the archaeological context were, at some point, objects of work, instruments of work or waste of one or more productive processes. In archaeological activity, we cannot observe the processes of living work. Instead, work processes are recorded in artefacts, available for the observer to see, while the activities that produced artefacts/objects can be inferred by studying areas of activity, evaluating workspaces and areas of production, consumption and waste. Artefacts themselves define their life histories since both objects and archaeological contexts keep traces of activities of the past.

2.3   *The Traceology as a Social Memory*

Prior to Semenov's *Prehistoric Technology* in 1964, lithic studies were focused on ordering lithic assemblies in geographic and chronological terms, while the function of each of the artefacts was not a main focus of research in the field.[21] Although some specialists described certain functional aspects in a speculative way, they basically relied on morphological and technological criteria.[22]

Semenov's publication encouraged new perspectives in the field of trace-use analysis by basically demonstrating the need to systematise the use of experimental tools and the analysis of traces of use in the microscope. During the beginning of the discipline, its questions dealt with methodological aspects, while descriptions of traces produced by different subjects, worked through different kinematics of use, laid the foundations for the microscopic analysis of archaeological material. But it wasn't until 1977 that the first expert meeting on traces of use was held, titled 'Lithic Use-Wear Analysis'.[23] This meeting was organised by Bryan Hayden in Burnaby, British Columbia, to broadly deal with issues of a theoretical-methodological nature, such as the use of micro-

---

21   Semenov 1981.
22   Vaughan 1985.
23   With this first meeting, we can say that the first steps towards methodological studies for the maturity of the discipline are beginning.

scopic devices, nomenclatures, methodology of experimentation, as well as the characterisation of traces or traces of use.[24]

In recent years, with the intention of studying traces produced by raw matter as objectively as possible, scholarship aimed at quantifying certain traces of use, especially micro-polishes, has increased. At the same time, since the late eighties, interest in ethnographic research has also increased. Through this, it has been possible to better know the use of certain artefacts that were assigned to the work on different vegetal, animal and mineral materials. In addition to the use of ethnographic methods to evaluate functions of archaeological artefacts, archaeological theory has provided bases for interpretative proposals related to societies of the past.[25]

One of the main objectives of functional analysis over the last two decades has been the identification and quantification of different wear characteristics associated with all possible processes that altered the edges of artefacts,[26] such as human use, natural fractures and post-depositional processes in different types of lithics – including chert, quartz, quartzite and obsidian.[27]

Recently, the combined analysis of traces of use and micro-residues was popularised to identify not only activity but also processed material.[28] In this way, various techniques have been used to identify residues of both animal and plant origin from archaeological objects. Commonly preserved organic materials include blood, fats, hair, feathers, starch grains and a variety of plant and animal tissues. Because of the above, methods have been developed to analyse micro remains using techniques adapted from microscopy, histology, biochemistry, immunological chemistry, forensic science and molecular biology.[29]

2.4   Perspectives and Applications of Functional Analysis

As we have mentioned previously, since the investigations carried out by Semenov[30] there have been considerable developments in functional analyses of

---

24   Hayden 1979.
25   Mansur-Franchomme 1987; Ramseyer 1987; Kamminga 1988; Pelegrin et al. 1988; Owen and Porr 1999; Kimura et al. 2001; Rots and Williamson 2004; Perry 2005; Weedman 2006; Briz i Godino et al. 2014; Malainey et al. 2015.
26   Grace 1996.
27   Yamada 1993.
28   Atchison and Fullagar 1998; Field and Fullagar 1998; Lombard 2006; Buonasera 2007; Haslam et al. 2009; Blee et al. 2010.
29   Marreiros et al. 2015.
30   Semenov 1968.

lithic archaeological materials. However, at least in Mexican archaeology, little has been done to incorporate this type of analysis into the basic aspects of research. The above does not mean that the investigations are poorly done. Nevertheless, we consider there to have been little uniformity of research when it comes to variables used in the analysis of traces of use. In this way, the challenge basically lies in making a more homogeneous methodology in functional analyses, supported by microscopic techniques and experimental archeology.

As we know, the studies carried out by microscopic analysis are intended to infer the probable functionality of a certain class of artefacts, but it is important to point out the fact that not every form corresponds to a certain content.[31] However, the foregoing, the theoretical and morphologically defined functionality of an artefactual set can be inferred through microscopic studies of traces of use.[32]

Then we can say that, from a correct functional analysis of any lithic assemblage, we cannot only evaluate the functionality of the artefacts; we must also determine their role in the production process as instruments used during the work process.[33]

It is vital to note that, since the final products obtained are dedicated to consumption, these tools also constitute an important means to quantify the volume of production. Therefore, in any archaeological investigation that attempts to determine what, when, how and how much a society produced, it is necessary to first define the technical means of production implemented, among which lithic artefacts occupy an important place.

In this way, this field of research should seek significant correlations between macroscopic typological attributes and microscopic analyses of use traces, complemented by micro-residue analyses as well as contextual associations, to broaden the hypotheses that lead to the characterisation of a much more specific functionality.[34]

---

31 Bate 1998, p. 124.
32 Within the theoretical position of social archeology, an artefactual set refers to all those objects that distinguish each other by their raw material and functionality (Fournier 1997, p. 5).
33 The means or instruments of work 'are the elements that the human being interposes between the simple work force and the work objects. This allows to multiply the capacities and energy of work force or to carry out operations that surpass their natural capacities of movement' (Bate 1998, p. 59).
34 Bate 1998, p. 193.

3 Work, Value and Hunter-Gatherer Societies

3.1 *The Organisation of Work in Hunter-Gatherer Communities*

There have been diverse efforts and theoretical proposals from anthropology, ethnoarchaeology and archeology to understand the differences in social organisation between collecting-hunter groups. Traditionally, explanations about these types of communities have tended to classify them as societies that are not very complex in their behaviour, including their social and symbolic spheres, accepting less elaborate behavioural interpretations as satisfactory. In contrast, we start from the fact that hunter-gatherer groups do not all belong to the same phase of social development. Therefore, we cannot consider them 'less complex', and, taking up the proposal of Felipe Bate, we distinguish between pre-tribal hunter-gatherers and tribalised hunter-gatherers. Likewise, there may be hunter-gatherer or food-producing societies in different phases of historical development, since the term 'hunter-gatherer' refers only to a form of techno-economic organisation, not to a mode of production itself.

Although the theoretical proposals on hunters remain strongly deterministic in an ecological sense – mainly in models of the type 'optimal foraging' where hunters are seen as inevitably destined to maximise energy resources and minimise risks[35] – there is a growing interest in assessing the internal causality of these societies, assigning them a more active rather than passive role in historical processes (a move that rejects the simplistic attitude that 'if the environment changes, society changes'). On the other hand, different authors agree that there is no single form of hunter, though some variability in their structural characteristics can be distinguished, which have generally been grouped into two types of societies. These proposals differ in their take on whether such differences can be attributed to ecological or social factors; therefore, the typologies summarised in the following table are not exactly equivalent, since they consider different causal factors for their classification (Table 2.1).

From a Marxist perspective, we assume that the evolution of human society implies different social formations and that the concept of 'hunter-gatherer' simply defines aspects of the techno-economy of a society. Therefore, we prefer to distinguish other fundamental elements that characterise said societies, such as the social relations of production.[36]

---

35 Bettinger 1987.
36 Marx 1984.

TABLE 2.1 Types of hunter-gatherer societies[a]

Author	1st group	2nd group
Service	Bands	Tribes
Binford	Foragers	Collectors
Testart	Hunters without storage	Hunters with storage
Ingold	Mode of production hunter-gatherer	Pastoralist mode of production
Woodburn	Immediate-return societies	Delayed-return societies
Bate	Pre-tribal hunter-gatherers	Tribal hunter-gatherers

a   Service 1962; Woodburn 1982; Testart et al. 1982; Ingold 1983; Bate 1986; Binford 1996.

Therefore, we chose to characterise hunters 'without storage' or 'immediate return'[37] simply as a primitive community of hunter gatherers[38] to differentiate them from tribalised hunter societies. These pre-tribal hunters are defined in a way that has been compared to a 'primitive communism', since the relations of production are based on the absence of private ownership of the territory.

Another of the central elements of this social formation was the precariousness of the economy.[39] Since these societies depended entirely on natural production, their productivity was subjected to the conditions of resource availability. Therefore, the production-consumption cycles were short and with a practical absence of social storage.[40] To reduce the risk of deficiencies, domestic units established strong reciprocity relationships,[41] giving them the right to be assisted in case of shortage, forcing them, in turn, to grant the same favour to those in an equivalent situation.[42]

On the other hand, high mobility and low population density are very interrelated aspects with the previous social formations. The low population density is not only due to the limitations of the production system subject to seasonal productivity, but it is a social strategy, using contraceptive methods, linked to the avoidance of overexploiting resources. In addition, although the absence of storage allows for high mobility, breastfeeding tends to reduce it, so strategic spacing between births leads to a lower birth rate.

37   Woodburn 1982.
38   Bate 1998, p. 83.
39   Bate 1986.
40   Ingold 1983.
41   Sahlins 1965.
42   Bate 1998, p. 84.

Finally, although the precariousness of the economy tends to generate very strict social rules, particularly intended for the reduction of social differences, birth control and mating rules, the observance of roles defined by sex and age or in compliance with taboos, there is always place for agents to act individually. However, this action operates at a low level in individuals, since there are no true rulers; but at a higher level of action as a group, decisions are usually agreed or consulted with the elders or characters with leadership roles. In this sense, hunter gatherers 'vote with their feet', with fission and migration as means to resolve conflicts within communities and, possibly, as bases for cultural and historical divergence.

3.2 The Structure of Archaeological Sites and Their Activities

In studies on collecting hunter groups, the use of surface survey data is commonly compared to those materials from controlled excavations in extensive areas. This is largely understood if we compare the low economic cost of surface study with respect to excavation analysis. However, it seems that surface studies have supplanted the inferences evaluable only by excavation. This has been particularly notable in the arid and semi-arid regions of northern Mexico, in arguments that low sedimentation allows surface observation of 'original' occupations. The analysis of survey data, however, does not allow for the evaluation of contexts such as volumes and surfaces in specific sequences, and only obtains an occupational palimpsest that may correspond to different temporalities and cultural groups, which may potentially in turn be naively considered as a singular occupation. The above also applies to the typology of sites.[43]

Some authors such as Leticia González Arratia[44] have made attempts to define parameters and indicators that allow for the inference of the functionality of hunter-gatherer sites. However, the impossibility of directly dating lithic surface materials makes it practically impossible to discern whether the spatial links of materials on the surface of a given site correspond with chronological similarities. The study area, in any case, will remain an important tool for assessing settlement preferences and for analysing locations and movements of hunter-gatherer groups, but such data should be complemented with an analysis of excavated materials.

In this way, to evaluate the possibility of distinguishing between populations or the functionality of the sites, it is necessary to consider the formation and

---

43   Acosta 2008.
44   González Arratia 1992a, and 1992b.

TABLE 2.2 Equivalences in the typology of hunter-gatherer sites

Type of site	Binford (1996)	Dillehay (2000)	Features
1. *Base camp*	Residential base	Long-term base camps	High intensity High redundancy High variability
2. *Secondary camp*	Location	Short-term base camps	Variable intensity Moderate redundancy Moderate variability
3. *Specialised sites*			
a. Quarry		Quarries	
b. Station	Station	Transitory stations	Variable intensity Low redundancy Very low variability
c. Kill site	*Field camp*	*Butchering stations*	
Others			
	Cache		

transformation processes of the sites of hunter-gatherers, as well as the reliability in the recovery of field data. The variability of the materials located in the sites of hunter gatherers may be due to various causes, such as: a) differences in the functionality of the site; b) the intensity of settlement; and c) the redundancy of occupations.

Both the intensity of occupation (the duration of singular events) and the redundancy of occupations (the number of repeated occupations at a given site) produce the density of artefacts that we observe in a H-G archaeological site. On the other hand, the characteristics of the materials will be determined by the daily activities carried out in them. In this way, we can group H-G sites into at least three different types (see Table 2.2):

a) *Base camps*, where the core of subsistence and reproductive activities will be carried out. Hunting or gathering games originate there in addition to much of the work of processing, manufacturing and various other activities of the group.

b) *Secondary camps*, which are usually stations of shorter duration and intensity than base camps. They may be temporary camps between two base camps, or sites near areas of low or seasonal productivity, occupied for a short period of time.

c) *Specialised sites*. In this category we integrate various types of sites aimed at obtaining resources or processing specific materials. These sites are usually ephemeral, often in the open sky, except for those located in strategic resource banks (such as the so-called 'workshops'), as well as the sites of rock representations not associated with base or secondary camps. In most of them redundancy is generally very low.

The specific qualities of the base camps allow for a greater diversity of artefacts and areas of activity, while specialised sites (a kill site, for example) may have only one area of activity and will tend to have low artefactual variability. Only a small part of the characteristic materials of such a society are represented (Table 2.2). In order to evaluate the possibility of distinguishing populations or 'cultural traditions' in a given area, it is first necessary to distinguish the functionality of the sites used in the analysis.[45]

4   Santa Marta as a Case Study: Analysis Methodology

4.1   *The Santa Marta Rock Shelter at the End of the Pleistocene: Chronology and Location*

Caves and rock shelters, dry caves with good sedimentation in particular, are excellent places to obtain information due to their optimal conditions for the preservation of a great variety of archaeological indicators. Possibly the best location for this type of cave in southeastern Mexico is the Central Depression of Chiapas, characterised by an area of orographic shadow whose dominant vegetation is scrubland and medium sub-deciduous forest with less rainfall than the rest of the state (Figure 2.1).

These conditions were observed by those who conducted previous projects seeking occupations of hunter gatherers or incipient agriculture, such as Richard S. MacNeish[46] or Joaquín García-Bárcena,[47] who noticed that, particularly in the Ocozocoautla area, caves were located with good sedimentation and preservation of materials, such as the Santa Marta rock shelter.

---

45   Binford 1983, and 1996.
46   MacNeish and Peterson, 1962; MacNeish 1961.
47   García-Bárcena and Santamaría 1984.

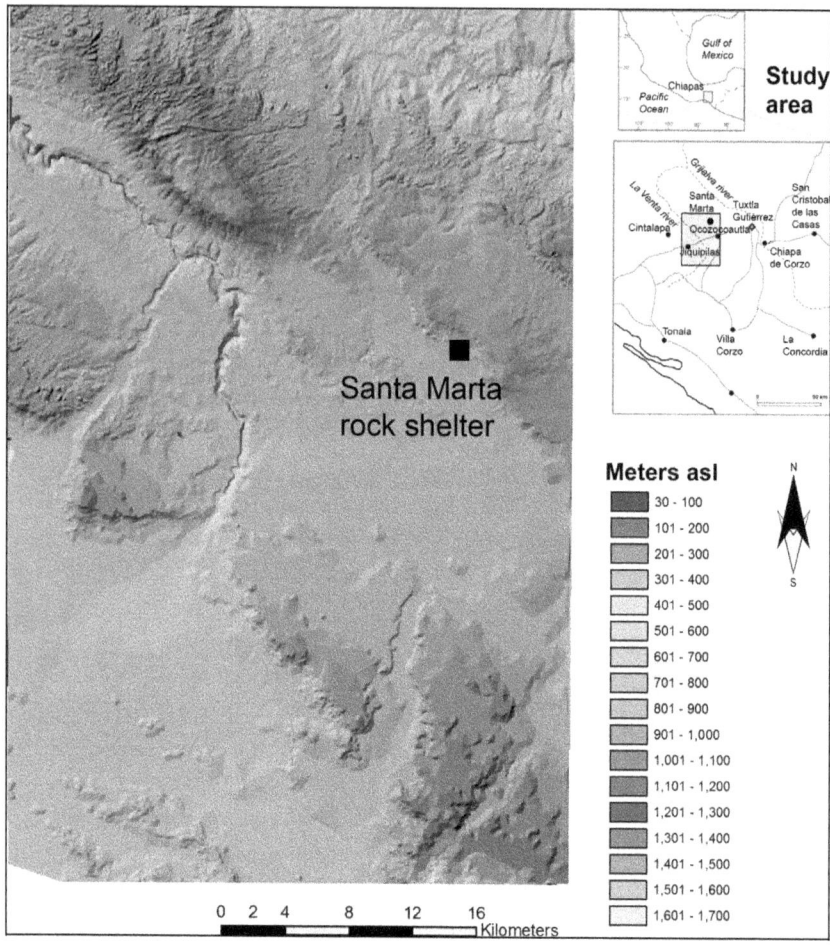

FIGURE 2.1 Study area

With this background, Guillermo Acosta Ochoa, in the Institute of Anthropological Research (UNAM) project 'Hunters of the Tropic', excavated the rock shelter in 2005 to examine the cultural variability of the Pleistocene and the beginnings of the Holocene in the southeast of Mexico and to furthermore identify early occupations associated with hunter-gatherers from the late Pleistocene in the region.[48] During this investigation, new information on the rock shelter was obtained, including new dates, ranging from 12,450–11,266 cal BP,

---

48   Acosta 2008.

for the levels associated with the final Pleistocene, which make it the earliest site registered in the Mexican southeast. In the occupation floors corresponding to these dates, palaeo-ethnobotanic and archaeo-zoological data was recovered that complemented the information available in the region for the Pleistocene-Holocene transition.

The earliest occupation corresponds to layer XVI. This is a layer of preceramic occupations that has the presence of reddened sands, burned rocks and patches of ash and coal. Layer XVI is divided into seven occupancy floors that have very similar characteristics, only varying in the distribution of archaeological materials and in the amounts of ash that are present in the floors. The layer represents the highest occupation of the coast due to the qualities and quantities of the materials found; therefore, it was selected for the application of a series of macro- and micro-analyses to gather data on the media of subsistence during the Pleistocene-Holocene transition.

The study shows that in Santa Marta there was a subsistence oriented towards the hunting of modern fauna, such as deer [*Odocoileus* and *Mazama*], armadillo [*Dasypus*], rabbit [*Sylvilagus* sp.], pecarí [*Dicotyles* sp.] and turtle [*Kinosternon* sp.].[49]] Meanwhile, the palaeo-ethnobotanical data shows pollen from plants that suggests the exploitation of different tropical forests, as well as the introduction of plants, such as teosinte [*Zea mays*] and cocoa [*Theobroma cacao*], suggesting a marked importance in plant collection during the period.[50] These results place hunter gatherers as the first human groups in the tropical regions of southeastern Mexico, with a highly diversified subsistence predating the emergence fluted-points technology in Central America by at least 500 years.[51]

4.2 Work Processes, Activity Areas and Daily Activities

We will begin the discussion on the theoretical aspects that support this work by explaining the meaning of 'everyday life'. In our case, we return to the definition of the Marxist sociologist Agnes Heller,[52] who argues that '[d]aily life is the set of activities that characterise the reproduction of men, which, in turn, create the possibility of social reproduction'.[53] If, then, we conceive of everyday life as the totality of activities linked to the particular reproduction of individuals (persons), we must clarify that these activities integrate productive (economic

---

49 Eudave 2008.
50 Rivera Irán 2013.
51 Acosta 2008, and 2010; Acosta and Pérez 2012; Acosta et al. 2013.
52 Agnes Heller 1985, and 1998.
53 Heller 1998, p. 19.

in the strict sense), reproductive (which include both biological reproduction such as leisure and recreation, being, in short, the restitution of the workforce) and ideological (assuming that ideology is more than simply 'false consciousness').

This social reproduction at a particular level must be observed as a continuous dialectic, the result of the tension between all the limitations and restrictions operating in the structure of the community as well as unique aspects of creativity, innovation and leadership. This approach seeks a reconsideration of the strongly deterministic characteristics of some historical materialist models (at least in the structural sense), which leave little space for autonomous subjective agency, except for class subjects, establishing individualistic models in which the ontology of the subject is seen as fixed.[54]

In this way, the category of work process allows for a better explanation of the so-called 'artistic creations' and 'technical feats' evidenced in an object or in archaeological material – whose uniqueness sometimes gives it the dabbler merit as a 'piece worthy of a museum' – and where leadership roles and individual technical achievements and aesthetic creations, canonised from an established 'tradition', can be satisfactorily explained by the dialectical relationship between the individual and the collective.[55]

Work processes of past societies have correlations in the archaeological context – for example, the analysis of traces of use in lithic material will give us information related to the handling of plants or animals, lithic technology, techniques for food processing, etc. Thus, this proposal aims to lay the foundations for the production of data on work processes related to the use of timber and plant resources that are adequate for the reliable reconstruction of subsistence strategies of societies that inhabited the rock shelter of Santa Marta and to more generally aid studies of subsistence strategies in hunter-gatherer societies.

Previously, there has been less interest in the analysis and registration of hunter-gatherer plant resources, stemming both from a belief that there is a lack of preserved botanical remains as well as from prejudices regarding the importance of that for which they were used. Such prejudices are usually accompanied by preconceptions about the social agents who managed plant resources, as, typically, men are considered to have been in charge of hunting and of the manufacture and use of lithic materials, while women are considered to have been collectors and in turn related to motherhood and baby care.

---

54   Gándara 1994, p. 101.
55   Acosta 1999.

In this way, the analysis of the domestic spaces of the Santa Marta rock shelter, focusing on the occupation levels at the end of the Pleistocene and at the beginning of the Holocene (layers XVI and XVII; 12,450–11,266 cal BP) allows us to have a better idea about its territoriality, cycles of activities and effects on the environment. The results enable us to consider that the rock shelter was occupied as a base camp at levels 2 to 7 of layer XVI (Figures 2.3–2.8), while level 1 of layer XVI (Figure 2.2) and level 2 of layer XVII (Figures 2.9) appear to be the initial and final occupations of the main occupational period at the site. The density and variability of the artefacts indicate that the place was used as a refuge during the time, when the weather was wetter and cooler and the land more forested than today.

We do not rule out that other open-pit sites have complemented the mobility cycle during the dry season. Unfortunately, the difficulty of dating the surface sites leaves us with only an outline of this cycle of mobility. The analysis of raw materials and operational chains based on the lithic artefacts of Santa Marta indicates that the reservoir workshops located west of the shelter were exploited since this time and were part of the exploitation of important lithic resources for communities in a zone rich – for the pre-ceramic period – in tropical, mesophilic and deciduous forest species.

The distribution of archaeological features and materials through occupational surfaces of Santa Marta indicates a diversity of daily activities – which had the fireplace as a focal point, as noted in ethnographic studies of hunters in tropical regions – the most obvious of which being the manufacture of lithic tools and the consumption of animals (see Figure 2.9).[56]

In particular, the analysis of lithic technology indicates that the artefacts manufactured in the rock shelter were poorly elaborated, with little preparation of the cores, often on very particular modified flakes, used with sharp edges or with simple marginal retouching (Figure 2.10). The constant appearance of concave or notched scrapers (spoke shavers) along with traces of use in the artefacts suggests regular work of wood or other plant resources.[57] The absence of lithic projectile points may indicate that the tools were either manufactured with other materials, that prey was captured by traps, or the use of techniques, such as the use of blowpipes, that have not been previously considered.

---

56   Politis 1996.
57   Pérez 2010.

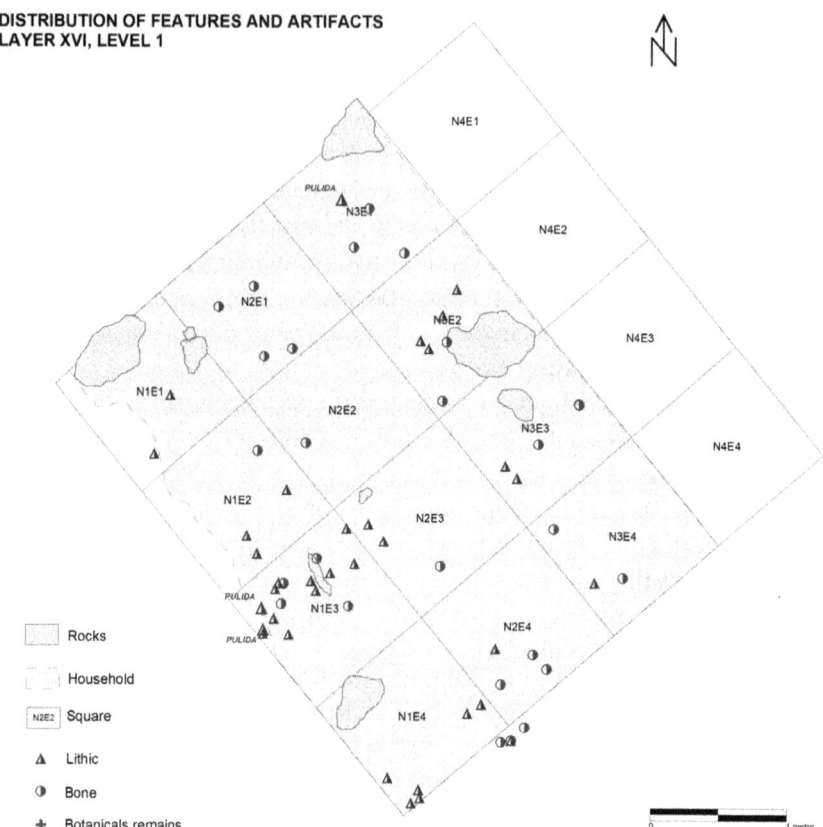

FIGURE 2.2 Santa Marta: activity areas, Layers XVI, level 1

On the other hand, chemical analyses of occupation surfaces allow us to infer other activities that leave no trace in macro remains and suggest discrete areas of transit, plant management and the possible processing of animal prey (Figure 2.13). Other studies, such as the analysis of microfossils in stone tools (starch granules and phytoliths) or the study of traces of use in lithics, have allowed us to expand our observations towards an even more complete idea of the daily life of the human groups that inhabited the Santa Marta rock shelter ten thousand years ago, making it clear that they come out of the stereotype of the specialised hunters with fluted points that were supposedly the colonisers of the Central American tropical regions.

WORK AND SUBSISTENCE IN PRECERAMIC GROUPS OF MEXICO 57

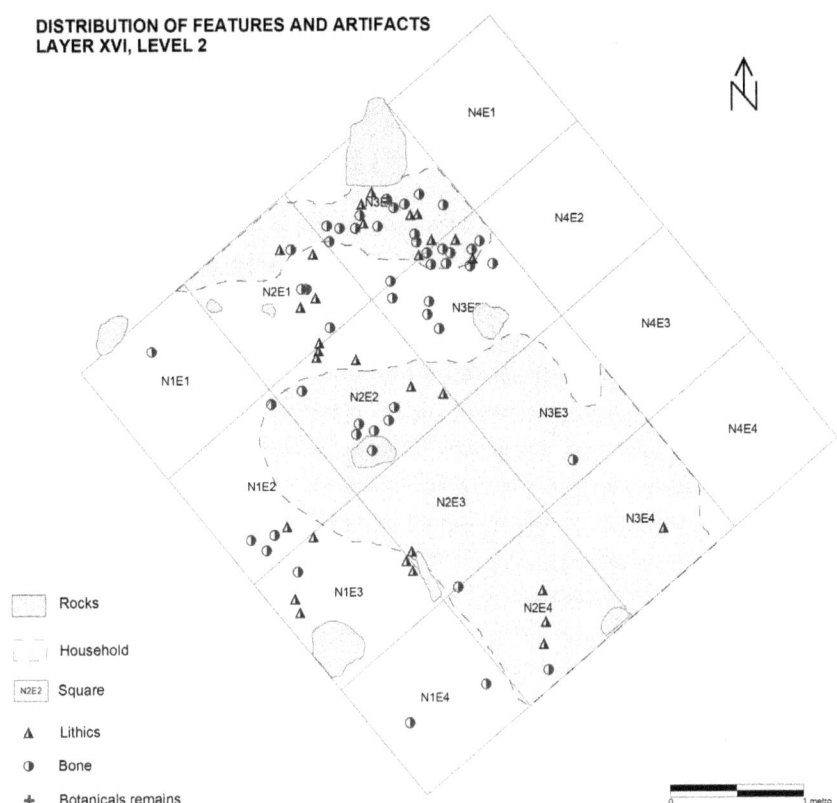

FIGURE 2.3 Santa Marta: activity areas, Layers XVI, level 2

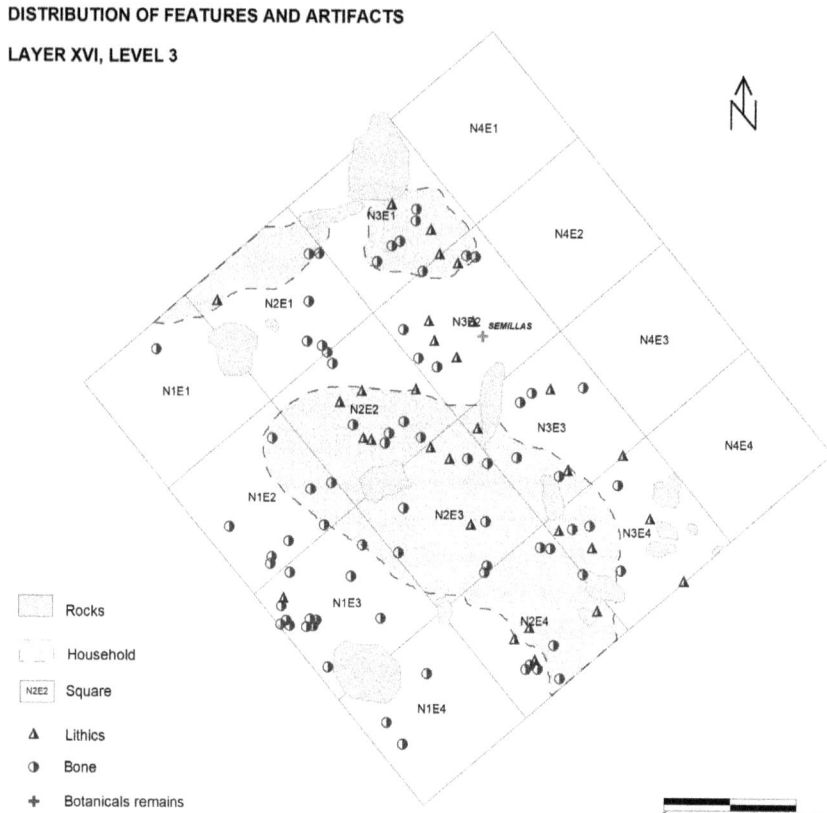

FIGURE 2.4 Santa Marta: activity areas, Layers XVI, level 3

WORK AND SUBSISTENCE IN PRECERAMIC GROUPS OF MEXICO 59

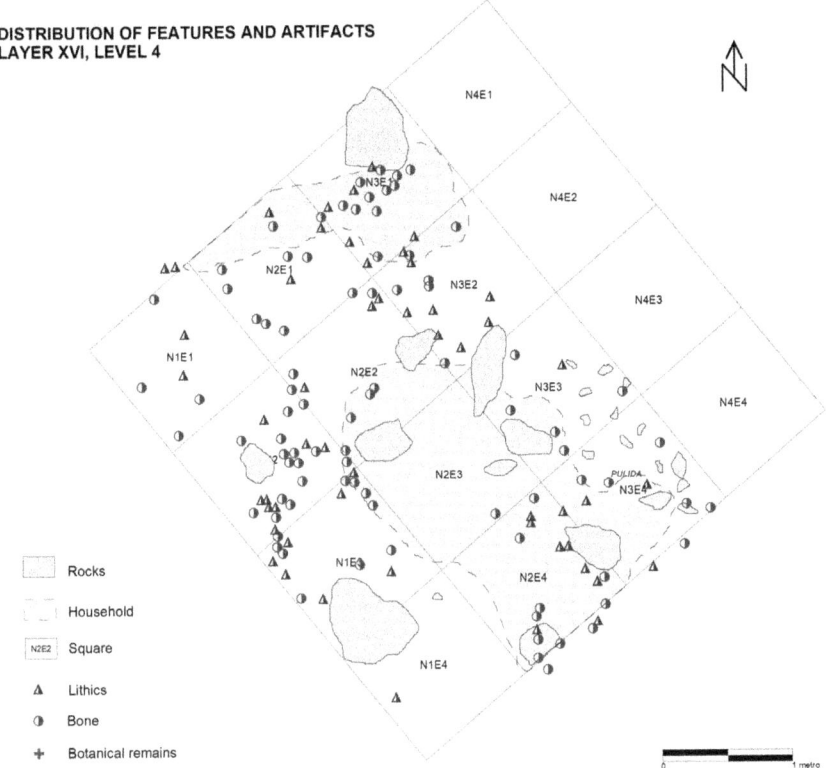

FIGURE 2.5 Santa Marta: activity areas, Layers XVI, level 4

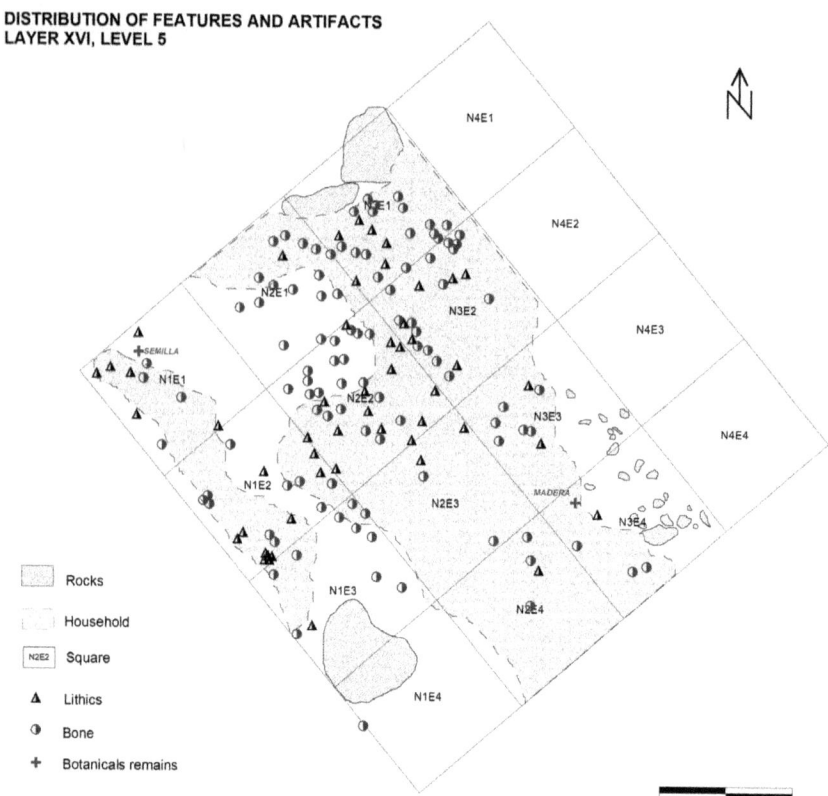

FIGURE 2.6 Santa Marta: activity areas, Layers XVI, level 5

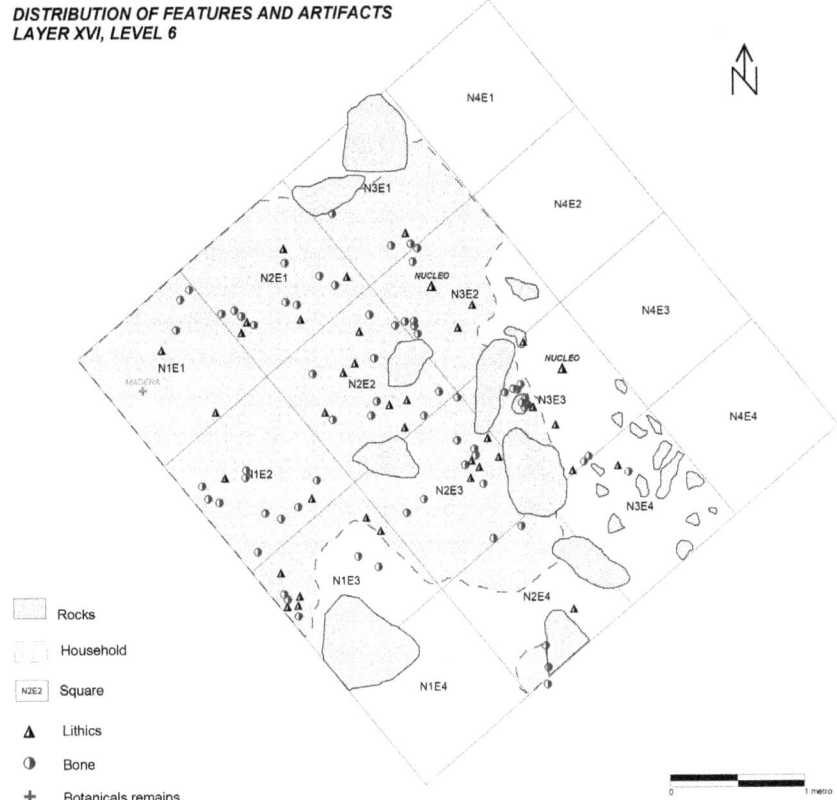

FIGURE 2.7 Santa Marta: activity areas, Layers XVI, level 6

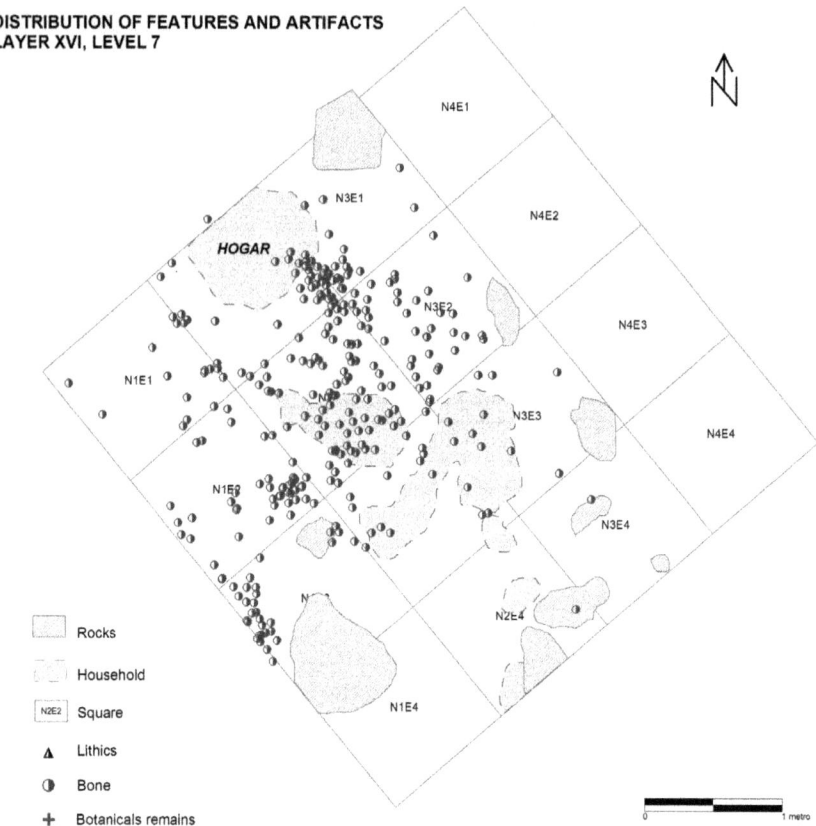

FIGURE 2.8 Santa Marta: activity areas, Layers XVI, level 7

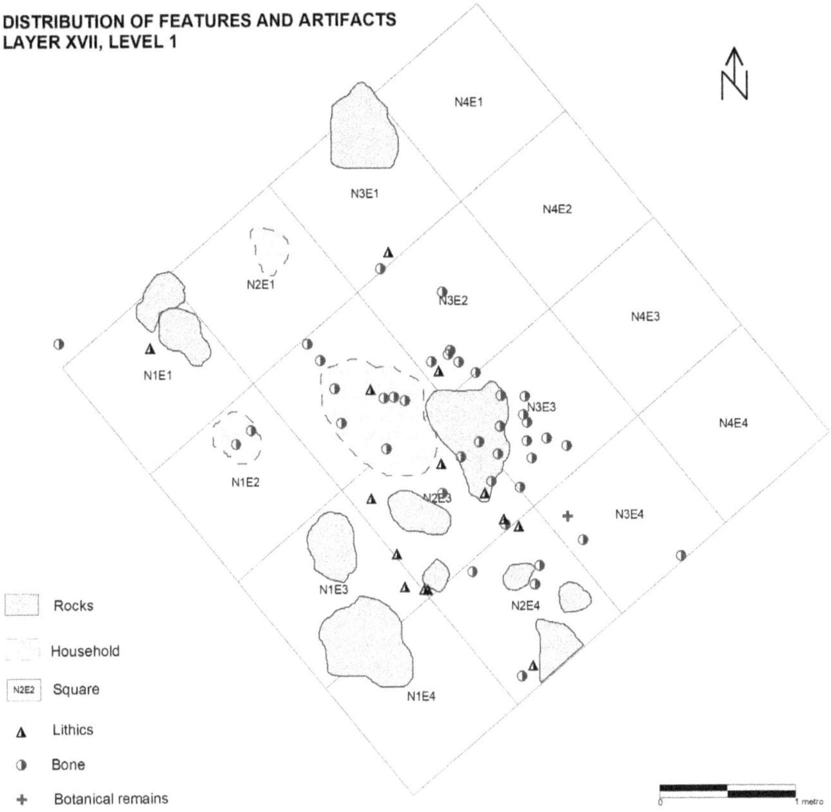

WORK AND SUBSISTENCE IN PRECERAMIC GROUPS OF MEXICO

**DISTRIBUTION OF FEATURES AND ARTIFACTS
LAYER XVII, LEVEL 1**

FIGURE 2.9 Santa Marta: activity areas, Layers XVII, level 1

FIGURE 2.10 Spoke shavers recovered from Santa Marta

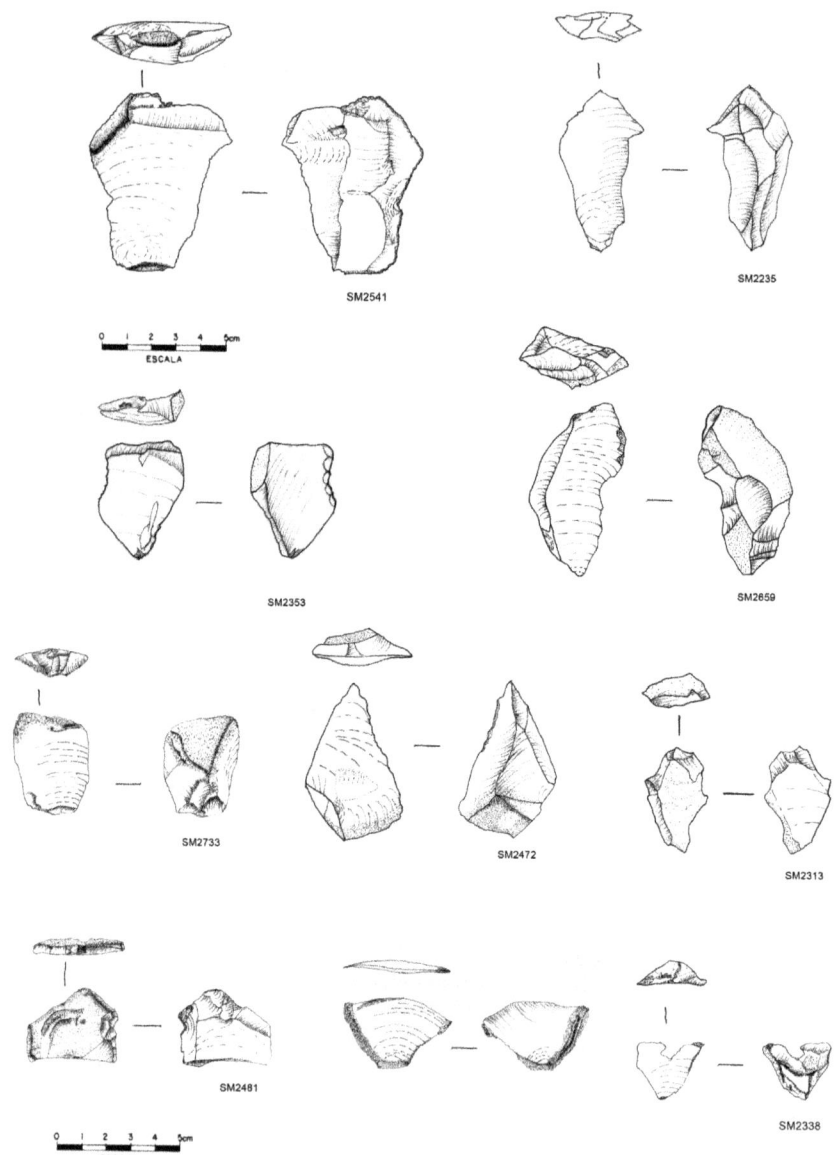

FIGURE 2.11   Pleistocene lithics from Santa Marta

WORK AND SUBSISTENCE IN PRECERAMIC GROUPS OF MEXICO 65

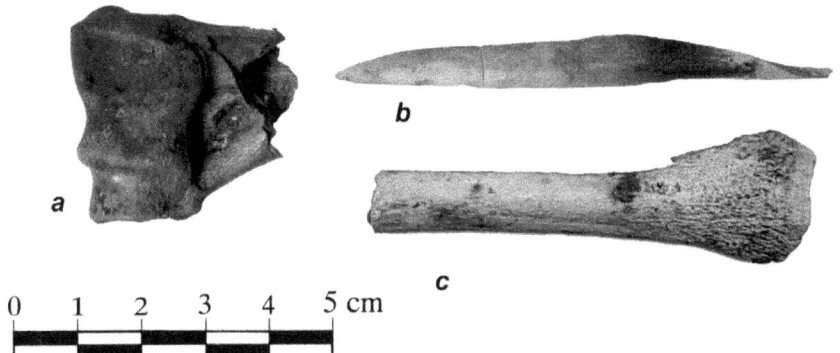

FIGURE 2.12   Faunal remains from Santa Marta: a. distal epiphysis of right humerus of brocket deer with intentional fracture; b. left tibia diaphysis of white-tailed deer, with cleaning and polishing traces on the active edge; c. proximal epiphysis of left cervical metacarpus, bone-point without active edge, with edge polish.

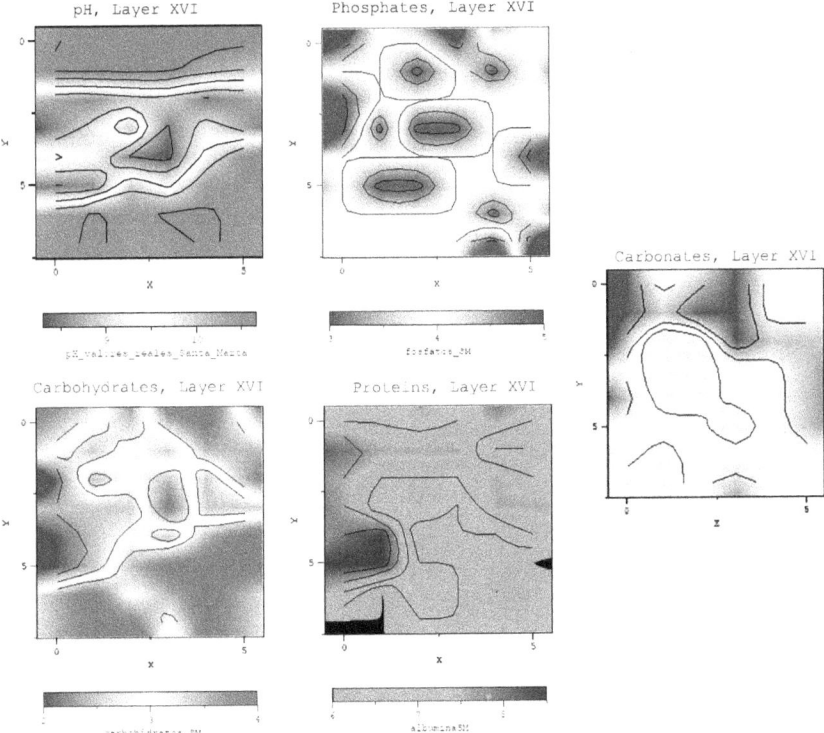

FIGURE 2.13   Chemical analysis of occupation surfaces at Santa Marta, Layer XVI

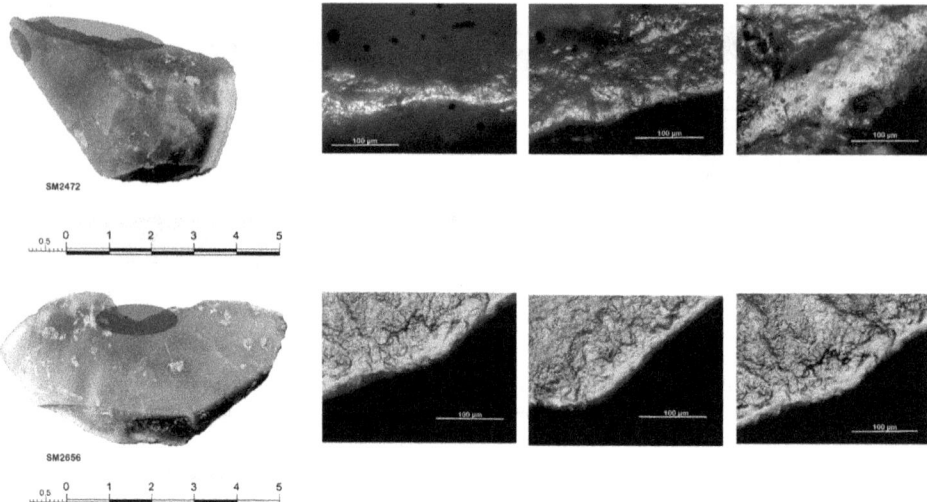

FIGURE 2.14   Santa Marta lithic artefact (SM 2472) with presence of wood cutting marks and artefact SM 2656 associated with the scraping work of plant tissue

4.3   *The Traceology of Artefacts*

From a functional point of view, there have been few investigations focused on lithic assemblage, even in light of the decisive role played by work instruments in carrying out multiple activities in hunter-gatherer societies. Thus, the processing of plant resources and the work done on skin or wood are some of the production processes that depended to a greater or lesser extent on the use of lithic tools. Many of these activities can only be detected in the archaeological record through recovered lithic instruments.

In addition, it is important to note that since the final products obtained are dedicated to consumption, these tools also constitute an important means to quantify the volume of production. For all this, it should be emphasised that any archaeological approach that seeks to determine how, what, when and how much a society produced must necessarily define the technical means of production implemented, among which lithic artefacts again occupy an important place.

In our case, for microscopic-based analyses, the methodology used by Álvarez,[58] as well as by Pérez Martínez and Acosta was applied through an OlympusBX52 microscope, with micro-polishes recorded at 200x. However, from the analyses performed both in the identification of micro residues as well as

---

58   Álvarez 2003.

traceological ones, we noticed that the most common trace of use found was the rounding of the active edges, as well as the presence of brightness, which was observed in most artefacts. Surface polish was observed towards the ventral face in five of the artefacts, while it was possible to identify stretch marks in none and edge retouching was noticed in eleven. Artefacts with micro-polishes also had active edges rounded (Figure 2.14).

From this lithic set, a sample of eight artefacts for the extraction and identification of waste was taken, and in most of them fibers and parenchyma remains could be identified, which seems to indicate the processing of wood. Although other types of residue were observed – such as phytoliths, bone fragments and other filaments, which look like animal hairs – we have not been able to relate these residues to the characterised use traces observed in the lithic artefacts. They are likely to have come from post-depositional contamination found on the context.

The artefacts that have micro-polishes in the ventral face are associated (Table 2.3) with the presence of fibers, parenchyma and raffidia. The raffidia and the possible presence of phytoliths seem to indicate an activity predominantly at work in wood or rigid stems, possibly for the manufacture of tools such as construction materials, traps etc.

The presence of phytoliths, *drusen* or raffidia have already been reported in other investigations, and it has been confirmed that work on plants and the presence of these elements produce micro-polishes in lithic artefacts.[59]

We can observe three probable processes of determined work. The first one is related to obtaining raw material; a second work process corresponds to obtaining timber materials for the subsequent manufacture of other tools, such as darts, traps or spears; and a final process corresponds to the processing of plant resources for consumption, such as the use of barks for medicinal use or the extraction and scraping of tubers for consumption.

From the analysis of traces of use, as well as the experimental work carried out, we have been able to characterise the presence of micro-polishes associated with the work of fresh wood. It is likely that the tools used for this type of activity were the same for all work processes related to the processing of wood and plant resources, and that there is no morphological specialisation, since the analysis identified several functional edges. Therefore, we assume that these tools were multifunctional, which would indicate little formalised and expeditious technology that was used for various work processes.

With reference to previous analyses of micro residues and traces of use, and guided by a Marxist theoretical perspective, it is possible to characterise the

---

59   Kamminga 1979, pp. 143–57.

TABLE 2.3   Association of traces of use and identification of micro-remains

Artefact	Plant remains	Faunal remains	Mineral remains	Non identified remains	Traces of use	Artefact functionality
SM 1894	Fibers, tissue	Filament, bone remains	None		Micro-polish, bone-processing work	Scrape
SM 1912		Fat			Micro-polish, bone-processing work	Scrape
SM 2146	Fibers	None	Red ochre		Micro-polish, plant-processing work	Scrape / scratch
SM 2353	Fibers, plant tissue, raffidia	Filament	None	Probable phytoliths	Micro-polish, plant-processing work	Scrape / scratch
SM 2447	Fibers, raffidia	None	None	Probable phytoliths	Micro-polish	Scrape / scratch
SM 2472	Fibers, plant tissue	None	None	Probable phytoliths	Micro-polish, timber work	Cutting
SM 2659	Fibers, plant tissue	Filament	Red ochre	Probable phytoliths	Micro-polish, timber work	Scrape
SM 2753	Fibers, plant tissue	None	none		Micro-polish, timber work	Scrape

social dynamics of a human group. In this sense, we start from the fact that archaeological artefacts are initially inserted into an economic cycle. By evaluating the characteristics of the artefacts and their relations with the archaeological context, it is possible to establish the basis of how these materials are inserted into daily life and to establish the elements that characterise its mode of production.

Based on the foregoing, our methodological proposal for the analysis of lithic sets has the purpose of recognising the relationships between production and consumption cycles. We recognise that there are some constants in the way of organising the consumption of certain products if we analyse them from a Marxist perspective, transforming them from raw materials to specific use, and that the functional context of lithic artefacts is the basis for establishing significant associations between the technological characteristics and their function, and to thus identify the social relations established between human groups, or between them and their environment.

We can affirm that functional analysis is a tool of great explanatory capacity to reveal the relationships that occur in this dialectical relationship of production and consumption – a form of analysis to be understood not only as an isolated technique that generates data, but also as an axis that will guide us to the understanding of economic rationality and exploitation of resources in hunter-gatherer societies.

5 Concluding Remarks: Work and Subsistence in Hunter-Gatherer Societies

So far, the excavations in Santa Marta suggest that the inhabitants of the site had a way of life, lithic technology and subsistence pattern very different from that associated with typical Clovis hunters, presenting expeditious lithics (mainly touch-up lacquers marginal), but whose dates precede by almost a millennium the appearance of groups with fluted points in the area (12,500–11,000 cal BP). For the moment, it will be enough to be able to frame the materials and domestic contexts of the Early Holocene of Santa Marta in a more general structure and to know the role that the group played in the socioeconomic processes of the last glacial period. In this sense, it is difficult to mark the differences in lithic technology, rationality of exploitation and subsistence systems between hunters of pointed tips and those of expeditious technology – such as those observed on the coast of Ecuador,[60] the Savanna de Bogotá in Colombia[61] and Santa Marta, Mexico[62] – which may be due only to differences in the availability of raw materials in the different regions as suggested by Cooke.[63] The results seem to indicate that these groups, which inhabit Neotropical regions at the end of the Pleistocene, correspond to societies with an expedited technology and a highly diversified resource exploitation pattern, much more oriented to small and medium-sized hunting, with high use and consumption of timber and vegetable resources. The above seems to be corroborated with the botanical remains recovered in Santa Marta, suggesting a deep knowledge held by the groups about the tropical resources of the area, which include *Zea* pollen [teosinte] and *Theobroma* sp. [cocoa] in addition to *Phaseolus* [bean] and *Ipomoea* [sweet potato] starches at the end of the Pleistocene.[64]

As discussed, the debate on global variability of gatherer hunters indicates greater variability than recognised until a decade ago. However, the interest in studying those hunter-gatherers linked to early domestication, particularly in the Neotropics, is still scarce.

From our point of view, there is a trap in the use of these indicators to investigate social complexity. Working only with the presence or absence of diagnostic elements is similar, in form and function, to the elaboration of the old lists of cultural traits, although that procedure is somewhat inevitable in

---

60 Stothert 1985.
61 Correal 1990.
62 Acosta 2010.
63 Cooke 1998.
64 Acosta 2008; Cruz 2015; and Rivera Iran 2013.

an initial approach to studying hunther-gatherer societies. However, archaeological research must go further, aiming to analyse how peculiarities arise in non-stratified societies.

We consider that the hunter-gatherer groups do not all belong, de facto, to the same phase of social development. We therefore cannot simply type them as less or more 'complex', and we prefer to distinguish them, returning to Felipe Bate's proposal, as non-tribal hunters or tribal hunters, assuming in the same way that there may be hunter-gatherer or food-producing societies at different stages of historical development. In this sense, the transition from collection to food production, as well as cultural variability in this type of society, is a central issue for archaeological research. However, as paleoethnobotanical, archaeological and chronological evidence accumulates, there seems to be ever less consensus as to when and where the dividing line should be drawn in that developing continuum.

From this perspective, through the implementation of a research design that integrates an adequate theoretical framework and the methodology necessary to systematically recover diverse evidence on the use of the environment by hunter-gatherers, it will be possible to propose and evaluate new alternatives on the initial colonisation of the tropical regions of the New World.

References

Acosta, Guillermo 1999, 'Procesos de trabajo determinado: la configuración de modos de trabajo en la cultura arqueológica', *Boletín de Antropología Americana*, 35: 17–35.

Acosta, Guillermo 2000, *Entre lagos and volcanes, La cultura arqueológica asociada a la cerámica azteca I*, Tesis de Licenciatura en Arqueología, México D.F.: Escuela Nacional de Antropología e Historia.

Acosta, Guillermo 2006, *Proyecto Cazadores del Trópico Americano. Informe de actividades: Excavaciones en dos cuevas secas de la Región de Ocozocoautla, Chiapas*, México D.F.: Instituto de Investigaciones Antropológicas, Universidad Nacional Autónoma de México.

Acosta, Guillermo 2008, La *cueva de Santa Marta y los cazadores-recolectores del Holoceno temprano en las regiones tropicales de México*, Tesis de Doctorado, Universidad Nacional Autónoma de México.

Acosta, Guillermo and Patricia Pérez Martínez 2012, 'El Poblamiento de Chiapas a Fines del Pleistoceno', in *Arqueología Reciente de Chiapas: Contribuciones del Encuentro Celebrado en el 60.° Aniversario de la Fundación Arqueológica Nuevo Mundo*, edited by Lynneth Lowe and Mary E. PyeProvo, Utah: Brigham Young University.

Acosta, Guillermo, Patricia Pérez Martínez and Irais Rivera Irán 2013, 'Methodology for the Study of Plant Food Processing in Hunter-gatherer Societies: A Case Study', *Boletim do Museu Paraense Emílio Goeldi, Ciências Humanas*, 8, 3: 535–50.

Álvarez, Myrian 2003, *Organización tecnológica en el Canal Beagle. El caso de Túnel I* (Tierra del Fuego, Argentina), Tesis de Doctorado, Universidad de Buenos Aires, Facultad de Filosofía y Letras.

Atchison, Jennifer and Richard Fullagar 1998, 'Starch Residues on Pounding Implements from Jinmium Rock-shelter', in *A Closer Look: Recent CLR Australian studies of stone tools*, edited by Richard Fullagar, Sydney: Archaeological Computing Laboratory, University of Sydney.

Bate, Luis Felipe 1977, *Arqueología y materialismo histórico*, México D.F.: Ediciones de Cultura Popular.

Bate, Luis Felipe 1978, *Sociedad, formación económico social y cultura*, México D.F.: Ediciones de Cultura Popular.

Bate, Luis Felipe 1986, 'El modo de producción cazador recolector o la economía del salvajismo', *Boletín de Antropología Americana*, 13: 5–31.

Bate, Luis Felipe 1998, *El proceso de investigación en arqueología*, Barcelona: Crítica.

Binford, Lewis 1996, 'Willow smoke and dog's tails: hunter gatherer settlement system and archaeological site formation', *American antiquity*, 45: 4–20.

Binford, Lewis R. 1983, *In Pursuit of the Past*, New York: Thames and Hudson.

Blee Alisa, Keryn Walshe, Allan Pring, Jamie Quinton, and Claire Lenehan 2010, 'Towards the Identification of Plant and Animal Binders on Australian Stone Knives', *Talanta*, 82, 2: 745–50.

Bettinger, Robert L. 1987, 'Archaeological approaches to hunter-gatherers', *Annual Review of Anthropology*, 16, 1: 121–42.

Buonasera, Tammy 2007, 'Investigating the Presence of Ancient Absorbed Organic Residues in Groundstone Using GC-MS and Other Analytical Techniques: A Residue Study of Several Prehistoric Milling Tools from Central California', *Journal of Archaeological Science*, 34, 9: 1379–90.

Briz i Godino, Iván, Débora Zurro, Myrian Álvarez, and Marco Madella 2014, 'Ethnoarchaeology and Residue Analysis in Fisher-Hunter-Gatherer Sites', in *The Cultural Dynamics of Shell Middens and Shell Mounds: A Worldwide Perspective*, New México: University Press.

Cooke, Richard G. 1998, 'Human Settlement of Central America and Northernmost South America (14,000–8,000 BP)', *Quaternary International*, 49–50: 177–90.

Correal, Gonzalo 1990, 'Evidencias culturales durante el Pleistoceno y Holoceno de Colombia', *Revista de Arqueología Americana*, 1: 69–89.

Cruz, Jorge Ezra 2015, *Extracción, identificación y análisis de almidones en artefactos líticos y pisos del abrigo de Santa Marta con ocupación precerámica en la Depresión Central de Chiapas*, Tesis de Maestría en Antropología, México D.F.: Universidad Nacional Autónoma de México.

Dillehay, Thomas, 2000, *The Settlement of the Americas*, New York: Basic Books.

Eudave, Itzel 2008, *Subsistencia de los cazadores recolectores, un estudio de los restos faunísticos de la cueva de Santa Marta, Chiapas*, Tesis de Licenciatura en Arqueología, Escuela Nacional de Antropología e Historia, México.

Field, Judith and Richard Fullagar 1998, 'Grinding and Pounding Stones from Cuddie Springs and Jinmium', in *A Closer Look: Recent Australian studies of stone tools*, edited by Richard Fullagar, Sydney: Archaeological Computing Laboratory, University of Sydney.

Flannery, Kent v. 1973, 'Archaeology with a Capital S', in *Research and Theory in Current Archaeology*, edited by Charles L. Redman, New York: Wiley.

Gándara, Manuel 1990, 'Algunas notas sobre el análisis del conocimiento', *Boletín de Antropología Americana*, 22: 5–19.

Gándara, Manuel 1981, 'La vieja "nueva arqueología" (segunda parte)', *Boletín de Antropología Americana*, 3: 7–70.

Gándara, Manuel 1992, 'El análisis teórico: aplicaciones al estudio de la complejidad social', *Boletín de Antropología Americana*, 25: 93–104.

Gándara, Manuel 1994, 'Consecuencias metodológicas de la adopción de una ontología de la cultura: una perspectiva desde la arqueología', in *Metodología y cultura*, edited by Jorge González and Jesús Galindo, México D.F.: Pensar la Cultura CNCA.

García-Bárcena, Joaquín and Diana Santamaría 1984, *La Cueva de Santa Marta Ocozocoautla, Chapas. Estratigrafía, cronología y cerámica*, Colección Científica 111, México D.F.: Instituto Nacional de Antropología e Historia.

García-Bárcena, Joaquín, Diana Santamaría, Ticul Álvarez, Manuel Reyes, and Fernando Sánchez 1979, *Excavaciones en el abrigo de Santa Marta, Chiapas*, México D.F.: Departamento de Prehistoria, Instituto Nacional de Antropología e Historia.

González Arratia, Leticia 1992a, 'Estudio integrado arqueológico del Bolsón de Mapimí: Parte arqueológica', in González Arratia, Leticia, *Ensayo sobre la arqueología en Coahuila y el Bolsón de Mapimí*, Saltillo: Archivo Municipal de Saltillo.

González Arratia, Leticia 1992b, 'El problema de la arqueología de superficie y la movilidad de los grupos cazadores-recolectores', in González Arratia, Leticia, *Ensayo sobre la arqueología en Coahuila y el Bolsón de Mapimí*, Saltillo: Archivo Municipal de Saltillo.

Haslam, Michael, Gail Robertson, Alison Crowther, Sue Nugent and Luke Kirkwood (eds.) 2009, *Archaeological Science under a Microscope: Studies in Residue and Ancient DNA Analysis in Honour of Thomas H. Loy*, Canberra: ANUE Press.

Heller, Agnes 1985, *Historia y vida cotidiana: aportación a la sociología socialista*, México D.F.: Grijalbo.

Heller, Agnes 1998, *Sociología de la vida cotidiana*, Barcelona: Península.

Ingold, Tim 1983, 'The Significance of Storage in Hunting Societies', *Man*, 18, 3: 553–71.

Kamminga, Johan 1979, 'The Nature of Use-Polish and Abrasive Smoothing on Stone

Tools', in *Lithic Use-Wear Analysis*, edited by Bryan Hayden, New York: Academic Press.

Kamminga, Johan 1988, 'Wood Artefacts: A Checklist of Plant Species Utilised by Australian Aborigines', *Australian Aboriginal Studies*, 2: 26–59.

Kimura, Brigitta, Steven A. Brandt, Bruce L. Hardy, and William W. Hauswirth 2001, Analysis of DNA from Ethnoarchaeological Stone Scrapers, *Journal of Archaeological Science*, 28, 1: 45–53.

Lombard, Marlize 2006, 'Direct Evidence for the Use of Ochre in the Hafting Technology of Middle Stone Age Tools from Sibudu Cave', *Southern African Humanities*, 18, 1: 57–67.

MacNeish, Richard S. and Frederick A. Peterson 1962, *The Santa Marta Rock Shelter, Ocozocoautla, Chiapas, México*, New World Archaeological Foundation Papers 14, Provo, UT: Brigham Young University.

Malainey, Mary, Myrian Álvarez, Iván B. Briz i Godino, Débora Zurro, Ester Castelló and Timothy Figol 2015, 'The Use of Shells as Tools by Hunters-Gatherers in the Beagle Channel (Tierra del Fuego, South America): An Ethnoarchaeological Experiment', *Archaeological and Anthropological Sciences*, 7, 2: 187–200.

Mansur-Franchomme, María Estela 1987, *El análisis funcional de artefactos líticos*, Volume 1, Buenos Aires: Instituto Nacional de Antropología.

Marreiros, Joan Manuel, Juan F. Gibaja and Nuno Ferreira Bicho (eds.) 2015, *Use-Wear and Residue Analysis in Archaeology*, London: Springer.

Marx, Karl 1984 [1859], *Contribución a la crítica de la Economía Política*, México D.F.: Quinto Sol.

Marx, Karl 1946 [1867], *El Capital*, tomo I, México D.F.: Fondo de Cultura Económica.

Morgan, Lewis 1891, *La sociedad primitiva*, México D.F.: Colofón.

Owen, Linda R. and Marín Porr (eds.) 1999, *Ethno-Analogy and the Reconstruction of Prehistoric Artefact Use and Production*, Urgeschichtliche Materialhefte 14, Tübingen: Mo Vince Verlag.

Patterson, Thomas C. 1994, 'Social Archaeology in Latin America: An Appreciation', *American Antiquity* 59, 3: 531–37.

Pelegrin, Jacques, Claudine Karlin and Pierre Bodu 1988, 'Chaînes opératoires: un outil pour le préhistorien', *Technologie préhistorique, Notes et Monographies Techniques*, 25, 55–62.

Pérez-Martínez, Patricia 2010, *Arqueología experimental*, Tesis de Licenciatura, Escuela Nacional de Antropología e Historia, México.

Pérez-Martínez, Patricia and Acosta-Ochoa, Guillermo 2018, 'Análisis funcionales en artefactos líticos de grupos cazadores-recolectores en regiones tropicales durante la transición Pleistoceno final-Holoceno temprano: el abrigo Santa Marta, Chiapas, México', *Arqueología Iberoamericana*, 37: 23–30.

Perry, Linda 2005, 'Reassessing the Traditional Interpretation of "Manioc" Artifacts in the Orinoco Valley of Venezuela', *Latin American Antiquity*, 16, 4: 409–26.

Politis, Gustavo 1996, *Nukak*, Bogotá: Instituto Amazónico de Investigaciones Científicas SINCHI.

Ramseyer, Denis 1987, 'Emmanchements de l'outillage lithique néolithique de quelques stations littorales du canton de Fribourg (Suisse occidentale)', *MOM Éditions*, 15, 1: 211–18.

Rivera Iran, Irais 2013, *Modo de vida en el bosque tropical del sureste mexicano: un acercamiento al uso de la vegetación por sociedades cazadoras-recolectoras*, Tesis de Maestría, Facultad de Filosofía y Letras, Universidad Nacional Autónoma de México.

Rots, Veerle and Bonny S. Williamson 2004, 'Microwear and Residue Analysis in Perspective: The Contribution of Ethnoarchaeological Evidence', *Journal of Archaeological Science*, 31: 1287–99.

Sanoja, Mario 1983, 'Siete temas de debate en Arqueología Social', *Cuadernos de Antropología: Revista Digital del Laboratorio de Etnología 'María Eugenia Bozzoli Vargas'*, 2, 1: 1–68.

Semenov, Sergei Aristarkhovich 1981 [1964], *Tecnología prehistórica: estudio de las herramientas y objetos antiguos a través de las huellas de uso*, Madrid: Akal.

Service, Elman 1962, *Primitive Social Organization: An Evolutionary Perspective*, New York: Random House.

Sahlins, Marshall 1965, 'On the Sociology of Primitive Exchange', in *The Relevance of Models in Social Anthropology* edited by Michael Banton, London: Tavistock.

Stothert, Karen 1985, 'The Preceramic Las Vegas Culture of Coastal Ecuador', *American Antiquity*, 50, 3: 613–37.

Tantaleán, Henry and Miguel Aguilar (eds.) 2012, *La arqueología social latinoamericana: De la teoría a la praxis*, Bogotá: Universidad de los Andes.

Testart, Alain, Richard G. Forbis, Brian Hayden, Tim Ingold, Stephen M. Perlman, David L. Pokotylo, Peter Rowley-Conwy and David E. Stuart 1982, 'The Significance of Food Storage Among Hunter-Gatherers: Residence Patterns, Population Densities, and Social Inequalities', *Current Anthropology*, 23, 5: 523–37.

Vargas-Arenas, Iraida 1985, 'Modo de vida: categoría de las mediaciones entre formación social y cultural', *Boletín de Antropología Americana*, 12: 5–16.

Vargas-Arenas, Iraida 1990, *Arqueología, ciencia y sociedad*, Caracas: Abre Brecha.

Vargas-Arenas, Iraida and Mario Sanoja 1999, 'Archaeology as a Social Science: Its Expression in Latin America', in *Archaeology in Latin America*, edited by Gustavo Politis and Benjamin Alberti, London: Routledge.

Veloz Maggiolo, Marcio 1984, 'La arqueología de la vida cotidiana: matices historia y diferencias', *Boletín de Antropología Americana*, 10: 5–21.

Weedman, Kathryn J. 2006, 'An Ethnoarchaeological Study of Hafting and Stone Tool Diversity among the Gamo of Ethiopia', *Journal of Archaeological Method and Theory*, 133: 188–237.

Woodburn, James 1982, 'Egalitarian Societies', *Man*, 17, 3: 431–51.

Yamada, Shoh 1993, 'The Formation Process of Use-wear Polishes', in *Traces et fonction: Les Gestes Retrouvés*, ERAUL 50, Volume 2, edited by Patricia C. Anderson et al., Liège: Éditions Centre de Recherches Archéologiques du CNRS, Études et Recherches Archéologiques de l'Université de Liège.

CHAPTER 3

The Mode of Production of the Chalcolithic Period in Palestine

Ianir Milevski, Bernardo Gandulla and Pablo Jaruf

1   Introduction

In this chapter we will try to define the socio-economic formation and possible socio-political forms in Palestine during the Chalcolithic period; this period has been largely discussed in the anthropological literature of the late prehistory in the Levant.

In the 1960s, the discussion of modes of production resulted in the examination of prehistoric and early historic societies around the world to determine their socio-economic forms. The works by Karl Marx and Friedrich Engels[1] were re-evaluated not only by Marxists but also by the entire community of scholars dealing with prehistory and ancient history. The revision of the writings of Marx and Engels were directed mainly against Stalinism and his 'steps' in the development of pre-capitalistic societies.[2] Besides, scholars related to the neo-evolutionism like Sahlins attempted to define what he termed a 'domestic mode of production' and to apply it to societies organised at the local or family level, which Sahlins identified with the Neolithic period.[3] Earle, to some extent continuing the work of Sahlins, tried to define the political economy of the Bronze Age in Eurasia, viewing it as a sort of transitional period between chiefdoms and agricultural states.[4] While Sahlins's work was mainly based on Marx's 'primitive form', and was followed in this sense by others,[5] Earle's interpretation for the Bronze Age could be compared with the 'Asiatic mode of production'.[6]

---

1   Marx 1970; Engels 1972; and Marx 1993.
2   See Hobsbawm 1965.
3   Sahlins 1972.
4   Earle 2002, pp. 1–18.
5   See Service 1962.
6   The utilisation of the term and the discussion of the 'Asiatic mode of production' have continued for a while around the world (see Hobsbawm 1965, and Hindess and Hirst 1975), and in particular among French anthropologists and sociologists such as Godelier (1975). The debate on this mode of production was especially developed as a critique of the Stalinist dogma. Stalinist ideas attempted to negate the existence of such a mode of production (McGuire

However, the ideas put forward by Marx did not suggest a linear model in which all societies must develop. Marx suggested that mankind has followed an uneven and combined development, which negates a mechanical application of the evolution of socio-economic formations.[7] Less developed social forms do not need to pass through all the historic steps and could skip some of them. There is not one but a series of 'pictures' of various forms of property types and modes of production that have taken place in various forms of communities, from ancient to modern forms, based on the exploitation of labour and the exchange of goods.[8] Still, different social formations can co-exist for a while within the same territory, until a new system replaces an older one.[9]

2 The Chalcolithic Period in Palestine

The Chalcolithic period (c. 4,500–3,700 BC) of Palestine (southern Levant) (Figure 3.1) is one of the most studied periods of late prehistory in the Near East in the last decades.[10] Its chronological scope extends between the Neolithic period with the domestication of plants and animals and the the beginning of the Early Bronze IA, rendering it a key time to understand social development in the southern Levant. This period marks the beginning of copper metalwork in this region and a vast iconography reflecting not only the subsistence base but also a system of ideas associated with life and death.[11]

2002). Wittfogel (1957, pp. iii, vi, 382–412), in a different approach, criticised the lack of treatment of this mode of production in the literature of Lenin and Stalin (and even in the late works of Marx), suggesting 'totalitarian Communist' leaders did not care to see themselves in the role of oriental despots.

7   McGuire 2002.
8   Godelier 1975. In letters Marx wrote in 1881 to Vera Zasulich (Marx and Engels 1992, p. 71), he stressed that the development that applied to Western Europe was never intended to be a rigid framework of unilinear evolution for all societies. Therefore, Marx sought laws of evolution without being evolutionary in the mode of Spencer. He furthermore had reservations about the adaptation of Darwinian theories on the evolution of species for the study of society.
9   Novack 1974.
10 Though there is almost no discussion regarding the beginning of this period, its end has been debated; while Gilead (2011) proposes that the end of this period occurred around 3800 BC, Burton and Levy (2011a) propose that it ended around 3600 BC, which coincides with the date suggested as the beginning of the Early Bronze I.
11 Bourke 2001; and Rowan and Golden 2009.

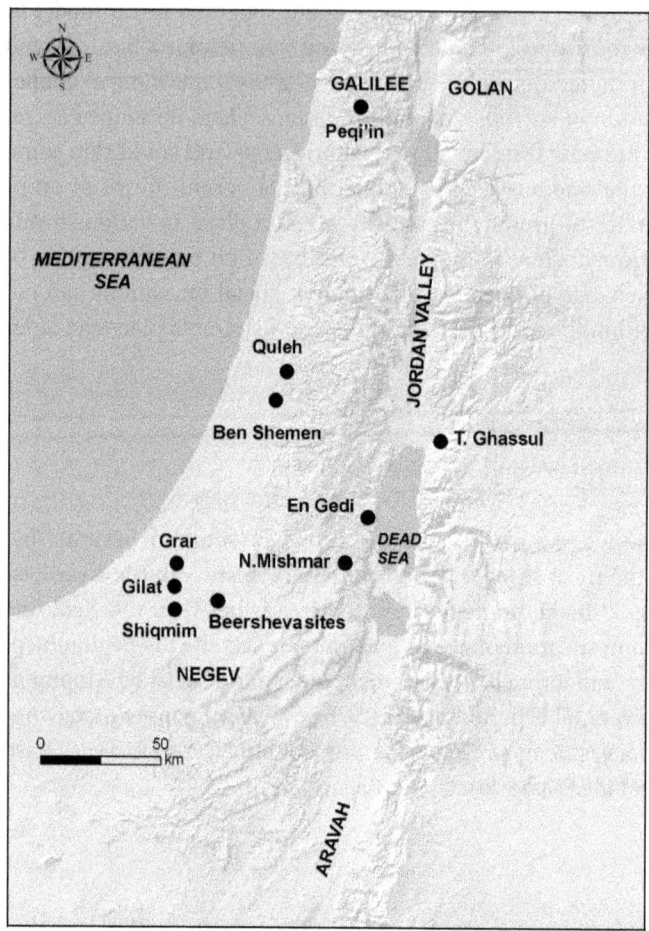

FIGURE 3.1 Map with the location of main sites and regions mentioned in the text

From the point of view of the nomenclature accepted for the area under consideration, we are referring to the Chalcolithic period, or 'Copper Age', associated with the Ghassulian and Golan cultures,[12] labelled sometimes as the late Chalcolithic period,[13] which many scholars consider this period to be the last chapter of the prehistory of that region.[14]

12 Gilead 2011.
13 Garfinkel 1999.
14 Joffe and Dessel 1995.

TABLE 3.1 Accepted chronology of the late prehistory in Palestine

Years BC	Period
Pre-Pottery Neolithic	9,500–6,500
Pottery Neolithic	6,500–4,500
Chalcolithic	4,500–3,700
Early Bronze I	3,700–3,100/3,000
Early Bronze II	3,100/3,000–2,800
Early Bronze III	2,800–2,500

Several archaeological schools have addressed the problem of defining the type of society of the Chalcolithic. The neo-evolutionist schools have defined the period through an anthropologic comparison, using the terms 'chiefdom', 'ranked' and 'stratified society' following Service and Fried.[15] Sometime earlier, Finkelstein made an attempt to use a new political terminology and proposed the term 'Proto-urban I' for the Chalcolithic period.[16]

However, Gilead has contested the possible existence of a social hierarchy during this period and prefers to talk about a more egalitarian society based on social forms of domestic religion or practices guided by shamans,[17] and Banning has suggested analysing the Chalcolithic period as a 'house society'.[18] In previous works, attempts have been made to provide a view that explains all aspects of Chalcolithic society, taking into consideration modes of production, changes in material culture and the iconographic and religious expressions pertaining to the period.[19] The present essay is a continuation of the research conducted on the Chalcolithic society and the transition from this period to the Early Bronze I (c. 3,700–3,000 BC) in the southern Levant (Table 3.1).

Discussion of the possible socio-political forms that took shape during the Chalcolithic period, as was said before, is especially significant, given that the period is comprised of the time between the end of the so-called 'Neolithic revolution' (tenth to seventh millenniums BC) and the 'urban revolution' that took place towards the end of the fourth millennium BC.[20]

---

15 Levy 1998, based on Service 1962 and Fried 1967.
16 Finkelstein 1996.
17 Gilead 1993; and see Gošić and Gilead 2015.
18 Banning 2010.
19 Milevski 2013.
20 Childe 1942, and 1950.

Additionally, two other 'revolutions' are believed to have occurred during this period: one is the so-called 'secondary products revolution' (milk, wool, draft animals) and the other is the 'metal revolution' characterised by the production of the first copper objects.[21] But, according to Gordon Childe, these revolutions were epiphenomena of the 'Neolithic revolution' and almost amount to a prerequisite for the urban revolution.[22]

3 Evolution Theories, Modes of Production, Pre-state Forms of Social Organisation

As a means of addressing the classification of the type of society in the Chalcolithic of Palestine, the proposals made by the neo-evolutionist anthropologists Service and Fried were taken by Levy and in general by Verhoeven in what he called a 'contextual approach'.[23]

We could agree to put it between what these authors identify as 'ranked societies' and 'stratified societies', i.e. between a society in which the degree of differences is small and another in which access to means of subsistence by all is clearly uneven. For instance, in the category of 'ranked societies' there seems to have been high labour mobility preceded by a greater division of labour. However, in order to fine tune this idea, we still have to determine who held or administered the means of production and how this was carried out.

Our methodology does not consist in the application of a type of society borrowed from an ideal evolutionary model but rather in a relational analysis of the components of a specific socio-economic formation. This type of procedure enables us to infer – amongst the different modes of production that coexist in every particular socio-historical situation – the presence of a dominant form that leaves its imprint and influence on all others. This analysis of a specific socio-economic formation leads to the concept of a mode of production, where a specific formation consists of a dynamic coexistence of modes of production, one of them generally dominating the others.[24] In this respect, we agree with Hobsbawm that 'we are not obliged to accept Marx's list

---

21 For the 'secondary products revolution', see Sherratt 1981; for 'metal revolution', see Levy 2007.
22 Childe 1942.
23 Levy 1998; Verhoeven 2010.
24 Marx 1993.

of historical epochs as given in the *Preface* or in the *Formen*.[25] But what we certainly should stress is that we utilise Marxist methods of dialectical materialist analyses based on the material evidence provided by the archaeological methods.

Without going into complex definitions, what is relevant for our subject is the assumption that, broadly speaking, the Chalcolithic can be described as a late expression of Marx's 'primitive form' of production, prior to the 'Asiatic mode of production' that could be identified with the Early Bronze Age.[26] The Chalcolithic probably fits with what Wolf and Rosenswig defined as kin-ordered modes of production.[27] The study of kin organisation is one of the keys in order to understand the mode of production in these communities. The kin-ordered mode of production is defined by its use of kinship as the key to mobilising resources rather than economy/technology of mode or political/military of the tributary mode.

According with these definitions, we need to remember that we are dealing with a pre-state form of social organisation. In archaeology, definitions regarding these forms of social organisation have not been very explicit but rather vague. For instance, in the introduction to a volume on the topic, Bolger and Maguire define these entities as 'small-scale societies which preceded the emergence of the earliest states in the Near East'.[28]

Nevertheless, in order to attempt to define a pre-state form of social organisation we must define the notion of state. Far from setting out to discuss this issue within the context of this chapter, we nevertheless wish to make clear several aspects that will serve as guidelines. We are naturally very far from the apparently naïve definitions such as that proposed by Cicero in Book I of *De Republica*, in the sense that the state is simply a multitude of people united by the community of law and utility as a means of attaining the 'common good', or

---

25 Hobsbawm 1965, p. 19.
26 See Milevski 2013 on this topic. In the 'Asiatic mode of production', the social entity stands above a number of small communities and appears as the main or sole proprietor of communal resources; hence, the real communities are only hereditary possessors. The superior social entity is the real proprietor and the real presupposition of communal property; the individual is, in fact, propertyless, or property appears by the individual's membership in the community. The realisation of the superior unit may take the form of a despot, the supposed father of many communities, a dynasty, a palace or a temple (Marx 1993). On the 'Asiatic mode of production', see also Hobsbawm 1965; Mandel 1974; and Godelier 1975. On a negation of such a mode of production, see Anderson 1974.
27 Wolf 2001, pp. 349–51; Rozenswig 2012, pp. 9–10.
28 Bolger and Maguire 2010, p. 1.

the Hegelian notion of the (modern) state as the realisation of 'reasoned freedom'.[29] Contrarily, we clearly adopt the notion set forth by Marx and Engels when they defined the state as 'the form in which the individuals of a ruling class assert their common interests, and in which the whole *civil society of an epoch is epitomized*'.[30]

The state, as explained by Engels, is therefore a product of human society at a particular stage of development; it is the probe that this society has involved itself in a contradiction and social antagonisms. In order that these antagonisms, social classes with conflicting economic interests, shall not consume themselves, a power, apparently standing above society, has become necessary to moderate the conflicts, i.e. the state.[31]

We do not ignore recent contributions made by other colleagues in terms of defining the different types of ancient states, either in Mesopotamia or in Egypt.[32] However, we believe that these definitions should consider the class component of the state – the existence of which depends, consequently, on class contradictions. The thought of Karl Marx was precisely to pay attention to the contradictions as a method: 'As soon as they are reduced to specific questions they are already explained'.[33] For this, a dialectical materialist analysis should avoid schematism.

For those archaeologists dedicated to the study of Levantine prehistory, the closest thing to the creation of a state for the first time is Gordon Childe's definition of the 'urban revolution'.[34] The notion of the state in the Bronze Age implies a solution to the contradictions present in late-prehistoric communities through the establishment of a bureaucratic administration capable of bridging the division between rural communities and urban centres, solving conflicts through the new relations of production according to the model developed by Marx.[35] For their part, neo-evolutionists such as Earle defined the Bronze Age state as an 'agricultural state', indicating its rural nature despite it being an institution of domination and exploitation of one social group over others.[36]

In the last decades, the question of the state has been discussed for antiquity. Some archaeologists have proposed some other possible developments label-

---

29 Hegel 1991.
30 Marx and Engels 1970, p. 80.
31 Engels 1972.
32 Campagno 2006; Di Bennardis 2014.
33 Marx 1970, p. 216.
34 Childe 1950.
35 Marx 1970.
36 Earle 2002.

led as 'alternative states', while others have even wanted to abandon the concept of state.[37] However, Lull and Micó have formulated a several parameters to the rising of the state from a Marxist perspective, based on clear elements which should be searched in the archaeological record.[38]

Of course, the question of the state and the passage of the Chalcolithic to the Early Bronze Age in Palestine should be discussed in relation to local material evidence. This evidence could be on several levels, one of them being the existence of surplus accumulation, social differences, physical violence or military specialisation, as recently was elaborated by a series of archaeologists,[39] but this violence should be proved to be related to social clashes.[40]

It is worth noting that several colleagues have stressed the differences between the Chalcolithic and the subsequent Early Bronze Age. For instance, Joffe and Dessel point out that the Bronze Age completes a long tradition at the end of a trajectory that began in the Paleolithic era and finished at the end of the Chalcolithic.[41] Joffe and Dessel believe that a line should be drawn between both periods. We understand that this line probably lies between the pre-state communities and those that led to the creation of a state in the southern Levant after a process that extended over a period of several hundred years.

There is a discussion amongst several authors regarding whether this passage or transition was continuous or abrupt. Though this is not the topic under consideration in this paper, it is worth noting that Gilead[42] supports the idea of an 'abrupt transition' with a marked discontinuity between the Chalcolithic and the Early Bronze Age on the grounds that the former had come to an end after 3,800 BC, and there is a hiatus between both periods, whereas Braun[43] and, to a certain degree, van den Brink[44] have proposed the existence of multiple links between both periods.

In another publication, we proposed that the transition from one period to another occurred abruptly in northern and southern regions, like Galilee and

---

37   And see Chapman 2008 for a discussion on several understandings of the rising of the state in Bronze Age Spain.
38   Lull and Micó 2007, pp. 237–61; and see Lull et al., this volume. These parameters include the division of labour, the division of classes with a certain society and the place of politics within the production process.
39   García-Piquer and Vila-Mitjà 2016.
40   And see Lull et al., this volume.
41   Joffe and Dessel 1995.
42   Gilead 2011.
43   Braun 2011.
44   van den Brink 2011.

Beersheva valley, but also that a part of the elements of the Chalcolithic continued to exist in the Early Bronze Age, like some pottery, flint industry and the casting of utilitarian tools in pure cooper.[45] This situation suggests that the transition took place in an uneven and combined way, in the sense that some regions adopted a new mode of production earlier than others, giving rise to a dynamic in which growth of the economy and social forces occurs faster or slower based on natural conditions and historical connections.[46]

Significantly, Diakonoff has pointed out that when society passes from a historically conditioned socio-economic stage – what is known as socio-economic formations – to the next stage of development (or formation) of mankind, it preserves, to a certain extent, the class (or pre-class) structure that characterised the preceding formation, albeit modified.[47]

4   Material Evidence for a Socio-Economic Definition of the Chalcolithic Period

While knowledge of the finds of the Chalcolithic period in Palestine are relatively established within their respective material cultural contexts, this is not sufficient to achieve an adequate understanding of the society that produced them or of the form of its political organisation. What is required is familiarity with both the conditions in which these artefacts were produced and the social structures that enabled their production, which involves a process of reconstruction and interpretation based on certain models. The material base of the Chalcolithic period is shown below in Table 3.2. The Chalcolithic is characterised by its rural aspect, which, nevertheless, differs from the rural aspects of the previous Pottery Neolithic period and the subsequent Early Bronze I, with a certain emphasis on the settlements in the south (principally in the Negev), but also in the coastal plain, the central hill country, the Jordan valley and the Galilee and Golan heights (Figure 3.1). The key issue is that during this period there was a change in the division of labour and in the way products circulated.

The ensuing discussion considers archaeological artefacts as potential economic goods that have both use value and exchange value, as described some

---

45   Milevski 2013.
46   And see Milevski et al., 2022, for a case of the Early Bronze I. For the uneven and combined processes in history, see Novack 1974, pp. 75–122.
47   Diakonoff 1975.

TABLE 3.2 Parameters for the Chalcolithic period and the Early Bronze Age in Palestine, economics and social relations

Parameters	Chalcolithic period	Early Bronze Age
Craft specialisation	Part time	Part time
Labour division		Full time
Agriculture	Hoes, dig sticks?	Plough?
Husbandry		
Networks of Exchange	Small and medium distances	Medium to long distances
Transport		Donkeys, major circulation of goods
Settlement patterns	Galilee	Breakup of the Chalcolithic settlement system
	Golan	Galilee
	Jordan valley	Jordan valley
	Southern coastal plain	Southern coastal plain
	Judean desert	Dead Sea plain
	Shephela	Aravah
	Northern Negev	
Social organisation	Village communities	Pre-urban and urban communities

time ago – still, it is evident that not all objects were traded.[48] The study of these artefacts and their spatial distribution can shed light on the type of social organisation that enabled them to be manufactured and distributed. Bearing in mind this organisation, we shall attempt to understand the social and cultural implications reflected in iconographic and ideological components in the archaeological record, such as burial customs. The following parameters were considered: 1) settlement patterns and architecture; 2) agriculture and animal husbandry; 3) storage of foodstuffs; 4) crafts; 5) iconography; and 6) burial modes.

---

48 Milevski 2011. The exchange of basic products in ancient times does not imply a form of capitalist production as some authors have suggested – for example, Silver 1983, and 1985. In our opinion, this point of view was refuted successfully some time ago by Salvioli (1979), followed by Gaido (2003), who each argued against the opinion of historians and economists who believed (under the influence of modern conditions) that capitalism existed in ancient societies.

4.1 Settlement Patterns

Chalcolithic settlements were concentrated in the Northern Negev, the coastal plain, the Jordan valley, the Galilee and the Golan plateau. The Central Hill Country and the Shephela were inhabited as well. Major sites during the period were near or very close to water streams.[49] Site distribution maps point out to a sharp break between the Chalcolithic and EB I periods, as has been suggested by Gophna and Portugali.[50] While the centre of the Chalcolithic settlement was the Irano-Turanian zone, the Early Bronze I dominated the Mediterranean phytogeographical zone. Finkelstein and Gophna[51] suggested that the Chalcolithic expansion of settlements in the Hill Country may well be linked to horticulture.

Settlement patterns changed greatly from the Chalcolithic to the Early Bronze IA.[52] Gophna and Portugali[53] concluded from the size and distribution of settlements in the Chalcolithic and the Early Bronze I (with a projection onto the Early Bronze II and III) that a comparison of rank-size distribution of sites shows the hierarchal nature of the pre-urban and urban periods (i.e. Early Bronze I and II–III) against the non-hierarchal distribution of countryside Chalcolithic settlements.[54]

The Chalcolithic architectural units were composed of a single room, located on the narrow side of a rectangular or trapezoidal walled courtyard (e.g. Teleilat Ghassul, Fasa'el, Meser, Golan sites). These rooms are rectilinear in shape and often termed 'broad room' or 'broad house',[55] indicating that the entrance to the structures was in one of the long walls. Installations such as hearths and silos are usually located in front of these structures, sometimes enclosed by courtyard walls. The small structures were probably used for sleeping and storage, while other daily activities were carried out in the courtyards or adjacent to the dwelling unit.[56]

4.2 Agriculture and Husbandry

Primary Chalcolithic innovations were horticulture, including the cultivation of olives [*Olea europea*] – completing the domestication of plants that occurred

---

49 Winter-Livneh et al. 2010.
50 Gophna and Portugali 1988.
51 Finkelstein and Gophna 1993.
52 Gophna and Portugali 1988; Lovell 2002; and Rowan and Golden 2009.
53 Gophna and Portugali 1988, pp. 18–19.
54 Winter-Livneh et al. 2010.
55 Gilead 1988, p. 416; Porath 1992, p. 41; and Rowan and Golden 2009, p. 29.
56 Winter-Livneh et al. 2010.

in the previous Neolithic period – the improvement of food storage systems and the milk and wool industries, including the production of butter.

While the utilisation of irrigation for farming and true domestication (not merely utilisation) of olives in the Chalcolithic[57] has been not accepted by all scholars,[58] it is evident that olive production existed in the Chalcolithic period,[59] and olive oil is traced even earlier.[60]

It is also evident that milk and wool industries, secondary products derived from ovicaprine husbandry, are one of the characteristics of the south Levantine Chalcolithic (albeit with antecedents in the Pottery Neolithic period), with strong indications not only in the faunal register,[61] but also in the pottery repertoire and the iconography of the period.[62] This is the completion of the 'secondary products revolution'.[63]

4.3 Storage Devices

Storage devices were markedly developed during the Chalcolithic period, even in its early stages (Pre-Ghassulian horizon), such as at Tel Tsaf.[64] Other sites, such as Teleilat Ghassul, show considerable facilities for storage.[65] However, large-scale storage were created only in Early Bronze I. Silos in every settlement and large-scale complexes (larger than those at Tel Tsaf) at several sites – including the Halif Terrace,[66] Amazyia[67] and 'En Zippori[68] – emphasise the importance of surplus goods. Some of those complexes are proto-types of the granaries of the Early Bronze II–III period.[69]

4.4 Crafts

Chalcolithic pottery in some way represents a continuation of Late Neolithic traditions, but it is notable for having more standardised parameters. According to petrographic studies, few ceramic groups existed in the Galilee and the

---

57 Suggested by Zohary 1975.
58 Gilead 1988; Liphschitz and Bonani 2000.
59 Epstein 1998; Meadows 2001; Lovell et al. 2010; and Milevski 2012.
60 Namdar et al. 2015.
61 Grigson 1995, and 2006.
62 Milevski 2009.
63 Sherratt 1981; but see also Marciniak 2011.
64 Garfinkel et al. 2009.
65 Bourke 2002.
66 Dessel 2009.
67 Milevski et al. 2012.
68 Milevski et al. 2014.
69 Mazar 2001.

Golan Heights,[70] and five ceramic groups have been distinguished in the central and southern regions as having been distributed through small to medium inter-regional networks.[71] Patterns of distribution were longitudinal and transversal, but in restricted areas – the Galilee, the Jordan valley, the Judean/Shephela area and the Beersheva Basin – probably reflecting limited exchange networks, with distribution of wares not exceeding a radius of 20 kilometres.

Furthermore, copper metallurgy first existed in the Chalcolithic times in the southern Levant, from which two different copper metalworking techniques have been identified: one based on casting of utilitarian tools and another that used the 'lost-wax' technique to produce elaborate prestige items, particularly for ritual use, such as 'sceptres', 'crowns', mace-heads and other objects.[72] The latter technique combines copper with small amounts of arsenic and antimony. The 'lost-wax' technique may have received foreign influence and may have even involved some movement of populations, given the use of non-local materials such as antimony and arsenic. Unfortunately, we cannot address this topic in depth in this paper.[73]

Metallurgy also had a social influence that resulted in the creation of a sort of 'fetishism' of copper objects.[74] Decades earlier, the mysterious character of copper objects was noted by Gordon Childe, who claimed that metal commodities were produced by means of a process 'unknown' to most sectors of society at the time.[75]

We are assuming that the introduction of new techniques of farm work and work in new branches of production, including copper working, required specialised groups.[76] These craftspeople could have been workers comprised within the kin or community system in several cases, such as potters, i.e. with certain independence, but others such as copper workers seem to have been controlled by or attached to elites, who centralised production in the area during the Chalcolithic and later controlled the distribution of metal products.[77]

Conversely, metalworking had an expanding effect on the division of labour during the Chalcolithic as a prologue to the 'urban revolution' in the Early

---

70 Shalem et al. 2019.
71 Goren 2006; Roux and Courty 1998.
72 Golden 2010.
73 And see Gandulla and Jaruf 2017.
74 See Anfinset 2010.
75 Childe 1930.
76 Golden 2010.
77 Shalev 1994. And see for craft specialisation and social contexts of artisans, see Costin 1991.

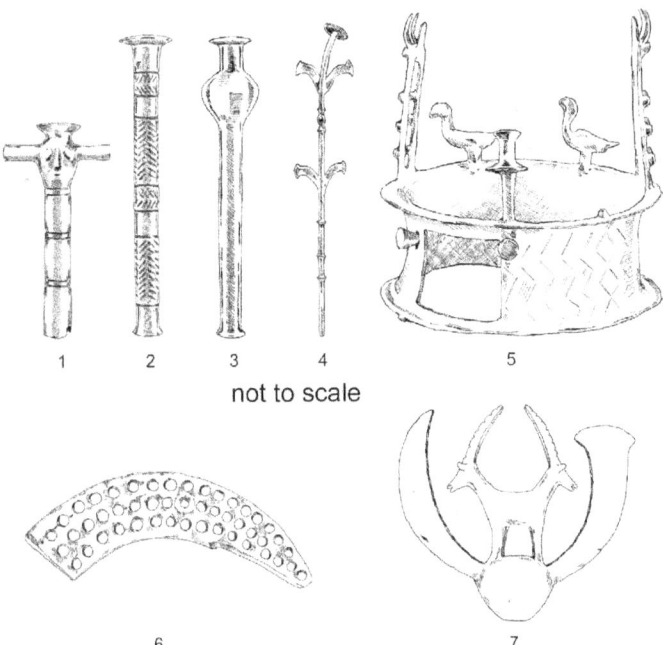

FIGURE 3.2 Copper and other objects from Nahal Mishmar: 1. standard n° 21; 2. standard n° 41; 3. standard n° 50; 4. sceptre n° 126; 5. crown n° 7; 6. ivory tusk n° 2; 7. zoomorphic decorated mace-head n° 153.
ADAPTED AND REDRAWN FROM BAR-ADON 1980

Bronze Age, when metalworking developed into a craft associated with the controlling groups in society. Metallurgy and flint knapping changed the way in which production and distribution were organised in those periods.[78]

4.5 Iconography

In many cases, the objects of the Chalcolithic (Figure 3.2) such as 'standards', mace-heads, 'crowns' and 'sceptres' or 'ceremonial staffs' found at Nahal Mishmar seem to be associated with the figure of some sort of 'ruler'.[79] However, Gilead has suggested that some of these objects do not seem to be associated exclusively with a specific social group differentiated in terms of political concentration or ritual power, as could be inferred from the mural of the procession at Teleilat Ghassul.[80]

---

78   Shalev 1994; Rosen 1997.
79   Bar-Adon 1980.
80   Gilead 2002. For the mural painting, see Cameron 1981, figure 14.

FIGURE 3.3
Ossuaries: 1. ossuary from Peqi'in; 2. ossuary from Peqi'in; 3. ossuary from et-Taiyiba; 4. ossuary from Benei Beraq.
1. ADAPTED FROM GAL ET AL. 2011, FIGURE 9; 2. ADAPTED AND REDRAWN FROM GAL ET AL. 2011, FIGURE 10; 3. ADAPTED AND REDRAWN FROM YANNAI AND PORATH 2006, OSSUARY N° 9; 4. ADAPTED AND REDRAWN FROM PERROT AND LADIRAY 1980, FIGURE 141

In any case, the iconographic motifs associated with these objects are also present in other contexts. For example, this iconographic repertoire also appears in objects with religious significance, such as the ossuaries found in several cemeteries including Ben Shemen and Peqi'in[81] (Figure 3.3), and apparently reflects a symbolic system centered on fertility, reproduction and the cycle of life, be it human, plant or animal (Figure 3.4).[82]

However, the fact that parts of the repertoire, particularly the metal objects, are associated with symbols of power such as 'crowns' and 'sceptres' may point to a process of symbolic concentration through which certain individuals asserted their dominion.

The concentration of certain iconographic motifs and artefacts may also amount to the material expression of a specific cultural identity and the media that human groups resorted to in order to reproduce their identity and define it in relation to a specified territory.[83] It is on this basis that we shall attempt to identify the members of the Ghassulian culture that is similar yet different to

---

81   Perrot and Ladiray 1980; Gal et al. 1999.
82   Milevski 2002; Shalem 2008.
83   Milevski 2010; Milevski and Gandulla 2014.

THE MODE OF PRODUCTION OF THE CHALCOLITHIC PERIOD IN PALESTINE   91

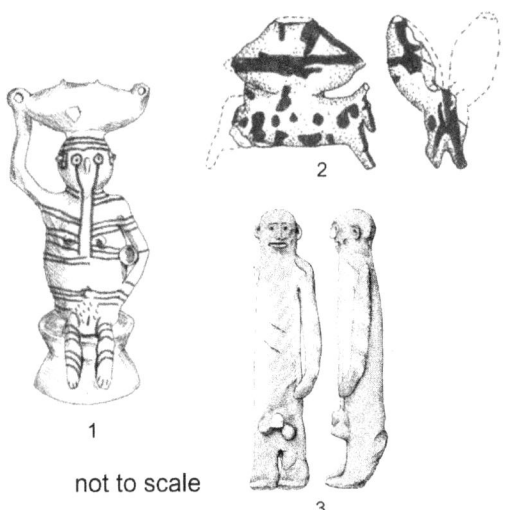

FIGURE 3.4
Figurines: 1. female figurine from Gilat; 2. zoomorphic figurine from En Gedi; 3. Male figurine from Quleh.
1. ADAPTED FROM ALON AND LEVY 1989, FIGURE 8; 2. ADAPTED FROM USSISHKIN 1980, FIGURE 11; 3. ADAPTED FROM MILEVSKI 2002

other Chalcolithic societies such as the Golan culture or the Timnite culture in the Negev and Aravah.[84]

There has been much discussion regarding the existence of specific constructions for sanctuaries. The only cases that have apparently not given rise to discussion are En Gedi on the Dead Sea and Teleilat Ghassul.[85] Gilat has been subject to more consideration.[86] Naturally, Levy's proposal includes sanctuaries amongst the forms in which chiefdoms exercised their power. We suggest, as Ilan and Rowan have done, that ceremonial rites were also conducted in the caves used as secondary cemeteries in the Chalcolithic.[87] By way of example, we can mention the cultic burial of the Quleh figurine (Figure 3.4: 3), a symbol of fertility and the cycle of life associated with agriculture.[88] It is therefore difficult to prove the existence of a central cult with temple constructions. Obviously, those who deny the existence of chiefdom-like societies in the Chalcolithic suggest that the cult was also conducted at a domestic level.[89]

In any case, the Chalcolithic can be deemed to be the last expression of prehistory even from an iconographic point of view since it involves a symbolic

---

84   Esptein 1998; Rosen 2011.
85   Mallon et al. 1934; Ussishkin 1980; Seaton 2008; and Ussishkin 2014.
86   Levy 2006.
87   Ilan and Rowan 2012.
88   Milevski 2002.
89   Gilead 2002; Joffe 2003; and Ilan and Rowan 2012.

system that reproduces and deepens the characteristics of Neolithic religion, the origins of which can even be traced to the Natufian culture.[90]

The fact that the Chalcolithic iconographic motifs disappeared concurrently with the socio-economic 'collapse' suggests the existence of a close relationship between them, enabling the application of a metaphor of the relationship between superstructure and infrastructure, a relationship that is not mechanical but dialectical. The increasing social divisions registered during the Chalcolithic seems to have gone hand in hand with a greater number and diversity of iconographic motifs and artefacts.

4.6 Burial Modes

The study of funeral customs, what we call 'burial modes' (Figure 3.5), could lead us to also understand social relations within communities.[91] In studies of the Pre-Pottery Neolithic period, there are burials under the houses, which mark clear forms of household burials.[92] Things change when we get to the Chalcolithic, in which there are primary burials within sites, 'home burials'; however, bones were subsequently removed, placed in containers or ossuaries and re-buried in cemeteries – generally in burial caves. This is to say that such burials were of the community.

The latest studies on three Chalcolithic cemeteries in the southern Levant, Peqi'in, Horvat Qarqar and Quleh-Mazor indicate that the sites were not ascribed to a single settlement but to numerous, whose distances could vary by several tens of kilometres. This multiple affiliation results from petrographic studies, indicating that ossuaries and utensils of ceramics buried there originated in different areas around the secondary cemeteries.[93] If this is so, the Chalcolithic burial caves were an extension of the villages and a gathering place that also operated on the larger regional scale, like the notion of interconnecting Ghassulian Chalcolithic communities.[94]

5 Discussion

As we pointed out earlier, the problem for archaeologists and historians is how to identify, based on the analysis of material records, the social entities – com-

---

90 Shalem 2008.
91 And see Milevski 2019.
92 For example, Kuijt and Goring Morris 2002; Kuijt 2008.
93 Boness et al. 2015; Milevski et al., in press. See also Golding-Meir and Iserlis 2013.
94 Milevski et al., in press.

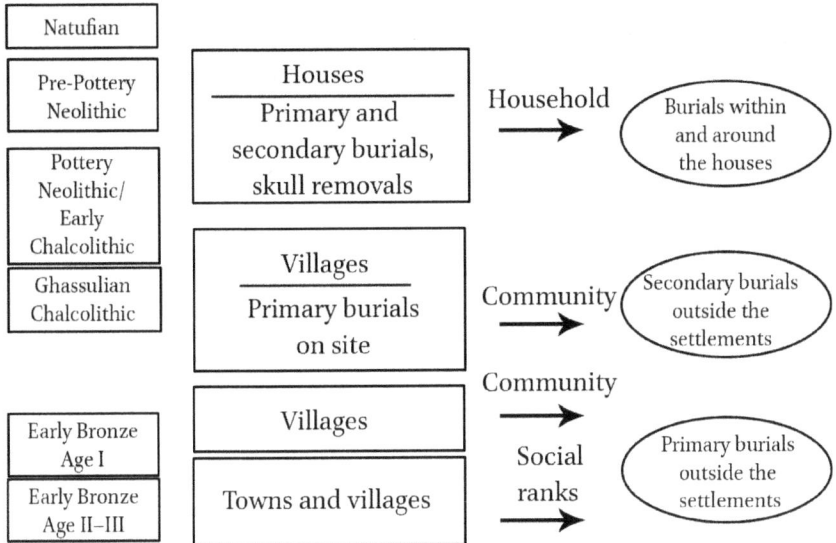

FIGURE 3.5 Burial modes in the late prehistory of Palestine.
ADAPTED FROM MILEVSKI 2019

munities, clans, tribes or individuals – that participated in socio-economic developments as well as the social tensions that arose between such groups. We suggest to include the Chalcolithic of Palestine in the villager community-based mode of production, one of the forms of the 'primitive community' as defined by Marx.[95] We prefer to use the term 'communal', which we believe provides the best description of the types of property relations that we are discussing.[96] Based on the above, we believe that despite the fact that the Chalcolithic of Palestine was characterized by a community-symbolic system, this did not prevent the emergence of a process involving the organisation into social hierarchies of certain individuals, which surely would have included patriarchal family heads (though we should not rule out the possibility that women also played this role). However, we presume that this hierarchical organisation took place within the family framework and responded to the positions of prestige determined by kinship relationships.

The process involving the organisation into social hierarchies went hand in hand with the rise in productivity, the emergence of new production branches and the expansion of exchange networks. As regards productivity, silos were

---

95   Marx 1993.
96   And see Suret-Canale 1964.

larger in number and size as a result of an increase in grain production, and there are many indications of an intensification of horticulture (shown in the multiplication of olive pits and olive oil containers), and craftwork (pottery, flint and basalt tools). Also worth noting is the multiplication of evidence regarding secondary products, particularly textiles and milk.[97] Moreover, according to studies we have conducted, Chalcolithic product exchange networks became more regular over distances involving several dozens of kilometres and involved pottery, basalt tools and copper products.[98] In any case, despite the increase of exchange networks, the circulation of goods was probably still limited.

The Chalcolithic of Palestine (Figure 3.6: 1) constituted a communal form of socio-economic organisation based on villages with their attendant agropastoral activities and crafts. The Chalcolithic elites that controlled these activities were village elites. There may have been another elite, a sort of priestly class associated with the sanctuaries.

On several occasions we have considered Bourke's suggestion regarding the existence of two elites in Chalcolithic society, namely a traditional elite which drew its power from control of a specialised knowledge and religion, and an emerging elite that based its power on the control of agricultural surpluses.[99]

Though the transition from the Chalcolithic to the Early Bronze Age in Palestine (c. 3,700 BC) assumed multiple forms, its main aspects involved the collapse of settlements of the Chalcolithic Ghassulian culture and their substitution by a new type of community. This was an uneven process that occurred in different ways in different regions, as may be seen in the distinctions between settlements in the Beersheva Valley, the Negev, Galilee, the Golan, etc. The transition was more abrupt in the northern regions of Palestine than in the central regions. It was so abrupt in the south that no Early Bronze settlements have been found in the Beersheva Valley.[100]

According to the new chronology, socio-economic systems went from agropastoral communities in the Chalcolithic, with relatively developed secondary production branches, to an urban revolution towards 3,100 BC.[101] Agricultural

---

97   Grigson 1995; Levy and Gilead 2012; and Milevski 2013.
98   Milevski and Barzilai 2017.
99   For the archaeological correlates for this control, see Bourke 2001. Although this author suggested the existence of two elites, their socio-economic contexts are unclear, and it is not known whether they represent one or two different social orders.
100 Milevski 2013.
101 Regev et al. 2012.

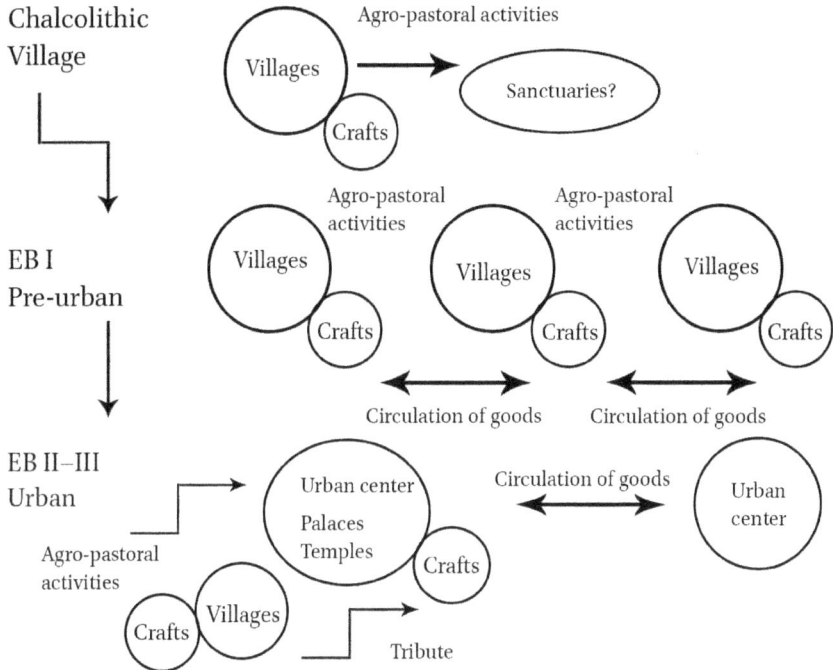

FIGURE 3.6 Model of socio-economic formations for the Chalcolithic and Early Bronze Age in the southern Levant.
ADAPTED FROM MILEVSKI 2013

and pastoral activities changed at a slower pace, but some important changes probably occurred during this transition, such as the complete domestication of the olive tree – though it is possible that exploitation of olives and the use of the plough started before.[102] Transportation was radically transformed with the domestication of the donkey, and the circulation of goods increased during the Early Bronze Age.[103] Finally, burial practices were greatly altered, as were the iconographic elements associated with religious beliefs.

According to certain authors, the situation ended in violent conflicts towards the end of the Chalcolithic, or the 'Terminal Chalcolithic'.[104] Burton and Levy have suggested that the final phase of the Chalcolithic can be explained

---

102   Zohary 1975; Grigson 1995; Namdar et al. 2015.
103   Milevski 2011; Milevski and Horwitz 2019.
104   Joffe and Dessel 1995; Yekutieli 2012. This is not the place to discuss in detail the evidence supporting these contentions, which are closely associated with the determination of end dates for the Chalcolithic period, some of them new, others old and no longer valid. The reliability of the association of the data with the transition period is problematic.

by a *dénouement* of the Negev as part of the loss of control over the production and exchange of copper and also by climate change that caused the drying of areas that previously enjoyed better rainfall.[105]

In another article, we suggested that Chalcolithic elites acquired their 'power' from the villages by expropriating clan control of agriculture and animal husbandry as well as by controlling crafts and even copper work.[106]

Upon the collapse of the Chalcolithic society, new elites in the Early Bronze Age villages began developing, from a lower level, new village-based forms of production and distribution.[107] The economies of the first Early Bronze Age communities were mostly based on agro-pastoral activities (Figure 3.6: 2). However, unlike the Chalcolithic, the Early Bronze Age elites probably obtained their surpluses not only from these activities but also from the exchange profits of goods that rose towards the middle of the fourth millennium BC.[108] Crafts developed both independently and within circles attached to the elites. The trend towards full-time specialisation increased in some cases. Food storage systems that were developed during the Chalcolithic (even during its early stages) experienced a significant concentration of agricultural surpluses during the Early Bronze Age.[109]

This process led to the development of a primary urbanisation where social elites garnered power and created their own institutions. The urbanisation occurred at the end of the Early Bronze I / beginning of the Early Bronze II (c. 3,100/3,000 BC) (Figure 3.6: 3) and constitutes a radical change in all social relations; power was then concentrated in the hands of the urban elites and 'superior units', i.e. institutions such as palaces and temples.[110]

The most important change developed during the Early Bronze Age was the restructuring of the division of labour with a differently organised system of crafts and a revolution in the circulation of goods due to the changes mentioned above. In its contribution to improved transportation methods, the domestication of donkeys allowed for a greater volume of exchange.[111]

The rapid reproduction of means and a greater division of labour enabled the development of the urban phase at the end of the Early Bronze Age I. This urban phase represented not only the creation of the first urbanisation in the

---

105   Burton and Levy 2011b; Milevski et al. 2016.
106   Milevski 2009.
107   Ibid.
108   Milevski 2011.
109   Garfinkel et al. 2009; Golani and Yannai 2016; and Milevski et al. 2012.
110   de Miroschedji 2013, pp. 186–92.
111   Milevski 2011; Milevski and Horowitz 2019.

southern Levant (different from what occurred in the north that was more closely linked with Mesopotamia), but also the creation of the first state or states in the territory under research. The Early Bronze Age state created bureaucratic institutions and constructed public buildings and even external walls that outlined the areas dominated by the ruling classes in a specific territory.[112]

6   Summary

Summing up, the late-prehistoric social formations in Palestine ranged from the so-called 'primitive' forms in one of their late variants during the Chalcolithic to the forms associated with some aspects present in the theoretical model of the 'Asiatic mode of production' during the Early Bronze Age.

There is no question that surplus values existed in some way, although they were probably redistributed in some form or used by social groups or community leaders.

In other terms, these surpluses were not converted into private property. It is not a matter of whether social differences existed, including those based on the division of labour and access to resources or to means of production such as land and livestock.[113] There is no question that there were leaders making decisions based on some control over the population of communities. And it is not that there was no violence or no group that tried to monopolise violence. Perhaps all of these existed in the Chalcolithic period; the situation, however, was not solved and led to social contradictions and tensions, which can be measured in political and social terms.

Finally, these contradictions and tensions are likely to have rendered the Chalcolithic as a dynamic era characteristic of transitional periods in which the old communal forms went into crisis. The social transformation was uneven and highly localised, and its dynamics varied spatially, even in a small territory such as the southern Levant.

Acknowledgements

We thank Cecilia Mizraji for the translation of a first version of this paper and the Fund for Science and Technology (FONCYT) of Argentina that generously

---

112   Shalev 2018.
113   Risch 2018.

funded the research presented within it (PICT 2010-0883). We also are indebted to three anonymous reviewers who helped to improve a previous version of the paper with their critical comments.

References

Alon, David and Thomas E. Levy 1989, 'The Archaeology of Cult and the Chalcolithic Sanctuary at Gilat', *Journal of Mediterranean Archaeology*, 2, 2: 163–221.

Anderson, Perry 1974, *Lineages of the Absolutist State*, London: New Left Books.

Anfinset, Niels 2010, *Metal, Nomads and Culture Contact: The Middle East and North Africa*, London: Equinox.

Banning, Edward B. 2010, 'Houses, Households, and Changing Society in the Late Neolithic and Chalcolithic of the Southern Levant', *Paléorient*, 36, 1: 49–87.

Bar-Adon, Pessah 1980, *The Cave of the Treasure*, Jerusalem: Israel Exploration Society.

Di Bennardis, Cristina 2014, 'Un acercamiento al problema del poder político y el estado en las sociedades antiguo-orientales: reflexiones sobre teorías e interpretaciones', in *Diversidad de formaciones políticas en Mesopotamia y el Cercano Oriente. Organización interna y relaciones interregionales en la Edad del Bronce*, Barcino Monographica Orientalia 1, edited by Cristina Di Bennardis, Eleonora Ravenna and Ianir Milevski, Barcelona: Institut del Pròxim Orient Antic, Universitat de Barcelona.

Bolger, Diane and Louis C. Maguire (eds.) 2010, *Development of Pre-State Communities in the Ancient Near East*, Oxford: Oxbow Books.

Boness, Doron, Naama Scheftelowitz, Peter Fabian, Isaac Gilead and Yuval Goren 2015, 'Petrographic Study of the Pottery Assemblages from Ḥorvat Qarqar South, a Ghassulian Chalcolithic Cemetery in the Southern Levant', *Bulletin of the American Schools of Oriental Research*, 375: 185–213.

Bourke, Stephen J. 2001, 'The Chalcolithic Period', in *The Archaeology of Jordan*, edited by Bruce Macdonald, Russell Adams and Piotr Bieliński, Sheffield: Sheffield Academic Press.

Bourke, Stephen J. 2002, 'The Origins of Social Complexity in the Southern Levant: New Evidence from Teleilat Ghassul, Jordan', *Palestine Exploration Quarterly*, 134, 1: 2–27.

Braun, Eliot 2011, 'The Transition from Chalcolithic to Early Bronze Age I. A "Lost Horizon" Slowly Revealed', in *Culture, Chronology and the Chalcolithic: Theory and Transition*, edited by Jaimie L. Lovell and Yorke M. Rowan, Oxford: Oxbow Books.

van den Brink, Edwin C.M. 2011, 'Continuity and Change – Cultural Transmission in the Late Chalcolithic – Early Bronze Age I: A View from Early Modi'in, a Late Prehistoric Site in Central Israel', in, *Culture, Chronology and the Chalcolithic: Theory and Transition*, edited by Jaimie L. Lovell and Yorke M. Rowan, Oxford: Oxbow Books.

Burton, Margie M. and Thomas E. Levy 2011a, 'The End of the Chalcolithic Period (4500–3600 BC) in the Northern Negev Desert, Israel', in *Culture, Chronology and the Chalcolithic: Theory and Transition*, edited by Jaimie L. Lovell and Yorke M. Rowan, Oxford: Oxbow Books.

Burton, Margie M. and Thomas E. Levy 2011b, 'Chalcolithic Social Organization Reconsidered: Excavations at the Abu Hof Village, Northern Negev, Israel', *Mitekufat Haeven – Journal of the Israel Prehistoric Society*, 42: 137–92.

Cameron, Dorothy O. 1981, *The Ghassulian Wall Paintings*, London: Kenyon-Deane.

Campagno, Marcelo 2006, *Estudios sobre parentesco y estado en el antiguo Egipto*, Buenos Aires: Ediciones del Signo.

Chapman, Robert 2008, 'Alternative States', in *Evaluating Multiple Narratives: Beyond Nationalist, Colonialist and Imperialist Archaeologies*, edited by Junko Habu, Clare Fawcett and John M. Matsunaga, Oxford: Oxbow Books.

Childe, Vere Gordon 1930, *The Bronze Age*, Cambridge: Cambridge University Press.

Childe, Vere Gordon 1942, *What Happened in History*, London: Penguin Books.

Childe, Vere Gordon 1950, 'The Urban Revolution', *The Town Planning Review*, 21: 3–17.

Cicero, Marcus T. 1995 [51 AD], *De Republica*, Cambridge: Cambridge University Press.

Costin, Cathy L. 1991, 'Craft Specialization: Issues in Defining, Documenting, and Explaining the Organization of Production', *Archaeological Method and Theory*, 3: 1–56.

Dessel, Jack P. 2009, *Lahav I: Pottery and Politics: The Halif Terrace Site 101 and Egypt in the Fourth Millennium B.C.E.*, Winnnona Lake, IN: Winona Eisenbrauns.

Diakonoff, Igor 1975, 'The Rural Community in the Ancient Near East', *Journal of the Economic and Social History of the Orient*, 18, 2: 121–33.

Earle, Timothy 2002, *Bronze Age Economics: The First Political Economies*, Boulder, CO: Westview Press.

Engels, Friedrich 1972 [1884], *The Origins of the Family, Private Property and State*, New York: Pathfinder.

Epstein, Claire (ed.) 1998, *The Chalcolithic Culture of the Golan*, IAA Reports 5, Jerusalem: Israel Antiquities Authority.

Finkelstein, Israel 1996, 'Toward a New Periodization and Nomenclature of the Archaeology of the Southern Levan', in *The Study of the Ancient Near East in the Twenty-First Century: the William Foxwell Albright Centennial Conference*, edited by Jerold S. Cooper and Glenn M. Schwartz, Winona Lake, IN: Eisenbrauns,

Finkelstein, Israel and Ram Gophna 1993, 'Settlement, Demographic and Economic Patterns in the Highlands of Palestine in the Chalcolithic and Early Bronze Periods and the Beginning of Urbanism', *Bulletin of the American Schools of Oriental Research*, 289: 1–22.

Fried, Morton H. 1967, *The Evolution of Political Society: An Essay in Political Anthropology*, New York: Random House.

Gaido, Daniel 2003, 'Karl Kautzky on Capitalism in the Ancient World', *The Journal of Peasant Studies*, 30: 146–58.

Gal, Zvi, Dina Shalem and Howard Smithline 2011, 'The Peqi'in Cave: A Chalcolithic Cemetery in Upper Galilee, Israel', *Near Eastern Archaeology*, 74, 4: 1–16.

Gal, Zvi, Howard Smithline and Dina Shalem 1999, 'New Iconographic Aspects of Chalcolithic Art: Preliminary Observations on Finds from the Peqi'in Cave', *'Atiqot*, 37: 1–16.

Gandulla, Bernardo and Pablo Jaruf 2017, 'Otherness and Interaction in Copper Metallurgy in the Chalcolithic of the Southern Levant: The Transcaucasian Connection', *Claroscuro*, 16: 1–22, available at: http://ppct.caicyt.gov.ar/index.php/claroscuro/issue/view/700.

García-Piquer, Albert and Assumpió Vila-Mitjà (eds.) 2016, *Beyond War: Archaeological Approaches to Violence*, Cambridge: Cambridge Scholars Publishing.

Garfinkel, Yosef 1999, *Neolithic and Chalcolithic Pottery of the Southern Levant*, Qedem 39, Jerusalem: The Hebrew University of Jerusalem.

Garfinkel, Yosef, David Ben-Shlomo and Tali Kuperman 2009, 'Large-scale Storage of Grain Surplus in the Sixth Millennium BC: The Silos of Tel Tsaf', *Antiquity*, 83: 309–25.

Gilead, Isaac 1988, 'The Chalcolithic Period in the Levant', *Journal of World Prehistory*, 2, 4: 397–443.

Gilead, Isaac 1993, 'Sociopolitical Organization in the Northern Negev at the End of the Chalcolithic Period', in *Biblical Archaeology Today, Supplement*, edited by Avraham Biran and Joseph Aviram, Jerusalem: Israel Exploration Society.

Gilead, Isaac 2002, 'Religio-Magic Behavior in the Chalcolithic Period of Palestine', in *Aharon Kempinski Memorial Volume: Studies in Archaeology and Related Disciplines*, Beer Sheva Volume 15, edited by Shmuel Ahituv and Eliezer D. Oren, Beer Sheva: Ben-Gurion University of the Negev Press.

Gilead, Isaac 2011, 'Chalcolithic Culture History: Ghassulian and Other Entities in the Southern Levant', in *Culture, Chronology and the Chalcolithic: Theory and Transition*, edited by Jaimie L. Lovell and Yorke M. Rowan, Oxford: Oxbow Books.

Godelier, Maurice 1975, 'Modes of Production, Kinship and Demographic Structures', *Marxist Analyses in Social Anthropology*, edited by Maurice Bloch, New York: Wiley.

Golani, Amir and Eli Yannai 2016, 'Storage Structures of the Late Early Bronze I in the Southern Levant and the Urbanization Process', *Palestine Exploration Quarterly*, 148, 1: 8–41.

Golden, Jonathan 2010, *Dawn of the Metal Age: Technology and Society during the Levantine Chalcolithic*, London: Equinox.

Golding-Meir, Nissim and Mark Iserlis 2013, 'Petrographic Examination of Ceramics', in *Late Chalcolithic and Early Bronze Age I Remains at Nesher-Ramle Quarry*, edited by Vladimir W. Avrutis, Haifa: University of Haifa & Bouky Ltd.

Gophna, Ram and Juval Portugali 1988, 'Settlement and Demographic Processes in Israel's Coastal Plain from the Chalcolithic to the Middle Bronze Age', *Bulletin of the American Schools of Oriental Research*, 269: 11–28.

Goren, Yuval 2006, 'The Technology of the Gilat Pottery Assemblage', in *Archaeology, Anthropology and Cult: The Sanctuary at Gilat, Israel*, edited by Thomas E. Levy, London: Equinox,

Gošić, Milena and Isaac Gilead 2015, 'Unveiling Hidden Rituals: Ghassulian Metallurgy of the Southern Levant in the Light of the Ethnographical Record', in *Copper and Trade in South-Eastern Mediterranean: Trade Routes of the Near East Antiquity*, edited by Karolina Rosińska-Balik, Agnieszka Ochał-Czarnowicz, Marcin Czarnowicz and Joanna Dębowska-Ludwin, Oxford: Archaeopress.

Grigson, Caroline 1995, 'Plough and Pasture in the Early Economy of the Southern Levant', in *The Archaeology of Society in the Holy Land*, edited by Thomas E. Levy, London: Leicester University Press.

Grigson, Caroline 2006, 'Farming? Feasting? Herding? Large Mammals from the Chalcolithic of Gilat', in *Archaeology, Anthropology and Cult: The Sanctuary at Gilat, Israel*, edited by Thomas E. Levy, London: Equinox.

Hegel, Georg W.F. 1991 [1821], *Elements of the Philosophy of Right*, edited by Allen W. Wood, Cambridge: Cambridge University Press.

Hindess, Barry and Paul Q. Hirst 1975, *Pre-Capitalistic Modes of Production*, London: Routledge.

Hobsbawm, Eric 1965, *Introduction to* Pre-Capitalist Economic Formations *by Karl Marx*, New York: International Publishers.

Ilan, David and Yorke M. Rowan 2012, 'Deconstructing and Recomposing the Narrative of Spiritual Life in the Chalcolithic of the Southern Levant (4500–3600 B.C.E.)', *Archaeological Papers of the American Anthropological Association, Special Issue – Beyond Belief: The Archaeology of Religion and Ritual*, 21, 1: 89–113.

Joffe, Alexander H. 2003, 'Slouching toward Beersheva: Chalcolithic Mortuary Practices in Local and Regional Context', in *The Near East in the Southwest: Essays in Honor of William G. Dever*, edited by Beth Alpert Nakhai, Boston, MA: American Schools of Oriental Research.

Joffe, Alexander H. and J.P. Dessel 1995, 'Redefining Chronology and Terminology for the Chalcolithic of the Southern Levant', *Current Anthropology*, 36: 506–18.

Kuijt, Ian 2008, 'The Regeneration of Life: Neolithic Structures of Symbolic Remembering and Forgetting', *Current Anthropology*, 49: 171–97.

Kuijt, Ian and Nigel Goring-Morris 2002, 'Foraging, Farming, and Social Complexity in the Pre-Pottery Neolithic of the Southern Levant: A Review and Synthesis', *Journal of World Prehistory*, 16, 4: 361–440.

Levy, Janet and Isaac Gilead 2012, 'Spinning in the 5th Millennium in the Southern Levant: Aspects of the Textile Economy', *Paléorient*, 38, 1–2: 127–39.

Levy, Thomas E. 1998, 'Cult, Metallurgy and Rank Societies – Chalcolithic Period (ca. 4500–3500 BCE)', in *The Archaeology of Society in the Holy Land*, 226–44, edited by Thomas E. Levy, London: Leicester University Press.

Levy, Thomas E. (ed.) 2006, *Archaeology, Anthropology and Cult: The Sanctuary at Gilat, Israel*, London: Equinox.

Levy, Thomas E. 2007, *Journey to the Copper Age: Archaeology in the Holy Land*, San Diego, CA: San Diego Museum of Man.

Liphschitz, Nili and Giorgio Bonani 2000, 'Dimensions of Olive (*Olea europaea*) Cultivation in the Old World: A Reassessment', *Journal of Archaeological Science*, 18, 441–53.

Lovell, Jaimie L. 2002, 'Shifting Subsistence Patterns: Some Ideas about the End of the Chalcolithic in the Southern Levant', *Paléorient*, 28, 1: 89–102.

Lovell, Jaimie L., John Meadows and Geraldine E. Jacobsen 2010, 'Upland Olive Domestication in the Chalcolithic Period: New 14C Determination from el-Khawarij (Ajlun), Jordan', *Radiocarbon*, 52: 364–71.

Lull, Vicente and Rafel Micó 2007, *Arqueología del Origen del Estado: Las Teorías*, Barcelona: Bellaterra.

Mallon, Alexis, Robert Koeppel and René Neuville 1934, *Teleilat Ghassul I, 1929–32*, Rome: Pontifical Biblical Institute.

Mandel, Ernest 1974, *The Formation of the Economic Thought of Karl Marx: 1843 to Capital*, London: Monthly Review Press.

Marciniak, Arkadiusz 2011, 'The Secondary Products Revolution: Empirical Evidence and its Current Zooarchaeological Critique', *Journal of World Prehistory*, 24: 117–30.

Marx, Karl 1970 [1859], *A Contribution to the Critique of Political Economy*, New York: International Publishers.

Marx, Karl 1993 [1939], *Grundrisse: Foundations of Political Economy (Rough Draft)*, London: Penguin Classics.

Marx, Karl and Friedrich Engels 1970 [1846], *The German Ideology*, New York: International Publishers.

Marx, Karl and Friedrich Engels 1992, *Collected Works*, Volume 46, New York: International Publishers.

Mazar, Amihai 2001, 'On the Significance of the Early Bronze III Granary Building at Beit Yerah', in *Studies in the Archaeology of Israel and Neighboring Lands in Memory of Douglas L. Esse*, edited by Sam R. Wolff, Chicago, IL and Atlanta, GA: Oriental Institute, University of Chicago.

McGuire, Randall H. 2002, *A Marxist Archaeology*, New York: Percheron Press.

Meadows, John 2001, 'Olive domestication at Teleilat Ghassul', in *The Ancient Near East: An Australian Postgraduate Perspective*, edited by Liza Hopkins and Anna Parker, Sydney: Sydney University.

Milevski, Ianir 2002, 'A New Fertility Figurine and New Animal Motifs from the Chalcolithic in the Southern Levant: Finds from Cave K-1 at Quleh, Israel', *Paléorient*, 28, 1: 133–42.

Milevski, Ianir 2009, 'Review: The Copper Age and Inequality in the Southern Levant', *Mitekufat Haeven: Journal of the Israel Prehistoric Society*, 39: 159–80.

Milevski, Ianir 2010, 'Visual Expressions of Craft Production in the Chalcolithic of the Southern Levant', in *Proceedings of the 6th ICAANE*, Volume 3, edited by Paolo Matthiae, Francis Pinnock, Lorenzo Nigro and Nicolo Marchetti, Wiesbaden: Harrassowitz Verlag.

Milevski, Ianir 2011, *Early Bronze Age Goods Exchange in the Southern Levant: A Marxist Perspective*, London: Equinox.

Milevski, Ianir 2012, 'The Barter of Olives during the Early Bronze Age', in 'On the Shadow of the tree: Olive Trees, Olive Oil and Their Products' – conference organised by the Ben-Gurion University in the Negev and Israel Antiquities Authority, Beersheva [Hebrew].

Milevski, Ianir 2013, 'The Transition from the Chalcolithic to the Early Bronze Age of the Southern Levant in Socio-Economic Context', *Paléorient*, 39: 193–208.

Milevski, Ianir 2019, 'Burial Customs in the Southern Levant during the Late Prehistory and the Concept of *Burial Modes* as a Research Tool', in *Worship and Burial in the Shefela and Negev Regions Throughout the Ages*, edited by Daniel Varga, Yael Abadi-Reiss, Gunnar Lehman and Daniel Vainstub, Beersheva: Israel Antiquities Authority and Ben-Gurion University of the Negev, Beersheva [Hebrew].

Milevski, Ianir and Omry Barzilai 2017, 'Redes de intercambio en los finales de la prehistoria del Levante meridional', in *Si un Hombre desde el Sur ... / Šumma Awīlum ina Šūtim ...: Escritos de Alumnos, Colegas y Amigos en Homenaje a Bernardo Gandulla*, Tomo I, edited by Ianir Milevski, Luciano Monti and Pablo Jaruf, Buenos Aires: Editorial de la Facultad de Filosofía y Letras, Universidad de Buenos Aires.

Milevski, Ianir and Bernardo Gandulla 2014, 'Minor Arts and Society in the Chalcolithic of the Southern Levant', in *Proceedings of the 8th ICAANE*, Volume 1, edited by Piotr Bieliński, Michał Gawlikowski, Rafał Koliński, Dorota Ławecka, Arkadiusz Sołtysiak and Zusanna Wygnańska, Wiesbaden: Harrassowitz Verlag.

Milevski, Ianir and Liora Kolska Horwitz 2019, 'Domestication of the Donkey (*Equus asinus*) in the Southern Levant: Archaeozoology, Iconography and Economy', in *Animals and Human Society in Asia: Historical, Cultural and Ethical Perspectives*, edited by Rotem Kowner, Guy Bar-Oz, Michal Biran, Meir Shahar and Gideon Shelach-Lavi, Cham: Palgrave Macmillan.

Milevski, Ianir, Bernardo Gandulla and Pablo Jaruf 2016, '"Eco-systems" or "Socio-systems"? The Case of the Chalcolithic of the Southern Levant', in *Proceedings of the 9th International Congress on the Archaeology of the Ancient Near East*, Volume 3, edited by Rolf A. Stucky, Oskar Kaelin and Hans-Peter Mathys, Wiesbaden: Harrassowitz Verlag.

Milevski, Ianir, Nimrod Getzov and Yitzhak Paz 2022, 'Uneven and Combined: The Synchronization of the Early Bronze Age I and the First Urbanization in the Southern Levant', in *Transitions during the Early Bronze Age in the Levant*, edited by Matthew J. Adams, Felix Höfflmayer and Valentine Roux, Münster: Zaphon.

Milevski, Ianir, Roy Liran and Nimrod Getzov 2014, 'The Early Bronze Town of Ein Zippori in the Galilee, Israel', *Antiquity*, 88, available at: http://www.antiquity.ac.uk/projgall/milevski339/.

Milevski, Ianir, Ronit Lupu and Anat Cohen-Weinberger, in press, *Excavations at Quleh and Mazor (West). Burial Practices and Iconography in Southern Levantine Chalcolithic Cemeteries*, Wien: Austrian Academy of Sciences.

Milevski, Ianir, Eliot Braun, Daniel Varga and Yigal Israel 2012, 'A Newly-Discovered Early Bronze Age Settlement and Silo Complex at Amaziya, Israel', *Antiquity*, 86, available at: http://www.antiquity.ac.uk/projgall/milevski331/.

de Miroschedji, Pierre 2013, 'La ville au Proche-Orient ancien: approches archéologiques', in *De la maison á la ville dans l'Orient ancien: La ville et les début de l'urbanisation*, edited by Cécile Michel, Nanterre: CNRS.

Namdar, Dvory, Alon Amrani, Nimrod Getzov and Ianir Milevski 2015, 'Olive Oil Storage during the Fifth and Sixth Millennia BC at Ein Zippori, Northern Israel', *Israel Journal of Plant Sciences*, 62: 1–2.

Novack, George E. 1974, *Understanding History: Marxist Essays*, New York: International Press.

Perrot, Jean and Daniel Ladiray 1980, *Tombes à ossuaries de la region côtiere palèstinienne au IVème millénaire avant l'ère chrétienne*, Paris: Association Paléorient.

Porath, Yosef 1992, 'A Chalcolithic Building at Fasa'el', *'Atiqot*, 17: 1–19.

Regev, Joana, Pierre de Miroschedji and Elisabetta Boaretto 2012, 'Early Bronze Age Chronology: Radiocarbon Dates and Chronological Models from Tel Yarmuth (Israel)', *Radiocarbon*, 54, 3–4: 505–24.

Risch, Roberto 2018, 'Affluent Societies of Later Prehistory: Surplus without the State', in *Überschuss ohne Staat: Polticische Formen in der Vorgeschite – Surplus without the State: Political Forms in Prehistory*, edited by Harald Meller, Detlef Gronenborn and Roberto Risch, Halle (Saale): Landesmueseum für Vorgeschigte Halle.

Rosen, Steven A. 1997, *Lithics after the Stone Age: A Handbook of Stone Tools from the Levant*, Walnut Creek, CA: Altamira.

Rosen, Steven A. 2011, 'Desert Chronologies and Periodization', in *Culture, Chronology and the Chalcolithic: Theory and Transition*, edited by Jaimie L. Lovell and Yorke M. Rowan, Oxford: Oxbow Books.

Rosenswig, Robert M. 2012, 'Materialism, Mode of Production, and a Millennium of Change in Southern Mexico', *Journal of Archaeological Method and Theory*, 19: 1–48.

Roux, Valentine and Marie-Anne Courty 1998, 'Identification of Wheel-Fashioning

Methods: Technological Analysis of 4th–3rd Millennium BC Oriental Ceramics', *Journal of Archaeological Science*, 25: 747–63.

Rowan, Yorke M. and Jonathan Golden 2009, 'The Chalcolithic Period of the Southern Levant: A Synthetic Review', *Journal of World Prehistory*, 22: 1–92.

Sahlins, Marshall 1972, *Stone Age Economics*, Chicago, IL and New York: Aldine.

Salvioli, Giuseppe 1979 [1906], *Le capitalisme dans le monde antique*, Paris: Giard et Brière.

Seaton, Peta 2008, *Chalcolithic Cult and Risk Management at Teleilat Ghassul: The Area E Sanctuary*, Oxford: Archaeopress.

Service, Elman 1962, *Primitive Social Organization: An Evolutionary Perspective*, New York: Random House.

Shalev, Sariel 1994, 'The Change in Metal Production from the Chalcolithic Period to the Early Bronze Age in Israel and Jordan', *Antiquity*, 68: 630–37.

Shalev, Omer 2018, 'The Fortification Wall of Tel Erani: A Labour Perspective', *Tel Aviv*, 45, 2: 193–215.

Sherratt, Andrew G. 1981, 'Plough and Pastoralism: Aspects of the Secondary Products Revolution', in, *Pattern of the Past: Studies in Honour of David Clarke*, edited by Ian Hodder, Glyn Isaac and Norman Hammond, Cambridge: Cambridge University Press.

Silver, Morris 1983, *Prophets and Markets: The Political Economy of Ancient Israel*, Boston, MA: Kluwer-Nijhoff.

Silver, Morris 1985, *Economic Structures of the Ancient Near East*, London: Croom Helm.

Shalem, Dina 2008, *Iconography on Ossuaries and Burial Jars from the Late Chalcolithic in Israel in the Context of the Ancient Near East*, PhD Thesis, University of Haifa [Hebrew].

Shalem, Dina, Anat Cohen-Weinberger, Bernardo Gandulla and Ianir Milevski 2019, 'Ceramic Connections and Regional Entities: The Petrography of Late Chalcolithic Pottery from Sites in the Galilee (Israel)', in *Isaac Went Out ... to the Field (Genesis 24:63): Studies in Archaeology and Ancient Cultures in Honor of Isaac Gilead*, edited by Hayim Goldfus, Meyer I. Gruber, Shamir Yona and Peter Fabian, Oxford: Archaeopresss.

Suret-Canale, Jean 1964, 'Les societés traditionnelles en Afrique noire et le mode de production asiatique', *La Pensée*, 177: 19–42.

Ussishkin, David 1980, 'The Ghassulian Shrine at Ein Gedi', *Tel Aviv*, 7: 1–44.

Ussishkin, David 2014, 'The Chalcolithic Temple in Ein Gedi: Fifty Years after its Discovery', *Near Eastern Archaeology*, 77, 1: 15–26.

Verhoeven, Marc 2010, 'Social Complexity and Archaeology: A Contextual Approach', in *Development of Pre-State Communities in the Ancient Near East*, edited by Diana Bolger and Louise C. Maguire, Oxford: Oxbow Books.

Winter-Livneh, Rona, Tal Svoray and Isaac Gilead 2010, 'Settlement Patterns, Social

Complexity and Agricultural Strategies during the Chalcolithic Period in the Northern Negev, Israel', *Journal of Archaeological Science*, 37: 284–94.

Wittfogel, Karl 1957, *Oriental Despotism: A Comparative Study of Total Power*, New Haven: Yale University Press.

Wolf, Eric 2001, 'The Mills of Inequality: A Marxian Approach', in *Pathways of Power: Building an Anthropology of the Modern World*, edited by Eric Wolf, Berkeley, CA: University of California Press.

Yannai, Eli and Yosef Porath 2006, 'A Chalcolithic Burial Cave at Et-Taiyiba', *'Atiqot*, 53: 1–44.

Yekutieli, Yuval 2012, 'Egypt and the Southern Levant during the Naqada Period – Contact and Resistance', from 'Imports During the Naqada Period: A Workshop Investigating Two Sides of an Egyptian and Southern Levantine Phenomenon' – conference held at the W.F. Albright Institute of Archaeological Research, November 29, 2012, Jerusalem.

Zohary, Daniel 1975, 'Beginnings of Fruit Growing in the Old World', *Science*, 587: 319–27.

CHAPTER 4

An Exceptional Case of the Urban Revolution? A Marxist Perspective on the Preclassic Maya

Marcus Bajema

1   Different Hemispheres, Different Worlds?

The destruction of the pre-Columbian civilisations of the Americas through a combination of mass murder, territorial conquest, enslavement and infectious diseases must rank among the top crimes of European imperialism. In his essays 'On cannibals' and 'On coaches', Michel de Montaigne penned his *j'accuse* against this crime. In the latter essay, he imagines a Greco-Roman encounter with the Americas and contrasts its beneficial, if hypothetical, effects with the early modern conquest, which was based on the profit motive:

> We, on the contrary, took advantage of their ignorance and lack of experience to pervert them more easily towards treachery, debauchery and cupidity, toward every kind of cruelty and inhumanity, by the example and model of our own manners. Whoever else has ever rated trade and commerce at such a price? So many cities razed to the ground, so many nations wiped out, so many millions of individuals put to the sword, and the most beautiful and the richest part of the world shattered, on behalf of the pearls-and-pepper business! Tradesmen's victories![1]

To contrast with these European vices, Montaigne describes not just the 'cannibals' of Brazil but also the kingdoms of Peru and Mexico. The latter civilisation was singled out for its complex cosmological ideas as well as for its scale.[2] Collectively, the cultures of the Americas offer a mirror to European greed and trickery, highlighting the reality of a genuinely alternative course of social development. One further notable aspect of Montaigne's writings on the Americas is the connection he makes between its discovery and the Epicurean

---

1   Montaigne 1991, p. 1031.
2   Amnistía Internacional, pp. 1035–6.

doctrine of the plurality of worlds. The connection is made in 'On coaches' and twice in 'An apology for Raymond Sebond'.[3] Two key points can be derived from these passages:

- No law covering everything that exists can be posited. Instead, humans can only know laws covering parts of the whole. Hence, no template can be formulated for other worlds, as they are both similar and dissimilar to ours, just as the Americas differ from Europe and Asia.
- These differences between worlds and continents have also to be understood temporally, recalling the memory of past civilisations disparate from the contemporary ones known. A distinction in the temporality of the New and Old Worlds can also be noted, as the former is said to be younger in age than the latter.

These passages can also be placed alongside an invocation of Lucretius on how time and nature compel changes to all things in the world, irrevocably altering their character.[4] As such, contingency and diversity seem to characterise his views of the history of civilisations on different continents, as well as an appreciation that no abstract theoretical grid can be imposed on them. The exceptionality of Montaigne's ideas can be readily grasped when contrasted to the stadialist schemes of the Enlightenment.[5] In them, the Americas were invariably placed at the lower rungs of a fixed scheme of societal development, with clear negative connotations for the status and worthiness of its cultures in European eyes. Needless to say, such valuations formed part of the core of imperialist ideologies.[6] It's important for Marxist historians and archaeologists to take note of this episode of intellectual history, for Montaigne's ideas can be placed within the broader framework of the so-called aleatory current of philosophy identified by Louis Althusser.

Like Montaigne, Althusser invoked Epicurean atomism, though in his case not to grasp the plural histories of different worlds and continents, but rather to think through the philosophical sources of Marxism. According to him, Marx has to be located within a series of thinkers, starting with Epicurus and Lucretius, moving on to Machiavelli, Hobbes, Spinoza and Rousseau.[7] The common denominator between these varied thinkers, articulated in clearly distinct systems, is held to be the primacy of the encounter over form. That is, determinat-

---

3 Montaigne 1991, pp. 587–8, 646.
4 Montaigne 1991, p. 681.
5 Meek 1976, pp. 37–67.
6 See Anievas and Nisancioglu 2015, Chapter 5, for a strong, recent argument on the role of the Americas in the development of European capitalism.
7 Althusser 2006, pp. 168–88.

ive historical events are held to be aleatory in their starting point as well as in their subsequent effects. In basic terms this can be seen in the encounter of the owners of money and of labour power that resulted in capitalism. Yet whether this meeting of elements 'takes hold' (i.e. results in structural changes) or not depends on a host of contingent factors and cannot be predicted in advance.

There are a good number of examples, as in late medieval Italy, where the encounter between money and labour took place but didn't produce the lasting effect of capitalism.[8] Furthermore, it's impossible to predict what specific form would result from an encounter that lasts, as this cannot be deduced from the elements taking part in it: hence, such an encounter is aleatory in its effects too. The capitalist mode of production, then, was neither prefigured in the process of history nor was its specific form determined by an iron necessity. With regard to historical change, another aspect of the Althusserian theory of the encounter is that of plural temporality.[9] That is, different elements taking part in an encounter have distinct temporal rhythms and cannot be reduced to an absolute, singular measure of time. Instead, it's important to think in terms of conjunctures, the 'taking hold' of different elements in a particular combination. And although these different conjunctures cannot be reduced to a single template, they share enough 'constants' to allow them to be compared to each other.[10]

In contrast to this aleatory perspective, there is the logic of the 'accomplished fact', the unfolding of a historical sequence of modes of production according to a pre-determined order. A good example of this can be found in the adaptation by Engels of Morgan's evolutionist series of stages of world history. Morgan paid a great deal of attention to the Americas, based in part on his early study of the Iroquois in New York state. One notable feature of his work was his polemic argument against the existence of urban civilisations in Mexico.[11] According to him, the conquistadores, and those who followed in their wake, had inappropriately applied the template of feudal Europe to societies that were in fact radically different. Instead, Morgan proposed to understand all American Indian societies according to another template, that of the system ordered by kinship, which he had first discovered to exist among the Iroquois.[12]

---

8   Althusser 2006, p. 198.
9   Morfino 2015, pp. 153–64.
10   Althusser 2006, p. 278.
11   Morgan 1965, Chapter 10 and Chapter 11.
12   This is the famous *gens*, a form of social organisation based on kin relations. On its Iroquois variant, see Morgan 1964, Part II, Chapter 2.

For Morgan, this system contrasted sharply with state society. Thus, in his evolutionist scheme, no state had emerged in the Americas before Columbus. Instead, the most advanced cultures in the pre-Columbian Americas were the so-called 'military democracies', as found in Mexico.[13] These societies had elaboration of chiefly offices but were still structured by the democracy inherent in a kin-based order. Even though important nuances and qualifications can be found in Morgan, according to his evolutionist scheme the highest level attained by any American Indian culture was the stage of 'Middle Barbarism'.[14] He recognised important differences between the New and Old Worlds, especially in the contrast between the use of irrigation in the former and of domesticated animals in the latter. Yet, in the end, these hemispherical distinctions yielded to the universalist straitjacket of the sequence of development from 'savagism' to 'civilisation'. Engels took over Morgan's scheme with few qualifications, including the view of a lack of state development in the Americas.[15] However, he did emphasise to a greater degree the importance of animal domestication in the Old World, noting how, together with metallurgy, it had spurred on the development of slavery and property.[16]

The adaptation of Morgan's stadialism by Engels can be understood as part of the broader thrust of his late work, especially considering the historical determinism of *Anti-Dühring*.[17] Marx's understanding of Morgan, as part of his recognition of a plurality of pathways of development, was in this sense distinct from that of Engels. In particular, he discounted the notion that a general 'historico-philosophical theory' could be derived from the outline of Western European development in his *Capital*, which would prescribe the course of history everywhere.[18] Instead, using the metaphor of geological stratigraphy, Marx outlined an intricate trajectory of the commune from the archaic form studied by Morgan to more complex forms, the latter holding out potential for an alternative, revolutionary path for Russia.[19] The attention to multilinear development can be traced back to the time during which Marx was working on *Capital*, as scattered references on the pre-Columbian cultures of Mexico and Peru show.

---

13   Morgan 1964, pp. 181–7.
14   Morgan 1964, p. 17.
15   Engels 1990, pp. 136–9.
16   Engels 1990, pp. 162–5.
17   In the argument that ancient slavery was a necessary condition for modern socialism to develop, Engels 1987, p. 168.
18   Marx 1983a, pp. 135–6. See Anderson 2016, Chapter 6, for the broader context of these drafts, including the notes made by Marx on Morgan's *Ancient Society*.
19   Marx 1983b, pp. 107–10.

In the *Grundrisse* and the different volumes of *Capital*, Marx mostly uses the Americas to draw up counterfactuals to established wisdom. Notable in particular is his observation that gold and silver were not used as money in Mexico and Peru, but rather used for ornaments, disproving monetary value as an inherent property of these materials.[20] Marx here also cited Peter Martyr on how the cacao currency of pre-Columbian Mexico prevented hoarding and, consequently, the avarices of wealth. Marx was especially drawn to the Inca of Peru. There, a system with an advanced division of labour had emerged without money or commodity exchange, thus disproving Adam Smith's vision of such a division as the originary act of political economy.[21] Inca communism, as it were, can been grasped as the 'natural community in the form of the state', echoes of which can be recognised in the work of Luxemburg as well.[22] Leaving aside this complex issue, which would demand an article in itself,[23] what is important here is the use of the Americas by Marx to question uniform patterns of social development and to point to alternative pathways.

In the third volume of *Capital*, Marx criticised the assumption that present relations of distribution are features of human production in general, which leads to a view of pre-capitalist forms as mere underdeveloped variants of capitalism.[24] He argued that social production is the generic combination of reproductive and surplus labour, but that the social uses of the latter are not predetermined by human nature. He mentions the 'more ingeniously developed communism' of Peru in this context, and goes on to argue in Montaignesque fashion for the transience of capitalism and its specific distribution relations:

> On the other hand, scientific analysis of the capitalist mode of production demonstrates the contrary, that it is a mode of production of a special kind, with specific historical features; that, like any other specific mode of production, it presupposes a given level of the social productive forces and their forms of development as its historical precondition: a precondition which is itself the historical result and product of a preceding process, and from which the new mode of production proceeds as its given

---

20 Marx 1987, p. 211.
21 Marx 1987, pp. 299–300.
22 Krader 1975, table 1, p. 136; Luxemburg focuses on the Inca: see Luxemburg 2013, pp. 199–203.
23 With particular regard to the similarities and differences between the early London notebooks, containing excerpts from Prescott's histories of the conquests of Mexico and Peru, and the later notebooks on Morgan.
24 Marx 1998, pp. 863–4.

basis; that the production relations corresponding to this specific, historically determined mode of production – relations which human beings enter into during the process of social life, in the creation of their social life – possess a specific, historical and transitory character; and, finally, that the distribution relations essentially coincide with these production relations are their opposite side, so that both share the same historically transitory character.[25]

2 Urban Revolutions and Modes of Production

One of the more interesting observations that can be made about contemporary debates on ancient civilisations is how denunciations of past scholarship coexist with even worse forms of the same mistakes. Today it is not hard to find ample grounds for criticising Morgan's terminology of savagism, barbarism and civilisation, or his ambivalence about races or the inadequacy of his source material. Yet we can find in his work a keen sense of the aleatory alongside the evolutionism. At the end of his *Ancient Society*, Morgan notes that the stage of 'Middle Barbarism' wasn't surpassed until metallurgical experimentation led to the discovery of iron.[26] This 'accident of circumstances' could have easily not taken place, delaying the development of civilisation by millennia. Present-day authors, while not speaking of savages and barbarians, have fewer qualms about pressing a more deterministic view of development. Moreover, they have moved from singular cases, that is, specific civilisations, to comparing larger cultural or geographical units such as notions of West and East or of continents.[27]

In his bio-geographical account of history, Jared Diamond posited that distinctions in plant and animal domesticates, terrain and climate can account for the slower or faster paces of change on different continents.[28] Comparing the development of different regions according to a simple empirically based stadialist scheme, he argued that the Americas lagged 5,000 years behind Western Eurasia in regards to the emergence of villages with food production.[29] Together with an inferred smaller scope for long-distance exchange in the Americas, based on geographic and climatic factors, this lag would explain why

---

25   Marx 1998, p. 864.
26   Morgan 1964, p. 468.
27   Diamond 1997; Morris 2015.
28   Diamond 1997, p. 87.
29   Diamond 1997, pp. 361–4.

the Old World conquered the New and not the other way around. The nuance of Diamond that intersocietal interaction might reduce the time for a society to pass from one stage to the next[30] are not found in the adaptation of his model by Morris. Comparing eight regions, Morris calculated that it would take 2,000 years to move from initial cultivation to full domestication, an average 4,000 years more to the first states, followed 1,000 years later by empires and another 2,500 years for industrialisation.[31]

Based on this view of history as unfolding according to a railroad timeline, the first Mesoamerican and Andean states lagged 3,000 years behind those of Western Eurasia. Notions of fixed intervals between stages crumble, however, when we consider the trajectories of singular cases, like that of the Maya below. Gordon Childe's outline of prehistoric revolutions, developed in the 1930s through 1950s,[32] is more amenable to this perspective than other theories. The notion of a revolution as a qualitative change, involving many factors, comes closest to Althusser's notion of the encounter discussed above. This will become more apparent when focusing on the specific revolution discussed in this article: the urban revolution. Superficially, this revolution, as discussed by Childe, can be grasped as a checklist of ten elements that define an urban state-level society – for example, thresholds of so many thousand inhabitants, monumental architecture and systems for recording.[33]

Yet the true core of the urban revolution is a Marxist conception of class society based on surplus appropriation.[34] In that sense, it is close to Eric Wolf's notion of the tributary mode of production, as a variant both in terms of substance and in its dialectical approach.[35] Childe's dialectics allowed him to move away from stadialism. He understood the relations between the patterns reconstructed by archaeologists not as mechanical and one sided, but rather as reflecting the interconnections between different aspects, constrained not just by biological needs but also by knowledge and forms of cooperation.[36] Hence, we can see here a looser causal framework, one that can recognise the impact of contingencies while also providing a coherent framework from the forces and relations of production to the socio-political, religious and ideational aspects. Behind the abstraction from the archaeological record, therefore, lies a creative and sophisticated Marxist perspective.

---

30   Diamond 1997, p. 362.
31   Morris 2015, pp. 151–4.
32   See Trigger 1980 for an overview of Childe's work from a Marxist perspective.
33   Childe 1950 is the classic reference.
34   Childe 1950, pp. 11–12.
35   See Rosenswig 2017 for an archaeological application of Wolf's ideas.
36   Childe 1979, pp. 93–4.

It is important here to recall that the urban revolution initially developed as the result of a broader effort by Childe to understand technological and social development in prehistoric Western Eurasia. The structuring effects of metallurgical innovations played an important role in this, and Childe sought to understand the social consequences of the transitions represented by the coming of the Bronze and Iron Ages.[37] Crucial in the development of a metallurgical industry of even a modest size, Childe observed, was the existence of a surplus to support specialist craft workers. Such a surplus and the question of its appropriation immediately brings up the possibility of the emergence of a class society and, concomitant with it, the rise of the state. Both are present in Childe's urban revolution and provide structure to the other elements, even if they could themselves take distinct forms, as in the different methods of extracting surplus in the Mesopotamian and Egyptian states.[38]

Furthermore, the interaction between the different societies in Western Eurasia precluded the recognition of an ideal developmental trajectory in any of the cases.[39] The Americas, being outside the Old World sequence of metallurgical development altogether, presented even greater challenges. Childe notes that the Maya fit the criteria for the urban revolution, yet the 'essential preconditions' of Eurasian development were missing, mainly metallurgy and the use of domesticated animals.[40] Once again, the Americas throw a wrench into the theoretical machinery of stadialism, and later studies using the Childean theory of urban revolution have found more clues for distinctly American patterns. Two works from the 1960s found important differences in the trajectories of New and Old World cases.[41] The most detailed of these was that of Robert M. Adams, who focused in particular on class and socio-political organisation, using new evidence from the large-scale settlement surveys then taking place in Iraq and Mexico. He saw a greater degree of discontinuity in central Mexico compared to Mesopotamia, and, more importantly, he also recognised distinct patterns in his two cases with regard to settlement, technological innovation and forms of economic integration.[42]

Another important work, written in the spirit of Childe, was the monumental comparison of seven early civilisations by Bruce Trigger.[43] Covering a

---

37 Childe 1944.
38 Childe 1954, pp. 47–50.
39 As comprehensively explored in Childe 1951.
40 Childe 1950, p. 9.
41 Braidwood and Willey 1962; Adams 1966.
42 Adams 1966, pp. 171–4.
43 Trigger 2003.

broad range of topics, he focused on similarities in class structures and surplus appropriation, much as Adams did. Trigger found interesting patterns for land ownership. In his New World cases, collective and institutional (mainly state) ownership can be seen as the sole forms, while for the Old World cases a trajectory to private forms of ownership can be recognised, if at different speeds.[44] He cautioned, however, against seeing one form of ownership as superior over the others, for all are conducive to surplus appropriation by an elite. More can be made here of the connection between forms of land ownership and the main productive forces of early civilisations: agricultural production, which was left underexplored by the work of Adams and Trigger. One Soviet study had emphasised this, recognising three distinct climatic adaptations, which for Masson was influential in shaping the trajectories and structures of the urban revolutions that took place in these regions.[45]

Detailed settlement-pattern studies in Mesoamerica and the Mediterranean allow for a more precise understanding of the impact of the different agronomic properties of the main staple crops, which are, respectively, maize and wheat.[46] The characteristics of maize are such that the main way to increase surplus is through irrigation, investing labour in the productivity of land. On the other hand, wheat surpluses are more readily increased by decreasing the amount of labour that is necessary to plant or harvest it, using ploughing, metal sickles and other implements. As a result, different patterns of population and settlement growth can be seen, as well as notably different ways in which states and their ruling elites appropriated agricultural surpluses.[47] In particular, states in the Mediterranean were dependent on naval expansion in order to grow, for unlike Mesoamerican states, they could not deploy large-scale labour for agricultural intensification. The *chinampa* irrigation of the Aztecs and the naval grain imports of Classical Athens can be taken as exemplary cases of this.

One topic not covered in these studies, however, is the precise connection between the forces and relations of production. Again, there are clues. Somewhat vindicating Engels, a large-scale sample revealed inequality in house sizes to be much greater in Eurasia than in Mesoamerica and North America.[48] The authors precisely attribute this to the greater availability and use of domest-

---

44   Trigger 2003, pp. 334–7.
45   Masson 1988, figure 33, p. 129.
46   Blanton 2004, pp. 210–13.
47   Blanton 2004, pp. 226–8.
48   Kohler et al. 2017, figure 3, p. 621.

icated animals in Eurasia, which made not just a greater surplus of staple crops possible by saving labour input, but also increased the range of available products. Such surpluses would have formed the basis for greater inequality, further exacerbated by metallurgy and means for warfare. Their conclusion is of particular note:

> Greater wealth differentials are more strongly associated with increasing settlement size, regional population size and regional population density in the Old World than in the New World ... Although explaining these differences in scaling behaviour is not our primary objective, it seems likely that they are connected with more economic specialization and long-distance exchange, in conjunction with lower frictions for long-distance transport by wheeled vehicles and more efficient water transportation in the Old World. The differential availability of large mammals that could be domesticated in the Old and New Worlds seems to have had diverse and far-reaching implications for the differing trajectories of societies in these two hemispheres.[49]

These findings are most damning for the stadialist view of development based on a correlation between a growth in scale and the intensification and expansion of class society. While it supports some of the ideas of Morgan and Engels, it also invalidates their notion of a uniform scale or series of historical change. Rather, it points to the general correctness of the theses of aleatory materialism on the encounter of specific elements, recognising a plurality of pathways that can be grasped and compared from this perspective. Of course, it is necessary to move beyond this general overview and establish how the inferred hemispherical patterns actually worked in singular cases. To that end, the case of the Preclassic lowland Maya urban revolution will be briefly discussed and related to patterns that can be found in Mesoamerica as a whole.

3   Plural Temporality and the Preclassic Lowland Maya

The long-term history of the lowland Maya area is defined by terms that are in fact derived from a Eurocentric obsession with 'the Classical', itself a result from Winckelmann's periodisation of Greek art. Accordingly, the main divisions are between a Preclassic, Classic and Postclassic period, even if these terms

---

49   Kohler et al. 2017, p. 621.

are stripped from their normative connotations by contemporary archaeologists.[50] The focus here lies on the Preclassic period, itself divided into different phases,[51] as follows:

1. Early Preclassic, 2000–1000 BC, earliest indications of complexity.
2. Middle Preclassic, 1000–400 BC, the emergence of the first states.
3. Late Preclassic, 400 BC – AD 150, apogee of the first states.
4. Terminal Preclassic, AD 150–250, decline of the first-generation states.

The best way to approach this trajectory of more than two millennia is not, however, to make these four phases the main unit of analysis. Rather, it is useful to trace the developmental histories of both local-level (village) communities and (city) states, making them, and especially the interaction between them, the mainstay of analysis. Maya archaeologists have long recognised two distinct kinds of economy, a social one focused on communities and a political economy that derives from state actors.[52] In the Maya area, the former economy persists alongside the latter form, each having their own temporal rhythm.[53] The relations between them are not just important for understanding the workings of established Maya states but are also especially important for grasping their beginnings. In some way or another, the political economy emerged out of a communal setting, forming the basis for the overall process of the urban revolution. Table 4.1 below summarises the different elements of the urban revolution according to their presence in communal and state settings.[54]

In an earlier work, I used these patterns to grasp the structural properties and dynamics of the Late Preclassic period, when the state had already emerged.[55] States are here distinguished by degree in terms of scale and distinguished qualitatively by kingship and a nexus of features associated with it: military organisation, monumental artistic expression and large-scale labour mobilisation. The concern in this article is, however, with the first beginnings of these distinctions and what they can tell us about the long-term trajectory of the Maya area. An abundance of evidence has more recently become available for the earliest phases of human activity in the Maya lowlands, leading to revisions in our ideas of the emergence of the state in this part of Mesoamerica.[56] In fact,

---

50   Evans 2012.
51   The following is based on Sharer and Traxler 2017, table 1.1, p. 4.
52   Sharer and Traxler 2006, p. 631.
53   Iannone 2002, table 1, p. 75.
54   Adapted with modifications from Bajema 2017, table 6.2, p. 175.
55   Bajema 2017, pp. 173–6.
56   For a comprehensive overview of the state of research, see the papers in Traxler and Sharer 2017.

TABLE 4.1 State and community in the Preclassic period lowland Maya region

	State level	Community level
Economic elements		
Agricultural means of production	Large scale water management	Terrace-building households
Urbanism	Very large (16 km²)	A few hundred inhabitants
	Extensive ceremonial core	Small ceremonial core
	Network of causeway roads	
Economic relations	Large scale labour mobilisation	Household based production
	Tribute?	
Long-distance exchange	Rare goods imported	Rare goods imported
Socio-political elements		
State form	Kingship	No state, communal organisation
	Regional hegemonic power?	
Military organisation	Large scale defensive works	No conclusive evidence
	Captive taking?	
Class and inequality	Larger compounds as social foci	Small distinctions, lineage based
World-view related elements		
Monumental architecture and art	Multiple large pyramids	Small plaza-focused core
Specialised knowledge	Astronomical orientation	Astronomical orientation
	Writing, artistic expression	
Feasting and cycle public festivals	Large-scale processions	Community-based feasting

given the evidence becoming available to reconstruct this trajectory, it is the development of the community, rather than the state, that may be seen as the most decisive change from a long-term perspective.

It was at the communal level that the basic relations of production of the ancient Maya were developed, which, with significant modifications, persisted throughout the pre-Columbian era.[57] To be more precise in defining community, it refers here to a co-residential group of sedentary farmers, in which kinship relations played an important structuring role. Sedentary lifeways only started long after the first traces of cultigens like maize appear, dated to the turn of the third millennium BC. In fact, the earliest recognisable 'villages' only gradually became 'durable', with mobile populations co-existing with more permanent groups, as at the site of Ceibal before 700 BC.[58] This is particularly notable, as at this site an early monumental focus with valuable religious deposits

---

57 See especially McAnany 1995, now supplemented by Ensor 2013 for tracing kin-based social patterns.
58 Inomata et al. 2015.

has been found that is dated to 950 BC.[59] A similar situation can be seen at the site of Cival, where little evidence for a concentration of population can initially be seen, even if a massive mobilisation of labour took place to construct its central plaza, which, too, contained significant religious offerings.[60]

The aleatory character of this process seems highlighted by the complex interaction between the environment, agricultural strategies and social interaction, a process of multiple centuries that only 'took hold' during the Middle Preclassic. Apart from Ceibal and Cival, many other sites testify to this development, showing differences and similarities at the local and regional level. This variation can be connected to the ecological and geographical distinctions in the southern Maya lowlands, notably for the Preclassic between the Petén region of northern Guatemala and the coastal area of Belize.[61] Obviously, precise site-based patterns form the backbone of archaeological reconstruction. What a Marxist analysis adds is precisely the understanding of the causal factors that have shaped the patterns reflected in Table 4.1, working from the forces to the relations of production. Following Althusser and Childe, however, to start with the forces of production doesn't imply that they have a determining role in everything that follows.

As with any Mesoamerican culture until the late Postclassic period, the Maya didn't practice any kind of metallurgy and can be seen as a stone-working, agriculturally based society. It has been pointed out that the basic material resources for a Maya community to reproduce itself can be found within a 25-kilometre radius.[62] Obviously, this does not include materials found in only a few locales, such as obsidian, jadeite and other precious stones, as well as salt and marine resources. As for any pre-industrial society, the basis for Maya economic life was agriculture. Although a wide variety of plants were cultivated or gathered, the main staple crop was maize, which stands out for its high productivity, especially if fostered by some form of irrigation.[63] Early Maya farmers, still partly depending on gathering and hunting, seem to have been drawn to wetland areas that were conducive to higher yields.[64]

Water was also a crucial resource in farming, and water works can be found early in the Preclassic period. At the small site of Chan, terrace-based agriculture can already be detected in the Middle Preclassic period, and these terraces

---

59   Aoyama et al. 2017.
60   Estrada-Belli 2012, pp. 207, 214.
61   King 2017, p. 448.
62   Demarest 2004, pp. 149–52.
63   Blanton 2004, pp. 210–3.
64   King 2017, pp. 425–32.

seem to have been constructed and maintained by cooperating households.⁶⁵ Occurring before the rise of states, and without clear indications for class distinctions, the terraces of Chan point to the capabilities of Maya farmers for independent economic development within a communal framework. A lack of elite supervision and control can be seen for the relations of production more broadly as well, with most craftwork based at the household level.⁶⁶ The long-distance exchange of rare materials like obsidian, jadeite, salt and aquatic resources also preceded the emergence of elites, and their wide availability later, even in small communities, points to the persistence of 'open loop' exchange networks.⁶⁷

In fact, craftworkers in Maya communities seem to have gained a more exalted, independent status.⁶⁸ Furthermore, one of the exceptions to household-based production in fact proves its rule of elite non-interference. For at the Late Preclassic period site of Colha, situated in an area of Belize blessed with high quality chert deposits, chert working was not household based but rather took place in workshops according to standardised procedures.⁶⁹ Exports can be found far afield in Belize and even further away for special objects like chert eccentrics. Again, no interference by patrimonial elites and/or the state seems probable. Rather, the communal focus of the craft can be seen in a cache in a small pyramidical structure, cut into a preceding Middle Preclassic platform.⁷⁰ Among many other precious finds, this cache contained a chert blade with blood residue, interpreted as the result of a bloodletting ritual, indicating that the craft was a central communal focus.

Other examples of community-wide specialisation can be found, including salt at Komchen.⁷¹ Such communities have the advantage of exclusive access to special resources, but their actual development may be more accidental. It has been pointed out that the focus of chert working at Colha was in fact the result of an agricultural crisis threatening the viability of the community, resulting in a communal response.⁷² As such, sites like Colha and Komchen can be understood as having been independent of state intervention, taking

---

65 Wyatt 2012, pp. 86–7.
66 Hendon 1999, p. 118.
67 King 2017, pp. 445–6.
68 For example, at Chan shell, working debris was found in two of the more elaborate burials and in residence structures close to the site centre; see Keller 2012, pp. 266–7.
69 Hester and Shafer 1994, p. 60.
70 Barrett et al. 2011, p. 24.
71 Sharer and Traxler 2006, p. 275.
72 King 2017, pp. 453–4.

part in 'open loop' exchange networks that had preceded the Late Preclassic period. Another negative case of elite intervention in the relations of production comes from the Mirador basin, which has low-quality chert deposits. There, the Middle to Late Preclassic record shows little evidence for the control of craftwork or import of chert, with a poor record of tools, despite a more advanced chert-working industry nearby at Tikal.[73] Overall, the basic production processes of Maya economic life can be located at the household and communal level, with little evidence of state actors intervening in this after the state had emerged.

We turn now from the forces and relations of production to the superstructure of socio-political and ideological factors. Being so distinctive from Eurasian cases, it seems best to start an historical-materialist analysis with Maya world views. The most detailed information on Maya world views comes from ethnography and the texts and iconography of the Classic and Postclassic periods. These findings can, with due caution, be extrapolated back to the Preclassic period, when similar practices can be recognised.[74] Of particular interest in the later record is the Maya conception of materiality. As noted by Althusser, matter from an aleatory perspective is not to be conflated with brute matter. Rather, it can be a trace, gesture or even a phoneme.[75] The Maya case offers a particularly suitable demonstration of the validity and usefulness of this perspective.

A recent study by Houston shows a particular convergence with Althusser, noting the prioritising of form over matter in Western philosophy, itself a break with the etymological roots of matter in Indo-European concepts of growth processes.[76] In a world-view where things are not defined by matter but by flow and energy, it is perhaps less surprising to see all kinds of metaphoric connections being made between what for Western eyes are essentially distinct things.[77] A good example of this can be seen in Houston's analysis of the conceptual linkages between humans, jadeite and maize,[78] which can be summed up in this way:

1. According to the Maya sacred book the *Popol vuh*, recovered in the colonial era but with clear connections to the pre-Columbian era, the current

---

73 King 2017, p. 436.
74 Houston and Taube 2008, p. 134.
75 Althusser 2006, pp. 262–3.
76 Houston 2014, pp. 8–9.
77 Yet not without rulers – see, for example, the distinction between additive crafts (e.g. ceramics) and reductive ones (e.g. lithics), Houston 2014, p. 98.
78 Houston 2014, pp. 11–12, 93–4, 127.

human race was created from maize by the gods. Linguistics and iconography further suggest a broad contiguity between humans and plant life, with a particular focus on maize.

2. Jadeite in Classic-period texts can be referred to as *yaxtuun*, a combination of stone [*tuun*] and a blue-green colour [*yax*], which extends to related greenstones. Metaphorically, *yax* points to freshness and growth, as for example in a still green sprouting maize plant, as well as moisture or a shining surface and breath.

3. Jadeite was thought to be able to capture and preserve a human's spirit or breath, preserving his or her energy and potential to persist to some extent beyond death.

Significantly, *yax* occupies a central position in the basic Maya cosmogram in a quincunx outline of a centre and four cardinal directions, each signified by a colour, which is analogous to a farmer's field or *milpa*.[79] Here, the presence of such ideas in the Preclassic period can be demonstrated, as caches and burials from the period seem to reflect similar ideas. Recent discoveries at Ceibal have revealed early caches dated to 1000–850 BC that contain jadeite objects, in shapes that would later be adopted at the major Olmec site of La Venta.[80] These caches were dug into the first outline of the civic-ceremonial centre of Ceibal, and notably one of the caches was laid out in the cruciform or quincunx outline of the Maya cosmogram. This was not an isolated phenomenon, for another elaborate cache has been found from somewhat later in Middle Preclassic Cival, containing, among other things, jadeite celts laid out in the quincunx pattern.[81] As a bowl from K'axob and a somewhat later cache from Chan attest, the Maya cosmogram was a common motif in communal rituals.[82]

A more complex ideology, shaped partly by contacts with the wider Mesoamerican world, can thus be seen in the southern Maya lowlands before the emergence of any state. It is, in fact, crucial for understanding the social relations within Maya communities. Ethnographers have developed the notion of a covenant or moral community to capture the reciprocal relations between the landscape, plant and animal life, humans and the gods.[83] Of course, all of these have to be understood as part of the conceived flow of energy and potentialities. Hierarchy is evident as well, for example in the necessity to 'feed' ancestors and deities through offerings. The evidence from caches, as well as

---

79 For further analysis of this, see Tate 2012, pp. 58–61, 186–7.
80 Aoyama et al. 2017, pp. 706–8.
81 Estrada-Belli 2006, pp. 59–62.
82 Headrick 2004, pp. 370–1.
83 This account draws upon Monaghan 2000; see also McAnany 2010, pp. 90–5.

the re-entering of burials, points to the presence of such conceptions in the Preclassic era. Not only is such evidence of a moral community in these offerings significant, but also their focus in the civic-ceremonial centres of the different communities.

As noted earlier, these communal foci took considerable labour to be constructed in a landscape that was still only partially composed of sedentary groups. We also saw the cooperation of households for constructing terraces at Chan, or the community-wide specialisation at Colha, all involving the coordination of labour. Labour is to be understood as part of a broader set of social and religious obligations within the moral community, as amply documented by Maya ethnographers.[84] Hence, it is less surprising to see here an already complex society, which needs to be understood in its own terms socially rather than as containing 'emergent elites' foreshadowing later states. Even so, inequality is clearly possible within the moral community, for as the gods and ancestors demand things from the present generation of community members, so might these members demand things from each other. Social differentiation can be seen in different communities, which can be related to different lineages establishing their positions with regard to land or traditions of craftwork.[85]

However, such intra-community differentiation does not naturally and inevitably lead to states and classes. The nearly two millennia of history of the small site of Chan shows that Maya communities had trajectories of their own, which cannot be reduced to stadialist templates. During the Classic period, the settlement expanded and the population rose from a few hundred to over a thousand people.[86] Evidence for elites is now also clearer, but the leadership they provided obviously had a communal and religious focus rather than any kind of self-aggrandising representation.[87] Furthermore, craft activity remained at the household level, and access to rare materials like jadeite has been noted for non-elite areas as well.[88] All of this points to the capability of Chan to survive as a community within a landscape that was dominated by states. In this sense, the moral community co-existed with the 'divided society',[89] which arose with the urban revolution at the turn from the Middle to Late Preclassic.

In fact, we may conceive of this revolution as Althusser conceived of the aleatory encounter of the owners of money and the proletariat, solely possess-

---

84 King 2017, pp. 450–2.
85 McAnany 1995, p. 111.
86 Robin et al. 2012a, pp. 28–37.
87 Robin et al. 2012b, pp. 147–8.
88 Blackmore 2012, pp. 187–91.
89 Houston and Inomata 2009, p. 28.

ing labour, that resulted in capitalism.⁹⁰ For the Preclassic Maya, the encounter was between the community with its associated values and the new phenomenon of kingship and royal ideology as foci of the state. As with capitalism, this encounter failed to take place, or to take hold, many times, leading to the persistence of pre-existing communal patterns such as at Chan. Perhaps the best way to understand this encounter is to consider the ideological focus of the moral community, as it can be seen in the burials and caches in the civic-ceremonial centres of sites. The significance there of jadeite, especially its metaphoric connections to maize and the quincunx cosmogram, is carried over to the fledgling ideology of the state and its embodiment in representations and conceptions of figures of royal authority.⁹¹

A good example from the Preclassic period can be seen in Cival. Here, at the turn from the Middle to the Late Preclassic period, a stela was erected near the earlier cache with jadeite celts laid out in a quincunx pattern.⁹² On this stela, a striding figure can be seen, with iconographic features pointing to the maize deity and other indicators of kingship. Concurrently, a new Triadic group of pyramids was built, their art also featuring the maize god, as well as the emergence of the quincunx shaped cosmos. These pyramids and the stela reoriented the civic-ceremonial centre of Cival away from a communal focus to one dominated by royal ideology. However, from the focus on maize and the quincunx cosmogram, it is clear that there are important contiguities between the new ideology and that which preceded it at the communal level. Such similarities can be even better grasped from the wall paintings of Late Preclassic period San Bartolo, which survive in a fairly extensive form.

Briefly, the overall iconography of the San Bartolo murals shows phenomena such as the emergence of the first humans, a cycle of death and rebirth of the maize god, as well as four self-sacrificing youths at the four cardinal directions.⁹³ Overall, an important theme concerns relations between maize, the gods, and what may be interpreted as kingship, with the accessibility of the building in which they were housed possibly pointing to 'ideological education'.⁹⁴ One primary point of evidence is a scene from the west wall, showing a figure seated on a platform receiving an elaborate headdress from an attending figure. The seated figure may or may not have been an actual historical king. Yet

---

90   Althusser 2006, pp. 197–203.
91   Analogies between farming and kingship can be seen in the Classic period; see Houston and Inomata 2009, p. 145.
92   Estrada-Belli 2006, pp. 61–5.
93   Saturno 2009 gives an overview of the themes evident in these wall paintings.
94   Saturno 2009, p. 130.

even if it is just a mythological representation of authority as such, the recurrence of the so-called 'Jester God' motif in other forms of art from the same period bolsters the case for royal ideology.[95] As such, it is possible to recognise the presence of a figure of authority that we may term royal – even if these figures are more generic and closer to mythology than to history, for none have the individual features that their counterparts from the Classic period have.[96]

A key question, of course, concerns the process by which such figures of authority emerged. Here it is important to recall from the earlier discussion that the community had great success in the use of communal labour for constructing civic-ceremonial centres. Also, certain lineages could become distinguished from others within such communities, occupying a prominent position relative to others but still within the framework of the moral community. For the emergence of royal ideology at Cival, it has been proposed that it was precisely the large-scale mobilisation of labour that acted as the catalyst for a new form of authority to appear.[97] The evidence for the important early site of Nakbé provides more insights for this.[98] In the early part of the Middle Preclassic period (800–600 BC), the site was already quite extensive at fifty hectares, with stone architecture and the usual imported obsidian, jadeite and shell. Also notable are cases of cranial deformation and dental inlays that are characteristic of later elites, and which are not seen at all at smaller sites like Chan, as well as the mat motif on pottery that is later associated with royal ideology.

In the later part of the Middle Preclassic period (600–400 BC), two notable features can be seen. The first concerns the mobilisation of labour for constructing a civic-ceremonial centre with large pyramids and a ballcourt, as well as the first causeways, and quite importantly in various forms of agricultural intensification as well. Some terraces are associated with larger elite residences, one of which has been identified as a possible royal palace. Finally, although the evidence here is less pronounced, the monumental art at least shows various elements of ideology that would later be representative of kingship. What we can see here, then, is how the communal strategies for labour mobilisation and for the elaboration of social distinctions within and between lineages encounter each other.

---

95 For an overview of the parallels, see Bajema 2017, pp. 210–12.
96 Classic period iconography not only shows more individualised kings, but they also seem to have a more directing role in the flow of things, of their energy and potentiality; see Houston 2014, pp. 83–7.
97 Estrada-Belli 2012, pp. 219–22.
98 The outline of the Mirador basin trajectory below is based on Hansen 2017.

The result of this in the Late Preclassic period was the emergence of states in the Mirador basin, with the central focus passing from Nakbé to El Mirador. A true urban revolution can be seen in this period, with El Mirador reaching an extent of 16 square kilometres, with massive causeways reaching far into its hinterland, and the construction of some of the largest pyramidical structures of the Americas.[99] Clear evidence for elites can now be seen in the burial and residential record. Evidence of warfare also emerges in the form of substantial defensive works. Yet the Danta pyramid, which took an estimated to 10–12 million working days to construct, still follows the quincunx cosmogram in its outline, showing contiguity in ideology with the moral community. This shouldn't be taken to imply that Maya state and kingship were in any way prefigured in the community, but rather that in the encounter between the two, the latter is not completely subsumed into the former.

4   The Broader Mesoamerican World

Having discussed a singular case in some detail, the next step is to consider its impact on general ideas about social change, as discussed earlier in this chapter in the section on the urban revolution and the mode of production. First of all, the Maya trajectory makes a mockery of the 'railroad timetable' template that it takes a fixed amount of time to move from one stage to the next. The 2,000 years from initial cultivation to complete domestication and the 4,000 years from that point to the first states were completed by the Maya in a mere 1,500 years, making them something of the Stakhanovites among early civilisations. While there were some influences from other parts of Mesoamerica, the evidence does point to an indigenously driven trajectory. Furthermore, the co-existence of farmers and foragers, community and state make a stadial framework unsuitable for understanding this trajectory. The main question, however, concerns the finding, discussed in the same section on the urban revolution, that the scaling between population size and indications of inequality was not as strong in the Americas as it was in Eurasia.

While no Gini index was calculated for the Preclassic lowland Maya, the evidence discussed above provides important qualitative clues as to why this scaling would have been less powerful. As we saw, the basic relations of production can be understood on the household and communal level, for agricultural

---

99 More research is needed on the layout of the non-monumental structures of El Mirador, especially in light of its importance for discussions of low-density urbanism, a crucial feature for understanding Maya social organisation; for this, see Isendahl 2012.

intensification and craftwork as well as for the construction of monumental structures. It was even possible to see community-wide specialisation in craftwork, as with chert working at Colha. No elite intervention was apparent in this, even if distinctions between households can be noted, nor can it be recognised in the long-distance exchange of important materials. It was the community and its moral-ideological framework that structured this, not self-aggrandising individuals. When elites do emerge, they draw upon the potential for mobilising labour of the community to achieve public works on a wholly different scale, within the new framework of an urban state. Accordingly, the limits of political economy here can be summed up as follows:

1. Parts of the landscape containing communities rather than states were effectively outside the domain of political economy.
2. The predominant form of political economy involved large-scale labour mobilisation, which itself carried with it a more communal ethos and limited possibilities for self-aggrandising economic behaviour on the part of elites.
3. There are no indications that elites managed to gain comprehensive control over the basic production activities, which largely remained at the household level.

All three factors would work against the scaling of inequality relative to population increases, with the contiguities between communal and royal ideology enabling more egalitarian structures to persist at the newly emerged urban centres and realms of the state. A key question, nevertheless, is in what form such communal patterns persisted, considering the elaborate expressions of royal ideology in this period, together with recognisable strata of nobles.[100] A further question concerns how these broader changes impacted the relations of production, given that important features of the political economy had now emerged, or in some cases had perhaps merely become more visible. Among them are the collection by the state of 'bundles' of wealth, involving goods such as cacao, jadeite, textiles, quetzal feathers and shells, some of them through means closely associated with warfare.[101] Some have also posited elite control over obsidian exchange, but this remains an outstanding debate.[102]

Labour use in monumental constructions also changed, with less emphasis on massive constructions and more on smaller architectural spaces with se-

---

100 Houston and Inomata 2009, Chapter 6.
101 McAnany 2010, p. 286.
102 See Aoyama 2001 for the argument in favour based on evidence from Copan, and the critique in Clark 2003.

cluded access patterns.[103] Certain kinds of craftwork are also limited to elite contexts, involving esoteric knowledge.[104] Yet, another recurrent point of multiple studies emphasises that household-based production remained the primary form, and that such households continued to retain access to rare materials such as jadeite.[105] Elite intervention in this sphere was limited, if not unheard of, as certain groups of commoners may have depended on corvée labour for their economic reproduction.[106] The Classic Maya were far from a society of equals, yet at the same time important aspects of communal society persisted. Furthermore, after the collapse at the end of the Classic period, new states emerged in the Postclassic period with a greater emphasis on communalism over the elaboration of elites and royal figures.[107] Kingship remained as well, but in a different, more corporate form.

Such corporate forms of rulership and political organisation are also recognised in central Mexico, notably in the Classic metropolis of Teotihuacan. It has proven difficult to recognise a clearly distinct ruler in Teotihuacan art, and its apartment compounds have been used to calculate that it had a very low Gini score.[108] Such arguments are enticing but can only be decided if more evidence becomes available for the relations of production at this site, which so far has remained limited. It is possible to recognise some tantalising clues, however. One study has pointed to the relation between Teotihuacan's state ideology and that of preceding communal settings such as Tetimpa,[109] in a clear parallel to the Maya case discussed above. Study of obsidian production shows the presence of both smaller workshops of relatively well-off craft workers and large-scale, state-administered production of weaponry.[110] From Aztec parallels, a religious system of labour obligations may well have supplied the necessary workers for the larger workshops. Much more research is needed on Teotihuacan, but it certainly seems to provide another powerful case against linear scaling between inequality and population size in Mesoamerica.

Alongside communities and states, a third factor can be recognised: the role of marketplaces and long-distance exchange in Maya economics. Given that marketplaces have been hard to identify in the archaeological record, their role

---

103   Houston and Inomata, p. 87.
104   McAnany 2010, pp. 214–15.
105   Houston and Inomata 2009, Chapter 9.
106   Ensor 2013, p. 96.
107   The differences between individualised and corporate forms of elite representation for the Maya have been placed in a broader Mesoamerican context in Blanton et al. 1996.
108   Smith et al. 2014.
109   Urunuela and Plunket 2007.
110   Carballo 2007; Hirth et al. 2019.

has been underestimated despite clear evidence from the early colonial period that markets played an important role in Mesoamerican economies. One study has traced the long-term trajectory of different kinds of exchange, from simple forms of exchange to administered and competitive markets, finding that it only partly correlated with the cycles of the political economy.[111] Hence, there is much more to be learned of different exchange types and how they connect both to the social and political-economic spheres. Due attention in this regard is also to be given to the productive forces, as attempts to trace their growth are now developed as well.[112]

With regard to the late Postclassic introduction of metallurgy, it is important to recall from the theses of aleatory materialism how the initial encounter sets the terms of what comes after. This was certainly true for Mesoamerican metallurgy, which was conceived of in the previous section along the lines of Mayan views on materiality as part of the flows of energy and potentiality.[113] This implies also that it was embedded as a social technology in a different framework than the metallurgy of western Eurasia, which had developed much earlier in its trajectory. Using Renfrew's notion of the 'commodity nexus', I have argued elsewhere that the consequence of such different starting points is that distinct forms of political economy emerged, as there existed different determinants for the formation of class systems in the two hemispheres.[114] Of course, this includes other factors as well, such as the different domesticated plants and animals noted above. As has been discussed, these differences did not just play out within bounded cultural areas, but also in larger social fields encompassing a multiplicity of social forms.[115]

The European encounter with the Americas cut short the different indigenous American pathways of social development. While the pre-Columbian civilisations of the Americas were not perfect, as the evidence for human sacrifice shows,[116] José Mariátegui's point that they were far superior to the exploitative colonial constructs that followed seems valid.[117] Rejecting the teleological ideas implicit in stadialism, we may instead view the European conquest of

---

111   Braswell 2010, pp. 132–5.
112   Stark et al. 2016.
113   A shift can be seen from the valuation of jadeite to metallic sheen; see Houston 2014, p. 127. However, this should be seen as an extension of already existing ontologies; see Saunders 2002, pp. 218–19. Metallurgy, significantly, also does not seem to have fallen under the sway of elite control; see Stark et al. 2016, p. 265.
114   Bajema 2017, pp. 298–300.
115   Kohl and Chernykh 2003.
116   Tiesler and Cucina 2006.
117   Mariátegui 1988, pp. 35–6.

the Americas according to the Epicurean answer to the Stoic conception of the universe as a perfectly steered vessel: 'Consequently, my interesting friend, your comparison of the ship would seem to have capsized for the want of a good captain'.[118] Unlike in Adam Smith's conception of society as an 'immense machine' that provides a providential order,[119] Marx recognised the transient character of capitalism, partly from his recognition of the different characteristics of ancient Mexico and Peru.

The general observation that the scaling between population size and degrees of inequality was different in the New World and in the Old is crucial and of great significance for the understanding of world history. This finding confirms the validity of Marx's use of the Americas as a counterfactual to a universalist scheme in which all pre-capitalist forms are merely foreshadowing capitalism. While recognising the worth of some of the ideas of Morgan and Engels, most notably the role of domesticated animals in fostering a different property regime in Eurasia, their stadialism is too blunt an instrument to properly capture the plurality of world history. Instead, a Marxism conceived along the lines of aleatory materialism can recognise how in different world regions, different conditions and the sequence of historical encounters resulted in distinct patterns. Further studies on the persistence of more equal social forms relative to increased social scale will also be of great interest to those efforts seeking to bring out reversals of the processes that resulted in class societies, not in the ancient but in the modern world.[120]

Another important question related to this is the encounter between the different hemispheres, which resulted in the widespread destruction of human beings and their political and religious systems. As brought out in the Montaigne quotation at the beginning of this article, such destruction cannot be set apart from the sequence of encounters that led to the global capitalism of today. In order to capture this meeting of hemispheres, the notion of 'uneven and combined development' that was originally formulated by Trotsky[121] can be of great use. Whereas aleatory materialism provides the alternative to stadialism in the conception of temporality, combined and uneven development does the same for geography by showing that regional trajectories can never be understood in isolation from each other. As a recent study has shown, the European plundering and colonisation of the Americas had a significant, per-

---

118   In Lucian's dialogue *Zeus Rants*; see Harmon 1915, p. 165.
119   Smith 1976, p. 316.
120   As cogently argued in Trigger 2006.
121   Trotsky 1974, pp. 3–15.

haps decisive, effect on the development of capitalism in Europe itself.[122] Furthermore, this mutual process of development is important to understand the trajectories of Latin American societies as well,[123] and hence is important for the political strategies that seek to undo the destructions wreaked by the conquistadores and their modern capitalist epigones.

References

Adams, Robert M. 1966, *The Evolution of Urban Society: Early Mesopotamia and Prehispanic Mexico*, Chicago, IL: Aldine Publishing.

Althusser, Louis 2006, *Philosophy of the Encounter: Later Writings, 1978–1987*, London: Verso.

Anderson, Kevin B. 2016, *Marx at the Margins: On Nationalism, Ethnicity, and Non-Western Societies*, Expanded Edition, Chicago, IL: University of Chicago Press.

Anievas, Alexander and Kerem Nisancioglu 2015, *How the West Came to Rule: The Geopolitical Origins of Capitalism*, London: Pluto Press.

Aoyama, Kazuo 2001, 'Classic Maya State, Urbanism, and Exchange: Chipped Stone Evidence of the Copan Valley and its Hinterland', *American Anthropologist*, 103: 346–61.

Aoyama, Kazuo, Takeshi Inomata, Flory Pinzon, and Juan M. Palomo 2017, 'Polished Greenstone Celt Caches from Ceibal: The Development of Maya Public Rituals', *Antiquity* 91, 357: 701–17.

Bajema, Marcus J. 2017, *Bodies of Maize, Eaters of Grain: Comparing Material Worlds, Metaphor and the Agency of Art in the Preclassic Maya and Mycenaean Early Civilisations*, Oxford: Archaeopress.

Barrett, Jason W., Harry J. Shafer and Thomas R. Hester 2011, 'Lessons from the Field: The Contribution of Colha to Lowland Maya Lithic Research', in *The Technology of Maya Civilization: Political Economy and Beyond in Lithic Studies*, edited by Geoffrey Braswell, Sheffield: Equinox Publishing.

Blackmore, Chelsea 2012, 'Recognizing Difference in Small-Scale Settings: An Examination of Social Identity Formation at the Northeast Group, Chan', in *Chan: An Ancient Maya Farming Community*, edited by Cynthia Robin, Gainesville, FA: University Press of Florida.

Blanton, Robert E. 2004, 'Settlement Pattern and Population Change in Mesoamerican and Mediterranean Civilizations: A Comparative Perspective', in *Side-by-side survey:*

---

122   Anievas and Nisancioglu 2015, Chapter 5, especially pp. 162–8.
123   Novack 1976.

Comparative Regional Studies in the Mediterranean World, edited by Susan E. Alcock and John F. Cherry, Oxford: Oxbow.

Blanton, Robert E., Gary M. Feinman, Stephen A. Kowalewski and Peter N. Peregrine 1996, 'A Dual-Processual Theory for the Evolution of Mesoamerican Civilization', *Current Anthropology*, 37, 1: 1–14.

Braidwood, Robert J. and Gordon R. Willey 1962, 'Conclusions and Afterthoughts', in *Courses Toward Urban Life: Archaeological Considerations of Some Cultural Alternates*, edited by Robert J. Braidwood and Gordon R. Willey, Chicago, IL: Aldine Publishing Company.

Braswell, Geoffrey E. 2010, 'The Rise and Fall of Market Exchange: A Dynamic Approach to Ancient Maya Economy', in *Archaeological Approaches to Market Exchange in Ancient Societies*, edited by Christopher P. Garraty and Barbara L. Stark, Boulder, CO: University Press of Colorado.

Carballo, David M. 2007, 'Implements of State Power: Weaponry and Martially Themed Obsidian Production Near the Moon Pyramid, Teotihuacan', *Ancient Mesoamerica*, 17: 173–90.

Childe, Vere G. 1944, 'Archaeological Ages as Technological Stages', *The Journal of the Royal Anthropological Institute of Great Britain and Ireland*, 74: 7–24.

Childe, Vere G. 1950, 'The Urban Revolution', *The Town Planning Review*, 21, 1: 3–17.

Childe, Vere G. 1951, *Social Evolution*, London: Collins.

Childe, Vere G. 1954, 'Early Forms of Society', in *A History of Technology*, edited by Charles Singer, Eric J. Holmyard and Alfred R. Hall, Oxford: Clarendon Press.

Childe, Vere G. 1979, 'Prehistory and Marxism', *Antiquity*, 53: 93–5.

Clark, John E. 2003, 'A Review of Twentieth-Century Mesoamerican Obsidian Studies', in *Mesoamerican Lithic Technology: Experimentation and Interpretation*, edited by Kenneth G. Hirth, Salt Lake City, UT: University of Utah Press.

Demarest, Arthur A. 2004, *Ancient Maya: The Rise and Fall of a Rainforest Civilization*, Cambridge: Cambridge University Press.

Diamond, Jared 1997, *Guns, Germs and Steel: A Short History of Everybody for the Last 13,000 Years*, London: Vintage.

Engels, Friedrich 1987 [1878], *Anti-Dühring*, in *Marx and Engels Collected Works*, Volume 25, Moscow: Progress Publishers.

Engels, Friedrich 1990 [1884], *The Origin of the Family, Private Property and the State: In the Light of the Researches by Lewis H. Morgan*, in *Marx and Engels Collected Works*, Volume 26, Moscow: Progress Publishers.

Ensor, Brian E. 2013, *Crafting Prehispanic Maya Kinship*, Tuscaloosa, AL: University of Alabama Press.

Estrada-Belli, Fernando 2006, 'Lightning Sky, Rain, and the Maize God: The Ideology of Preclassic Maya Rulers at Cival, Peten, Guatemala', *Ancient Mesoamerica*, 17, 1: 57–78.

Estrada-Belli, Fernando 2012, 'Early Civilization in the Maya lowlands: Monumentality and Placemaking, a View from the Holmul Region', in *Early New World Monumentality*, edited by Richard L. Burger and Robert M. Rosenswig, Gainesville, FL: University Press of Florida.

Evans, Susan T. 2012, 'Time and Space Boundaries: Chronologies and Regions in Mesoamerica', in *The Oxford Handbook of Mesoamerican Archaeology*, edited by Deborah L. Nichols and Christopher A. Pool, New York: Oxford University Press.

Hansen, Richard D. 2017, 'Cultural and Environmental Components of the First Maya States: A Perspective from the Central and Southern Maya Lowlands', in *The Origins of Maya States*, edited by Loa P. Traxler and Robert J. Sharer, Philadelphia, PA: University of Pennsylvania Museum of Archaeology and Anthropology.

Harmon, Austin M. 1915, *Lucian*, Volume II, London: William Heinemann.

Headrick, Annabeth 2004, 'The Quadripartite Motif and the Centralization of Power', in *K'axob: Ritual, Work and Family in an Ancient Maya Village*, edited by Patricia A. McAnany, Los Angeles: Cotsen Institute of Archaeology, University of California.

Hendon, Julia A. 1999, 'The Pre-Classic Maya Compound as the Focus of Social Identity', in *Social Patterns in Pre-Classic Mesoamerica*, edited by David C. Grove and Rosemary A. Joyce, Washington, D.C.: Dumbarton Oaks Research Library and Collection.

Hester, Thomas and Harry J. Shafer 1994, 'The Ancient Maya Craft Community at Colha, Belize, and its External Relationships', in *Archaeological Views from the Countryside: Village Communities in Early Complex Societies*, edited by Glenn M. Schwartz and Steven E. Falconer, Washington, D.C.: Smithsonian Institution Press.

Hirth, Kenneth G., David M. Carballo, Mark Dennison, Sean Carr, Sarah Imfeld and Eric Dyrdahl 2019, 'Excavation of an Obsidian Craft Workshop at Teotihuacan, Mexico', *Ancient Mesoamerica*, 30: 163–79.

Houston, Stephen D. 2014, *The Life Within: Classic Maya and the Matter of Permanence*, New Haven: Yale University Press.

Houston, Stephen D. and Karl A. Taube 2008, 'Meaning in Early Maya Imagery, in Iconography Without Texts', edited by Paul Taylor, London: Warburg Institute.

Houston, Stephen D. and Takeshi Inomata 2009, *The Classic Maya*, Cambridge: Cambridge University Press.

Iannone, Gyles 2002, '*Annales* History and the Ancient Maya State: Some Observations on the "Dynamic Model"', *American Anthropologist*, 104, 1: 68–78.

Inomata, T., Jessica MacLellan, Daniel Triadan, Jessica Munson, Melissa Burham, Kazuo Aoyama, Hiroo Nasu, Flory Pinzon and Hitoshi Yonenobu 2015, 'The Development of Sedentary Communities in the Maya Lowlands: Co-Existing Mobile Groups and Public Ceremonies at Ceibal, Guatemala', *Proceedings of the National Academy of Sciences* 112, 14: 4268–73.

Isendahl, Christian 2012, 'Agro-Urban Landscapes: The Example of Lowland Maya Cities', *Antiquity* 86, 334: 1112–25.

Keller, Angela H. 2012, 'Creating Community with Shell', in *Chan: An Ancient Maya Farming Community*, edited by Cynthia Robin, Gainesville: University Press of Florida.

King, Eleanor M. 2017, 'Rethinking the Role of Early Economies in the Rise of Maya States: A View from the Lowlands', in *The Origins of Maya States*, edited by Loa P. Traxler and Robert J. Sharer, Philadelphia, PA: University of Pennsylvania Museum of Archaeology and Anthropology.

Kohl, Philip L. and Evgeny N. Chernykh 2003, 'Different Hemispheres, Different Worlds', in *The Postclassic Mesoamerican World*, edited by Michael E. Smith and Frances E. Berdan, Salt Lake City: University of Utah Press.

Kohler, Timothy A., Michael E. Smith, Amy Bogaard, Gary M. Feinman, Christian E. Peterson, Alleen Betzenhauser, Matthew Pailes, Elizabeth C. Stone, Anna M. Prentiss, Timothy J. Dennehy, Laura J. Ellyson, Linda M. Nicholas, Ronald K. Faulseit, Amy Styring, Jade Whitlam, Mattia Fochesato, Thomas A. Foor and Samuel Bowles 2017, 'Greater Post-Neolithic Wealth Disparities in Eurasia than in North America and Mesoamerica', *Science*, 551: 619–22.

Krader, Lawrence 1975, *The Asiatic Mode of Production. Sources, Development and Critique in the Writings of Karl Marx*, Assen: Van Gorcum.

Luxemburg, Rosa 2013 [1909–10], 'Introduction to Political Economy', in *The Complete Works of Rosa Luxemburg*, Volume I, London: Verso.

Mariátegui, José C. 1988 [1928], *Seven Interpretive Essays on Peruvian Reality*, Austin, TX: University of Texas Press.

Marx, Karl H. 1983a [1877], 'A Letter to the Editorial Board of Otechestvennye Zapiski', in *Late Marx and the Russian Road: Marx and the Peripheries of Capitalism*, edited by Teodor Shanin, New York: Monthly Review Press.

Marx, Karl H. 1983b [1881], 'Drafts of a Reply to Vera Zasulich', in *Late Marx and the Russian Road: Marx and the Peripheries of Capitalism*, edited by Teodor Shanin, New York: Monthly Review Press.

Marx, Karl H. 1987 [1857–58], *Economic Manuscripts of 1857–58*, in *Marx and Engels Collected Works*, Volume 29, Moscow: Progress Publishers.

Marx, Karl H. 1998 [1894], *Capital*, Volume III, in *Marx and Engels Collected Works*, Volume 37, Moscow: Progress Publishers.

Masson, Vadim M. 1988, *Altyn-Depe*, Philadelphia, PA: University Museum.

McAnany, Patricia A. 1995, *Living with the Ancestors: Kinship and Kingship in Ancient Maya Society*, Austin, TX: University of Texas Press.

McAnany, Patricia A. 2010, *Ancestral Maya Economies in Archaeological Perspective*, Cambridge: Cambridge University Press.

Meek, Ronald L. 1976, *Social Science and the Ignoble Savage*, Cambridge: Cambridge University Press.

Monaghan, John D. 2000, 'Theology and History in the Study of Mesoamerican Religions', in *Handbook of Middle American Indians, Supplement 6: Ethnology*, edited by John D. Monaghan, Austin, TX: University of Texas Press.

Montaigne, Michel 1991, *The Complete Essays*, translated by Michael A. Screech, London: Penguin.

Morfino, Vittorio 2015, *Plural Temporality: Transindividuality and the Aleatory between Spinoza and Althusser*, Chicago, IL: Haymarket Books.

Morgan, Lewis H. 1964 [1877], *Ancient Society*, Cambridge, MA: The Belknap Press of Harvard University Press.

Morgan, Lewis H. 1965 [1881], *Houses and House-life of the American Aborigines*, Chicago, IL: University of Chicago Press.

Morris, Ian 2015, *Foragers, Farmers, and Fossil Fuels: How Human Values Evolve*, Princeton, NJ: Princeton University Press.

Novack, George 1976, 'The Law of Uneven and Combined Development and Latin America', *Latin American Perspectives* 3, 2: 100–6.

Robin, Cynthia, Andrew R. Wyatt, Laura J. Kosakowsky, Santiago Juarez, Ethan Kalosky and Elise Enterkin 2012, 'A Changing Cultural Landscape: Settlement and GIS at Chan', in *Chan: An Ancient Maya Farming Community*, edited by Cynthia Robin, Gainesville, FA: University Press of Florida.

Robin, Cynthia, James Meierhoff and Laura J. Kosakowsky 2012, 'Nonroyal Governance at Chan's Community Center', in *Chan: An Ancient Maya Farming Community*, edited by Cynthia Robin, Gainesville, FA: University Press of Florida.

Rosenswig, Robert M. 2017, 'The Tributary Mode of Production and Justifying Ideologies: Evaluating the Wolf-Trigger Hypothesis', in *Modes of Production and Archaeology*, edited by Robert M. Rosenswig and Jerimy J. Cunningham, Gainesville, FL: University of Florida Press.

Saturno, William A. 2009, 'Centering the Kingdom, Centering the King: Maya Creation and Legitimization at San Bartolo', in *The Art of Urbanism: How Mesoamerican Kingdoms Represented Themselves in Architecture and Imagery*, edited by William L. Fash and Leonardo López Luján, Washington, D.C.: Dumbarton Oaks Research Library & Collection.

Saunders, Nicholas J. 2002, 'The Colours of Light: Materiality and Chromatic Cultures of the Americas: Colouring the Past', in *The Significance of Archaeological Research*, edited by Andrew Jones and Gavin MacGregor, Oxford: Berg.

Sharer, Robert J. and Loa P. Traxler 2006, *The Ancient Maya*, 6th ed., Stanford, CA: Stanford University Press.

Sharer, Robert J. and Loa P. Traxler 2017, 'The Origins of Maya States: Problems and Prospects', in *The Origins of Maya States*, edited by Loa P. Traxler and Robert J. Sharer, Philadelphia, PA: University of Pennsylvania Museum of Archaeology and Anthropology.

Smith, Adam 1976 [1759], *The Theory of Moral Sentiments*, Oxford: Clarendon Press.

Smith, Michael E., Timothy Dennehy, April Kamp-Whittaker, Emily Colon and Rebecca Harkness 2014, 'Quantitative Measures of Wealth Inequality in Ancient Central Mexican Communities', *Advances in Archaeological Practice*, 2, 4: 311–23.

Stark, Barbara L., Matthew A. Boxt, Janine Gasco, Rebecca B. Gonzalez Lauck, Jessica D. Hedgepeth Balkin, Arthur A. Joyce, Stacie M. King, Charles L.F. Knight, Robert Kruger, Marc N. Levine, Richard G. Lesure, Rebecca Mendelsohn, Marx Navarro-Castillo, Hector Neff, Michael Ohnersorgen, Christopher A. Pool, L. Mark Raab, Robert M. Rosenswig, Marcie Venter, Barbara Vorhies, David T. Williams and Andrew Workinger 2016, 'Economic Growth in Mesoamerica: Obsidian Consumption in the Coastal Lowlands', *Journal of Anthropological Archaeology*, 41: 263–82.

Tate, Carolyn E., 2012, *Reconsidering Olmec Visual Culture: The Unborn, Women, and Creation*, Austin, TX: University of Texas Press.

Tiesler, Vera and Andrea Cucina 2006, 'Procedures in Human Heart Extraction and Ritual Meaning: A Taphonomic Assessment of Anthropogenic Marks in Classic Maya Skeletons', *Latin American Antiquity*, 17, 4: 493–510.

Traxler, Loa P. and Robert J. Sharer (eds.) 2017, *The Origins of Maya States*, Philadelphia, PA: University of Pennsylvania Museum of Archaeology and Anthropology.

Trigger, Bruce G. 1980, *Gordon Childe: Revolutions in Archaeology*, London: Thames and Hudson.

Trigger, Bruce G. 2003, *Understanding Early Civilizations: A Comparative Study*, Cambridge: Cambridge University Press.

Trigger, Bruce G. 2006, 'All People are (not) Good', in *The Politics of Egalitarianism*, edited by Jacqueline Solway, New York: Berghahn Books.

Trotsky, Leon 1974, *The History of the Russian Revolution*, Ann Arbor, MI: University of Michigan Press.

Urunuela, Gabriela and Patricia Plunket 2007, 'Tradition and Transformation: Village Ritual at Tetimpa as a Template for Early Teotihuacan', in *Commoner Ritual and Ideology in Ancient Mesoamerica*, edited by Nancy Gonlin and Jon C. Lohse, Boulder, CO: University Press of Colorado.

Wyatt, Andrew R. 2012, 'Agricultural Practices at Chan: Farming and Political Economy in an Ancient Maya Community', in *Chan: An Ancient Maya Farming Community*, edited by Cynthia Robin, Gainesville, FA: University Press of Florida.

CHAPTER 5

Violence in the Prehispanic Andes: Materialities, Social Practices and the Moche Case

Alex Gonzales-Panta and Henry Tantaleán

1   Introduction

Until a few decades ago, Latin America was plagued by a series of dictatorships, guerrillas and 'subversive' groups. With the fall, deactivation and/or capture of those social expressions, alleged democratic and non-violent periods were initiated.[1] However, the reality is different. Under the umbrella of the so-called 'democratic governments', this supposed moment of 'peaceful' progress has only hidden other forms of violent social relations that take place throughout the continent, where the poor, ancestral ethnic groups, immigrants, women and children remain the most recurring victims.[2] The forms acquired of this violence are different and more 'subtle': overwork, job insecurity, exclusion, marginalisation, xenophobia, invisibility, corruption, embezzlement, dispossession, destruction of territories, citizen insecurity, criminality, gender violence and so on. Despite proclaimed democracy, freedom and respect for human rights, many of these forms of violence are hidden by public and economic policies designed and/or promoted by political, economic and religious elites of each country.[3] From a social perspective, these forms of violence are legitimated in some academic elaborations, including the social sciences, which present scientific 'truths' that serve to validate or hide the current violence.

---

1 One of the most recent is the peace agreement reached by the FARC-PC and the Colombian government; despite this, many of the former combatants have been killed by paramilitary groups. See: https://www.eldiario.es/politica/partido-FARC-asesinato-excombatiente-guerrilla_0_907460209.html.
2 Amnistía Internacional 2014.
3 Lobbies, 'revolving doors' and bribes are the most recurrent forms of these practices; this is documented in different journalistic and academic research. It can be reviewed for the Peruvian / South American case: https://ojo-publico.com/tag/odebrecht and, Crabtree and Durand 2017.

However, in recent years, anthropological and sociological studies have increased their investigation of violence.[4] In archaeology, this concern has been materialised in some volumes.[5] Thus, why is it important to conduct a research of violence from archaeology?

As we know, archaeology is the study of societies, its history. This study includes violence, a universal phenomenon that has deeply impacted, conditioned and canceled the social life of human beings. Archaeology is powerful because it approaches violence and other phenomena through material objects: cause and consequence (products and producers) of all social practice. Because of this dialectical process, the study of objects brings us closer to social relations without intermediaries (oral and/or written). Therefore, archaeological research is more transparent than historical sources that may contain biases or partitions. We believe that a study of these characteristics allows us to know the past in its fullness, without reducing it to representations of some contemporary theoretical models, loaded with ideologies in most cases.

Therefore, from a historical materialist approach, we can respond and/or problematise the discussion of violence into three broad themes: 1) To deny the essentiality behind some archaeological explanations, whether biological, religious or cultural; 2) To see to what extent the presence of violence is related to forms of political and economic organisation of each historical situation; and 3) To reveal mechanisms, especially ideology, that deny, alienate or hide violence.

For all the above, observing when and how the violent episodes occurred, who benefited from them, who suffered them and how such situations could be overcome can help to better understand the phenomenon of violence and act accordingly.

Now, why propose the usefulness of Marxist archaeology? We believe that the theoretical and methodological elements of historical materialism are significant in this effort, since this approach indicates that people and their production and reproduction are the basis for any explicit social development (material and ideal). In addition, Marxism is useful because it understands that knowledge is not a form of struggle in itself, but rather a tool (among others) of human understanding, criticism, denunciation and social transformation.[6]

---

4   For an introduction at the Latin American level, see Solís and Moriconi 2018. For the Peruvian case, see Manrique 2002; Klarén 2003; and Cotler and Cuenca 2011.

5   For the South American case, see López Mazz and Berón 2014; and Landa and Hernández 2014. Globally, this concern has already had a certain history for 20 or 30 years, which has intensified in the last decade; see Keeley 1996; Walker 2001; Arkush and Allen 2006; and Nielsen and Walker 2009, among others.

6   Marx 1975.

Thus, we believe certain narratives that assess and investigate the violence of the Andean past are problematic. Mainly, we detect a series of contradictions between the explanatory proposals and the social materiality of the past. In order to overcome these contradictions in part, we expose possible theoretical-methodological research routes based on the same archaeological materials. In order to exemplify the viability of our theoretical-methodological approach, we present a study of Prehispanic violence based on the archaeological materiality of the Moche society (100–800 AD). Finally, we will present a series of issues related to the archaeological study of violence for future works.

2 Archaeological Research on Violence in the Prehispanic Central Andes

So far, investigations of violence in the Central Andes have attempted to explain the evidence of the past from political, sociological and anthropological models, constructed from ethnohistoric and ethnographic records.[7] However, these investigations, often contain ideological, economic and political premises originated in liberal philosophy and economics.[8] Those archaeological explanations place practices of violence in ahistorical ideas that run between human and Andean essentialisms. These essentialisms can be tracked from two different models.

The first model, that of human essentialism, comes from an approach to the state of nature, where competition between humans gave rise to a political entity that warranted order among individuals, namely the state.[9] Thus, violence in the Andean past is explained as a response to competition for scarce resources caused by different elements: lack of land for cultivation, population growth, environmental catastrophe, etc. Some examples are the works of Robert Carneiro (1970), Shelia Pozorski (1987) and David Wilson (1988). These proposals place individualism and competition as necessary forms for social survival, order and human progress, and we may associate them with principles operating in capitalism and neoliberalism.

The second model, an Andean cultural essentialism, has origins in the romanticism of the nineteenth century.[10] This romanticism is later reinforced by

---

7   Carneiro 1970; Topic and Topic 1997; and Ghezzi 2006, and 2007. For a critique of these models from anthropology, in the case of ritual warfare in Peru, see Remy 1991.
8   For a general review, see Lull and Micó 2007.
9   Hobbes 2005.
10 The romanticism is a 'movement' that tries to cope with the Enlightenment and its uni-

work done by ethnographers and anthropologists during the twentieth century, such as by Marcel Mauss (2010) and Karl Polanyi (1991). Although both authors recognised the original economic forms of certain Precapitalistic or non-capitalist human groups, their writings also ended up being input for romantic or idyllic visions of these groups. We can link certain aspects of indigenism practiced by Julio C. Tello and other anthropologists with Romanticism. However, there will be the proposals of John Murra on the uniqueness of Andean economic organisation and social relations,[11] which will be freely used by other researchers to generate a particularistic vision of the Andean world ('Lo Andino'). In the same vein, a particular history of different expressions of violence in Andean societies end in their denial or positive valuation. In this way, the evidence that could indicate episodes of violence is interpreted as the materialisation of a 'world-view', where being sacrificed (killed) was an 'honour' and a 'privilege', since it would allow reproduction, order and social survival.[12] Both models of explaining violence coexist in the present, but with positive, spiritual and religious explanations.[13]

This tight synthesis is not intended to delegitimise or belittle the works that have been developed in the Pre-Hispanic Andes under these premises. It is, rather, one way to point out critically that all models of explanation find their fundamental premises in cultural, economic, political and, most often, ideological assumptions. Operating in this way conditions the possibilities of knowledge, suggesting that all forms of expression that human societies can achieve are limited to a few that are already known today. Even worse, the existence of a spirit, be it a universal human *being* or, specifically, a transcendental and ahistorical Andean *ethos*.

On the contrary, we believe that the violence of the present, which is a consequence (among others) of capitalism, should not be naturalised in the material record of the past. Likewise, its denial must not be sought in immutable cultural ideas supposedly generated in a particular territory.

We consider it necessary to discuss violence from the historical situation in which these practices took place and to recognise their role in the social, eco-

---

versal rationalist goals, placing the focus on the cultural particularities; for a discussion on this, see Berlin 2015.

11   Murra 1972, and 1975.

12   For example: Hocquenghem 1987; Topic and Topic 1997; Ghezzi 2007 and Castillo 2007. In addition, generally, and especially in the Moche case when talking about sacrifices, it was men (warriors) who would help to recover environmental, cosmogonic and social order. While the sacrifice of women is linked to their role as companions or servants of great lords and, though rarely, of ladies. The ideological premises underlying these ideas are evident.

13   A discussion on both perspectives appears in Quilter 2002 and in Arkush 2012.

nomic and political relations of the Andean past. In what follows, we discuss how we could undertake this form of research.

3   A Historical Materialist Investigation of Violence

As noted above, explanations of evidence of violent practices in the Andean past most frequently refer to human and Andean essences. Unlike them, we believe that the practice of violence responds to specific historical situations. For that reason, this research should be located at every historical moment, and social phenomena must be explained in relation to the objective and subjective conditions in which they occur.

From the historical materialism developed by Karl Marx and Friedrich Engels,[14] we know that social life and the materialisation of different forms of organisation and of social, economic and political relations are historically constituted and do not respond to immutable essences (ideas):

> The mode of production of material life determines the process of social, political and intellectual life in general. It is not the conscience of men that determines reality; on the contrary, social reality is what determines their conscience.[15]

This premise is demonstrated empirically from the basic primary fact that to think and be aware, you must be alive, and that one can only live materially and socially. This dialectic of human life is the necessary condition for any historical development/process.[16] The forms of how this occurs determine social relationships. Because relationships are produced in different ways, they involve a variety of interests that sometimes cause contradictions with the productive

---

14   Developed in Marx 1970; Marx 1971, especially in the introduction; and Marx and Hobsbawm 1979.
15   Marx 1970, p. 37.
16   There are common places of criticism of historical materialism for supposedly being mechanistic and for its emphasis on the economic (for a review of these criticisms, see Eagleton 2015). However, from the beginning, Engels already pointed out that: 'According to the materialist conception of history, the factor that ultimately determines history is the production and reproduction of real life. Neither Marx nor I have ever affirmed more than this. If someone misrepresents it by saying that the economic factor is the only determinant, it will turn that thesis into an empty, abstract and absurd phrase' (Marx and Engels 1977, p. 75). This is not the place to expand on this issue. For a deeper review in archaeology, see Lull 2005 and Lull in this volume. See also Milevski, this volume.

community or between different communities. These social contradictions are solved through politics, negotiation and consensus; or they are resolved using force or coercion. The latter can lead to conflicts if those who suffer from it resist. Repression is one mechanism to ensure that conflict does not break out and can be exercised physically or ideologically. Repression can reach undetectable levels, even for those suffering such violence. This social network is embodied in all the materiality produced or used in the social becoming, regardless of whether its materialisation is a consequence of a voluntary act. Consequently, the investigation of violence from a historical materialist perspective must rely on objective, material and concrete reality:[17] the objects.

Currently, much of the timely debate about violence in the pre-Hispanic Andes can be expressed in the following question: why should some social practices of the past be considered violent based on violent practices in current times? The question (of an epistemological order) is pertinent, but the answer must be based on the operability of the concept (of an ontological order). Any concept or category we use to capture some social relationship is theoretical and becomes real in research practice.

Violence is a form of human relationship that occurs and reproduces in relation to the productive developments of each historical situation. Therefore, the levels of violence are not abstractions of some metaphysical entity yet to be discovered; they are linked to the ways in which production is organised and to the social relationships that it enables. We do not deny that there could be different triggers for episodes of violence (religious, cultural, political, etc.). However, these could only be possible based on and through existing material conditions.

Thus, a social relationship of violence requires at least two individuals or groups: one that exerts violence and another that suffers. Between the two is the means to exercise or reject violence, which can be enacted by the body itself or with objects intended exclusively for its purpose. When those who suffer violence react, conflict breaks out. However, conflict often does not erupt, since the material and ideological means to produce the submission of the victims is so effective that it cancels any possibility of resistance (e.g. by coercion) and alienates those who suffer (e.g. by persuasion and ideology).

Vicente Lull and associates (2015) point out that a third party would be present in violent relationships: the rest of the society, which neither exercises nor suffers violence but observes it. Individuals in a society may try to

---

17 We understand by objective reality the relationship of the human being (women and men), the natural environment and the objects produced. These three objective fields (human, nature and objects), in intense and constant dialectical movement, produce objective and subjective consequences, which can be traced from the material correlates they generate in their historical display.

explain violence objectively, assess it based on traditions (ethical and moral) and norms (legal and ideological), or they may not recognise it and/or they might sanction it based on moral and ideological principles.[18] Researchers of our present who study violence can be included in the latter group and be subject to similar contradictions. Thus, the dependence of interpretations based on tradition, intersubjective consensus and political position to identify and punish (or not) causes violence to seep into social recognition and, as noted above, also into academic formulations. Faced with this situation, should we assume that there are no relations of violence beyond those who claim them? We think not.

The way to escape the situation above is to locate the reality of violence in its causes and consequences, materialised in the objects. Through investigation we can define violent social relations, regardless of those who exercise them, suffer them or observe them. In this direction, Lull and colleagues (2006) propose a qualitative and quantitative investigation of the materials (objects), organised in effects, means and representations, which we here try to redefine in **subjects**, **means** and **spaces**; as a way of materially specifying the evidence that allows us to identify relationships of violence. The sense (direction) of this violence will allow us to define the forms of violence and resistance, oppression and so on, and this will depend on the location of the agents and victims of violence as well as the social, economic and political context in which they are inserted.

Subjects, means and spaces of/for violence are dynamic and can change their position according to the place from which violence is exercised and experienced. In such a way, they are not closed categories. For example, one **subject** of violence may also be one **means** for violence, especially if it is a warrior specialist used by an elite to coerce several subjects. In the same way, a fortress is a **means** of defence and attack, but it can also be a **space of control** when it limits the free movement of those who live inside. This same fortress can be a **subject** of violence if we can recognise the damage done to it, such as, for example, its intentional destruction or a fire that cancels its useful 'life', etc. In the same way, a room or any building can become a space of violence; for example, the torture spaces such as the Víctor Jara stadium in Chile.[19] This determination of uses will always be the result of an archaeological investigation that contextualises all the objective elements indicated in such historical situations, which we will characterise in detail below.

---

18   Lull et al. 2015, p. 33.
19   San Francisco et al. 2010.

3.1 *Subjects of/for Violence*

We are referring here to the subjects who exercise violence and those who suffer from it. The latter, the victims, are the subjects most 'feasible' to be recognised archaeologically by the observable marks on their bodies, mainly osteological. In addition, it is also possible to find a way to identify the aggressors. The third element, observers of violence (complainants, witnesses and/or accomplices) are indirectly inferred from the presence of the two main actors.

3.1.1   Subjects of Violence, or Victims

Thanks to the advancement of bioanthropology, it is possible to identify traces/marks of violence left on bodies themselves and to link them to potential patterns of hits and determine their severity.[20] It has even been possible to associate the means with which certain individuals were violated. However, this type of analysis is the most restricted, because the work in cemeteries is limited to patterns of burial and to their associated grave goods, especially in the case of important personages in tombs.[21] On the other hand, the existence of mass graves, battlefields and places of execution are issues that have been little investigated because of different problems. First, because their spatial identification is difficult. Second, because they respond to burial spaces not institutionalised and/or formalised. For example, the archaeological context of a possible mass grave was located at the Pacatnamú site in the Jequetepeque valley;[22] another context, at the Punta Lobos site in the Huarmey valley, showed the presence of executed subjects in a non-formal space.[23]

Furthermore, it is possible to identify traces of violence in buildings, fields of crops, roads, etc., which allows sites to also be treated as 'subjects' of violence. However, the human being will be the main and unique reference point when we discuss victims of violence.

3.1.2   Agents of Violence or Aggressors

Usually, the specialists referred to as 'warriors' are defined by the artefacts that accompanies them in their graves.[24] An osteological investigation will uncover

---

20 Vega 2016.
21 Alva 1994; Alva and Donnan 1993; Castillo 2000; and Franco 2016, among others.
22 Verano 1986.
23 Verano and Toyne 2011. In the case of mass graves in recent history, especially in South America, there is an interesting and very important bibliography (see Funari and Zarankin 2006). In the context of the political violence in Peru from 1980–2000, Ricardo Uceda (2004) has presented important arguments to understand the logic and the way in which the perpetrators and organisers of people's disappearances operated.
24 Strong and Evans 1953; Bourget and Newman 1998; Alva and Chero 1999; and Franco 2016.

indicators of violence such as marks, traumas of conflict or indications of musculoskeletal patterns related to specialised violent activity. With a set of archaeological data that exposes the possibility of a group or collective linked exclusively to the exercise of violence, it can be established that said violence was structural.[25] Here we will have to differentiate between subjects for effective violence and subjects who lead violence. Thus, some individuals or groups, such as kings, emperors or some elite class, lead violence without 'getting their hands dirty'. However, how to establish this passes for determining subject roles as 'king', 'emperor' or 'social class'. In the last instance, it is important to determine the person who organises and forces other subjects to exercise violence.

3.2 Means to Exercise or Reject Violence

Clearly, artefacts or objects that can be identified as weapons have been the best and most used indicator to demonstrate the existence of violent practices. Likewise, it remains critical to define which elements, in addition to artefacts, may have been used as weapons. Many times, simple elements taken from nature, such as rocks or tree trunks, can be offensive artefacts. On the other side, elements of nature can be used to repel aggression.

Other types of means involve the communication of violence. Representations of violence could have well served to 'educate', discipline and intimidate potential groups that tried to subvert existing orders, or it could have simply served to reproduce the social conditions where violence is common in the daily life.[26] Its 'role' as a means must be proposed in relation to other elements of identification of violence.

As we said, human bodies themselves, as disciplined by elites to become specialists in the exercise of violence, are a means for subjects who organise violence.

3.3 Spaces for the Exercise of Violence

The places where these violent practices occur can be built. But these spaces can also be open areas used in a spontaneous or consensual manner. Facilities prepared for violent purposes can be more easily traced, starting with architectural spaces like the so-called 'temples' to the large plazas in the archaeological sites where sacrificial ritual activities are carried out. Perhaps these are the

---

25 We define structural violence as a form of social inequality guaranteed by a collective specialised in the exercise of physical violence (for example, the military or police).

26 However, the dependence on ethnohistoric, ethnographic and 'common' ideas limits historical potential, placing iconographic analyses in a very thin line between history and fable.

most obvious places in our archaeological research; but we must also remember that, as history shows, conflicts often erupt in the least expected places. Battlefields outside the cities are the best examples. The identification of these spaces is very difficult in archaeology. For example, there is no knowledge of any battlefield archaeologically identified in the case of the Incas. However, we know from ethnohistorical documentation that battles and wars were recurrent as institutionalised practice.[27] Corroborating this information materially is still a pending task.

On the other hand, the existence of spaces of confinement, where people were retained prior to the 'ritual sacrifice', has rarely been considered. These spaces of violence are significant because such 'sacrificial rituals' would occur in public spaces, during specific dates, and therefore it was necessary to retain the subjects. In more recent times, these spaces have been identified in contexts of dictatorships and civil wars – for example, spaces of torture and forced confinement (prisons and concentration camps) prior to extrajudicial executions. These spaces are important because they allow us to reconstruct the intensity and sophistication of violence.[28]

To exemplify possible lines of research and work, we will indicate some of the available evidence and social practices that imply exercises of violence in what has been defined as the Moche society or culture. We discussed this evidence in relation to the organisation and social relationships of production, because, as we have pointed out, it is difficult to determine and understand isolated violence, since these practices respond to concrete historical conditions. While the organisation and social relationships of production do not necessarily act as triggers of violence, they are the necessary condition for it to occur.

4   The Moche

The Moche was a social group that has been characterised as a state,[29] as groups of states[30] and as a series of social groups integrated by a common ideology.[31] The entity spread over a large part of the Peruvian north coast (Figure 5.1), approximately between 100 and 800 AD. This society is known in the media for the lavish burials found, the monumentality of its buildings and its icono-

---

27   Rostworowski 1983, and 1999.
28   Funari and Zarankin 2006.
29   Lumbreras 1981; Stanish 2001.
30   Shimada 1994a; Donnan and Castillo 1994; and Rosas 2017.
31   Bawden 1994; Quilter 2010; Quilter and Koons 2012; and Swenson 2015.

FIGURE 5.1 Location of the main Moche sites mentioned in the text.
PRODUCED BY GONZALES-PANTA

graphic representations in different types of materials. The study of ceramics has contributed to the determination of the chronology of the two Moche states (North and South), organised into two sequences.[32] However, the real scope of the Moche is far from uniform, as ceramic styles do not necessarily reflect coherent stratigraphic relationships. The absence of radiocarbon dating series to validate these chronologies is also problematic.[33] What we know well is that there was a distinct materiality shared between several valleys on the Peruvian northern coast during that period, which allows us to speak of a Moche 'territory'.

Below, we summarise some examples of materiality that suggest Moche violent practices, which we then associate with the organisation of production and of social relationships.

4.1   *Materiality of Moche Violence*

There is no updated and comprehensive work that synthesises the large number of burials related to the Moche phenomenon and includes an exhaustive bioanthropological analysis associated with its funerary goods and tomb types. The existence of such a study could help us to propose more robust hypotheses about social relations and their impact on the bodies themselves. However, there are some studies that allow us to begin understanding the materiality of the Moche human bodies. A first account was made by Christopher Donnan from the funerary contexts excavated until 1991.[34] For his part, Luis Jaime Castillo conducted studies in the same direction, but he mainly associated the graves with iconographic representations. In this way, Castillo identified what he calls 'The Mochica rituals of death'.[35] Finally, the work of François Millaire attempts to define social differences from the characterisation of tomb types, associated objects and bodies.[36] Other significant work that is bioanthropological are analyses made by John Verano, especially in contexts of sacrifices or elite personages.[37]

The main contexts studied to date correspond to people who were killed to serve as offerings in the burials of important personages or who were victims during rituals; in both cases they are regarded as 'sacrificial'. In addition, there are some burial contexts in cemeteries or tombs of elite where the cause

---

32   Castillo and Donnan 1994a.
33   See in this regard Aimi et al. 2016, and Rosas 2017.
34   Donnan 1995.
35   Castillo 2000.
36   Millaire 2002.
37   Verano 1997, 2001a.

of death of the main individual is probably identified as violent due to their participation in fighting.[38] Here, we note some of the archaeological context reporting on bodies that act as sacrifices/offerings in the burials of elite individuals and sacrifices/offerings in rituals.

William Duncan Strong and Clifford Evans provide a first example of graves with 'sacrificed' individuals. Within the framework of the Virú Project, they excavated the first tomb of what will be considered a personage from the Moche elite. The tomb was located in Huaca de la Cruz in the Virú Valley. It contained a male individual, deposited in a cane coffin, accompanied by a large number of objects and the bodies of a 12-year-old child and two young women. The women and child were 'sacrificed', probably killed by suffocation, as they would have been, depending on the position in which they were found, thrown into the tomb during the burial process.[39] This form of burial, a main personage 'accompanied' by sacrificed people, recurred in different valleys and chronologies of the north coast. Among the most well-known, we can point out the grave of 'Lord of Sipán' (640–680 AD), who was buried in the burial platform of Huaca Rajada in the Lambayeque Valley. This personage was 'accompanied' by three young women of between 15 and 20 years.[40] Another funerary context is that which contained the 'Lady of Cao' (400 AD), exhumed from the *huaca* of the same name in the Chicama Valley. The funerary camera or mausoleum contained the mummy bundle of the main personage, 'Lady of Cao', and four 'accompanying' individuals located in different fosses. The main female personage (Lady of Cao) had a teenaged person (undetermined sex) who was strangled with a reed rope as part of her offerings.[41] One of the 'accompanying' individuals, another 'offering' located in the central fosse adjacent to the Lady of Cao tomb, was an individual of 12 or 13 years, sex also not determined. This individual was exhumed with a reed rope still around their neck.[42] We also take note of the 'Tomb of reused camera' located on the west side of the upper pyramid, which presented a woman sacrificed as offering, also killed by strangulation.[43] Likewise, the

---

38 Franco 2016, p. 69; Verano 2014.
39 Strong and Evans 1952; seen at Castillo 2007, p. 18.
40 Alva and Donnan 1993; Alva and Chero 2008; and Aimi et al. 2016. Shimada suggests that these women could correspond to secondary burials (Shimada et al. 2006, p. 231).
41 Mujica et al. 2007, p. 223.
42 Mujica et al. 2007, p. 215.
43 Mujica et al. 2007, p. 187. Since the discovery of the Lady of Cao, some interpretations have been made that assume that there was gender equality in the Moche era. In addition, it has been celebrated that a woman 'achieved the same power as men'. This does nothing but simplify and trivialise a social struggle. These approaches are unfortunate if we consider the teenage girls murdered in the same context as Lady of Cao. This leads

funeral contexts located in San José de Moro (500–600 AD) in the Jequetepeque Valley[44] and Huaca de la Luna (300–700 AD) in the Moche Valley are relevant.[45]

The other group of archaeological contexts are those in which bodies were placed in plazas without a burial procedure. The best detailed cases are those recorded in Huaca de la Luna (Figure 5.2) in the lower valley of the Moche River. In the Plaza 3C, dated around the third and fourth centuries AD, 25 'complete' or 'almost complete' skeletons were found along with 46 sets of incomplete human remains and isolated bones.[46] It could be established that bodies do not corresponded to a single deposition event.[47] In all cases in which it was possible, bone analysis determined that the individuals were male and aged between adolescence and adulthood. Some showed fractures of the forearm, shoulder blade, ribs and hand bones, which were in the first healing stages at the time of death, suggesting prior injuries of perhaps a few weeks. As Verano points out,[48] fractures are consistent with those expected from fighting with blunt weapons such as clubs, so individuals could have been to be brought to the site after battle, or, if the fighting occurred in the same settlement, the individuals were held in place for a while before being killed. Cutting marks are also present in almost all of the bones, which suggests a process of flesh removal, not necessarily for direct human-consumption purposes.[49] Also, in some cervical vertebrae, cuts that are consistent with slaughter practices have been identified.[50] Some bodies had their arms tied behind their backs (Figure 5.3) and ropes on the neck, ankles and trunk,[51] which makes it possible to assume that they were forcibly held in some position. In fact, Steve Bourget found traces of wood posts that could be evidence of the 'display' of these prisoners (Figure 5.4).[52]

In the same building of the Huaca de La Luna, in Plaza 3A, the bodies of 35 male individuals were located, with evidence of wounds to ribs that were in the process of healing at times of death. In addition, it is suggested that fracture

---

us to an uncritical celebration of violence and power relations in general. For a critique of this simplification in the Moche case, see de la Torre and Lapi 2014, and for a more general framework, see Escoriza et al. 2014, especially the introduction and presentation.

44   Castillo and Donnan 1994b; Castillo 2000.
45   Uceda 2018.
46   Verano et al. 2007, p. 226.
47   Tufinio 2006.
48   Verano et al. 2007, p. 252.
49   Verano et al 2007, p. 250.
50   Verano et al. 2007, figure 271, p. 227.
51   Verano et al. 2007, figure 271, p. 228.
52   Bourget 2001, p. 101.

VIOLENCE IN THE PREHISPANIC ANDES   151

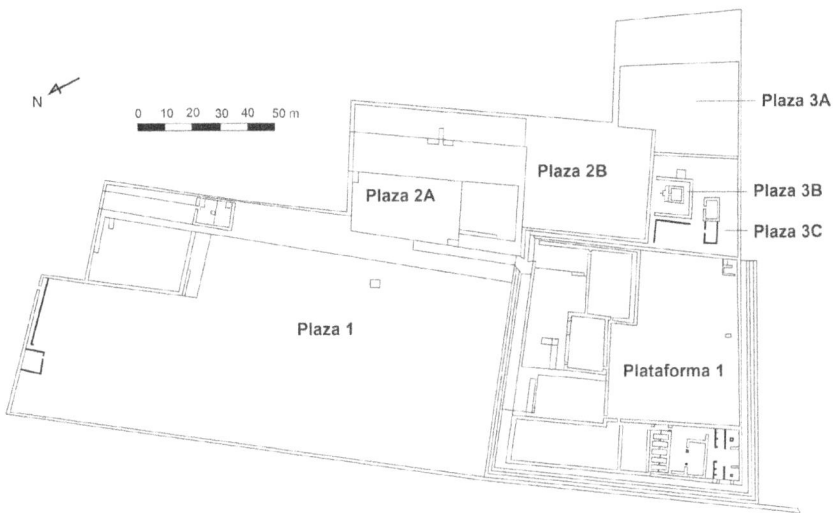

FIGURE 5.2 Map of Huaca de la Luna.
REDRAWN FROM SHIMADA ET AL. 2006

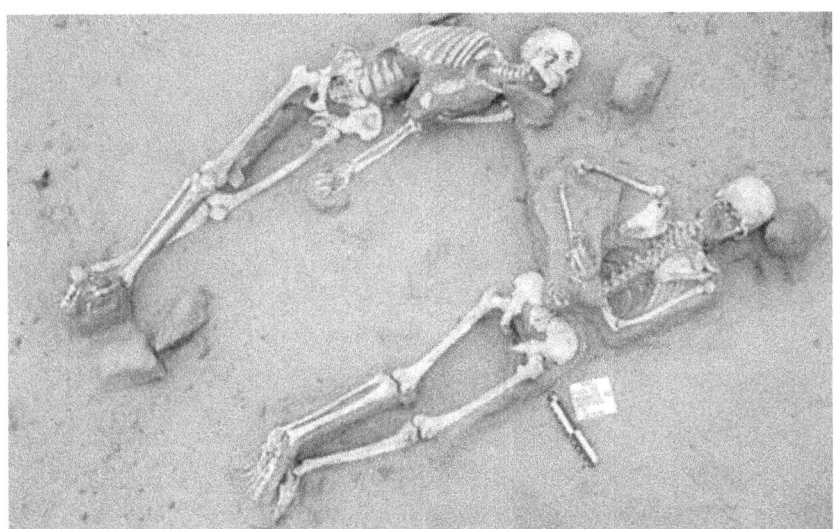

FIGURE 5.3 View of complete articulated individual, with their hands tied behind their back.
AFTER UCEDA ET AL. 2016, P. 172

FIGURE 5.4
Modelled ceramic vessel representing a prisoner tied to a tree and attacked by birds.
THE METROPOLITAN MUSEUM OF ART

marks on the hands could be evidence of torture,[53] which makes it possible to state that these individuals were treated as prisoners of war.[54]

A similar situation is seen on the main platform of the Huaca Cao Viejo, where male adult individuals with similar characteristics to those at Huaca de la Luna were found.[55] Similar contexts to those just mentioned (associated with monumental architecture) do not exist in other places, or, if they do, they have not been located or excavated. An example that could resemble the latter case is the fosse found in Pacatnamú, where bodies still retained reed ropes to their hands and feet; however, in this case, the bodies were not left in plazas.[56]

A very common discussion in Moche archaeology has to do with the identity or cultural belonging of the sacrificed and of elite individuals as determ-

53   Bourget and Millaire 2000; Verano 2001b, and 2007; and Bourget 1997, and 2001.
54   Quilter 2002, p. 167.
55   Franco 2019.
56   Verano 1986.

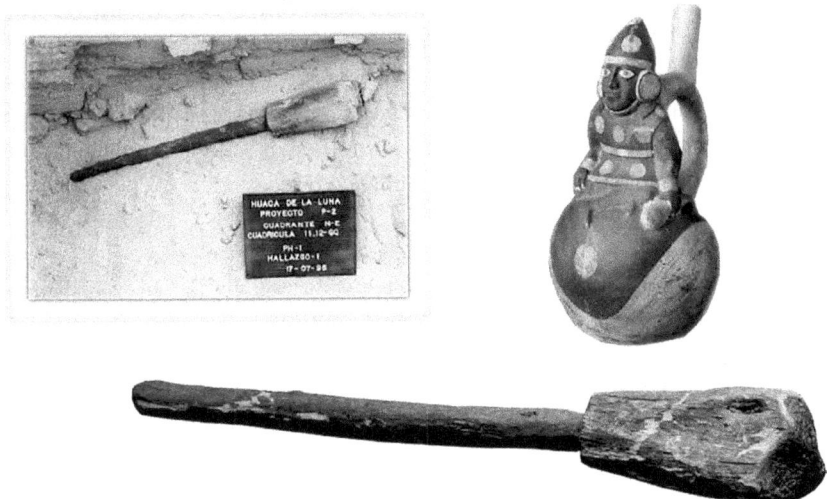

FIGURE 5.5 Modelled ceramic vessel and wooden mace recovered from Tomb 1 of Platform II in Huaca de la Luna.
AFTER UCEDA ET AL. 2016, P. 169

ined from mitochondrial DNA[57] and isotopic studies.[58] However, it is rarely considered that the relationship between victims (the sacrificed) and elite personages does not necessarily have to do with biological proximity but with social class. For example, lords and commoners can share the same isotopic marks when living in the same region, and mitochondrial DNA studies report on phylogenetic traits that do not strictly correspond to social classes or other types of social differentiation.

Aggressors or subjects who enacted violence, called warriors, have been defined in relation to the artefacts associated with their graves. When these grave goods are extraordinary, they are the defined as 'warrior-priests'.[59] Elements considered as means of violence are not only associated with men, but also women, the more spectacular case being that of the Lady of Cao. Moreover, a burial has been recorded of two individuals, associated with ceramic representations of sacrifice and fighting, on Platform II of Huaca de la Luna. One of them (Tomb 1) showed, as part of the offerings, a wooden mace that had a thin layer of human blood (Figure 5.5).[60]

57 Shimada et al. 2006.
58 Toyne et al. 2016.
59 Alva and Chero 1999.
60 Bourget and Newman 1998; Uceda et al. 2016, p. 170.

Despite the evidence discussed here, it is necessary to raise new research questions based on human bone analysis that can link activity patterns directly in the bone – such as the recurrent use of slingshots, maces or spear throwers – and, if possible, what manner and in what range of feasibility these activities can be identified osteologically. Currently, there is a large sample of human remains available for the development of such research.

4.2 Means for Violence

In Moche society, a great quantity of objects were created to serve exclusively as movable and immovable weapons of attack and defence. Among the movable were those that involved medium- and long-distance confrontations, mainly throwing-weapons such as arrows, slings, spears, etc., and fighting body-to-body, such as daggers, shields, brass knuckles and clubs.[61] However, many of these do not have corresponding analyses, or their exact origin is unknown. Almost all the attack and defence weapons, especially the clubs, have been found on the surface and in burials, even without being characterised chronologically and contextually.[62] In addition, the vast majority comes from looting remains. All this has greatly complicated the investigation of the means of violence. The most emblematic cases are those found in large tombs, although the ornaments that include these weapons have helped reinforce the idea that they correspond to warriors who participated in ritual battles.[63]

Immovable weapons, especially fortresses, are the most representative of immobile defence arms,[64] but they are not present in the entire Moche area. There are also surveillance posts, walls and checkpoints.[65] These were built around the third and fourth centuries AD,[66] although many fortresses have not been dated by radiocarbon and are associated with different chronologies by their surface ceramic materials. These fortifications include trench systems,

---

61   Chamussy 2012; Mayer 1988.
62   There are a large number of clubs and other weapons in national and international collections and museums. In Peru, one of the great collections for the Moche case is in the Larco Museum. For a general review of metal weapons from Peru and stored in different museums, consult Mayer 1998.
63   For example, within the grave goods of the Lady of Cao, 23 spear throwers and two clubs were collected (Mujica et al. 2007, p. 235).
64   Willey 1953; Wilson 1988; and Dillehay 2001.
65   Castillo 2007; Rosas 2007; Billman 1996; Wilson 1988; Giersz 2011. Although these are not strictly means of violence, they help propose hypotheses about the control of people and territories. The same can be mentioned for the valleys of Casma, Nepeña and Santa (Proulx 1968; Wilson 1995, and 1988).
66   Rosas 2007; Dillehay et al. 2009; and Wilson 1988.

ditches and high walls with parapets, with locations in strategically difficult-to-access places. This type of construction fulfilled different goals, ranging from protecting a sector of a community from local aggressors[67] to the protection of Moche territories against an external enemy.[68] A good example is the line of fortifications conveniently situated in the neck of the Virú Valley[69] that served to protect the frontiers of the Moche territories against other societies, such as the Cajamarca or Recuay.

On the other hand, there are iconographic representations of the exercise of violence in different types of support, including those that are movable (sculptures, ceramic representations) (Figure 5.4) and immovable (friezes and murals) (Figure 5.6). Some studies, like those of Christopher Donnan (1977) and Anne-Marie Hocquenghem (1987), have been important for their attempt to order the representations based on recurrent stylistic patterns and for trying to link them with ethnohistoric narratives. However, on some occasions, iconographic representations are used, by many researchers, to express explanations apart from actual violence.

Beyond the above discussion, there are two types of representations of violence: representations of torture, sacrifice and murder, and representations of fighting. Both kinds of activities are represented in a multitude of supports (ceramic, mud, lithic and textile). Depictions of fighting can be intra- or intergroup, and they are recognised by the attires worn by the combatants. In the case of intergroup fighting, the most frequent representations are of battles between the Moche and Recuay factions.[70]

The most impressive and relevant representations, due to their public nature, are those found on the walls of public spaces ('plazas') of monumental buildings like Huaca de la Luna and Huaca Cao. In the main plazas of these monuments, murals depict prisoners, bound and naked, driven straight to their death. These scenes even represent the blood of the victims. Likewise, in the Moche site of Pañamarca in Nepeña Valley, murals show scenes of sacrifice and fighting,[71] featuring clubs and shields. These examples show the importance not only of executing prisoners, but, above all, to expose the practice to a large audience. This can also be related to the practice of exposing the bodies after murder, as demonstrated by individuals found in the Huaca de la Luna.

---

67   Dillehay 2001.
68   Wilson 1987; Rosas 2007; and Lau 2016.
69   Lau 2016, p. 59.
70   Lau 2004, and Lau 2016, p. 64. See for example Pardo and Rucabado 2016, figures 11 and 76 a–b.
71   Bonavía 2007.

FIGURE 5.6 Mural depicting prisoners in Huaca de la Luna.
PHOTOGRAPHY BY ALEX GONZALES-PANTA

Therefore, beyond the interpretations that have been proposed, we can say that many representations are embedded in a communication system that supported violence as a transmission mechanism of information. Although this is evident, the meaning of such depicted practices is still far from being revealed. They can be commemorative representations of mythical character and, therefore, of religious or ritualistic significance. However, they can also be representations of ideological discourses that frame intimidating violence. Or, in another way, overexposures of violence could well have served as a form of invisibility, naturalising violent practices during the Moche period. In one sense or another, the relationships that can be established between these possible forms of violence and political-economic organisation can provide greater insights into their nature, which we will discuss later

4.3 Spaces for Violence

When we talk about the violated subjects of Huaca de la Luna (see 3.1.1 *Subjects of Violence, or Victims*), the analysis of bodies suggests that spaces existed for their detention and possible torture. However, exact locations have not been confirmed. On the other hand, the architectural spaces where the bodies mentioned in section 3.1.1 were found reveal to us that these sites were sufficiently unique, serving as places where murders were carried out, probably for 'public' exhibition. The most notable evidence is found in Plazas 3A, 3B and 3C of Huaca de la Luna[72] and in those of Huaca Cao.[73] Other buildings that could have the same archaeological contexts, given their architectural similarities, are those from Huaca Dos Cabezas in the Jequetepeque Valley and Pañamarca in the Nepeña Valley.

It's been hypothesised that in the Lambayeque Valley, on the Pampa Grande site, the forced labour of subjugated populations realised the work of ruling elites, including the construction of walls that separated and confined residential areas located south of the settlement. This sector differs from the northern sector, where the elite lived, in terms of architecture, work tools, ceramics and consumed resources.[74] It is postulated that the history of the location ended with a fire and subsequent abandonment of the site, possibly due to a revolt of the population of the southern sector.[75] A similar situation has been postulated for the Galindo site in the Moche Valley.[76] In this settlement, walls were built to separate and isolate sectors of the population in spaces called 'cercaduras'.[77] Just as in the Pampa Grande site, the situation is theorised to have ended with a revolt that ended with the site's abandonment.

---

72 Bourget 1997, and 2001; Bourget and Millaire 2000; Tufinio 2000, 2001, 2004, and 2006.
73 Franco 2019.
74 Shimada and Maguiña 1994, p. 56; Shimada 1994b, p. 208.
75 Shimada 1994b, pp. 249–54.
76 Bawden 1996.
77 For a definition and other cases of this type of structure, see Gamboa 2008.

5   Production, Social Relationships and Moche Violence

The elements linked to violence mentioned in this chapter did not exist in some kind of social vacuum. They were part of other much broader and more fundamental social relationships. Below, we give an approximation of these social relationships in Moche society.

In the case of the Moche, basic subsistence production was guaranteed by an important agricultural system.[78] Thus, many early Moche communities were related to the lands at the bottom of the valley as well as on the slopes on the hills.[79] This situation was accentuated with the passage of centuries, with some nuances in each of the northern coastal valleys, as fishing, livestock and hunting were added to subsistence production.[80] This basic production made possible the quantitative and qualitative growth of artisanal productions such as ceramics, metals, textiles and other objects, especially in some important sites such as Huaca de la Luna in the Moche Valley,[81] Cerro Mayal in the Chicama Valley,[82] and, towards the last stages of Moche development, in Pampa Grande in the Lambayeque Valley.[83] In these settlements, fancy ceramic vessels and metal objects were produced. There are other settlements of ceramic production, but not of the quantitative and qualitative characteristics of the above mentioned. Rather, these other sites were characterised by the production of utilitarian ceramics (domestic) and some decorative objects, such as in the case of Pampa Inca[84] in the Santa Valley.

Spatial and territorial studies of regional scope have defined several types of settlements, differentiated by their architectural characteristics (design and construction materials).[85] These settlements were associated with different work instruments and had access to different consumption goods. In addition, these sites show a growth of complexity in their architectural constructions: productive constructions (irrigation canals, dams) and public-ceremonial and domestic buildings.

---

78   Billman 2010, p. 181; Gamboa and Nesbitt 2012, p. 118.
79   Pozorski 1979, p. 175; Billman 1996; Canziani 2009; and Wilson 1988.
80   Pozorski 1982; Campbell 2000; Vázquez and Rosales 1998.
81   Gayoso 2011.
82   Russell et al. 1994.
83   Shimada 1994b.
84   Wilson 1988, p. 211.
85   Lambayeque valleys (Shimada and Maguiña 1994); Zaña valley (Boza 2006); Jequetepeque valley (Dillehay et al. 2009); Chicama and Moche valley (Billman 1996); Virú valley (Willey 1953); Santa valley (Wilson 1988); Nepeña valley (Proulx 1968, 1982); Casma valley (Wilson 1995); Culebras valley (Giersz and Prządka 2009).

Although the greatest efforts of archaeological excavation have been concentrated in the settlements that present monumental buildings (temples), private buildings (palace-houses), plazas, and elite domestic architecture, there are some works that account for settlements characterised as villages with the presence of domestic architecture (houses) of commoners.[86] Settlements with monumental architecture have, generally, a higher proportion of work instruments linked to the tools, ceramics, textiles and metal artefact production,[87] and an absence of agricultural production instruments[88] and fishing instruments. The 'village' settlements are mostly linked to tools for agricultural work. For example, in places in the Moche Valley such as Santa Rosa-Quirihuac and Ciudad de Dios, a large number of stone hoes were recovered.[89]

By the third and fourth centuries AD, sites traditionally considered as the center of the state of Moche reached a greater architectural volume and greater urban complexity (for example, Huacas de Moche, Mocollope and El Brujo). Furthermore, these settlements reached levels of craft production before unknown.[90] In fact, archaeological evidence suggests that craft production was specialised and concentrated in workshops of these sites, especially in Huaca de la Luna. Although there is evidence of ceramic production elsewhere, it is clear that there was a greater concentration of production in the settlements of the Chicama and Moche valleys. The absence of production sectors in other sites, although there was a presence of other elaborate artefacts, could indicate a control of the production of fancy ceramics and metals ornaments, distributed among the different social spaces with primary orientation towards the elites or dominant groups. It is true that this absence may also be due to the lack of more extensive archaeological works such as those developed in Huaca de la Luna. In any case, the evidence suggests that the control of production and, above all, the distribution of the most elaborated goods were directed primarily towards a specific group linked to architectural spaces and burials characterised as elite. This does not necessarily lead to the validation of a centralised state, because, as some researchers point out, there are many quantitative and qualitative differences that allow doubting of such centralisation.[91] As some novel proposals point out,[92] the existence of possible scenarios where elites

---

86 Shimada and Maguiña 1994; Gumerman and Briceño 2003.
87 Bennier 2019; Gayoso 2011; Shimada 2001; Fraresso 2008.
88 Chapdelaine 2001.
89 Billman 1997; Gumerman and Briceño 2003.
90 Bernier 2009; Gayoso 2011.
91 Castillo and Donnan 1994a; Shimada 1994a, and 2010.
92 Quilter 2010; Quilter and Koons 2012; Swenson 2015; and Rosas 2017.

of each valley, though related regionally, acted as independent social organisations can be a path of research. However, we also think that such proposals should be validated empirically and not only raised from a new model based exclusively in the ethnohistorical record.[93]

Beyond this discussion, it is possible to identify, with some differences, over seven centuries of occupation across the Moche valleys, featuring growths and abandonments of both monumental and residential elite and non-elite architecture built with precarious materials. The last social spaces were associated with production tools in agriculture as well. Although by around the third century AD in these valleys the growth of craft production can also be observed in fancy ceramic, control of distribution remained the same. In fact, this same growth continued to be greater in Huaca de la Luna, which only found a possible parallel in the Lambayeque Valley in the Pampa Grande site in the sixth century AD. It was also during these centuries that there was a greater presence of fine ceramics in the Santa, Nepeña and Culebras valleys.

The differentiated participation in production, organised and controlled by central or regional elites, concluded with uneven access to what was produced. These uneven social relationships could be defined as exploitation[94] and should not be obviated when we evaluate the archaeological evidence, especially when we are focused on research of violent practices. As we mentioned, these violent practices were materialised in the different elements: subjects, means and spaces of violence. This situation leads us to point out that the organisation of production, distribution and consumption in the Moche society was guaranteed by the effective control by the elites of the means of production and the labour force. This is evident in the case of the production of fine ceramics and metal ornaments, where control was had over the raw materials and the instruments and knowledge necessary to produce them.

On the other hand, the archaeological data suggesting effective violence, especially of violated subjects, shows an increase around the second and third centuries AD, and it is above all visible in settlements of the Chicama and Moche valleys, including public spaces. However, this data may be due to increased archaeological excavations in monumental sites of these valleys. The presence of buildings with similar features in other valleys suggests similar archaeological contexts.

The resources for these constructions, the distribution of spaces and means for violence, and the similarities in the tombs of elites with human offerings

---

93   For a discussion about the 'Southern Moche state', see Tantaleán 2015.
94   We understand exploitation as the 'process of practical usurpation of people's livelihoods in concrete conditions and by a defined class of individuals'. Lull 2005, pp. 13–14.

serve to indicate that the social relationships of exploitation were guaranteed by physical violence. Even these relationships of violence went beyond of the border of the valleys and helped to maintain the relations of exploitation in Moche society. This violence must have been accompanied by an ideological foundation, understood not as an epiphenomenon of the economic structure but as a social mechanism that consolidated asymmetrical social orders, always under the protection of means and production relations.

Archaeological data is still limited, and although it is mostly restricted to elites, it still allows us to propose as a hypothesis that an elite contributed, with a social class 'spirit', to maintaining exploitation relations thanks to the exercise of physical and ideological violence. This exploitation and these violent relations were accentuated around the third and fourth centuries AD, reaching a level of symbolic improvement suggested in the mural representations of the Moche sites – including Huaca de la Luna, Huaca Cao Viejo and, perhaps, Pañamarca – and to ritual practices designed to produce, reproduce and legitimise them. But, at the same time, these violent practices speak to a social group who were not passive actors, because the sophistication of their reaction informs us of the resistance that they could undertake. We do not know the scope of these forms of resistance, such as political negotiations, concessions or even violent revolts. All of these issues will require further archaeological research, posing similar types of questions to those that we have asked throughout this chapter.

6   Final Comments

This work is one approach to the research of violence in the Prehispanic central Andes. We have briefly outlined the problems faced by the various explanatory frameworks that are supported by anthropological and socio-political models. According to our approach, one way to escape this problem lies in starting from the study of archaeological objects as an objective way of historical approach. With this, we do not intend to delegitimise works that are developed from ethnographic and ethnohistoric sources. What interests us is to discuss their theoretical premises, the arguments for their validation and the theoretical and methodological consequences when transferring their models to the archaeological task.

We have raised the ways in which research on violence can be developed from a historical materialist approach. In this sense, our study is based on correlations of the objective materials of social life. As an example of the potential of our approach, we have focused on the social materiality that suggests relationships of physical and symbolic violence, which we have discussed in relation to the forms of production organisation and social relations of the Moche. This analysis also allows us to point out the social division of labour, the ownership of means of production and the consumption of goods that show relations of social inequality in the Moche world, inequality that can be characterised as one of exploitation. This exploitation was ensured by a strong government that used mechanisms of physical and ideological coercion for maintaining inequalities. Such ideological mechanisms were guaranteed by effective physical violence, a response to which – conflict – may be suggested by revolts that occurred in Pampa Grande[95] and Galindo.[96] At the same time, the Moche elites had sufficient capacity to maintain a territory apart from other social groups, through negotiations and, sometimes, through violent actions, probably conflicts or wars.

We are still in a process of organisation and analysis of all available archaeological evidence, so what is stated in this text does not exhaust the existing Moche social materiality. However, what we have proposed serves to exemplify the role of violence and its importance for the reproduction of social inequalities. We hope to in future synthesise the abundant Moche material to validate hypotheses here proposed.

7   Coda

We would not like to leave this text without paying attention to a little-warned consequence of the hypothesis about the violence of the past, especially of the Moche case. There is a kind of positive assessment of the 'great' Moche leaders (men and women), leadership that was guaranteed by effective violence. Such assessment can be seen daily on media and cultural levels. These assessments help to build or cement a common everyday sense that normalises oppression, exploitation and violence as legitimate means to achieve 'success', especially when this violence is exercised by leaders. The treatment of the personages found in the rich Moche tombs is proof of this, hiding the suffering of large social groups, especially commoners that maintained the position and social reproduction of these leaders. This 'common sense' pervades many of the cultural polities in the Andes and from there raises the positive assessments in the general public. Thus, actions of resistance, sometimes violent by communities

---

95   Shimada 1994b.
96   Bawden 1996.

or subaltern groups, are condemned by common sense and the media, denying political and practical response on legitimate interests of defence. Thus, erased from the past and present are those people (women and men) who were murdered to act as offerings in graves, in plazas and, currently, in public demonstrations, in prisons and in daily life.

References

Aimi, Antonio, Walter Alva, Luis Chero, Marco Martini, Francesco Maspero and Emanuela Sibilia 2016, 'Hacia una nueva cronología de Sipán', in *Lambayeque, Nuevos horizontes de la arqueología peruana*, edited by Antonio Aimi, Krzysztof Makowski and Emilia Perassi, Milan: Ledizioni.

Alva, Walter 1994, *Sipán, descubrimiento e investigación*, Lima: Backus & Johnston S.A., Colección Cultura y Artes del Perú.

Alva, Walter y Christopher B. Donnan 1993, *Royal Tombs of Sipán*, Los Angeles, CA: Fowler Museum of Cultural History, University of California.

Alva, Walter and Luis Chero 2008, 'La tumba del sacerdote-guerrero', in *Sipán: El tesoro de las tumbas reales*, edited by Antonio Aimi, Walter Alva and Emilia Perassi, Firenze: Giunti.

Amnistía Internacional 2014, *La larga lucha de los pueblos indígenas de América en defensa de sus derechos*, available at: https://www.amnesty.org/download/Documents/4000/amr010022014es.pdf.

Arkush, Elizabeth 2012, 'Violence, Indigeneity, and Archaeological Interpretation in the Central Andes', in *The Ethics of Anthropology and Amerindian Research*, edited by Richard Chacón and Rubén Mendoza, New York: Springer.

Arkush, Elizabeth and Mark Allen (eds.) 2006, *The Archaeology of Warfare: Prehistories of Raiding and Conquest*, Gainesville, FL: University Press of Florida.

Bawden, Garth 1994, 'La paradoja estructural: La cultura Moche como ideología política', in *Moche: Propuestas y perspectivas*: Actas del Primer Coloquio sobre la Cultura Moche, Travaux de l'Institute Français d'Etudes Andines 79, edited by Santiago Uceda and Elías Mujica, Lima: Universidad Nacional de la Libertad-Trujillo & Instituto Francés de Estudios Andinos.

Bawden, Garth 1996, *The Moche*, London: Blackwell.

Berlin, Isaiah 2015, *Las raíces del Romanticismo*, Madrid: Taurus.

Bernier, Helène 2009, 'La producción especializada de la cerámica ritual mochica', *Estudios Atacameños*, 37: 157–78.

Billman, Brian 1996, *The Evolution of Prehistoric Political Organizations in the Moche Valley, Peru*, Ph.D. dissertation, Department of Anthropology, University of California, Santa Barbara.

Billman, Brian 2010, 'How Moche Rulers Came to Power: Investigating the Emergence of the Moche Political Economy', in *New Perspectives on Moche Political Organization*, edited by Jeffrey Quilter and Luis Jaime Castillo, Washington D.C.: Dumbarton Oaks Research Library and Collection.

Bonavia, Duccio 2007, 'Pañamarca, Valle de Nepeña', in *Arqueología y vida: Duccio Bonavia*, edited by Enrique Vergara, Trujillo: Universidad Nacional de Trujillo, and Instituto Francés de Estudios Andinos.

Bourget, Steve 1997, 'Las excavaciones en la Plaza 3A de la Huaca de la Luna', in *Investigaciones en la Huaca de la Luna 1995*, edited by Santiago Uceda, Elías Mujica, and Ricardo Morales. Trujillo: Universidad Nacional de la Libertad-Trujillo.

Bourget, Steve 2001, 'Rituals of Sacrifice: Its Practice at Huaca de la Luna and its Representation in Moche Iconography', *Moche Art and Archaeology in Ancient Peru*, edited by Joanne Pillsbury, Washington, D.C.: National Gallery of Art.

Bourget, Steve and Margaret Newman 1998, 'A Toast to the Ancestors: Ritual Warfare and Sacrificial Blood in Moche Culture', *Baessler Archiv*, 46: 85–106.

Bourget, Steve and Jean-François Millaire 2000, 'Las excavaciones en la Plaza 3A y Plataforma II de Huaca de la Luna', in *Investigaciones en la Huaca de la Luna 1997*, edited by Santiago Uceda, Elías Mujica, and Ricardo Morales, Trujillo: Universidad Nacional de Trujillo.

Boza, María Fernanda 2006, 'La ocupación mochica en los valles de Lambayeque y Zaña', *Arkeos, Revista Electrónica de Arqueología* PUCP, 1, 4: 29–55, available at: https://www.academia.edu/37214431/La_ocupaci%C3%B3n_Mochica_en_los_valles_de_Lambayeque_y_Za%C3%B1a.

Campbell, Kendall 2000, *Fauna, Subsistence Patterns and Complex Society at the El Brujo Site Complex, Perú*, Master's Thesis, Department of Anthropology, Northern Arizona University.

Canziani, José 2009, *Ciudad y Territorio en los Andes: Contribuciones a la Historia del Urbanismo Prehispánico*, Lima: Pontificia Universidad Católica del Perú.

Castillo, Luis Jaime 2000, 'Los rituales mochica de la muerte', in *Los dioses del Antiguo Perú*, edited by Krzysztof Makowski, Lima: Banco de Crédito del Perú, available at: http://sanjosedemoro.pucp.edu.pe/descargas/articulos/LosMochicasMuerte.pdf.

Castillo, Luis Jaime 2007, *La Gesta del Guerrero*, Lima: Pontificia Universidad Católica del Perú, available at: http://sanjosedemoro.pucp.edu.pe/descargas/articulos/La_gesta_del_guerrero.pdf.

Castillo, Luis Jaime and Christopher Donnan 1994a, 'Los mochicas del norte y los mochicas del sur, una perspectiva desde el Valle de Jequetepeque', in *Vicús*, edited by Krzysztof Makowski, Lima: Banco de Crédito del Perú, Colección Arte y Tesoros del Perú.

Castillo, Luis Jaime and Christopher Donnan 1994b, 'La ocupación moche de San José de Moro, Jequetepeque', in *Moche propuestas y perspectivas: Actas del Primer*

Coloquio sobre la Cultura Moche, Travaux de l'Institute Français d'Etudes Andines 79, edited by Santiago Uceda and Elías Mujica, Lima: Universidad Nacional de la Libertad-Trujillo and Instituto Francés de Estudios Andinos.

Carneiro, Robert 1970, 'A Theory of the Origin of the State', *Science*, 169: 733–8.

Chapdelaine, Claude 2001, 'The Growing Power of a Moche Urban Class', in *Moche Art and Archaeology in Ancient Peru*, edited by Joanne Pillsbury, Washington, D.C.: National Gallery of Art.

Chamussy, Vincent 2012, 'Empleo de las armas arrojadizas del área centro-andina: ¿Armas de caza o de guerra?', *Arqueología y Sociedad*, 24: 43–87.

Cotler, Julio and Ricardo Cuenca (eds.) 2011, *Las desigualdades en el Perú, balances críticos*, Lima: Instituto de Estudios Peruanos.

Crabtree, John and Francisco Durand 2017, *Peru Elite Power and Political Capture*, London: Zed Books.

De la Torre, Juan Carlos and Bárbara Lapi 2014, '¿Dónde están las mujeres? Reflexiones desde la arqueología peruana', *Revista de Investigaciones del Centro de Estudiantes de Arqueología UNMSM*, 8: 47–62.

Dillehay, Tom 2001, 'Town and Country in Late Moche Times: A View from Two Northern Valleys', in *Moche Art and Archaeology in Ancient Peru*, edited by Joanne Pillsbury, Washington, D.C.: National Gallery of Art.

Dillehay, Tom, Alan Kolata and Edward Swenson 2009, *Paisajes culturales en el Valle del Jequetepeque: Los yacimientos arqueológicos*, Trujillo: SIAN.

Donnan, Christopher 1995, 'Moche Funerary Practice', in *Tombs for the Living: Andean Mortuary Practices*, edited by Tom Dillehay, Washington D.C.: Dumbarton Oaks Research Library and Collection.

Eagleton, Terry 2015, *¿Por qué Marx tenía razón?*, Barcelona: Península.

Franco, Régulo 2016, *Mocollope, Pasado Prehispánico*, Chiclayo: Editora general Clene Salles.

Franco, Régulo 2016, 'Prestigio, poder y nuevos escenarios ceremoniales Moche en el Complejo El Brujo, costa norte del Perú', Segunda parte, *Arkinka*, 250: 80–9.

Franco, Régulo 2019, 'Sacrificios humanos en el mundo Moche: Una nueva mirada a la iconografía y a los hallazgos arqueológicos', *Quingnam*, 5: 83–132.

Fraresso, Carole 2008, 'El "sistema técnico" de la metalurgia de transformación en la cultura mochica: Nuevas perspectivas', in *Arqueología mochica: Nuevos enfoques*, Actes & Memoires de l'Institute Français d'Etudes Andines 21, edited by Luis Jaime Castillo, Hélène Bernier, Gregory Lockard and Julio Rucabado, Lima: Pontificia Universidad Católica del Perú, and Instituto Francés de Estudios Andinos.

Funari, Pedro Pablo A. and Andrés Zarankin (eds.) 2006, *Arqueología de la represión y la resistencia en América Latina 1960–1980*, Córdoba: Encuentro.

Gamboa, Jorge 2008, 'Plazas y cercaduras: Una aproximación a la arquitectura pública Moche IV y V en los valles de Moche y Santa', in *Arqueología mochica: Nuevos enfoques*, Actes & Memoires de l'Institute Français d'Etudes Andines 21, edited by Luis Jaime Castillo, Helène Bernier, Gregory Lockard and Julio Rucabado, Lima: Pontificia Universidad Católica del Perú, and Instituto Francés de Estudios Andinos.

Gamboa, Jorge and Jason Nesbitt 2012, 'La ocupación Moche en la Margen Norte del Valle Bajo de Moche, Costa Norte del Perú', *Arqueología y Sociedad*, 25: 115–42.

Gayoso, Luis 2011, *Los artesanos de la Ciudad de Barro: La organización de la producción artesanal en la Ciudad de las Huacas de Sol y de la Luna*, Tesis de Doctorado, Universidad Pablo de Olavide, Sevilla.

Ghezzi, Iván 2006, 'Religious Warfare at Chankillo', in *Andean Archaeology III*, edited by William Isbell and Helaine Silverman, New York: Springer.

Ghezzi, Iván 2007, 'La naturaleza de la guerra prehispánica temprana: La perspectiva desde Chankillo', *Revista Andina*, 44: 199–226.

Giersz, Miłosz 2011, 'Los guardianes de la frontera Sur: La presencia Moche en Culebras y Huarmey', *Andes*, 8: 271–310.

Giersz, Miłosz and Patrycja Prządka 2009, 'Cronología cultural y patrones de asentamiento prehispánico en el Valle del Rio Culebras, costa norcentral del Perú', *Arkeos, Revista Electrónica de Arqueología PUCP*, 4, 11: 1–40, available at: http://www2.congreso.gob.pe/sicr/cendocbib/con4_uibd.nsf/83539A8C0484225505257D11005CA6FB/$FILE/Cronolog%C3%ADaCulturalPatronesAsentamientoPrehisp%C3%A1nico.pdf.

Gumerman, George and Jesús Briceño 2003, 'Santa Rosa-Quirihuac y Ciudad de Dios: Dos asentamientos rurales en la parte media del Valle de Moche', in *Moche: Hacia el final del milenio*, Tomo I, edited by Uceda Santiago and Elías Mujica, Lima: Pontificia Universidad Católica del Perú.

Keeley, Lawrence H. 1996, *War Before Civilization*, New York: Oxford University Press.

Klaren, Peter 2003, *The Time of Troubles (1980–2000). Modern Violence and the Long Sweep of Peruvian History*, London: Institute for Latin American Studies (ILAS).

Hobbes, Thomas 2005 [1651], *Del ciudadano y Leviatán*, Madrid: Tecnos.

Hocquenghem, Anne Marie 1987, *Iconografía mochica*, Lima: Pontificia Universidad Católica del Perú.

Lau, George 2004, 'Object of Contention: An Examination of Recuay-Moche Combat Imagery', *Cambridge Archaeological Journal*, 14, 2: 163–84.

Lau, George 2016, 'Culturas en Contacto: La Interacción entre Recuay y Moche en el Norte del Perú', in *Moche y sus Vecinos, Reconstruyendo Identidades*, edited by Cecilia Pardo and Julio Rucabado, Lima: Museo de Arte de Lima (MALI).

Landa, Carlos and Odlanyer Hernández de Lara 2014, *Sobre campos de batalla. Arqueología de conflictos bélicos en América Latina*, Buenos Aires: Aspha.

López Mazz, José y Mónica Berón (eds.) 2014, *Indicadores arqueológicos de violencia, guerra y conflicto en Sudamérica*, Montevideo: Comisión Sectorial de Investigación Científica and Universidad de la República de Uruguay.

Lull, Vicente 2005, 'Marx, producción, sociedad y arqueología', *Trabajos de Prehistoria*, 62, 1: 7–26.

Lull, Vicente y Rafael Micó 2007, *Arqueología del origen del Estado: Las teorías*, Barcelona: Bellaterra.

Lull, Vicente, Rafael Micó, Cristina Rihuete and Roberto Risch 2006, 'La investigación de la violencia: Una aproximación desde la arqueología', *Cypsela*, 16: 87–108.

Lull, Vicente, Rafael Micó, Cristina Rihuete and Roberto Risch 2015, 'Gewalt-ein Beitrag zu deren Wahrnehmung und Bedingungen', in *Krieg: Eine Archäologische Spurensuche*, edited by Harald Meller and Michael Schefzik, Halle (Saale): Theiss.

Lumbreras, Luis 1981, *Los orígenes de la civilización en el Perú*, Lima: Milla Batres.

Manrique, Nelson 2002, *El Tiempo del miedo, violencia política en el Perú. Los años oscuros. Violencia y racismo en el Perú*, Lima: Fondo Editorial del Congreso del Perú.

Marx, Karl 1970 [1859], *Contribución a la Crítica de la Economía Política*, Madrid: Alberto Corazón Editor.

Marx, Karl 1971 [1857–58], *Elementos fundamentales para la Crítica de la Economía Política (Grundrisse)*, México D.F.: Fondo de Cultura Económica.

Marx, Karl 1975 [1845], 'Tesis sobre Feuerbach', in *Marx and Engels Obras Escogidas*, Moscow: Progreso.

Marx, Karl and Frederic Engels 1970 [1846], *La ideología alemana*, Barcelona: Pueblos Unidos-Grijalbo.

Marx, Karl and Friedrich Engels 1977, *Selected Letters*, Peking: Foreign Language Press.

Marx, Karl and Eric Hobsbawm 1979 [1964], *Formas económicas precapitalistas*, Barcelona: Crítica.

Mauss, Marcel 2010 [1925], *Ensayo sobre el don, forma y función del intercambio en las sociedades srcaicas*, Madrid: Katz.

Mayer, Eugen Friedrich 1998, *Armas y herramientas de metal prehispánicas en Perú*, M.A.V.A. 55, Mainz: Verlag Phillip von Zabern.

Millaire, François 2002, *Moche Burial Patterns: An Investigation into Prehispanic Social Structure*, Oxford: Archaeopress.

Millaire, François and Magali Morlion (eds.) 2009, *Gallinazo: An Early Cultural Tradition on the Peruvian North Coast*, Los Angeles, CA: Cotsen Institute of Archaeology Press.

Mujica, Elías, Régulo Franco et al. 2007, *El Brujo. Centro Ceremonial Moche en el Valle de Chicama*, Lima: Fundación Wiese, ING Fondos and AFP Integra.

Murra, John 1972, 'El "control vertical" de un máximo de pisos ecológicos en la economía de las sociedades andinas', in *Visita a la Provincia de León de Huánuco en 1562, Iñigo Ortiz de Zúñiga*, edited by John Murra, Huánuco: Universidad Nacional Hermilio Valdizán.

Murra, John 1975, *Formaciones económicas y políticas del mundo andino*, Lima: Instituto de Estudios Peruanos.

Nielsen, Axel and William Walker (eds.) 2009, *Warfare in Cultural Context: Practice, Agency, and the Archaeology of Violence*, Tucson, AZ: University of Arizona Press.

Pardo, Cecilia y Julio Rucabado (eds.) 2016, *Moche y sus vecinos. Reconstruyendo identidades*, Lima: Museo de Arte de Lima (MALI).

Polanyi, Karl 1991 [1944], *La gran transformación*, México D.F.: Fondo de Cultura Económica.

Pozorski, Shelia 1979, 'Prehistoric Diet and Subsistence of the Moche Valley, Peru', *World Archaeology*, 11, 2: 163–84.

Pozorski, Shelia 1987, 'Theocracy vs. Militarism: The Significance of the Casma Valley in Understanding Early State Formation', in *The Origins and Development of the Andean State*, edited by Jonathan Haas, Shelia Pozorski and Thomas Pozorski, Cambridge: Cambridge University Press.

Pozorski 1982 'Early Social Stratification and Subsistence Systems: The Caballo Muerto Complex', in *Chan Chan: Andean Desert City*, edited by Michael Moseley and Kent Day, Albuquerque: University of New Mexico Press.

Proulx, Donald 1968, *An Archaeological Survey of the Nepeña Valley, Peru*, Research Report 2, Amherst, MA: Department of Anthropology, University of Massachusetts.

Quilter, Jeffrey 2002, 'Moche Politics, Religion, and Warfare', *Journal of World Prehistory*, 16: 145–95.

Quilter, Jeffrey 2010, 'Moche: Archaeology, Ethnicity, Identity', *Bulletin de l'Institut Français d'Études Andines*, 39, 2: 225–41.

Quilter, Jeffrey and Michele Koons 2012, 'The Fall of the Moche: A Critique of Claims for South America's First State', *Latin American Antiquity*, 23, 2: 127–43.

Remy, María Isabel 1991, 'Los discursos sobre la violencia en los Andes: Algunas reflexiones a propósito del Chiaraje', in *Poder y violencia en los Andes*, 265–71, compiled by Henrique Urbano, edited by Mirko Lauer, Cuzco: Centro de Estudios Regionales Andinos Bartolome de las Casas.

Rosas, Marco 2007, 'Nuevas perspectivas acerca del colapso Moche en el bajo Jequetepeque: Resultados preliminares de la segunda campaña de investigación del Proyecto Arqueológico Cerro Chepén', *Bulletin de l'Institut Français d'Études Andines*, 36, 2: 221–40.

Rosas, Marco 2017, 'La cultura mochica: Confrontando el modelo estatal con una perspectiva andina', in *Repensar el Antiguo Perú. Aportes desde la arqueología*, edited by Rafael Vega-Centeno, Lima: Pontificia Universidad Católica del Perú and Instituto de Estudios Peruanos.

Rostworowski, María 1983, *Estructuras andinas del poder: Ideología religiosa y política*, Lima: Instituto de Estudios Peruanos.

Rostworowski, María 1999, *History of the Inca Realm*, Cambridge and New York: Cambridge University Press.

Russell, Glenn, Leonard Banks and Jesús Briceño 1994, 'Cerro Mayal: Nuevos datos sobre la producción cerámica Moche en el Valle Chicama', *Moche propuestas y perspectivas*: *Actas del Primer Coloquio sobre la Cultura Moche*, Travaux de l'Institute Français d'Etudes Andines 79, edited by Santiago Uceda and Elías Mujica, Lima: Universidad Nacional de la Libertad-Trujillo and Instituto Francés de Estudios Andinos.

San Francisco, Alexander; Miguel Fuentes and Jairo Sepúlveda 2010, 'Hacia una arqueología del Estadio Víctor Jara. Campo de detención y tortura masiva de la dictadura en Chile (1973–1974)', *Revista de Arqueología Histórica Argentina y Latinoamericana*, 4: 91–116.

Shimada, Izumi 1994a, 'Los Modelos de organización sociopolítica de la cultura Moche: Nuevos datos y perspectivas', in *Moche Propuestas y Perspectivas*: *Actas del Primer Coloquio sobre la Cultura Moche*, Travaux de l'Institute Français d'Etudes Andines 79, edited by Santiago Uceda and Elías Mujica, Lima: Universidad Nacional de la Libertad-Trujillo, and Instituto Francés de Estudios Andinos.

Shimada, Izumi 1994b, *Pampa Grande and the Mochica Culture*, Austin, TX: University of Texas Press.

Shimada, Izumi 2001, 'Late Moche Urban Craft Production: A First Approximation', in *Moche Art and Archaeology in Ancient Peru*, edited by Joanne Pillsbury, Washington, D.C.: National Gallery of Art.

Shimada, Izumi 2010, 'Moche Sociopolitical Organization: Rethinking the Data, Approaches, and Models', in *New Perspectives on Moche Political Organization*, edited by Jeffrey Quilter and Luis Jaime Castillo, Washington, D.C.: Dumbarton Oaks Research Library and Collections.

Shimada, Izumi and Adriana Maguiña 1994, 'Nueva visión sobre la cultura Gallinazo y su relación con la cultura Moche', in *Moche: Propuestas y perspectivas: Actas del Primer Coloquio sobre la Cultura Moche*, Travaux de l'Institute Français d'Etudes Andines 79, edited by Santiago Uceda and Elías Mujica, Lima: Universidad Nacional de la Libertad-Trujillo, Instituto Francés de Estudios Andinos, and FOMCIENCIAS.

Shimada, Izumi, Ken-Ichi Shinoda, Walter Alva, Bourget Steve and Santiago Uceda 2006, 'Estudios arqueogenéticos de las poblaciones prehispánicas mochica y sicán: Resultados e implicancias', *Arqueología y Sociedad*, 17, 2006: 223–54.

Solís, Juan and Marcelo Moriconi 2014, *Atlas de la violencia en América Latina*, San Luis Potosi: Universidad Autónoma de San Luis Potosí, Mexico.

Stanish, Charles 2001, 'The Origin of State Societies in South America', *Annual Review of Anthropology*, 30: 40–64.

Strong, William and Cliford Evans 1952, *Cultural Stratigraphy in the Virú Valley, Northern Perú: The Formative and Florescent Epoch*, Columbia Studies in Archaeology and Ethnology 4, New York: Columbia University Press.

Swenson, Edward 2015, 'The Materialities of Place Making in the Ancient Andes: A Critical Appraisal of the Ontological Turn in Archaeological Interpretation', *Journal of Archaeological Method and Theory*, 22, 3: 677–712.

Tantaleán, Henry 2015, 'Hacia una arqueología dialéctica: Una heurística y una explicación del fenómeno Moche', *Revista Chilena de Antropología*, 31: 63–78.

Topic, John and Theresa Topic 1997, 'Hacia una comprensión conceptual de la guerra andina', in *Arqueología, antropología e historia en los Andes. Homenaje a María Rostworowski*, edited by Javier Flores and Rafael Varón, Lima: Instituto de Estudios Peruanos.

Toyne, Marla, John Verano, Christine White and Fred Logstaffe 2016, 'La vida de un guerrero: Un análisis isotópico del sacrificio y la guerra Moche', in *Moche y sus vecinos, Reconstruyendo Identidades*, edited by Cecilia Pardo and Julio Rucabado, Lima: Museo de Arte de Lima (MALI).

Trinidad, Escoriza Mateu, M. Juana López, and Ana Navarro Ortega (eds.) 2014, *Mujeres y arqueología: Nuevas aportaciones desde el Materialismo Histórico: Homenaje al Profesor Manuel Carrilero Millán*, Granada: Junta de Andalucía, Consejería de Innovación, Ciencia y Empresa.

Tufinio, Moisés 2000, 'Excavaciones en la Plaza 3C', in *Informe técnico 1999: Proyecto Arqueológico Huaca de La Luna*, edited by Santiago Uceda and Ricardo Morales, Trujillo: Universidad Nacional de Trujillo.

Tufinio, Moisés 2001, 'Excavaciones en la Plaza 3C', in *Informe técnico 2000: Proyecto arqueológico Huaca de La Luna*, edited by Santiago Uceda and Ricardo Morales, Trujillo: Universidad Nacional de Trujillo.

Tufinio, Moisés 2004, 'Excavaciones en la Plaza 3C de la Huaca de la Luna (1998–1999)', in *Investigaciones en la Huaca de la Luna 1998–1999*, edited by Santiago Uceda and Elías Mujica, Trujillo: Universidad Nacional de Trujillo.

Tufinio, Moisés 2006, 'Excavaciones en la Plaza 3C y sacrificios humanos en Huaca de la Luna', in *Proyecto arqueológico Huaca del Sol y de la Luna: Investigaciones en la Huaca de la Luna 2000*, edited by Santiago Uceda, Elías Mujica and Ricardo Morales, Trujillo: Facultad de Ciencias Sociales, Universidad Nacional de Trujillo and Patronato Huacas del Valle de Moche.

Uceda, Ricardo 2004, *Muerte en el Pentagonito: Los cementerios secretos del ejército peruano*, Bogotá: Planeta.

Uceda, Santiago 2018, 'Huacas del Sol y de la Luna: Cien Años Después de los Trabajos de Max Uhle', in *Proyecto Arqueológico Huaca de la Luna: Informe técnico 2006*, edited by Santiago Uceda, Ricardo Morales and Carlos Rengifo Trujillo: Universidad Nacional de Trujillo and Patronato Huacas del Valle de Moche.

Uceda, Santiago, Ricardo Morales and Elías Mujica 2016, *Huaca de la Luna, Templos y dioses*, Trujillo: World Monuments Found, Backus & Johnston S.A.

Vázquez, Víctor and Teresa Rosales 1998, 'Zooarqueología de la zona urbana Moche', in *Investigaciones en la Huaca de la Luna 1996*, edited by Santiago Uceda, Elías Mujica and Ricardo Morales, Trujillo: Universidad Nacional de Trujillo.

Vega, María del Carmen 2016, *A History of Violence: 3000 Years of Interpersonal and Intergroup Conflicts from the Initial to the Early Colonial Periods in the Peruvian Central Coast: A Bioarchaeological Perspective*, Electronic Thesis and Dissertation Repository 3836, available at: https://ir.lib.uwo.ca/etd/3836.

Verano, John 1986, 'A Mass Burial of Mutilated Individuals at Pacatnamu', in *The Pacatnamu Papers*, edited by Christopher Donnan and Guillermo Cock, Los Angeles, CA: Museum of Cultural History.

Verano, John 1997, 'Human skeletal remains from Tomb I, Sipán (Lambayeque river valley, Peru); and their social implications', *Antiquity*, 71, 273: 670–82.

Verano, John 2001a, 'War and Death in the Moche World: Osteological Evidence and Visual Discourse', in *Moche Art and Archaeology in Ancient Peru*, edited by Joanne Pillsbury, Washington D.C.: National Gallery of Art.

Verano, John 2001b, 'The Physical Evidence of Human Sacrifice in Ancient Peru', in *Ritual Sacrifice in Ancient*, edited by Elizabeth Benson and Anita Cook, Austin: University of Texas Press.

Verano, John 2014, 'Warfare and Captive Sacrifice in the Moche Culture', in *Embattled Bodies, Embattled Places: War in Pre-Columbian Mesoamerica and the Andes*, edited by Andrew Scherer and John Verano, Washington D.C.: Dumbarton Oaks.

Verano, John, Moisés Tufinio and Mellisa Lund 2007, 'Esqueletos humanos de la Plaza 3C de Huaca de la Luna', in *Investigaciones en la Huaca de la Luna 2001*, edited by Santiago Uceda, Elías Mujica and Ricardo Morales, Trujillo: Universidad Nacional de Trujillo.

Verano, John and Marla Toyne 2011, 'Estudio bioantropológico de los restos humanos del Sector II, Punta Lobos, Valle de Huarmey', *Andes*, 8: 449–74.

Walker, Phillip 2001, 'A Bioarchaeological Perspective on the History of Violence', *Annual Review of Anthropology*, 30: 573–96.

Willey, Gordon 1953, *Prehistoric Settlement Patterns in the Virú Valley, Perú*, Bureau of American Ethnology Bulletin 155, Washington D.C.: Smithsonian Institute.

Wilson, David 1987, 'Reconstructing Patterns of Early Warfare in the Lower Santa Valley: New Data on the Role of Conflict in the Origins of Complex North-Coast Society', in *The Origins and Development of the Andean State*, edited by Jonathan Haas, Shelia Pozorski and Thomas Pozorski, Cambridge: Cambridge University Press.

Wilson, David 1988, *Prehispanic Settlement Patterns in the Lower Santa Valley, Perú: A Regional Perspective on the Origins and Development of Complex North Coast Society*, Washington D.C.: Smithsonian Institution Press.

Wilson, David 1995, 'Prehispanic Settlement Patterns in the Casma Valley, North Coast of Peru: Preliminary Results to Date', *Journal of the Steward Anthropological Society*, 23, 1–2: 189–227.

CHAPTER 6

Marx, Marxism and Classical Antiquity

Steve Roskams

> Marxism is ... a philosophy, a tradition of thought, a mode of theoretical production, which has produced, and will produce many theories
> RANDALL MCGUIRE[1]

∴

> Marxism is, above all, a method of analysis – not analysis of texts, but analysis of social relations
> LEON TROTSKY[2]

∴

1   Introduction

Both of the above authors have made it clear in their writings that Marxism demands an integral relationship between political theory and practice: McGuire in *Archaeology as Political Action*,[3] Trotsky in nearly everything he published. Yet the two quotes encapsulate a debate at the heart of Marxism: does such an approach require the adoption of a particular philosophical position? Or does it rather involve specific ways of analysing society? In what follows, it will be clear that I am very much with Trotsky and the latter viewpoint. For me, historical materialism is about using analytical techniques to understand past and present society, with such understanding then being deployed to change the present world into something more fulfilling and sustainable in the future.

---

1   McGuire 2002, p. 9.
2   Trotsky 1906, p. 40.
3   McGuire 2008.

I have chosen to develop this argument in relation to antiquity in general, and the Roman Empire in particular, for two reasons. First, I know this period best archaeologically, at least for Britain and some other Roman provinces. Second, and more important, that empire has played a significant role in how modern society has constructed 'its' past and continues to do so. At the same time, this referential process studiously avoids any meaningful discussion of the material base on which these imperial systems were founded, an issue central to any Marxist approach.

Concerning the role of antiquity in the ideological structures of the Western world, advocates of liberal democracies portray Ancient Greece as diagnostic of European values such as civil rights and respect for learning. Yet such homage conveniently ignores Greek reliance on chattel slaves to support its citizens when voting, and to provide the intellectual space for aristocratic thinkers such as Plato and Aristotle to develop their perspectives. This agenda continues in attitudes to the Roman period. Thus, Beard's 'popular' account of Rome essentially mentions slaves in relation to their being freed, whilst even her more considered reflection on current themes in Classics, in its description of the lower members of society, concentrates only on attitudes towards ex-slaves.[4] In effect, she evades any proper consideration of the role of enslaved people *per se*, still less exploring the dire material circumstances in which this section of the population must have lived.[5]

In addition to supporting general values, the Roman Empire has also been used to justify the actions of modern imperialism by its apologists. Hence, classically educated rulers in the nineteenth century saw themselves as bringing 'civilisation' to other parts of the world when re-enacting Roman expansionism, for example with the French and Italian conquest of North Africa, or British control of the 'Middle East'. Indeed, the study of Roman archaeology was part of how English identity was established in relation to British imperialism at this time.[6] Such justifications have been reignited with the West's recent invasion of oil-rich territories in the latter region. This militarised process was portrayed in many media (without a hint of irony, it should be noted) as bringing civilisation to a region, Mesopotamia, which in fact witnessed the emergence of some of the earliest urbanised societies known to us.

In the course of nineteenth-century state formation in Europe, antiquity again played a role in the *Invention of Tradition*.[7] This is clearest in Germany,

---

4 Beard 2016, p. 46 for the former, Beard 2013, p. 17 ff. for the latter.
5 Joshel and Petersen 2014.
6 Hingley 2000.
7 Hobsbawn and Ranger 1983.

where the reconciliation of Roman and tribal Germanic pasts was a critical part of the state ideology that developed there after 1848. It is epitomised in the figure of Theodor Mommsen, an epigraphic expert on the Roman military who promoted a legal system for the emerging state modelled on Roman principles.[8] Finally, in recent decades, the very notion of a 'late antique period', distinguished from the Roman Empire at its height, resonates with the development of 'European identities' in the European Union,[9] especially when it draws on an overarching religious framework – early Christianity – as the glue that held the whole together.[10] In essence, therefore, Rome has been cited to support a range of political agendas in the last two centuries, making it important to appreciate the reality of social formations at that time.

In seeking to understand these real conditions, we must remember those facets of Roman society that contrast radically with anything seen in Western Europe before that time.[11] These differences include: the emergence of a professional army, which then conquered much of Western Europe and certain regions beyond; higher population densities and greater urbanisation than hitherto; increased division of labour, sometimes involving people working in 'state-run' factories; and a considerable escalation in the scale of long-distance, seaborne commerce.[12] Any explanation, therefore, must face the challenge of accounting for the qualitative distinctions between the Roman Empire and the rest of prehistory.

What follows seeks to argue that the Marxist concept of the slave mode of production provides a key analytical tool for exploring social dynamics at that time. Some recent writers have predicted (or at least hoped for) the return of Marx to this fray,[13] yet most scholars explicitly reject Marxism in trying to understand the past. Hence it is worth summarising first this non-Marxist conventional wisdom, both in wide-ranging analyses of past society, and in authors who consider the Roman period in particular.

---

[8] Hingley 2005, p. 31. Similar processes can be identified in Belgium with the historian Pirenne (James 2008) and in Italian unification (Mouritsen 1998).
[9] James 2008.
[10] Brown 1971.
[11] For details, see the various papers in Wacher 1987.
[12] Hopkins 1980. The latter development saw, inter alia, new foods replacing traditional counterparts in parts of Central Europe, first as luxuries but later as regular foodstuffs: Bekels and Jacomet 2003.
[13] Vanni 2017.

2   Conventional Descriptions of Classical Antiquity

A good example of the general approaches is Mann's account of *The Sources of Social Power: A History of Power from the Beginning to AD 1760*.[14] He interprets all pre-capitalist social development in relation to a mesh of military, ideological, political and economic factors, emphasising for Rome its martial aspects. Yet, to summarise bluntly his overall approach in this wide-ranging and accomplished commentary, Mann seems to give no concrete guidance on why one or another of these imperatives might have come to the fore at any particular time. Thus, he creates, in my opinion, detailed and fascinating, but ultimately descriptive, accounts of past social development.

Writers concerned solely with the Roman period have focused on a similar range of dynamics to those listed by Mann but tend to select one element over others. Unsurprisingly, their choices often align with the changing intellectual and political contexts in which they worked.[15] Thus, for much of the nineteenth century, the empire was interpreted in terms of bringing a civilising monumentality to different parts of Europe. Such vague cultural notions failed, however, to clarify how imperialism took over new regions and was able to impose its will thereafter. For such reasons, these perspectives increasingly gave way to highlighting military dynamics and accounts of imperial expansion, painting a picture of armed conquest and then consolidation across provinces. Archaeologically, evidence for marching camps and fortresses was emphasised and then, when imperial frontiers were set, included the investigation of large 'defensive' projects, as seen on the *Limes* in North Africa, Germany and Britain.

Yet this perspective, in turn, did not explain the desire to conquer in the first place. Many commentators thus rationalised Roman military expansion and its associated martial ideology as a product of political needs: Claudius invaded Britain in the first century CE because he required a victory to consolidate his authority, a similar motive lying behind Trajan's moves east and south in Europe in the second century CE. Political and administrative needs were also seen as dictating the subsequent development of infrastructure, notably roads for territorial control, in which Rome saw itself as conquering nature (and barbarians). Distances *en route*, measured by milestones incorporating epigraphically the emperor concerned with their construction, could be inter-

---

14   His aim is, in the process, 'to refute Marx and reorganise Weber' (Mann 1986, p. vii). How far he actually succeeds in this project has been questioned: Wickham 1988a.
15   Mattingly 2006 p. 3ff.

preted in political, rather than purely functional, terms.[16] Such imperatives were also seen in towns built along such routes, portrayed as places facilitating elite interaction to consolidate imperial identities, as much (or perhaps more so) in far off provinces as in the core.

If roads and associated towns were key politically, however, what underpinned their long-term stability? In the second half of the twentieth century, this question led, perhaps inevitably, to a greater emphasis on exploring the productive base of the empire in general and of landscape exploitation in particular: economic imperatives were seen as being of central importance.

The move between cultural, military, political and economic explanatory frameworks aligns with changes within archaeology as a whole,[17] as does the recent step in Roman archaeology beyond economic functionalism towards postmodern notions of identity.[18] This alternative focus has been underway for over a decade, perhaps part of a general paradigm shift in the humanities.[19] The trend is clearly evident in Mattingly's *magnum opus* discussing Roman Britain, which explains diverse social responses in terms of 'discrepant identities'.[20] Yet, within Romano-British archaeology, economic emphases still dominate interpretations, such imperatives taking a particular form: marketing opportunities. Hence, this perspective is discussed more fully next.

In this commercial paradigm, the Roman army was seen as not only providing infrastructure and landscape control, but also as creating demand and generating economic take off. Long-distance trade is portrayed as the empire's primary dynamic. Its scale is evidenced, for example, by the Monte Testaccio amphora rubbish dump outside Rome, with *tituli picti* and stamps on amphorae being held to show how systems of production and bureaucratic controls worked in practice.[21] Equally, at a more local level, shops and marketplaces found across the empire were thought to indicate communal market engagements, albeit with state involvement with weights and measures.

---

16 Laurence 1999; Laurence 2004. Roads, as 'gifts' to the Roman people, were part of a process of socially embedded exchange, reinforced by the naming of certain thoroughfares after state officials.
17 Trigger 1989.
18 Gardner 2016.
19 Pitts 2007 on the growing significance of the notion of identity; Snodgrass 2002 on paradigm shift.
20 Mattingly 2006. See also Mattingly 2004 for the specific notion of discrepancy. How shifting identities relate to socio-economic change remains problematic: see further discussion below.
21 Claridge 1998, p. 367 ff. Peacock and Williams 1986 provides a general discussion of amphorae.

Given this emphasis, it is surprising how little detail is actually known about economic operations under Rome. Aubert, who has spent a lifetime exploring Roman business mechanisms, admits in the end that these are 'far from clear' and 'too complex to grasp'.[22] In a similar vein, Greene, in a book entirely dedicated to *The Archaeology of the Roman Economy*, explicitly refuses to examine 'fundamental issues for which archaeology does not provide direct evidence'.[23] He nonetheless criticises Finley's 'primitivist' position for over-emphasising the socially embedded aspects of exchange, preferring a 'moderniser' approach, which sees capitalist enterprise at the core of empire. He further notes innovative Roman developments in water supply and architecture, but especially in food production and transport, and warns against underestimating the spread of Roman technology as facilitated by the army and associated state infrastructure.[24]

This desire to find capitalist relations in the Roman world is also expressed in the debate about town-hinterland relationships. Where Finley saw simple exploitation, others, noting the scale and complexity of the Roman trade, have attempted to step beyond his notion of 'the consumer city' by suggesting alternative models: the 'Service City', where taxing trade might generate sufficient wealth to support an urban settlement; the 'Organising City', in which surplus generated from managing the countryside allowed urban investment; and the 'Processor City' characterised by urban-industrial dynamics.[25]

Each of these models, particularly the last, can be questioned on empirical grounds. More important, they see economic activity in terms of servicing and organising, not producing, and all describe different types of towns rather than different forms of landscape exploitation. As stated initially, there is no doubt that the production of certain items increased in the Roman period, that urban markets flourished, and that products such as oil and wine were moved over long distances more regularly than hitherto, all in the process generating mercantile profits.

For Marxists, however, the critical issues concern what type of economic relationships underlay these developments and how any such profits might then be spent. Here it is interesting to note that Greene, although a proponent

---

22 Aubert 2001, p. 91. He therefore advises us not to speculate on such matters. Surprisingly, this does not stop him suggesting, on the very same page, that the empire represents '*the gradual globalisation of the market economy*'.
23 Greene 1986, p. 69.
24 Greene 1990 on innovation; Greene 2000 on the spread of technology.
25 Parkins 1997 for the general step; Whittaker 1995 for a summary of specific positions and references to supporting literature.

of Roman (proto-)capitalism, admits that mercantile gains were then devoted to good living and increased social status rather than to the type of productive investment seen in modern capitalism. Greene sees this as a product of aristocratic goals being constrained by caution about trade, thus limiting development of ideas about economic rationalism.[26] The same arguments appear in Wikander's discussion of Roman water power: landowners 'never attempted, or even had cause to attempt' anything like early modern industrialisation.[27] This admission, in turn, raises the issue of why elite ideology, which was transcended in recent centuries to allow industrial capitalism to develop, was retained in such a limiting way under Rome.

Issues such as the need to focus on production rather than distribution, and to develop a deeper understanding of the relationship between ideas and material circumstances, lie at the core of what follows in discussing Marxism. Before turning to this, however, it is useful to end this evaluation of conventional wisdom by reflecting on the problematic political consequences of the above interpretative schema for anyone critical of the present world. If the history of Rome is portrayed simply as *spreading civilisation* to barbarian societies, it can be used to justify any imperial intervention by 'advanced' states today, with the further implication that the *military* sphere was a key facet of Roman society. Equally, if elite *political contexts* are portrayed as dominant under Rome, the lesson for today is to improve matters by entering official politics (i.e. to adopt 'the reformist road'). Next, when emphasising *economic functionalism*, if we had a form of capitalism under Rome, then nothing much has changed in the two millennia since – hence nothing much can change in future. Finally, if *ideas* must develop before society can transform, as in postmodern discourse, we should give primacy to intellectual engagement today, not political action.

Thus, various aspects of current approaches – a lack of conceptual coherence or limited explanatory, rather than descriptive, value; a failure to fit what we know of trends in archaeological evidence; and their having unfortunate implications for those wishing to change the world today – make it necessary to step beyond these perspectives and to consider next what Marx, and Marxists, have to say about the Roman Empire. This is followed by an assessment of critiques of that position, then an argument over the centrality of slavery to antiquity, and finally of what all this might mean for understanding the end of the Roman Empire.

---

26   Greene 2000, p. 31 concerning lifestyle, and p. 54 on the impact of ideological structures.
27   Wikander 1984, p. 40.

3 Marxist Explanations of Classical Antiquity

Marx's writings only considered antiquity as an element in the arguments that occupied him most: explaining the unique character of capitalism in relation to all preceding socio-economic systems. Thus, he developed no dedicated discussion of social relations at that time.[28] Yet Marx had been brought up on the classics, a product of his bourgeois background and education.[29] He saw Aristotle as the greatest thinker of the ancient world (in fact, comparable historically only to Hegel) and remained deeply interested in antiquity throughout his life, saying at one point, when frustrated by reading contemporary commentators, 'these ancient writers, at least, remain ever new'.[30]

Such comments comprise more than bland eulogies. For example, Marx made use of the work of Titus Lucretius Carus, the poet who introduced Epicurean philosophy to a Roman audience in *De rerum natura* ('On natural things'), a framework with the notion of recycling in the natural world at its core. This perspective, when set beside his avid reading of the nineteenth-century soil chemist Liebig, was fundamental to Marx's notion of a metabolic rift being created under capitalism, something essential for understanding the current environmental crisis.[31]

More relevant to the present focus, Marx's approach to social analysis was influenced by the ideas of the Greek philosopher Heraclitus on change being fundamental to the universe: 'to be' is linked with 'to become'. The latter's perspectives concerning atomic materialism, when related to Marx's early student research into Democritus and Epicurus, can be connected to the notion of a monad pregnant with the future and laden with the past. Each monad was only definable in terms of other such entities, leading to an emphasis on relational properties. This perspective, resonating with what Marx took from Hegel's dia-

---

28 The main, consolidated source, the *Grundrisse* (a first 'rough draft' of *Capital*: Marx 1973), has just one section directly examining 'Forms which Precede Capitalist Production' (reiterated, in slightly more accessible form, in his explicit consideration of *Pre-Capitalist Economic Formations*: Marx 1964), comprising notes for what became *A Contribution to the Critique of Political Economy*, published in 1859. The whole discussion here, however, is simply part of his arguments on why capitalist dynamics are unique in human history, in particular concerning the increasing distancing of their labour from the control of producers, a process in which industrial capitalism is the ultimate outcome. Fortunately, a more well-rounded understanding of Marx's thinking about antiquity has been distilled from diverse sources by others since: see de Ste. Croix 1983 and Lekas 1988, plus further below.

29 de Ste. Croix 1983, p. 23.
30 MEW XXX, pp. 605–6.
31 Angus 2019, p. 55.

lectics emphasising inner contradiction, enabled him to move from 'dialectical idealism' to 'dialectical materialism'. Marx could thus portray change as a dialectical process and class as a social relationship between groups.[32]

It is widely acknowledged that Marx's writings were fundamentally influenced by contemporary episodes, for example his reorientation on the working class after his experiences in 1848, or his developing understanding of the nature of the state after the Paris Commune.[33] What the previous observations show is that, alongside particular historical events, his ideas were developed in an intellectual context. The latter was not only a product of engaging with and arguing against contemporary figures such as Smith and Ricardo, or of stepping beyond major intellects such as Hegel. Marx's thinking also involved assimilating Greek and Roman ideas into the heart of his perspectives. In essence, then, Marx may not have been concerned directly with analysing ancient society, but he did make incisive use of ideas derived from its philosophical output.

In order to present what Marx says about that world, it is useful first to clarify what I take to be the essence of historical materialism, not least because some of what I later portray as misconceptions derive from different views of what Marxist analyses actually involve. Marxism comprises an approach which has social production at its heart, different forms of such production defining different societies.[34] In particular, in all class societies, various modes of production can be defined as a relationship between the 'forces of production', i.e. knowledgeable producers acting collectively on nature (and, in the process, changing themselves), and corresponding 'relations of production', i.e. the distinct, and different, ways in which non-producers extract a proportion of the surplus created by those forces.

The notion of surplus extraction being at the core of a mode of production means that, for Marx, class is defined by an exploitative *relationship*, not by a specific type of work or consumption practice.[35] This whole approach is best summed up by Geoffrey de Ste. Croix: 'Class (essentially a relationship) is the collective expression of the fact of exploitation, the way in which exploitation is embodied in a social structure'.[36] Finally, Marx has a particular view of how social change occurs: as forces of production grow, relations of production may move from aiding to fettering development, resulting in social turmoil. In

---

32 See further below on how relational properties are embedded in the notion of a 'mode of production'.
33 Callinicos 1996, p. 12 ff.
34 Callinicos 1996, p. 65 ff.; Wood 2008.
35 McGuire 2002, p. 91 ff.
36 de Ste. Croix 1983, p. 43.

essence, therefore, this concept of a mode of production is an analytical device to study complex and contradictory data and explain social dynamics.

Turning from such generalities, Marx distinguished three such modes of production, of which the ancient or classical is pivotal here.[37] Two authors, Padelis Lekas and de Ste. Croix, provide, I suggest, the most coherent account of what Marx says about this period.[38] Unanimity between these two authors is, *prima facie*, surprising. The former is dedicated to showing the inadequacies of Marx's general analytical tools when applied to detailed historical contexts, accusing him of inconsistency and teleology (the latter critique is discussed – and dismissed – more fully below). The latter, in contrast, is a 'classical Marxist' arguing for the superiority of their analyses, in the process taking a hatchet to Weber's concept of social status.[39] The present article considers such frameworks only in outline: detailed arguments and links to primary sources are available in the two works cited above.

Marx suggests that the classical world was distinct from other societies, in that producers were part of a single community and controlled property collectively (hence the existence of state land: the *Ager publicus*) but also held land privately. 'Citizenship' fused these communal and private spheres, yet vast differences in wealth still existed within such citizenry, the impact of these disparities in the social fabric being mediated in towns. Marx summarised this distinctive formation to generate social cohesion under Greece and Rome as a 'being together' [*Verein*], rather than a 'gathering together' [*Vereinigung*], something that might occur in any prehistoric society.[40] The centrality of urban living explains, for Marx, why the polis was a legal entity in antiquity. It also accounts for the ideological mechanisms developed therein – for example, groups of citizens in the form of elite families and associated entourages, moving through carefully organised townscapes, usually with temporal control of the daily round, and the development of cognitive maps.[41]

---

37 The ancient/classical; the feudal and the oriental or Asiatic forms (the last has been much discussed, but is widely questioned today. See, however, the final section below on the tributary/peasant mode of production): Marx 1964. It is noticeable here that Marx describes each mode but does not define an explicit chronological sequence between them (Wood 2008), although, of course, his later writings do show that he sees feudalism as an immediate precursor to capitalism.

38 Lekas 1988 and de Ste. Croix 1983.

39 de Ste. Croix 1983, p. 89 ff. For me, de Ste. Croix provides the definitive answer to Love's (1991) attack on Marxism as being reductionist, thus countering the latter's espousal of Weberian concepts as generating multi-causal, historical explanations.

40 Hence his distinction between a 'community' and an 'association': Marx 1964.

41 See Walker (2000) on Rome and Rogers (1991) on Ephesus for some of the complex processes involved in establishing identities by movement in Roman townscapes.

De Ste. Croix describes how these tensions and attempts to overcome them played themselves out in the Greek world. Ultimately, however, in both Ancient Greece and more especially under Rome, conflict within the citizen body could be solved only by placing certain individuals entirely outside its structure: chattel slaves were not only non-citizens, but non-people. Deploying such producers allowed direct intervention in certain spheres – both in agriculture, notably wine and oil production, and in mining – whilst their use in domestic contexts ensured that no citizen had to work directly for their supposed equal. The 'slave mode of production' was therefore the foundation of ancient society, its fundamental fault line being between slaves and their owners.

Crises arose within an empire relying on slavery, their source not being difficult to define. Firstly, there was the obvious danger of slave rebellions. Owners may have intentionally drawn slaves from different sources in order to limit the development of any sense of class consciousness: The oppressed were divided by language, except that of their oppressor. Yet slave revolts are still well-known in the historical record. In addition, production beyond subsistence in all pre-capitalist societies was low, so, however it was procured, only a small surplus was available to support any non-productive elites: the ruling class was necessarily minute and had to compete for limited resources. Furthermore, much of the land and raw materials capable of intensive exploitation around the Mediterranean only existed in limited pockets.[42]

Finally, any intensification of the slave mode meant that owners were increasingly distanced from the point of production. This would have been a particular issue when consolidation of elite land had arisen in diverse historical circumstances, meaning that total holdings could be widely scattered. It is striking, here, that surviving agricultural manuals from the Roman world concern themselves with how absentee landlords might best handle their farms at arm's length. Nonetheless, the solution to such dispersed landholdings was to create slave managers, with important implications for how far technological development might then be implemented. In Marxist terms, such 'solutions' meant that slaves pivotal to the forces of production became increasingly central to the relations of production.[43]

If intensification in the slave mode was problematic, the logical ruling class solution was extensification: to attempt to dominate more and more territory. Thus, expansion was built into the logic of slavery, and conquest could generate

---

42   Horden and Purcell 2000.
43   Allowing some slaves to save up and buy their freedom, thus tying them to their owners in the course of their enslavement, might be some sort of solution to these problems – but see further below.

both land and further numbers of slaves. In addition, as territorial acquisition was procured initially by an army staffed solely of lower-order citizens, elites could increase their power at the core by taking over the plots of land then vacated.[44]

In the long term, imperial expansion required both a professional army and a bureaucracy to organise the exploitation of newly acquired areas.[45] Surplus might be extracted directly via the taking of booty and slaves or by taxation, or later by granting foreign lands to existing elites. These state representatives had every reason to procure such surplus from the provinces, but not necessarily to pass these products back to Rome: their material interests were not simply the same as those of the Italian aristocracy who originally put such officials in place. It is not surprising, therefore, that much of Roman history from when the empire started to conquer significant tracts of land across Europe involved leaders at the core, who rotated these administrative positions to prevent their authority from being set in stone. They also tried to bind these widely dispersed military leaders and state officials to a 'common' cause by supplying distinctive material culture, such as *terra sigillata* tablewares or olive oil and wine, across large swathes of empire. The state was prepared to allow these traded goods to 'pickaback' its official transport systems because it had a vested interest in ameliorating intra-elite tensions.[46]

Therefore, unlike interpretations promulgated by conventional wisdom, this approach suggests that activities such as exchanging ceramics to establish identities must be understood in the context of particular social tensions, not as a human need to truck and barter. More generally, conquest was not built into the Italian psyche, nor did martial ideologies simply drive the need for imperial expansion: each are facets of contradictions emerging within the slave mode of production. It is not surprising, then, that the ending of such expansion after the middle of the second century CE generated a playing out of contradictions. Yet the complex fragmentation of social relations could not, in the end, be avoided, and the fall of imperial systems over several centuries led, in diverse ways, into the Middle Ages (see the final section, below).

---

44 Hopkins 2004 charts this process in action in Italy, also referencing those who have both questioned and supported his model.
45 When moving from a citizen to a professional army, Rome created the first form of wage labour but, because it was directed towards conquest, this organisational form was qualitatively different from the use of wage labour under capitalism, a point not lost on Marx himself. See Marx 1973, p. 529n on the army not generating 'production values'.
46 Wickham 1988b draws out the implications of this prestige goods economy for later centuries.

4   Critiques of Marx on Classical Antiquity

This outline model of the development of classical antiquity has been criticised by various commentators. Perhaps the most detailed and trenchant is that of Padelis Lekas in his *Marx on Classical Antiquity*.[47] Despite agreeing with much of the above, he wishes to show that the application of Marx's analytical tools to empirical detail creates only reductionist and determinist accounts. He thus portrays all Marxist histories as simply unfolding teleologically, driven by gradual increases in productive forces. Whilst it is true that Marx's writings describe these historical processes in various ways for different audiences, some of which could be seen as mechanistic, Lekas maintains that this tendency derives equally from Marx's more considered theoretical work: all are aligned with, and are thus perhaps tainted by, the enlightenment notion of progress.

The foundations for this argument are created early in Lekas's account. He starts by suggesting, correctly, that changes in the forces of production impacting on increasingly outmoded relations of production are, for Marx, key in creating social turmoil (see above). Yet he then concludes that any new mode emerging after revolutionary change is '*determined* by the degree of growth that has been achieved by the forces of production',[48] such productive forces creating a new equilibrium 'at a higher level'.[49] As all change results from pre-existing conditions, historical development must be 'natural, continuous and orderly'.[50]

In reality, there is nothing in Marx's writings that portrays productive forces as determining what follows in a neat and tidy way, still less that whatever emerges will do so at a higher level (with the implication that, for Marxists, history must always move forward). To make his case, Lekas uses selective quotations to characterise Marx's view of base and superstructure, in particular the well-known formulation in the third volume of Capital that:

> The specific economic form (in which unpaid surplus-labour is pumped out of direct producers) ... determines the relationship of rulers and ruled, as it grows directly out of production itself ... It is always the direct relationship of the owners of the conditions of production to the direct pro-

---

47   Lekas 1988.
48   Lekas 1988, p. 19. Emphasis added.
49   Lekas 1988, p. 22.
50   Lekas 1988, p. 32.

ducers ... which reveals the innermost secret, the hidden basis of the entire social structure and with it the political form of the relation of sovereignty and dependence.[51]

What Lekas avoids quoting is the final sentence of that paragraph, which suggests a quite different conclusion to his own:

> This does not prevent the same economic basis – the same from the standpoint of its main conditions – due to innumerable different empirical circumstances, natural environment, racial relations, external historical influences, etc. from showing infinite variations and gradations in appearance, as the result of innumerable different empirical circumstances ... which can only be understood by analysing these empirically given conditions.[52]

Hence, Marx is quite clear that the notion of a base and superstructure defines an analytical tool to be used in exploring the real world, not a mechanism to predict the outcomes of social upheavals. Any other conclusion would make nonsensical the way in which Marx and Engels actively engaged with the struggles of their day, i.e. how they used their theory and analyses to guide their practice.

A second criticism, this time from a more sympathetic source, concerns Faulkner's account *Rome: Empire of the Eagles*.[53] This avowedly anti-imperialist narrative portrays Rome as 'a system of robbery with violence'.[54] Yet Faulkner then goes on to depict military dynamics, rather than slavery, as being at the core of this empire. His perspective, starting with the suggestion that tensions between clan and household required warriors for security, culminates in the development of a state-army nexus of power 'built on a tax-pay cycle'.[55] The resources to sustain this system over time, the principal ways by which surplus was pumped out of producers under Rome, derive, for Faulkner, from the glory, booty, indemnity payments and slaves that were accrued from military successes.

It is worth considering each of these 'rewards' in turn. Glory in itself can never sustain human society materially, even if it benefits the political posi-

---

51 Lekas 1988, p. 27.
52 Marx 1981, p. 927 (*Capital* Volume III).
53 Faulkner 2008.
54 Faulkner 2008, p. xii.
55 Faulkner 2008, p. 182.

tion of army leaders. Equally, booty, even if sold by aristocrats on the market to realise their profits from warfare, as Faulkner suggests it was, needs to be bought by consumers with the equivalent means at their disposal, hence raising issues about the source of the buyers' wealth. Next, indemnities paid by the conquered no doubt allowed elites to accumulate capital, but how was this to be deployed thereafter in relation to the economic process? Finally, slaves might allow intervention in production, but, as noted above, Faulkner has already at the start of his account dismissed the slave mode of production as being pivotal in antiquity.[56] The fundamental problem here is that, in separating the army from the rest of Roman society, it becomes unclear how the products of successful wars actually fed into the empire's productive base.[57]

A third commentator, the Marxist Ellen Wood, forthright in criticising any retreat from 'classical' Marxism, has taken issue with some conventional thinking on Rome, for example seeing the 'idle mob' in Rome as a creation of modern scholarship.[58] Yet, in her *Peasant-Citizen and Slave: The foundations of Athenian democracy*, she, like Faulkner, questions how pivotal slavery was in antiquity.[59] Whilst accepting that slaves were important for households and in mining, she argues that most slaves worked for rich men and that the countryside was the pre-eminent domain of the peasant producer. Thus, for Wood, landlord/peasant, rather than slave/owner, was the fundamental fault line in antiquity, the former combination being held together via political mechanisms.[60] With peasant producers dominating the rural economy and acting as a block on innovation, causes of change are, for Wood, necessarily large-scale and extra-systemic, for example population pressure, climate change or displacement of landholders.

This characterisation of Greek society, with its dominant peasantry, makes it difficult, however, to explain how Ancient Greece and its Roman successor differed fundamentally from broadly contemporary social formations elsewhere in Europe. Peasant producers were equally central to many prehistoric societies, but these lacked a professional army and the sort of infrastructure and urban development evident under Rome. Equally, martial prowess was still

---

56 Faulkner 2008, p. xii.
57 Such a stance, by portraying the army as an 'independent variable', implies that, today, we can separate military dynamics from the rest of capitalism and just export the more 'benign' elements.
58 Compare her view with, for example, Faulkner 2008, p. 124.
59 Wood 1988.
60 This general stance prefigures her subsequent move towards 'political Marxism', a journey which hinges on how one deploys the base/superstructure distinction noted previously: Callinicos 2009, p. 75 ff.

valued ideologically and warfare could involve the gathering of large forces, for example in reaction to Roman expansion under Julius Caesar in Gaul. Yet these were not imperial systems. How is that difference to be explained?

Here, it is worth recalling that a 'mode of production' defines how a dominant class sustained itself, not how the bulk of production happens. Thus, even if slaves worked mostly for the elite, as Wood accepts, they would still be essential for ruling class stability in the long term. The fact that peasants formed the majority of producers in antiquity does not, in itself, mean that the slavery was marginal to the empire.

5 The Centrality of Slavery

This last critique thus raises to two fundamentally empirical questions: what role did slaves play in social production under Rome? And what was the scale of that contribution? A huge amount has been written about slavery in antiquity.[61] This literature includes both authors who argue that it was central to the Roman Empire, notably Italian scholars working with Andrea Carandini who adopted an explicit Marxist viewpoint, and those who take a different position.[62] In confronting these questions, it should be noted that what matters is not simply the legal status of slaves and any gradations therein. Rather, it concerns what their material position in the landscape and in the home comprised.

Slavery allowed direct intervention in production in a way that was impossible using other economic relations, for example when taking rent from tenant households or using the labour of debt bondsmen or sharecroppers.[63] We know that slaves were used in temple building and maintenance, in mass-producing ceramic workshops and in domestic contexts, all things that were central to an elite lifestyle. They also had a role in the mining of precious metals, the one context where water power was applied in a 'true industrial application' (importantly, a technology not then extended to more mundane contexts such as the production of iron, textiles and food).[64]

It is not, however, temple building, ceramic production, mining or domestic households but, rather, agricultural production that was *the* pivotal context in

---

61 See, for example, the various contributions in Bradley and Cartledge 2011, plus their numerous references.
62 Carandini 1979 and 1988 versus Rathbone 1983. Wickham 1988b provides a useful perspective on this debate.
63 See Garnsey 1980 on non-slave labour.
64 Wilson 2000, p. 149.

all pre-capitalist societies. Use of slaves here no doubt varied across its empire and over time, yet slave estates clearly existed in the landscape: they are not only described directly by Roman authors,[65] but some have been excavated. The most quoted example of the latter, the site of Settefinestre in Italy, owned by the Volusii senatorial family, has been interpreted as evidencing a shift towards large-scale commercial farming based on the exploitation of slaves in the course of the first century CE.[66] More generally, a recent account suggests that, at its height, slavery might have accounted for about a quarter of the rural producers in Italy.[67] The broad correlation between this peak in the imperial core and the expansion of long-distance, Mediterranean trade, something at its heyday between c. 200 BCE and c. 200 CE, creates a circumstantial argument for the link between slavery and economic vibrancy.

Further, in determining the overall impact of slaves in the rural economy, it has often been assumed that such a male-dominated context would have made slavery quite inefficient, and thus that it could not have prevailed in the countryside. Yet this assumption about the landscape as an exclusively 'male' sphere may be a simple product of how women have been marginalised in historical and archaeological interpretations.[68] A recent account argues that women slaves, as reproducers, could organise childbirth and rearing alongside other tasks such as textile production (especially spinning), food preparation and crop processing.[69] Hence, they may have been more numerous than had been thought, making rural production by slaves more economically sound than sometimes suggested.[70]

That said, even where slavery was central to rural production, it may not have been used exclusively. Thus, opening up new tracts of land sometimes involved share coppers. More generally, it has been proposed, surely correctly, that the cyclical nature of parts of the agricultural economy makes sole reli-

---

65 Although see below, n. 612, on Cato.
66 Pucci 1985. The interpretation of this site and its implications have been contested, however (see above n. 608 on Carandini versus Rathbone). Marzano (2007, p. 129 ff.) questions the identification of slave quarters, the conventionally ascribed dating and the very idea that these large villas replaced medium-sized properties owned by free farmers. See also various contributions in Becker and Terrenato 2012 on evaluating evidence for the villa dell'Auditorium in Rome's suburbs, including Terrenato on Cato's *De agri cultura*: is the latter an accurate description of how to create a working estate or just an iconic model that an emerging social class might aspire to emulate?
67 Launaro 2011.
68 Rose 1993.
69 Roth 2003.
70 Fentress 2008 criticises Roth's methods but welcomes her overall conclusions.

ance on slave labour unlikely. A mixed-farming economy to spread out seasonal peaks seems probable, e.g. using free labour at harvest time to augment year-round slaves. Other spheres, however – for example, the production of 'cash crops' such as oil and wine – may have seen greater concentrations of slaves (see, for example, Settefinestre, above). The production of the latter commodities would also explain the need for the urban markets evident under Rome.

Whatever the scale of their use, slaves were expensive to buy initially, so it was necessary to create a certain level of subsistence in their lifetime in order to avoid wasting that investment. Allowing older slaves to finally buy their freedom might tie them to an owner as they saved up resources, providing a lump sum to then be spent on their replacement. This has led some commentators to suggest that slavery was not an economic necessity but rather a form of deferred socialisation: the way in which Rome assimilated people from newly conquered territories. This notion does not sit easily with the slave revolts known to have taken place, most famously under Spartacus.[71]

Also, concerning the buying of freedom, slaves working in domestic contexts in towns with markets, or in the countryside where they could access wild woodland (the *saltus*) to run their own herds, may have been able to use their initiative to generate the *peculium* required to pay off their owner. Yet slaves sent to the mines or into the navy would have had no such opportunities and were, in effect, being handed a death sentence. Thus, the evidence for freed men and women, mostly that subset who had the means and inclination to record their death epigraphically, can represent only a small proportion of the whole body of slave producers. The large numbers of freed people known to us from epigraphic sources gives some indication, paradoxically, of just how widespread slavery as a whole must have been.

On a number of grounds then, it can be suggested that slavery was central to certain sections of Roman society, including specialised production in some landscapes, albeit sometimes alongside non-slave labour, and in areas of production pivotal to the maintenance of imperial identities. Yet, as argued earlier, reliance on slaves limited the intensification of economic development and pushed Rome towards expansion, both to obtain new sources of such labour without the need to bring producers up from birth, and to gain control over tracts of land on which they could be deployed.[72] Thus, given the pivotal need to expand, it is not surprising that, after the Roman Empire created boundaries

---

71 Hunt 2018, p. 161 ff.
72 N.B. Woolf's conclusion (1992), that the only point at which the imperial economy became integrated above a local or, at best, regional scale coincided with the height of imperial expansion.

in the course of the second century CE, a number of tensions became apparent. To conclude this piece, Marxist attempts to confront this later period are considered next, albeit in outline.

6 Marxism and the End of Empire

As external supplies increasingly dried up and slave owning became more problematic, various solutions could have been adopted. One might have been to drive once 'free' producers into slavery. This is how the development of the late Roman colonate, in which peasants were tied more closely to the land, is interpreted by some.[73] Admittedly, this institution is seen by others as derived simply from the need to continue tax gathering. Yet, as taxation is really a mechanism for surplus extraction (see further below), binding generations of producers to specific parts of the landscape in order to facilitate their exploitation can still be seen as pushing them towards a form of slavery.

Alternatively, internal reproduction of slaves could have been developed to compensate for a lack of external sources.[74] Getting slaves to reproduce may have not been easy, however. Slave owners needed to regard these people as less than human to justify their degradation, and so created ideological structures to help generate such attitudes. Thus, famously, Varro described slaves as talking tools – *instrumentum vocale*[75] – and aristocratic children were trained at an early age to order slaves around using the imperative linguistic form rather than the present indicative.[76] Yet, despite these attempts to dehumanise them, slaves were in fact people who would not always reproduce to order.

More importantly, slave numbers could have been boosted by female slaves having children, whether willingly with male slaves that they saw as a spouse, or by forcing them to bear children of their owners.[77] Yet, either way, bringing up unfree producers from birth took more resources than capturing mature adults in war. It was not until about the age of five years that individuals became productive.[78] Thus, given the limited rate of production beyond subsistence in

---

73 de Ste. Croix 1983, p. 158 ff.
74 Bradley 1987.
75 But see Lewis 2013 for reservations on this usage and Roth 2007 for further discussion.
76 Beard 2013, p. 207.
77 Hunt 2018, p. 106 ff. Legal tracts concerning the status of any babies born to slaves imply that the latter was of significance, and perhaps commonplace.
78 Scheidel 1994.

antiquity and low average age at death, especially for slaves, it would be years before the losses involved in their upbringing could be recouped.

Maintaining slave numbers must have been challenging when Roman imperial expansion ceased, yet slaves were clearly still present in some numbers into the third and fourth centuries CE. Melania the Younger, for example, is said to have freed eight thousand individuals upon her conversion to Christianity.[79] Yet such large numbers may have been restricted to particular parts of that society – Melania was, after all, an aristocrat at the very pinnacle of that elite. Either way, slavery, in the form deployed under Rome in its heyday, did end over the course of later centuries, sometimes quickly and violently.[80] A recent lengthy consideration of detailed evidence describes the late Roman world as one of systems collapse, a coherent slave society fragmenting into 'a multitude of societies with (some) slaves'.[81]

The ending of imperial expansion and thus, ultimately, of aristocratic reliance on a slave mode of production poses considerable challenges for Marxists seeking to understand the transition of the late empire into the medieval period. Some have sought to explain this by suggesting that feudal social relations are evident from the third century CE, others by proposing that slavery continued to dominate up to the tenth century CE. Chris Wickham, correctly finding both these alternatives unconvincing, has tried to chart a different course in his magisterial Marxist work *Framing the Middle Ages*.[82] His key argument is that this period is defined not by feudal rents or by slave exploitation, but by taxation. The late Roman state thus becomes, for Wickham, the key nexus. Its appropriation of surplus allowed the military, administration and infrastructure of public works to continue, contrasting with Germanic societies, which had no regular army or urbanism to support. Crisis thus derived from a failure to maintain the system of taxation.

Much writing has been devoted to assessing and critiquing Wickham's frameworks, many commentators taking issue with his overarching interpretation of the state.[83] Yet, such discussions revolve, ultimately, around an aspect of political superstructure. In reality, different forms of exploitation, both di-

---

79 Harper 2011, p. 192 ff. This may be only a minority of her slave holdings and, where the Christian church inherited estates with large numbers of slaves, they continued their use without obvious moral reservations: Hunt 2018, p. 201. See Harper 2011, p. 209 ff. for further discussion of the 'Amelioration Thesis'.
80 Bonnassie 1991.
81 Harper 2011, p. 509.
82 Wickham 2005.
83 Banaji 2009; Innes 2009; Sijpesteijn 2009; and Whittow 2009.

rect and indirect, can occur beneath any state, each with a complex relationship with such an overlying organisation.[84] In sum, state taxation does not define a mode of production, something on which Trotsky is especially clear:

> The State is not an end in itself, but is a tremendous means for organizing, disorganizing and reorganizing social relations. It can be a powerful lever for revolution or a tool for organized stagnation, depending on the hands that control it.[85]

Other assessments of Wickham's *Frameworks* get closer to the mechanics of surplus extraction in the landscape, critical for the interpretation of archaeological evidence. Thus, Costambeys notes that the complex evolution from villa to village may happen independent of taxation systems, whilst Faith suggests that the change from pastoralism to agriculture in mid-Saxon Britain signals the point at which control over peasant labour occurred.[86] To incorporate such trends into a coherent account, however, we need to theorise the diverse ways in which peasantry can be exploited. As with the discussion of Roman slavery at its height, this will require more than an understanding of the legally defined degrees of freedom/slavery to which producers were subjected (tied, half-free, unfree, etc.) and how far these were inherited from the Roman world.

To understand this period, Wickham proposes the existence of a 'peasant mode of production'. In this, inhabitants may have had to fulfil external fiscal obligations, but any surplus not thus alienated externally may have been deployed in feasting and other mechanisms to enhance internal communal bonds.[87] Where dominant in landscape, such class relations might mark a return to lower social complexity, perhaps with less cultivation and smaller families with partible inheritance and local headmen. In contrast, the feudal mode of rent-taking from individual households would make producers more directly controlled by external landlords than in this peasant mode.[88]

This proposed addition of a new mode of production to our analytical toolbox alongside feudal and slave relations has not received universal acceptance.[89] Yet it is, I suggest, useful in helping us to distinguish between the

---

84   See, for example, Haldon 1993 on Byzantium.
85   Trotsky 1906, p. 38.
86   Costambeys 2009; Faith 2009.
87   Wickham 2005, p. 520 on fiscal aspect, p. 536 on social bonding.
88   Wickham 2005, p. 541.
89   Banaji 2010.

different ways in which surplus was extracted in the landscape. Such variations would impact on how power was exercised and on how forms of resistance arose, thus affecting the functioning and interaction of Wickham's other spheres: the state, aristocracy and exchange systems.[90] In sum, we might understand the ways in which the Roman Empire fragmented into myriad trajectories in the course of the third to ninth centuries CE by defining three modes of production:

- A slave mode, defined previously and seemingly increasingly less common in late antiquity
- A peasant (or 'tributary' – see below) mode, in which communities of producers regulated the landscape ('forces of production') and had some control over its surplus product, e.g. when using it to enhance internal social bonds, yet an overlying bureaucracy extracted some proportion through tribal allegiances ('relations of production'). Settlement, although subject to some limitations, might be mobile within the landscape (Wickham's 'fluid and fragmented' forms of organisation)[91]
- A feudal mode, in which individual households of producers controlled the landscape ('forces of production') and surplus was taken household-by-household, classically as rent for a plot, whether in kind or in coin, but also as labour service which allowed a feudal elite to direct parts of the labour process ('relations of production'). Even if peasant producers controlled individual properties and acted collectively beyond them, settlement space was ordered in much greater detail than under peasant relations: households would be tied down to specific plots, and the ability of people to move outside the settlement and utilise wider landscape resources curtailed, i.e. what has been termed 'the caging of the peasantry'[92]

Saunders charts exactly this process of change in England between the sixth and tenth centuries, for example in the move from non-nucleated to nucleated villages.[93] His study further suggests how the transition between tributary and feudal modes might be charted in Marxist terms. Tributary societies exploited by an external, likely itinerant, aristocratic authority would require local representatives to articulate those relationships (Wickham's 'headman'). Therefore, the latter, whilst still embedded in the settlement's forces of pro-

---

90   Haldon 1993 again provides a case study.
91   Wickham 2005, p. 517.
92   Wickham 2010.
93   Saunders 1990. His analysis uses the notion of a tributary mode, which I prefer for clarity to Wickham's more nebulous 'peasant mode' and which I will employ in what follows.

duction, could also play an increasingly significant role in the corresponding relations of production. Where surplus extraction was resisted by producers, stability would only be retained if representative headmen remained linked to an external, proto-state authority (tied in, for example, by the distribution of externally supplied prestige goods designed to consolidate these social alliances). Where such mechanisms failed, two broad outcomes might be predicted.

Firstly, the peasantry might throw off the yoke of external authority, perhaps returning to a fluidity of movement in the landscape. Reports of groups called *Bacaudae* could be evidence for this, perhaps one of the few examples of explicit class warfare in the Roman world.[94] References to such bands start in the late third century CE (i.e. not long after the ending of imperial expansion), but their impact reached crisis levels by the early fifth century CE, with swathes of landscape in Gaul and Spain no longer under imperial control. These were not just mobile, anarchic mobs; they may have rejected Roman Law, but they chose to live under 'woodland law' [*iura silvestria*], judgements being delivered beneath an oak tree and recorded on bones.[95] In marking an end to Roman surplus extraction, such groups must have played a significant role in the disintegration of the Western empire.

Alternatively, individual 'headmen' could recognise their growing position of authority in the process of exploitation and, making alliances with corresponding officials in other settlements, come together to reject the (proto-)state authority above them while retaining their control of surplus extraction locally. If successful in this strategy, they would then emerge as a feudal elite, with enhanced control of individual households set on specific settlement plots. In this way, feudal relations could emerge from contradictory trends embedded in the tributary mode.

The distinction between tributary and feudal modes is important, for the reasons given above, yet peasant households retained an integral relationship with the landscape in both cases. Thus, transitions between the two will be difficult to chart archaeologically.[96] Furthermore, both modes contrast markedly with the later development of capitalist wage labour. The breakup of any pre-

---

94   de Ste. Croix 1983, p. 478 ff.
95   de Ste. Croix 1983, p. 478. The choice to deliver legal judgements in 'natural' contexts rather than in monumental buildings, and for them to be inscribed on bones rather than written on documents, surely signifies a new relationship between culture and nature.
96   Perhaps best approached spatially: Saunders 1990. However, corresponding developments might also be traced in faunal patterning: Roskams and Saunders 2001.

capitalist imperial system makes the emergence of a complex patchwork of modes of production inevitable, particularly as various forms of surplus extraction would have existed alongside each other beforehand. It is only capitalism that is forced to drive out alternative systems so ruthlessly and completely. This has important implications for what pre-capitalist social crises might comprise and the timescales over which they may have operated.[97] Capitalism alone gives us a stark and increasingly immediate choice between socialism and barbarism. The fact that social interaction in pre-capitalist formations was complex does not, however, absolve Marxists from the need to come to terms with a range of trajectories in these developments.

7 Conclusion

This paper started by summarising mainstream approaches to the Roman world, arguing that they fail to fully conceptualise social dynamics. The subsequent text aimed to show that, both theoretically and empirically, Marxist modes of production – a slave mode at the core of Roman imperial expansion, and a complex interaction of this alongside tributary and feudal modes after imperial boundaries were drawn – provide a more convincing starting point to explore a diversity of responses in the past. Contrary to the accusations of many critics of Marxism, there is nothing in the latter formulations to suggest that social development must always go 'forward'. Indeed, across large swathes of the Roman Empire, there is plenty of empirical evidence of reduced levels of social complexity emerging between the third and ninth centuries – and perhaps most producers in the landscape were much the better for it.

References

Angus, Ian 2019, 'The Discovery and Rediscovery of the Metabolic Rift', in *System Change Not Climate Change: A Revolutionary Response the Environmental Crisis*, edited by Martin Empson, London: Bookmarks.

Aubert, Jean-Jacques 2001, 'The fourth factor: managing non-agricultural production in the Roman world', in *Economies Beyond Agriculture in the Classical World*, edited by David Mattingly and John Salmon, London: Routledge.

---

[97] Pasieka 2017.

Banaji, Jairus 2009, 'Aristocracies, Peasantries, and the Framing of the Early Middle Ages', *Journal of Agrarian Change*, 9: 59–91.

Banaji, Jairus 2010, *Theory as History: Essays on Modes of Production and Exploitation*, Leiden and Boston, MA: Brill.

Beard, Mary 2013, *Confronting the Classics: Traditions, Adventures and Innovations*, London: Profile books.

Beard, Mary 2016, SPQR: *A History of Ancient Rome*, London: Profile Books.

Becker, Jeffrey and Nicola Terrenato (eds.) 2012, *Roman Republican Villas: architecture, context, and ideology*, Ann Arbor: University of Michigan Press.

Bekels, Corrie and Stefanie Jacomet 2003, 'Access to luxury foods in Central Europe during the Roman period: the archaeobotanical evidence', *World Archaeology*, 34, 3: 542–57.

Bonnassie, Pierre 1991, *From Slavery to Feudalism in Southwestern Europe*, New York: Cambridge University Press.

Bradley, Keith 1987, 'On the Roman Slave Supply and Slave Breeding', in *Classical Slavery*, edited by Moses Finley, London: Routledge.

Bradley, Keith and Paul Cartledge (eds.) 2011, *The Cambridge World History of Slavery*, Volume 1, *The Ancient Mediterranean World*, Cambridge: Cambridge University Press.

Brown, Peter 1971, *The World of Late Antiquity: From Marcus Aurelius to Muhammad*, London: Thames and Hudson.

Callinicos, Alex 1996, *The Revolutionary Ideas of Karl Marx*, London: Bookmarks.

Callinicos, Alex 2009, *Imperialism and Global Political Economy*, Cambridge: Polity.

Carandini, Andrea 1979, *L'anatomia della scimmia: la formazione economica della società prima del capitale: con un commento alle Forme che precedono la produzione capitalistica dai Grundrisse di Marx*, Turin: Einaudi.

Carandini, Andrea 1982, 'Sottotipi di schiavitù nelle socieà schiavistiche greca e romana', *Opus*, 1: 195–8.

Carandini, Andrea 1988, *Schiavi in Italia: gli strumenti pensanti dei Romani fra tarda Repubblica e medio Impero*, Rome: Nuova Italia scientifica.

Claridge, Amanda 1998, *Rome: An Oxford Archaeological Guide*, Oxford: Oxford University Press.

Costambeys, Marios 2009, 'Settlement, Taxation and the Condition of the Peasantry in Post-Roman Central Italy', *Journal of Agrarian Change*, 9: 92–119.

Faith, Rosamond 2009, 'Forces and Relations of Production in Early Medieval England', *Journal of Agrarian Change*, 9: 23–41.

Faulkner, Neil 2008, *Rome: Empire of the Eagles*, Harlow: Pearson.

Fentress, Elizabeth 2008, 'Spinning a Model: Female Slaves in Roman Villas', *Journal of Roman Archaeology*, 21: 419–22.

Gardner, Andrew 2016, 'Debating Roman Imperialism: Critique, Construct, Repeat?', *Theoretical Roman Archaeology Journal*: 1–14.

Garnsey, Peter (ed.) 1980, *Non-Slave Labour in the Roman World*, Cambridge: Cambridge University Press.
Greene, Kevin 1986, *The Archaeology of the Roman Economy*, London: Batsford.
Greene, Kevin 1990, 'Perspectives on Roman technology', in *Oxford Journal of Archaeology*, 9, 2: 209–19.
Greene, Kevin 2000, 'Technological innovation and economic progress in the ancient world: M.I. Finley re-considered', *Economic History Review*, 53, 1: 29–59.
Haldon, John 1993, *The State and the Tributary Mode of Production*, London: Verso.
Harper, Kyle 2011, *Slavery in the Late Roman World, AD 275–425*, Cambridge: Cambridge University Press.
Hingley, Richard 2000, *Roman Officers and English Gentlemen: The Imperial Origins of Roman Archaeology*, London: Routledge.
Hingley, Richard 2005, *Globalizing Roman culture: Unity, Diversity and Empire*, London and New York: Routledge.
Hobsbawm, Eric and Terence Ranger (eds.) 1983, *The Invention of Tradition*, Cambridge: Cambridge University Press.
Hopkins, Keith 1980, 'Taxes and Trade in the Roman Empire (200 B.C. – A.D. 400)', *The Journal of Roman Studies*, 70: 101–12.
Hopkins, Keith 2004, 'Conquerors and slaves: the impact of conquering an empire on the political economy of Italy', in *Roman Imperialism: Readings and Sources*, edited by Craige Champion, Oxford: Blackwell.
Horden, Peregrine and Nicholas Purcell 2000, *The Corrupting Sea: A Study of Mediterranean History*, Oxford: Blackwell.
Hunt, Peter 2018, *Ancient Greek and Roman Slavery*, Malden, MA: Wiley.
Innes, Matthew 2009, 'Framing the Carolingian Economy', *Journal of Agrarian Change*, 9: 42–58.
James, Edward 2008, 'The Rise and Function of the Concept "Late Antiquity"', *Journal of Late Antiquity*, 1, 1: 20–30.
Joshel, Sandra and Lauren Petersen 2014, *The Material Life of Roman Slaves*, Cambridge: Cambridge University Press.
Launaro, Alessandro 2011, *Peasants and Slaves: The Rural Population of Roman Italy (200 BC to AD 100)*, Cambridge: Cambridge University Press.
Laurence, Ray 1999, *The Roads of Roman Italy*, London: Routledge.
Laurence, Ray 2004, 'Milestones, communications and political stability', in *Travel, Communication and Geography in Late Antiquity: Sacred and Profane*, edited by Linda Ellis and Frank Kidner, London and New York: Routledge.
Lekas, Padelis 1988, *Marx on Classical Antiquity: Problems of Historical Methodology*, Brighton: Wheatsheaf Books.
Lewis, Juan 2013, 'Did Varro Think that Slaves were Talking Tools?', *Mnemosyn*, 66: 4–5.
Love, John 1991, *Antiquity and Capitalism: Max Weber and the Sociological Foundations of Roman Civilization*, London and New York: Routledge.

Mann, Michael 1986, *Sources of Social Power from the Beginning to AD 1760*, Cambridge: Cambridge University Press.

Marx, Karl 1973, *Grundrisse: Introduction to the Critique of Political Economy*, translated by Martin Nicolaus, Harmondsworth: Penguin.

Marx, Karl 1964, *Pre-Capitalist Economic Formations*, translated by Jack Cohen, New York: International Publishing.

Marx, Karl 1981 *Capital*, Volume 3, Harmondsworth: Penguin.

Marzano, Annalisa 2007, *Roman Villas in Central Italy*, Leiden: Brill.

Mattingly, David 2004, 'Being Roman: Expressing identity in a provincial setting', *Journal of Roman Archaeology*, 17: 5–25.

Mattingly, David 2006, *An Imperial Possession: Britain in the Roman Empire, 54 BC – AD 409*, London: Penguin.

McGuire, Randall 2002, *A Marxist Archaeology*, New York: Percheron Press.

McGuire, Randall 2008, *Archaeology as Political Action*, California, University of California Press.

Mouritsen, Henrik 1998, *Italian Unification: A Study in Ancient and Modern Historiography*, London: Institute of Classical Studies.

Parkins, Helen (ed.) 1997, *Roman Urbanism: Beyond the Consumer City*, London: Routledge.

Pasieka, Paul 2017, 'Crisis, Marxism and Reconstruction of Time', *Theoretical Roman Archaeology Journal*: 165–78.

Peacock, David and David Williams 1986, *Amphorae and the Roman Economy: an Introductory Guide*, London and New York: Longman.

Pitts, Martin 2007, 'The Emperor's New Clothes? The Utility of Identity in Roman Archaeology', *American Journal of Archaeology*, 111, 4: 693–713.

Pucci, Guisepppe 1985, 'Il sistema della villa nell'Italia centrale', in *Settefinestre: Una villa schiavistica nell Etruria romana*, edited by Andrea Carandini, Modena: Edizione Panini.

Rathbone, Dominic 1983, 'The Slave Mode of Production in Italy', *The Journal of Roman Studies*, 73: 160–8.

Rogers, Guy 1991, *The Sacred Identity of Ephesos: Foundation Myths of a Roman City*, New York: Routledge.

Rose, Peter 1993, 'The Case for not Ignoring Marx in the Study of Women in Antiquity', in *Feminist Theory and the Classics*, edited by Nancy Rabinowitz and Amy Richlin, New York, NY: Routledge.

Roskams, Steve and Tom Saunders 2001, 'The Poverty of Empiricism and the Tyranny of Theory', in *Environmental Archaeology: Meaning and Purpose*, edited by Umberto Albarella, Dordrecht and London: Kluwer.

Roth, Ulrike 2003, *The Female Slave in Roman Agriculture: Changing the Default*, Unpublished PhD thesis, University of Nottingham, available at: http://eprints.nottingham.ac.uk/11181/1/403324.pdf.

Roth, Ulrike 2007, *Thinking Tools: Agricultural Slavery between Evidence and Models*, Bulletin of the Institute of Classical Studies Supplement 92, London: University College of London.

de Ste. Croix, Geoffrey 1983, *The Class Struggle in the Ancient Greek World*, London: Duckworth.

Saunders, Tom 1990, 'The Feudal Construction of Space,' in *The Social Archaeology of Houses*, edited by Ross Samson, Edinburgh: Edinburgh University Press.

Scheidel, Walter 1994, 'Columellas Privates ius liberorum: Literatur, Recht, Demographie. Einige Probleme', *Latomus*, 53: 513–27.

Sijpesteijn, Petra 2009, 'Landholding Patterns in Early Islamic Egypt', *Journal of Agrarian Change*, 9: 120–33.

Snodgrass, Anthony 2002, 'A Paradigm Shift in Classical Archaeology?', *Cambridge Archaeological Journal*, 12, 2: 179–94.

Trigger, Bruce 1989, *A History of Archaeological Thought*, Cambridge: Cambridge University Press.

Trotsky, Leon 1906, *Results and Prospects*, translated by Brian Pearce, London: Union Books.

Vanni, Edoardo 2017, 'Welcome-back Marx! Marxist Perspectives for Roman Archaeology at the End of the Post-Modern Era', *Theoretical Roman Archaeology Journal*: 133–49.

Wacher, John (ed.) 1987, *The Roman World*, London and Boston, MA: Routledge.

Walker, Susan 2000, 'The Moral Museum: Augustus and the City of Rome', in *Ancient Rome: The Archaeology of the Eternal City*, edited by Jon Coulston and Hazel Dodge, Oxford: Oxford University Press.

Whittaker, Charles Richard 1995, 'Do theories of the ancient city matter?', in *Urban Society in Roman Italy*, edited by Tim Cornell and Kateryn Lomas, London: UCL Press.

Whittow, Mark 2009, 'Early Medieval Byzantium and the End of the Ancient World', *Journal of Agrarian Change*, 9: 134–53.

Wickham, Chris 1988a, 'Historical Materialism, Historical Sociology', *New Left Review*, 171: 63–78.

Wickham, Chris 1988b, 'Marx, Sherlock Holmes and Late Roman Commerce', *The Journal of Roman Studies*, 78: 183–93.

Wickham, Chris 2005, *Framing the Middle Ages*, Oxford: Oxford University Press.

Wickham, Chris 2010, *The Inheritance of Rome: A History of Europe from 400 to 1000*, London: Penguin.

Wikander, Örjan 1984, *Exploitation of Water-Power or Technological Stagnation? A Reappraisal of the Productive Forces in the Roman Empire*, Lund: Gleerup.

Wilson, Andrew 2000, 'Industrial uses of water', in *Handbook of Ancient Water Technology*, edited by Örjan Wikander, Leiden: Brill.

Wood, Ellen 1988, *Peasant-Citizen and Slave: The Foundations of Athenian Democracy*, London: Verso.

Wood, Ellen 2008, 'Historical materialism in "Forms which Precede Capitalist Production"', in *Karl Marx's* Grundrisse: *Foundations of the Critique of Political Economy 150 Years Later*, edited by Marcello Musto, London: Routledge.

Woolf, Greg 1992, 'Imperialism, Empire and the Integration of the Roman Economy', *World Archaeology* 23, 3: 283–93.

CHAPTER 7

Marxism, Historical Archaeology and Capitalism's 'Laws of Motion'

LouAnn Wurst

1 Introduction

Marx's life's work was dedicated to understanding the inner workings of the capitalist system: 'to lay bare the economic law of motion of modern society'.[1] This seemingly innocuous statement is loaded with ideas that, when unpacked, get to the heart of Marx's philosophy: 'modern society' as the sum of the qualities that are peculiar to capitalism in general; 'motion' in the sense that everything is internally dialectically related and constantly changing in and through these relations; 'law' as a term referring to the strongest or most persistent tendencies deriving from central clusters of capitalist relations rather than inevitable outcomes; and finally, 'laying bare' is necessary because these laws of motion of capitalism are not immediately or directly apparent.[2]

Marx's goal is shared by many historical archaeologists, a subdiscipline dedicated to the archaeology of the capitalist world. Thus, it is no surprise that in the United States more Marxists work in historical archaeology than any other archaeological specialty, even though they are still a minority. In writing this paper, I found myself constantly wondering if Marx would find our research useful for his goals. Marx was, of course, a voracious reader, and anthropology figured prominently in the literature he consumed.[3] Of course, historical archaeology (or any modern discipline) did not exist at the time that Marx was reading and thinking, but this does not preclude wondering whether the specialised knowledge and understandings produced by what is typically considered an esoteric discipline can be of use in the wider Marxist struggle against capitalism.

My goal for this paper is to indicate how historical archaeology can contribute to this larger Marxist agenda. In what follows, I present what I see as the key aspects of Marx's philosophy that have guided my own archaeological research

---

1 Marx 1967, p. 20.
2 Ollman 2014.
3 Patterson 2009.

into capitalism's laws of motion, discuss the role of the historical archaeology of capitalism, and suggest the kind of contributions that historical archaeological research can make. Each is explored with an archaeological example to demonstrate how the particular craft of historical archaeology can make contributions to the larger Marxist project of creating a world without capitalism and its exploitation.

2   Marxism, Dialectics and a Philosophy of Internal Relations

Marx used a theory of internal relations based on the concept of the dialectic to understand capitalism. Patterson notes that different Marxist scholars have emphasised different aspects of the dialectic's most distinctive features.[4] Lukács prioritised the notion of totality, or the importance of the whole over the parts, while Mao Zedong focused on contradictions and Ollman has more recently emphasised abstractions.[5] But these are not mutually exclusive positions. Rather, they point to the key aspects of dialectics as the internal web of social relations that makes up the totality, that dialectical relations join contradictory forces internally as a unity of opposites, and that abstractions are an analytical approach to comprehending relations dialectically.[6]

Dialectical thinking is a very different approach than most common sense studies that begin with definitions of concrete entities (classes, society, economy, political systems, etc.) that interact as external relations. An approach based on external relations is the most common in the academy: we have departments that specialise in the study of political, economic and social systems, as if they were ontologically separate arenas. A philosophy of internal relations, in contrast, posits that it is the internal relation that actually defines and creates the surface appearance, and that the surface appearance, whether class, economy, anthropology, etc, does not and cannot exist apart from the internal web of social relations.[7] Thus, there is no such 'thing' as the economy or political system; rather, there is a complex web of dialectically related social relations which create the appearance of these things.

Dialectical relations always represent contradictions. Moore notes a 'mighty confusion between dialectics and interaction'.[8] Seeing external relations interacting or intersecting is not the same as dialectics which require the mutual

---

4   Patterson 2003, p. 8.
5   Lukács 1971, p. 27; Mao Zedong 1975, p. 311; Ollman 1193, p. 26.
6   Patterson 2003, p. 8. See also Ollman 1993, p. 35, and Moore 2017.
7   McGuire 1992, p. 94. See also Ollman 2003, Sayer 1987 and Harvey 1996.
8   Moore 2017, p. 15.

determination of historically grounded asymmetries.[9] This is why Marx could claim that capital and labour were 'expressions of the same relation, only seen from the opposite pole'.[10] Thus, one of the central facets of the dialectic is the unity of opposites, where dialectical relations unite opposites such as capital/labour, master/slave, production/consumption, agriculture/industry, etc. into single internally constituted wholes. These opposing entities or contexts have different intrinsic interests and material conditions; thus, dialectical social relations always contain conflict and contradiction within them.

Dialectical research emphasises social totality and focuses on the whole of real lived experience, connecting all aspects that 'common sense' understandings view as separate into a social totality. This Marxist focus on social totality has been vehemently rejected as part of the postmodern dismissal of universals, but this perspective is based on the confusion between a totalising theory and a totalising explanation. A totalising theory is necessary to even be able to see the systemic issues that characterise global capitalism – it is, after all, a totalising system.[11] The second is, of course, facile and easily rejected. Confusing and merging these two incapacitates us from making any kind of serious challenge or critique of capitalism, leading many to suggest that postmodernism actually functions as the dominant ideology of contemporary capitalism.[12]

Dialectical research focuses on the whole of real lived experience and then proceeds to an examination of the part to see where it fits and how it functions. Marx argued that his method started with the world as it presented itself and proceeded through abstraction, the intellectual process of breaking down the whole into component units.[13] All thinking is based on abstractions, but the key to Marx's process is realising that he abstracted relations and not 'things'. Even the commodity, the first object of analysis in *Capital*, and the most concrete of Marx's analysis, 'appears, at first sight, a very trivial thing, and easily understood'.[14] But as Marx shows, commodities are in fact bundles of contradictory relationships.

Marx's process of abstraction began with the use of concepts that refer to relations that are empirically open-ended rather than essentialist definitions that freeze and simplify reality.[15] Ollman shows how Marx used abstraction in

---

9   Ibid.
10 Cited in Ollman 2003, p. 77.
11 Wood 1995.
12 Eagleton 1996. See also Harvey 2000 and McGuire and Wurst 2002.
13 Marx and Engels 1970, p. 2.
14 Marx 1967, p. 76.
15 Sayer 1987, p. 147.

three different but closely related senses: 1) abstraction of extension; 2) abstraction of levels of generality; and 3) abstraction of vantage point. Abstractions of extension refer to delimiting both spatial and temporal boundaries around the subject of our studies, but unlike common temporal periodisation schemes familiar to archaeologists, abstractions of extension require abstracting relations or processes rather than simply events. Abstractions of levels of generality entail alternating the focus from the specifics of a particular context to more generalised levels. Lower levels may encompass all that is unique about a person, situation, or a particular context, while higher levels may entail all that is unique to people within capitalist society, the level of class society, or all that humans have in common. All of these levels are present simultaneously, but at each level different aspects of social relations are made visible. Vantage point refers to drawing abstractions from different sides of the same relation. Since dialectical relations represent a contradictory whole, both sides must be examined to understand that whole.[16]

The abstractions Marx used in any particular case were determined by the social relations and the part of the social whole he was trying to understand. In this sense, it was not simply the boundaries that were important to Marx's understanding, but the movement between the abstractions that made visible the inherent contradictions in society. This process is clear in the way that Marx shifted the *dramatis personae* when he moved from the analysis of exchange and commodities to questions of the labour process and absolute surplus value: 'he who was before the money-owner, now strides in front as capitalist; the possessor of labour-power follows as his labourer'.[17]

This emphasis on analytic abstraction based on relations is one of the most important and powerful aspects of Marx's philosophy. Holloway notes that Marxism is 'a solvent, an acid which dissolves the social rigidities that confront us'.[18] Bhaskar describes dialectics as the 'great loosener' of established binaries.[19] This is the method and theory that Marx used for the practical goal of laying bare the inner workings of the capitalist system, a goal shared by the field of historical archaeology. But not in the sense that capitalism is defined simply by the presence of money, markets, commodities or profit, nor as just a way to designate our economy. Capitalism, as Marx understood it, is not a thing but rather a dynamic totality; it is a complex set of social relations.

---

16   Ollman 2003, pp. 59–112.
17   Marx 1967, p. 172.
18   Holloway 2010, p. 87.
19   Bhaskar 2008, p. 354.

Another key aspect of Marx's philosophy of internal relations is that it dialectically integrated both theory and method into a single totality, a position at odds with most bourgeois science. The best statement of Marx's method is presented in this oft-cited quote:

> The premises from which we begin are not arbitrary ones, not dogmas, but real premises from which abstraction can only be made in the imagination. They are the real individual, their activity and the material conditions under which they live, both those which they find already existing and those produced by their activity.[20]

In other words, Marx and Engels started from a 'material' reality and derived relevant abstractions from this reality to grasp the significance and form of social relations. Thus, Marx's method focuses attention on the production and reproduction of everyday life in all of its varied aspects and manifestations. This focus on the production and reproduction of everyday life is the basic 'stuff' that archaeology deals with, and it has clear material referents. A Marxist archaeology must always begin with a human population that is active, historically situated, and whose activity is fundamentally associated with production.

Social relations are never completely of the present. Marx famously expressed this idea as 'men make their own history, but they do not make it just as they please; they do not make it under circumstances chosen by themselves, but under circumstances directly encountered, given and transmitted from the past'.[21] These circumstances include social relations, structures, material conditions, technology, etc. To fully understand a given society, it is necessary to place it within its historical and material context. In this, dialectical research cannot simply encompass the time period in question but must be framed as the dialectical integration of past, present and future. Ollman argues that Marx did this by studying history backwards, by beginning with the present *result* and looking to the past to consider its *preconditions*.[22] Bringing these understandings forward again allowed Marx to project this potential into the future and examine the present complete with its ties to the past, while simultaneously seeing the present as a precondition of the future.[23] This is a very different approach to bourgeois ideas of evolution, progress and linear causality, and

---

20 Marx and Engels 1970, p. 42.
21 Marx 1963, p. 15.
22 Ollman 2003, p. 125.
23 Wurst and Mrozowski 2014.

very different to the simplistic understandings of Marx's philosophy that have become enshrined in archaeology within the realm of post-processual theoretical approaches.

This dialectical connection of past, present and future is also key to understanding praxis, the political commitment to change the world. This overt political goal fundamentally distinguishes Marxism from the other social theories, a position summarised in Marx and Engels famous quote 'the philosophers have only interpreted the world, in various ways; the point is to change it'.[24] Marx undertook exhaustive empirical investigations of capitalism, not as a quest for abstract knowledge, but to subvert the capitalist system based on exploitative social relations. Praxis involves the dialectical interrelationship of critique, knowledge and action: critique reveals this oppression and how we as scholars are related to it; knowledge helps us understand the structure of how this oppression works; and critique and knowledge provides the basis to take action to transform society.[25]

The implications of Marxism as theory, method and political action are clear. As a philosophy of internal dialectical relations, a Marxist approach emphasises real, socially and historically conditioned contexts, centring research on issues and questions of the material production and reproduction of everyday life, dialectically integrating the past, present, and future, all with the political goal of bringing an end to capitalism and its social relations of oppression and exploitation. Following Marx, this focuses our attention on questions of class, labour, property and alienation – that is, issues of control over production. These are the aspects of Marx's work that have attracted myriad people to his philosophy. Archaeologists, whose research focuses on the scientific study of the material detritus of the production and reproduction of everyday life, are no exception.

3 Historical Archaeology and Capitalism's Laws of Motion

Historical archaeology is a relatively recent subdiscipline of archaeology that emphasises the capitalist world, the post-sixteenth-century context of European colonisation in all its manifestations that integrated the world into a single world system. The fact that historical archaeologists study capitalism makes the connection to Marx's work and Marxist thought both easier and

---

24 Marx and Engels 1970, p. 123.
25 See McGuire, O'Donovan and Wurst 2005 and McGuire 2008.

harder; easier since the actual connection is intuitively obvious, but harder because it is more difficult to articulate a special or privileged role for the archaeological knowledge of capitalism. Other articles in this volume[26] deal with pre-capitalist contexts where archaeological data may provide the only or strongest evidence for the material basis of everyday life, the mode of production, or labour and class relations, making the importance of archaeological research obvious. The strength of historical archaeology is the integration of material and textual evidence, but this also makes it difficult to discuss any unique contribution that archaeological research provides. Thus, historical archaeological understandings are not, or should not, be unique or privileged in any way.

This is a very different approach from that typically found in historical archaeology, where the utility is elaborated and explained as a form of disciplinary exceptionalism, a way to legitimate the existence of the discipline itself. At root, these arguments are based on reifying the existence of different disciplines and presenting arguments for the relevance of those discrete ways of knowing, ultimately presenting an argument for the importance of bourgeois science.[27]

McGuire has argued that 'archaeology is a weak weapon for political action, because it cannot be wielded directly in the struggles over land, life, liberty, and wealth that drive the political process'.[28] This is arguably true of any academic discipline, and I would suggest that the disciplinary boundaries themselves thwart this kind of understanding or praxis. Our struggle is not to justify the relevance of historical archaeology, but to find room for archaeology to participate in the collective project of creating a different life, one that subverts and transforms capitalist inequalities and oppression, and strives for social justice and dignity for all humans. This changes the question from 'how can archaeology help' (as a reified, discrete authentic discipline) to 'how can my research help further Marxist goals of creating a just world without capitalism?' I believe that historical archaeology can provide valuable insights into our collective efforts to understand capitalism's laws of motion.

The caveat is that it is not sufficient to just talk about capitalism or to simply use the term. There has been a recent explosion in discussion of capitalism, intensifying after contemporary financial crises and growing inequalities that

---

26 Pérez Martínez and Ochoa, Chapter 2; Milevski et al., Chapter 3; Bajema, Chapter 4; Gonzales-Panta and Tantaleán, Chapter 5; Roskams, Chapter 6.
27 See Wurst 2015.
28 McGuire 2008, p. 21.

have put open discussions of capitalism on the table once more.[29] These same patterns are evident in historical archaeology, where there had also been a dramatic increase in discussions of capitalism.[30] The irony is that few of these works make active use of Marx or his philosophy. What this suggests is that historical archaeologists are talking more about capitalism, but they may well be doing so without relying on Marx's insights.[31]

So, what role can historical archaeology inspired by Marx's philosophy of internal relations play in exposing capitalism's laws of motion? Some of the most powerful discussions of how capitalism works deal with broad strokes and high levels of generality – they largely deal with the mechanics of capitalism – and this is important.[32] The best known and widest cited aspects of Marx's theory of capitalism are based on his account of the general trends, laws and logic of the capitalist system. Abstract concepts such as compulsive accumulation, the exploitation of labour, tendency for rates of profit to fall, crises of overproduction and appropriation of surplus value, among others, are all crucial to understand the ever-expanding, dynamic and constantly changing capitalist system. But these abstract concepts tell us nothing about real concrete behaviour in particular times and places.[33] Historical-archaeological case studies dealing with lower levels of generality and unique or particular contexts help to make these large-scale abstract processes tangible by recognising the real and material consequences for people's everyday lives.

One advantage of archaeological research on capitalism is that the artefacts we recover from our sites are all commodities produced through capitalist forces that connect our separate sites to larger capitalist productive relations.[34] For example, every bottle represents the commodity form that lies at the heart of capitalist productive relations. Markings provide concrete data about what company produced it and when, and the fact that it was found in an archaeological context hundreds of miles from where it was manufactured serves as an entry point to examine how capitalism unfolds in various ways, including the implications of technological development on labour and productive class relations,[35] the distribution of global commodities,[36] or class dynamics

---

29 Eagleton 2011, p. xi.
30 Some examples include Croucher and Weiss 2011, Fracchia and Brighton 2015, Matthews 2012 and Pezzarossi 2019.
31 See Wurst and Lewis 2020.
32 See Harman 2009, McNally 2011 and, of course, Marx 1967.
33 Harman 2009, p. 72.
34 Wurst and Mrozowski 2014.
35 Paynter 1988.
36 Adams, Bower and Mills 2001. See also Roller 2019.

at household, community or regional scales.[37] In other words, a single artefact representing a commodity demonstrates how capitalism as a totalising system can be examined through the common detritus that archaeologists study.[38] This means that the dynamics of capitalism can be examined through any historic site, since all historic sites are/were part of the dialectic totality of the capitalist system, although some sites might be better for our purposes than others.

In the remainder of this paper, I want to develop these ideas with concrete case studies. While I have suggested that every historic-period site can be used to lay bare capitalism's laws of motion, there is utility in pointing toward particular kinds of research that directly further Marxist goals. In particular, I want to emphasise research geared toward: 1) making use of the class privilege that the discipline of archaeology affords; 2) producing detailed studies of the capitalist transformations of labour and class; 3) providing rich empirical contexts that challenge dominant ideologies, reified categories and common sense historical understandings that justify those in power and capitalism itself; 4) constructing shock effects that reveal the monstrosity of commodified life; and, finally, 5) reclaiming alternatives to and for the future. In what follows, I elaborate each of these contributions with an archaeological vignette (some brief, some detailed). In no way is this classification meant to be mutually exclusive or comprehensive, nor are these objectives limited to historical archaeology. I also do not mean to suggest that other Marxist archaeologists have not already done important work that lies outside of this classification. These thoughts would not be possible without the pioneering work 'laying bare' the ideological uses of archaeology for nationalist, colonialist and imperialist purposes.[39] There are probably many other ways where the particular craft of historical archaeology can make contributions to the Marxist agenda.

3.1   *Class Privileges*

One simple way that archaeology can help is to wield the class privilege that the discipline of archaeology affords for Marxist goals. It has been well documented that archaeology arose and continues as a form of middle-class practice.[40] This

---

37 Wurst 1999.
38 Of course, this process of connecting individual sites and artefacts to larger economic dynamics is a key facet of Marxist archaeology, regardless of the period in question. V. Gordon Childe's eponymous 'Man Makes Himself' (1936) is the classic demonstration of this process.
39 Trigger 1984. See also individual contributions in Schmidt and Patterson 1995 and Kohl and Fawcett 1995.
40 See Trigger 1989, Patterson 2002, Hamilakis and Duke 2007, and McGuire 2008.

class privilege confers opportunities to re-present the past by enacting our own archaeological pageants for Marxist ends. The very fact that archaeologists find a site worthy of research increases the visibility of that aspect of the past and lends authority and legitimacy to aspects of history that have been silenced, forgotten or ignored as part of the political uses of the past. An important example of this is the archaeological research of the Colorado Coalfield War including the Ludlow Tent Colony and massacre site. Dean Saitta, Randy McGuire, Phil Duke and other members of the Ludlow Collective clearly articulated this project as a form of emancipatory archaeology that emphasised class struggle, using their archaeological privilege to increase the legitimacy, awareness and importance of this site as an element of ongoing capitalist class warfare.[41]

3.2 *Transformations of Labour and Class*

The second clear contribution that we can make is producing detailed studies of the capitalist transformations of labour and class that go beyond simplistic statements at high levels of generality and which are geared, instead, toward elucidating the implications of structural changes on actual people's everyday lives. To clarify this, I provide a brief example on the labour transformations in the tourist industry based on archaeology data from one of the most eponymous tourist sites in the United States, Niagara Falls.

Literature on the history of tourism has burgeoned, but most of it is from a middle-class vantage point.[42] In this copious literature, we read all about the tourist's gaze, the creation of a consumer-oriented culture and the commodification of experience, yet there was scarcely a mention of the army of workers who made the middle-class experience possible.[43] Archaeological work for a bridge replacement project in Niagara Falls uncovered two privies, each with two temporally distinct artefact deposits associated with the Niagara House Hotel (Figure 7.1).[44] Nineteenth-century censuses document that hotels in Niagara Falls housed a large number of live-in employees, but between 1870 and 1880, these hotels reduced their live-in labour force by up to 75 percent. The 1880 census reveals many more households headed by hotel workers as well as

---

41 See Saitta 2007, Larkin and McGuire 2009, McGuire 2008, and Wood 2002.
42 Examples include Mackintosh 2019, Aron 1999, Brown 1995, Lofgren 1999, Urry 1990 and Withey 1997. All of these sources use the term 'middle class' in the common bourgeois sense.
43 Exceptions include Cocks 2001 and Sinclair 1997.
44 Wurst 2011.

FIGURE 7.1   The Niagara House
HOLDER 1882

an increase in workers living in the boarding houses scattered throughout the city. Most of the workers were either waiters or domestics, and this labour force was highly stratified in terms of occupation, sex and race. Without exception, the waiters were all men and the domestics were all women. The breakdown of employees based on race and sex reveals that the female workers were mostly white and Irish, while the males were black or mulatto, a structure reflecting stereotyped ideals of the Irish-immigrant domestic and the African-American waiter.[45] Having about 100 workers living in the same structure as the elite tourists they served must have created a situation rife with conflict and contradiction, and it seems obvious that management controlled the moral behaviour and sexual relations of the workers by manipulating existing hierarchies of race, class and gender.[46] The census records indicate a highly structured labour force living within the hotels, and one that was diminishing in numbers through time.

The privy deposit from the 1870s comprised a sample of over 7,000 artefacts and represents at least 184 unique ceramic and glass vessels. Analysis demon-

---

45   See Dudden 1985, Katzman 1981 and Cocks 2001.
46   Cocks 2001, p. 89.

strated that they were goods used in the hotel as well as those associated with the hotel's employees. Compared to other deposits from the site, these workers ate much cheaper foods from inexpensive dishes than the hotel guests. This is hardly surprising. More interesting is that this deposit yielded dominos and other gaming pieces, doll china and other doll fragments, showing that the workers found ways to occupy their probably limited off-duty hours. None of these workers had children living with them – the dolls and doll china may relate to the fact that many of these workers were themselves children. Female hotel servants range in age from 16 to 28, with an average age of 23. The privy, abandoned and capped around 1877, corresponds to the time when this hotel reduced their live-in staff. And this corresponds to developments in transportation that led to an increase in middle- and working-class tourism in Niagara Falls and a concomitant decrease in elite visitation. As visitors stayed for shorter periods of time, competition among Niagara's hotels must have become fierce. Hotel management responded to this competition by reducing their staff and no longer including board as part of the workers' wages. These savings in labour costs meant that the hotels could be competitive and still realise a profit. Of course, this meant that workers had to assume their own housing costs, representing a significant and dramatic decrease in absolute wages.[47] In this case, the abstract laws of capitalist motion – increasing both absolute and relative surplus value – attain an actual material and physical context while reminding us that capitalism has always had real-life casualties.

3.3 Everyday Life through Trash

The third kind of contribution I want to highlight is that an archaeological focus on mundane aspects of everyday life through the study of the trash that people left behind provides rich empirical contexts and data that make it easier to challenge the reified categories and common-sense understandings that permeate bourgeois reconstructions of the past. This empirical richness provides more compelling, intellectually satisfying explanations than theoretical arguments alone. In other words, our material data provides powerful ways to 'speak truth to power'.

One example is the research on the transformation of capitalist agriculture based on the archaeological investigation of 22 farms on the Hector Backbone in the Finger Lakes region of Central New York.[48] This area, settled in the early

---

47   Wurst 2011.
48   Wurst and Ridarsky 2014.

FIGURE 7.2 Resettlement Administration poster
RICHARD H. JANSEN, C. 1935

nineteenth century, was farmed extensively until the 1930s, when the Resettlement Administration began buying the farms as part of the New Deal's Submarginal Farms program. The literature justifies this dramatic intervention as 'saving farm families' who were 'stranded on sub-marginal farms', and that removing these farms from production saved farmers from their 'hopeless struggle' (Figure 7.2).[49] Historians argue that New York's agriculture experienced a slow but inevitable decline beginning around 1850, which resulted from the availability of better farmland in the West, transportation improvements, loss of soil fertility, and/or the unwillingness of northeastern farmers to adopt modern progressive farming practices.[50]

As a result of our work, we have documented hundreds of features, excavated over 800 square metres of surface area, and recovered more than 200,000 artefacts. All of this rich archaeological data, in conjunction with documentary evidence, contradicts the idea that the farmers of the Hector Backbone were engaged in a hopeless struggle and barely surviving. Instead, we have clear evidence of farm improvements, building and repair well into the twentieth century; historic farm-productivity data that reveals virtually no object-

---

49 Allen 1925; Foote et al. 1944, p. 1.
50 See Hedrick 1933 and Carlson 1974 as examples.

ive evidence for decline; analysis of soils that demonstrates that they were no different than other parts of the county; and artefact data that shows that these farmers were involved in an elaborate consumer culture which included farm equipment, automobiles or trucks, and telephone service installed at their own expense.[51] These contradictions show that rhetoric about saving poor and unproductive farmers trapped by their own ineptitude or the inevitable circumstances of bad soil was simply ideological, used to justify the government's New Deal resettlement policies. These policies worked through existing power and class structures to ensure that the farms that would be saved were those that met developing standards of industrial capitalist-style agriculture, while upland farms, such as those on the Hector Backbone, which were less suited to commercial agriculture, were sacrificed. Thus, this archaeological research on abandoned farms emphasises the dialectical connections between governmental land-planning policy, the class competition between different groups of farmers and the role of agriculture in capitalism, all of which ultimately highlight processes of capitalist dispossession. In the process, this research has exposed the ideology that hides these processes from view.

3.4   *Exploding the Continuum of History*

The fourth kind of contribution I want to highlight begins with Benjamin's theses on the philosophy of history. Benjamin contrasts historicism – easily recognised as bourgeois history that a Marxist 'cannot contemplate without horror' – with a historical materialism focused on the dialectical integration of past, present and future, whose goal is to 'brush history against the grain' and to 'explode the continuum of history'.[52] If historicism serves the victors and presents a view of history that hides the commodified capitalist nature of our existence, Marxism can 'construct shock-effects' that reveal the horror and monstrous nature of commodified existence.[53]

To explore the power of this approach, I want to tell a ghost story that has emerged from archaeological research at the Dunham 1 Farm Site on the Hector Backbone in New York's Finger Lakes. On July 25, 1878, the *Watkins Express* reported that 'a man by the name of McNish in the town of Hector committed suicide by hanging himself' in his barn 'when evidently in a condition of temporary insanity' (Figure 7.3). The following week, the newspaper described

---

51   Wurst and Ridarsky 2014, pp. 227–34.
52   Benjamin 1974.
53   McNally 2011, p. 7.

FIGURE 7.3 The McNish barn, photograph from the 1936 Acquisition Plan for the Township of Hector, Schuyler County, New York.
RECORDS OF THE NATURAL RESOURCES CONSERVATION SERVICE, UNITED STATES NATIONAL ARCHIVES, COLLEGE PARK, MD

Jesse McNish as 'a well to do farmer and respected by all, and no reason can be assigned for his rash act save temporary insanity'. He left a widow and three children to mourn his untimely death. While the editor of the newspaper, and perhaps their readers, could find no explanation for this senseless act, the dialectical optics of Marxism presents a different story.

Jesse McNish was born in 1825 in Orange County, New York. The 1850 federal census lists him as a young farmer with $500 in real estate, living next to his father with his wife, daughter, mother-in-law and a 24-year-old male labourer. In 1855, the McNish family was still living in Orange County, Jesse was listed as a grocer and a male clerk boarded with them. According to the 1860 Federal Census, the 35-year-old Jesse had relocated to Tioga County, New York, and he was listed as a merchant with $4,000 in both real and personal estate.[54]

McNish moved to Hector in 1864 after he acquired the Dunham Farm of upwards of a hundred acres for $3,100, subject to two mortgages of $600 each. After Jesse purchased the farm, he built a new house and barn complex. Our investigations documented the large dwelling with a full cellar, a porch addi-

54   Federal census records available through HeritgeQuest Online.

tion and a kitchen addition with a stone-lined well under the floor, as well as a smokehouse, box privy, small outbuilding, a spring house and a large barn complex. While Jesse constructed most of these features to establish the farm, very few of the over 11,000 artefacts can be associated with his occupation. A few scattered blue transfer-printed and hand-painted ceramic sherds and a Home-Rule smoking pipe are among the few artefacts that date to their fourteen-year occupation. The McNish family seem to have left little trace at the site, except for the structures and Jesse's ghost.

The *Watkins Express* described McNish as a well-to-do farmer, and census data confirms this. In 1870, Jesse was listed with $6,000 in real estate and $1,000 in personal estate. The McNish household also included a female domestic and male farm labourer. Information from the agricultural schedules offers more complexity. The farm was valued at $3,000 one year after McNish purchased the farm, and five years later the farm value had doubled to $6,000 when he reported a product value of $2,166. By 1875, however, McNish's farm value had dropped to $4,000 and his value of product plummeted to only $443. Other signs of fiscal stress can be gleaned from probate records. After his death, Jesse's goods were sold at public auction to settle his debt, and McNish's creditors filed suit in the New York Supreme Court on April 8, 1879, related to unpaid mortgages on the Dunham 1 farm. These records indicate that McNish repaid very little of the mortgages taken out on this farm. The final judgement was that all land be sold at public auction to pay the mortgages, unpaid interest and plaintiff costs.[55]

While we will never know the specific circumstances that led Jesse to such a 'rash act', the timing of his suicide within the Long Depression of 1873 to 1878, along with evidence for the sudden devaluing of his farm and products, indicates how this individual suicide story links to larger processes of capitalist dispossession. The Panic of 1873 represents the creative destruction that solved the crisis of overproduction, which resulted from the post-Civil War boom in productive capacity. This panic ultimately saw capitalism's credit and economic development shift from central Europe to the United States. Speculation in Germany and France expanded dramatically in the 1860s, as credit led to a building boom and sky-rocketing land prices. These shaky foundations were undercut by the importation of low-cost manufactured goods, in particular cheap grain produced by farmers in the American Midwest, in developments which became

---

55   Deed, mortgage, probate and census information available in the Schuyler County Clerk's Office, Watkins Glen, New York. Microfilm copies of the *Watkin's Express* available at the Schuyler County Historical Society, Montour Falls, New York.

known as the American Commercial Invasion. The European crash of May hit the United States in the fall of 1873. The banking crisis hit heavily bonded railroads first, but soon rippled through every corner of the political economy. Thousands of companies defaulted over a billion dollars in debt, nine out of ten railroad companies failed, all leading to double digit unemployment and a 25 percent drop in real wages.[56]

The agricultural sector was especially hard hit as crop prices plummeted. Cotton prices fell 50 percent in just six months, and other commodities followed suit. This decline was coupled with steady deflation, which meant that farmer's debts became more expensive at the same time they had less money for repayments because of plunging crop prices. Property sales and bankruptcies became common. Many farmers likely reacted as Jesse McNish did and took their own lives, although it is virtually impossible to find any statistics or literature to confirm this. Most understandings mimic those of the newspaper – as senseless acts related to temporary insanity.

What I do know, however, is that if you Google 'farmer suicide', you will learn about the contemporary epidemic of farmer suicides exploding worldwide. In the United States, farmer suicide occurs at twice the rate of the general population, mirroring the situation of farmers in Australia, the UK and France.[57] In the Indian state of Maharashtra, at least ten farmers have committed suicide every day for over ten years, and across India more broadly, more than 270,000 farmers have committed suicide since 1995. The literature on this epidemic is vast and contradictory. Claims that it is the fault of Monsanto's GM 'seeds of suicide', the World Trade Organization's structural-adjustment policies, US farm subsidies, the green revolution or global trading in farm commodities are all made while, at the same time, 'scientific' government reports emphasise individual psychological causes such as alcoholism and low self-esteem. Without defaulting to single or simple explanations, we do know that most of the suicide victims were small and marginal farmers with high levels of debt who were adversely affected by neoliberal economic policies.[58]

Under neoliberal capitalism, US crop surpluses have been dumped in foreign markets, undermining national food production capacity. As countries produce less of their own food, they become increasingly dependent on the vagaries of speculation in commodity futures and on the whims of global corporations. World Bank policies and structural adjustment are based on the agriculture

---

56   Nelson 2008.
57   Weingarten 2018.
58   Mohanty 2005, p. 276. See also Shiva 2009.

of corporate seeds that require pesticides and fertilisers, all to be purchased anew each year. Skyrocketing debt leading to skyrocketing food prices, hunger, starvation, and suicide have been the result.[59]

Juxtaposed in this way, we can see that Jesse McNish's suicide is the forehistory of the farmers in Maharashtra, presenting the 'tiger's leap … into the open sky of history' that explodes the linear continuum of history and forces the confrontation of past and present.[60] These are the dialectical optics based on the shock of recognising the precursors of the present no matter how distant or estranged they appear.[61] As Marx states, the student of history 'always finds his peasantry turning up again, although in diminished number, and always under worse conditions'.[62] Examining Jesse McNish's story side by side with the contemporary conditions of farmers provides a shock effect that manifests aspects of the social relations of capitalism, laying bare capitalism's laws of motion.

3.5 Alternatives to the Future

The final point I want to make is that historical-archaeological research can help to reclaim alternatives to/for the future by revealing the 'sprouts of communism' that already exist in capitalism. On the day I began to write this article, the Doomsday Clock was moved to 100 seconds, the closest that humanity has ever been to total annihilation, a state of affairs directly related to capitalism. It is commonly said that it is easier to imagine the end of the world than the end of capitalism, a sentiment, when coupled with the TINA doctrine (There Is No Alternative), works ideologically to incapacitate people from challenging the system that has created our dire condition. Ollman has argued that common interpretations of Marx's utopian ideas of communism are based on treating the past, present and future as separate and independent stages of history,[63] implying an inevitable movement through these stages, an idea that is very familiar to archaeologists. This common perspective is based on viewing communism as a totalising system from the perspective of communism itself – that is, as a not-yet-existing ideal. This makes it very easy to see why many people find it difficult to believe in such a society.

Instead, Ollman argues that Marx viewed communism from the vantage point of capitalism itself and that these 'sprouts' exist because capitalism is a

---

59   See Bello and Baviera 2009, Patel 2007 and Albritton 2009.
60   Benjamin 1974.
61   Buck-Morss 1991, p. 219.
62   Marx 1967, p. 700.
63   Ollman 2014, 64–5.

system fraught with contradictions internal to the dialectically related whole.[64] Thus, the eponymous quote from Marx and Engels, 'what the bourgeoisie therefore produces, above all, are its own grave-diggers',[65] is not a prediction of an inevitable future state, but rather the recognition of the internal contradictions of capitalism itself. Following Marx, we need to recognise that 'the sprouts of communism' already lie concealed in capitalism and that our goal as archaeologists should be to reveal them. These sprouts are hard to see, since revolutionary actions that did not lead to permanent social change are typically hidden, silenced or cast as failures. Holloway notes that this is wrong, for these acts have a validity of their own, independent of their long-term consequences: 'like a flash of lightning, they illuminate a different world ... the world that does not yet exist displays itself as a world that exists not-yet'.[66] Another problem is that most research on class struggle tends to emphasise unions and organised labour, a perspective that inadvertently reinforces the idea that there is no alternative, in the era of declining unions, by making other forms of class consciousness and activism literally unthinkable. Ironically, we have taken the idea of struggle in class struggle too literally – perhaps even adopting a bourgeois understanding of the term – and eschewed the real potential of Marx's internal relational understanding of class struggle that emphasises the dialectics of the two-fold nature of labour.

Marx himself claimed that this two-fold nature of labour, as abstract and useful or concrete labour, is 'the pivot on which a clear comprehension of Political Economy turns'.[67] Useful or concrete labour is the self-determined, purposive, conscious life activity that distinguishes humans from other animals – which lies at the very heart of our humanity, or species-being as Marx called it – while abstract labour is labour that produces abstract surplus value in capitalism. The strength of Marx's concept of the two-fold nature of labour is realising that concrete and abstract labour do not exist as separate acts, moments or events, but are simultaneous and contradictory relations. According to Holloway, 'concrete labour (potentially conscious life-activity) exists in the form of abstract labour, but exists in-against-and-beyond abstract labour'.[68] Rather than a totalising coherent system (that is daunting to face), capitalism is, by its very nature, inconsistent and contradictory, fraught with fissures and cracks; the sprouts of its undoing. These are the realisations that provide the frame-

---

64 Ollman 2008, p. 12.
65 Marx and Engels 1955, p. 22.
66 Holloway 2010, p. 30.
67 Marx 1967, p. 49.
68 Holloway 2012, pp. 517–18.

FIGURE 7.4 Photo of the workers at Coalwood (c. 1901).
MARQUETTE REGIONAL HISTORY CENTER, MARQUETTE, MICHIGAN

work to envision a different future and a place for our archaeological work: to highlight and expand the cracks that have always already been an essential part of capitalism.

As an example, I want to discuss archaeological research at Coalwood, a cordwood lumber camp operated by the Cleveland Cliffs Iron Company (CCI) from 1901 to 1912, now located in the Hiawatha National Forest in Michigan's Upper Peninsula. CCI was primarily an iron ore mining company, but they developed their cordwood operations to replace imported coal in their iron furnaces. CCI invested as little as possible in camp infrastructure to keep their labour costs low. They gave rights to people to construct and operate boarding houses and the camp store, or they built them themselves and then sold them to others to operate. CCI's only cost in establishing Coalwood was clearing the site and digging the well, and the tenants paid a fee to access the water. Thus, the camp largely formed itself as workers flocked to the area with their families and built their own dwellings (Figure 7.4).

The Finnish choppers who lived at Coalwood were paid by the cord. The figures for this piece work varied from .75 ¢ to $1.25, and the company tried to keep these figures as low as possible. CCI's annual reports are replete with statements bemoaning labour shortages, their inability to attract and retain productive workers, and competition with other area employers. When they were forced to increase wages because of shortages or competition, their strategy was to 'accumulate a safe reserve of wood' and then reduce wages again.[69]

There is a real contradiction in having labour concentrated to extract a finite resource and paying choppers by the cord produced. As timber resources diminished, productivity and wages would decrease as well, since the choppers would spend more time traveling to timber stands than cutting wood. The 1909 annual report states that 'the men have in nearly all cases been obliged to walk long distances to their work, a fact which has prevented the increase of their numbers', confirming that many workers resisted these conditions. By 1910, CCI 'reduced the choppers to actual family men ... working on very indifferent timber ... which under normal labour conditions, would be difficult to get out'. Men with families were less likely to engage in labour disputes and also allowed CCI to appropriate the unwaged labour of their wives and children.[70]

CCI's own business model created cracks that allowed the workers to control their concrete labour within the dictates of abstract capitalist production. Their everyday life within these cracks is evident in the large and diverse assemblage of domestic artefacts resulting from our archaeological excavations. Even though Coalwood was not a planned town, the site layout suggests a level of regularity, with even rows of houses along both sides of the road, which represents the creation of a worker community. Unidentified and architectural objects are the most common represented by the 68,000 artefacts, but a wide array of ceramics, bottles, cans and other materials are present across the site. Most of the tightly dated artefacts indicate that the workers brought very few goods with them; there is no evidence of heirlooms, unsurprising for recent immigrants. The site yielded a lot of evidence for premiums, objects that would come free with other purchases, such as stencilled blue cups, the style referred to as 'oatmeal pattern', that came in cereal packages, and Geisha Girl-pattern Japanese porcelain dishes which were free with tea purchases.

Among the more specialised artefacts are medicine bottles containing Finnish blood purifier, produced and marketed by August Edwards, a Finnish newspaper editor of Ashtabula, Ohio. Other evidence for the workers' concern for health and hygiene lies in their yards. The workers' houses had pristine yards with little topsoil – suggesting that the yards were frequently cleared and cleaned – and dense middens were spatially concentrated just outside of these

---

69   Annual Report 1899, p. 26. Cleveland Cliffs Iron Company annual reports available through the Cleveland-Cliffs Iron Company Historical Records Digitization Project, Northern Michigan University Archive. See: https://uparchives.nmu.edu/CCI/Index.html.
70   Howe 2015.

cleaned areas. The Finnish choppers at Coalwood also constructed a sauna that was centrally located along the row of worker houses, suggesting that it was used communally.

Aspects of communality are also evident in the alcohol bottles. Even though CCI did not prohibit alcohol in these camps, alcohol bottles were found in relatively low numbers within every feature area investigated, suggesting that alcohol was associated with community and sociability rather than the stereotypical drunken lumberjack. Frank Debelak recalls that communal events were very common, and people travelled to different camps for socialising events consisting of dancing, music and storytelling.[71] It is reasonable to assume that alcohol was a part of these communal events, explaining the widespread distribution of these bottles.[72] Another aspect of this communality is found in the large number and diversity of musical reed plates related to harmonicas, accordions and concertinas. We found so many of these that we were able to assess a minimum of 20 unique musical instruments recovered from every context across the site, indicating the importance of music to the workers' everyday lives.[73]

A small sample of artefacts relate to educating children and literacy. One worker's house site yielded fragments of an alphabet plate. Interestingly, ink bottles, slate fragments and pencils, all evidence of literacy, were concentrated in the worker houses rather than the store or camp office, where we would expect record keeping. Many artefacts relate to domestic labour and provide evidence of the productive roles of wives and children, including canning jars and stoneware crocks, fishing and hunting equipment, and spiles for tapping maple trees. All of this archaeological evidence provides rich details about these workers' everyday experiences and their efforts to control their own concrete labour within the dictates of abstract capitalist production.

The choppers' ability to live and work in their own houses with their families was undoubtedly an important reason for staying at Coalwood while timber resources diminished. What these workers sacrificed in the wages gleaned from 'indifferent timber' would have been more than compensated by the autonomy they had over their everyday lives. It is imperative that we recognise that the 'other doing' of Coalwood's choppers did not lie outside of capitalism in some utopian experiment, but was internal to capitalist production itself, a clear example of how, according to Holloway, concrete labour exists in the

---

71 A transcription of Frank Debelak's oral history is on file at the Hiawatha National Forest, Escanaba, MI.
72 Allen 2019.
73 Durocher 2018.

form of abstract labour, but also in-against-and-beyond it.[74] I doubt the Coalwood choppers were unique, and their privileging of concrete over abstract labour in everyday life was undoubtedly far more common than we recognise. The strength of archaeological case studies lies in the powerful and visceral materiality that makes the everyday life of alternatives imaginable. Historical-archaeological case studies can help battle the hopelessness of the TINA doctrine, enabling us to envision an end to capitalism that does not include the end of the world.

4   Conclusion

I have intentionally focused much of my allotted space on case studies, since I believe that this is the real contribution that historical archaeology can make to Marxism. Archaeology adds a richness and nuance to empirical understandings of the materiality of everyday life. Even so, it is important to recognise that all of the vignettes I have presented could just as easily have been told without historical archaeology at all. Recognising this does not disparage what our research can offer, but it does resist the temptation to legitimate the existence of the discipline itself or to argue that historical archaeology as a discipline has a unique or privileged standpoint.

However, I would also argue that none of these stories could have been told without Marxism. What Marxism adds is a dialectical philosophy that makes it possible to ask different questions that focus on the larger goal of laying bare the economic law of motion of modern society. Some of the most powerful discussions of how capitalism works emphasise broad strokes, high levels of generality and abstract concepts. But these abstract concepts tell us nothing and allow no conclusions about real concrete behaviour in particular times and places.[75] As Marx claimed, 'to be radical is to grasp the root of the matter. But, for man, the root is man himself'.[76] Historical-archaeological case studies – dealing as they do with lower levels of generality, unique or particular contexts and the materiality of everyday life – can help flesh out how capitalism unfolds and help us to see the real concrete implications of these large-scale abstract processes on people's actual lives.

In addition to highlighting capitalism's laws of motion, historical-archaeological research can make important contributions to Marx's goal of 'laying

---

74   Holloway 2012, pp. 517–18.
75   Harman 2009, p. 72.
76   Marx 1843.

bare'. Obviously, archaeologists 'lay bare' artefacts when they excavate them from the dirt, but this is not what Marx meant. Marx needs to 'lay bare' capitalism's laws of motion, since they are not obvious or immediately apparent but are rather distorted or disguised.[77] For any Marxist to 'grasp the root of the matter', efforts must be made to simply reveal capitalism. It is true that people have recently been talking more about capitalism, but many seem to be doing so without Marx's insights.[78] Ollman has argued that for capitalism 'to be noticed, let alone understood, people's attention has to be drawn to certain relations', since 'any effort to explain how it works must be accompanied by an equally strenuous effort to display it, to simply show that it exists and what kind of entity it is'.[79] McNally suggests that 'the very insidiousness of the capitalist grotesque has to do with its invisibility'.[80] Historical archaeology may not offer a unique or privileged position to combat capitalism, but it does offer a material viscerality that is hardly invisible. Whether the goal is to re-present the past, develop the richness of class and labour relations, challenge dominant ideologies, produce shock effects or alternative visions of the future in the past, historical-archaeological research has a great deal to offer, not because of any autonomous privileged positionality, but in collaboration with our comrades as we strive to create a world without capitalism.

References

Adams, William H., Peter M. Bowers and Robin Mills 2001, 'Commodity Flows and National Market Access: A Case Study from Interior Alaska', *Historical Archaeology*, 35, 2: 73–107.

Albritton, Robert 2009, *Let Them Eat Junk: How Capitalism Creates Hunger and Obesity*, New York: Pluto Press.

Allen, Tyler D. 2019, *Intemperate Men: Alcohol and Autonomy within the Lumber Camps of Michigan's Upper Peninsula*, Master's Thesis, Houghton, MI: Michigan Technological University.

Allen, William 1925, *The Utilization of Marginal and Sub-Marginal Hill Farm Land*, PhD, Ithaca, NY: Cornell University.

Aron, Cindy S. 1999, *Working at Play: A History of Vacations in the United States*, New York: Oxford University Press.

---

77 Ollman 2014b.
78 Wurst and Lewis 2020.
79 Ollman 2003, pp. 3–4.
80 McNally 2011, p. 2.

Bello, Walden and Mara Baviera 2009, 'Food Wars', *Monthly Review*, 61, 3: 17–31.
Benjamin, Walter 1974 [1940], 'On the Concept of History', Frankfurt: Suhrkamp Verlag, available at: https://www.marxists.org/reference/archive/benjamin/1940/history.htm.
Bhaskar, Roy 2008, *Dialectic*, New York: Routledge.
Brown, Dona 1995, *Inventing New England: Regional Tourism in the Nineteenth Century*, Washington: Smithsonian Institution Press.
Buck-Morss, Susan 1991, *The Dialectics of Seeing*, Cambridge, MA: MIT Press.
Carlson, Carolyn 1974, *Land and Life: Historical Ecology at Hector Land Use Area*, Master's Thesis, Cornell University.
Cocks, Catherine 2001, *Doing the Town: The Rise of Urban Tourism in the United States, 1850–1915*, Berkeley, CA: University of California Press.
Croucher, Sarah K. and Lindsay Weiss (eds.) 2011, *The Archaeology of Capitalism in Colonial Contexts*, New York: Springer.
Dudden, Faye 1985, *Serving Women: Household Service in Nineteenth-Century America*, Middletown, CT: Wesleyan University Press.
Durocher, Matthew 2018, *Music in the Northern Woods: An Archaeological Exploration of Musical Instrument Remains*, Master's Thesis, Houghton, MI: Michigan Technological University, available at: https://digitalcommons.mtu.edu/etdr/575.
Eagleton, Terry 1996, *The Illusion of Postmodernism*, Oxford: Blackwell Publishers.
Eagleton, Terry 2011, *Why Marx Was Right*, New Haven: Yale University Press.
Foote, Nelson, Walfred A. Anderson and Walter McKain 1944, *Families Displaced in a Federal Sub-Marginal Land Purchase Program*, Agriculture Experiment Station Bulletin, Cornell University.
Fracchia, Adam and Stephen A. Brighton 2015, 'Limestone and Ironstone: Capitalism, Value, and Destruction in a Nineteenth and Twentieth-Century Quarry Town', in *Historical Archaeologies of Capitalism*, edited by Mark P. Leone and Jocelyn E. Knauf, New York: Springer.
Hamilakis, Yannis and Philip Duke (eds.) 2007, *Archaeology and Capitalism*, Walnut Creek, CA: Left Coast Press.
Harman, Chris 2009, *Zombie Capitalism: Global Crisis and the Relevance of Marx*, Chicago: Haymarket Books.
Harvey, David 1996, *Justice, Nature and the Geography of Difference*, Oxford: Blackwell Publishers.
Harvey, David 2000, *Spaces of Hope*, Berkeley: University of California Press.
Hedrick, Ulysses 1933, *A History of Agriculture in the State of New York*, New York: Hill and Wang.
Holder, Thomas 1882, *A Complete Record of Niagara Falls and Vicinage*, Niagara Falls: Digital Collection of Niagara Falls Guidebooks from the 19th Century, Niagara University Library.

Holloway, John 2010, *Crack Capitalism*, London: Pluto Press.
Holloway, John 2012, 'Crisis and Critique', *Capital and Class*, 36, 3: 515–19.
Howe, Aaron 2015, *"Men of Good Timber": An Archaeological Investigation of Labor in Michigan's Upper Peninsula*, Master's Thesis, Kalamazoo, MI: Western Michigan University.
Katzman, D. 1981, *Seven Days a Week: Women and Domestic Service in Industrializing America*, Chicago: University of Illinois Press.
Kohl, Philip L. and Clare Fawcett (eds.) 1995, *Nationalism, Politics, and the Practice of Archaeology*, Cambridge: Cambridge University Press.
Larkin, Karin and Randall H. McGuire (eds.) 2009, *The Archaeology of Class War: The Colorado Coal Field Strike of 1913–14*, Boulder, CO: University Press of Colorado.
Lofgren, Orvar 1999, *On Holiday: A History of Vacationing*, Berkeley: University of California Press.
Lukács, Georg 1973 [1923], *History and Class Consciousness*, Cambridge, MA: MIT Press.
Mackintosh, Will B. 2019, *Selling the Sights*, New York: New York University Press.
Mao Zedong 1975 [1937], 'On Contradiction', in *Selected Works of Mao Tse-tung*, Volume 1, Peking: Foreign Language Press.
Marx, Karl 1843, *A Contribution to the Critique of Hegel's Philosophy of Right*, available at: https://www.marxists.org/archive/marx/works/1843/critique-hpr/intro.htm.
Marx, Karl 1963, *The Eighteenth Brumaire of Louis Bonaparte*, New York: International Publishers.
Marx, Karl 1967, *Capital*, New York: International Publishers.
Marx, Karl and Frederick Engels 1970, *The German Ideology*, New York: International Publishers.
Marx, Karl and Frederick Engels 1987, *Manifesto of the Communist Party*, available at: https://www.marxists.org/archive/marx/works/1848/communist-manifesto/index.htm. Marxist Internet Archive.
Matthews, Christopher N. 2012, *The Archaeology of American Capitalism*, Gainesville: University Press of Florida.
McGuire, Randall H. 1992, *A Marxist Archaeology*, San Diego: Academic Press.
McGuire, Randall H. 2008, *Archaeology as Political Action*, Berkeley: University of California Press.
McGuire, Randall H., Maria O'Donovan and LouAnn Wurst 2005, 'Probing Praxis in Archaeology: The Last Eighty Years', *Rethinking Marxism*, 17, 3: 355–72.
McGuire, Randall H. and LouAnn Wurst 2002, 'Struggling with the Past', *International Journal of Historical Archaeology*, 6, 2: 85–94.
McNally, David 2011, *Monsters of the Market: Zombies, Vampires and Global Capitalism*, Chicago: Haymarket Books.
Mohanty, B.B. 2005, '"We Are Like the Living Dead": Farmer Suicides in Maharashtra, India', *Journal of Peasant Studies*, 32, 2: 243–76.

Moore, Jason W. 2017, 'Metabolic Rift or Metabolic Shift? Dialectics, Nature, and the World-Historical Method', *Theory and Society*, 46, 4: 285–318.

Natural Resources Conservation Service Records, Record Group 114, College Park, MD: National Archives and Records Administration.

Nelson, Scott 2008, 'The Real Great Depression', *Chronicle of Higher Education*, available at: https://www.chronicle.com/article/the-real-great-depression/.

Ollman, Bertell 1993, *Dialectical Investigations*, New York: Routledge.

Ollman, Bertell 2003, *Dance of the Dialectic: Steps in Marx's Method*, Urbana: University of Illinois Press.

Ollman, Bertell 2008, 'Why Dialectics? Why Now?', in *Dialectics for the New Century*, edited by Bertell Ollman and Tony Smith, London: Palgrave MacMillan.

Ollman, Bertell 2014a, 'Communism: The Utopian "Marxist Vision" Versus a Dialectical and Scientific Marxist Approach', in *Communism in the 21st Century*, Volume 1, edited by Shannon Brincat, Santa Barbara, CA: Praeger.

Ollman, Bertell 2014b, 'Historical Archaeology, Dialectical Materialism, and "C.F.U.G. Studies"', *International Journal of Historical Archaeology*, 18, 2: 316–73.

Patel, Raj 2007, *Stuffed and Starved*, London: Portobello Books.

Patterson, Thomas C. 2002, *Toward a Social History of Archaeology in the United States*, Belmont, CA: Wadsworth Thomsen Learning.

Patterson, Thomas C. 2003, *Marx's Ghost: Conversations with Archaeologists*, Berg: Oxford.

Patterson, Thomas C. 2009, *Karl Marx, Anthropologist*, Oxford: Berg.

Paynter, Robert 1988, 'Steps to an Archaeology of Capitalism', in *The Recovery of Meaning: Historical Archaeology in the Eastern United States*, edited by Mark P. Leone and Parker B. Potter, Washington: Smithsonian Institution Press.

Pezzarossi, Guido 2019, 'Introduction: Rethinking the Archaeology of Capitalism: Coercion, Violence, and the Politics of Accumulation', *Historical Archaeology*, 53, 3–4: 453–67.

Roller, Michael P. 2019, 'The Archaeology of Machinic Consumption: The Logistics of the Factory Floor in Everyday Life', *Historical Archaeology*, 53, 1: 3–24.

Saitta, Dean J. 2007, *The Archaeology of Collective Action*, Gainesville: University Press of Florida.

Sayer, Derek 1987, *The Violence of Abstraction: The Analytical Foundations of Historical Materialism*, Oxford: Basil Blackwell.

Schmidt, Peter R. and Thomas C. Patterson (eds.) 1995, *Making Alternative Histories: The Practice of Archaeology and History in Non-Western Settings*, Santa Fe, New Mexico: School of American Research Press.

Shiva, Vandana 2009, 'Why Are Indian Farmers Committing Suicide and How Can We Stop this Tragedy?', *Voltairenet.org*, available at: https://www.voltairenet.org/article159305.html.

Sinclair, M. Thea (ed.) 1997, *Gender, Work, and Tourism*, London: Routledge.
Trigger, Bruce G. 1984, 'Alternative Archaeologies: Nationalist, Colonialist, Imperialist', *Man*, 19, 3: 355–70.
Trigger, Bruce G. 1989, *A History of Archaeological Thought*, Cambridge: Cambridge University Press.
Urry, John 1990, *The Tourist Gaze: Leisure and Travel in Contemporary Societies*, London: Sage Publications.
Weingarten, Debbie 2018, 'Why Are America's Farmers Killing Themselves?' *The Guardian*, available at: https://www.theguardian.com/us-news/2017/dec/06/why-are-americas-farmers-killing-themselves-in-record-numbers.
Withey, Lynne 1997, *Grand Tours and Cook's Tours: A History of Leisure Travel, 1750 to 1915*, New York: William Morrow and Company.
Wood, Ellen Meiksins 1995, *Democracy Against Capitalism: Renewing Historical Materialism*, Cambridge: Cambridge University Press.
Wood, Margaret C. 2002, 'Women's Work and Class Conflict in a Working-Class Coal-Mining Community', in *The Dynamics of Power*, edited by Maria O'Donovan, Carbondale, IL: Center for Archaeological Investigations and Southern Illinois University.
Wurst, LouAnn 1999, 'Internalizing Class in Historical Archaeology', *Historical Archaeology*, 33, 1: 7–21.
Wurst, LouAnn 2011, '"Human Accumulations": Class and Tourism at Niagara Falls', *International Journal of Historical Archaeology*, 15, 2: 254–66.
Wurst, LouAnn 2015, 'Toward a Collective Historical Archaeology', *Reviews in Anthropology*, 44: 118–38.
Wurst, LouAnn and Quentin Lewis 2020, 'Marxism, Historical Archaeology, and the Web of Life', in *The Routledge Handbook of Historical Archaeology*, edited by Charles E. Orser, Pedro Paulo A. Funari, Susan Lawrence, James Symonds and Andrés Zarankin, Oxford: Routledge.
Wurst, LouAnn and Stephen Mrozowski 2014, 'Toward an Archaeology of the Future', *International Journal of Historical Archaeology*, 18, 2: 210–23.
Wurst, LouAnn and Stephen Mrozowski 2016, 'Capitalism in Motion', *Historical Archaeology*, 50, 4: 81–99.
Wurst, LouAnn and Christine Ridarsky 2014, 'The Second Time as Farce: Archaeological Reflections on the New New Deal', *International Journal of Historical Archaeology*, 18, 2: 224–41.

PART 3

Balances and Perspectives

CHAPTER 8

Tangible Objects: Marxism, Production and Archaeology

Vicente Lull

1   The Tangible Object as Productive Force and Social Synthesis[1]

The object is a starting and end point. It is the ground on which archaeology develops. It is medium and vehicle, motive and objective. In archaeology, we work with tangible objects that make up the concrete synthesis of social relations. They have been produced by the relations between humans, and between these and the rest of nature. Material remains are perfect indicators of such relations and of their state and development. They establish our environment, reorder space and cancel or reshape pre-existing material relations. They build the silent surroundings that show us the limits of reason and the passion of each archaeological period. They establish the rules of contrast and geometry. Wherever language is absent, the resulting object is the wholeness, the link capable of recording experience and passing it on. Objects mobilise ideas.

To understand the object (as a whole) we must appeal to its history, which is at the same time inside and outside of it. The object's external history, of universal composition, seeks its presence and provides it with a material body; its internal history, which is its own history, enables it to be seen as active. The object may not be in charge or the protagonist of its own history, but it will become the protagonist and responsible for the history of everything else. As Marx already signalled:

> Relics of bygone instruments of labour possess the same importance for the investigation of extinct economical forms of society, as do fossil bones for the determination of extinct species of animals.[2]

---

1   This paper is based on two previous published works (Lull 2005 and 2007) but presents new arguments regarding the bonds between Marx's thought and archaeology.
2   Marx 2010, pp. 189–90.

Furthermore,

> It is not the articles made, but how they are made, and by what instruments, that enables us to distinguish different economic epochs. Instruments of labour not only supply a standard of the degree of development to which human labour has attained, but they are also indicators of the social conditions under which that labour is carried on.[3]

Archaeological objects are nothing but social-material remains which an erratic and hesitant discipline such as our own – perhaps like all disciplines – has considered and captured from a world populated by them – a world that would probably laugh at such a selection if it could. Objects recovered by archaeology constitute the objectified social relationship itself: at the same time, they *are* and *are not* what they shared and kept, or, if preferred, what they cancelled and overcame. Archaeological objects, like all objects, are not merely products, nor can they be considered the exclusive result of the material possibilities of societies. Overall, they are neither mere passive products nor submissive instruments in skilled hands that mediate in social production. Rather, they are determining subjects that enable gestures, thoughts and actions that will set the course and instruction for new hands and thoughts – thoughts that will emerge as the starting point for knowledge of a history they actively help to build. Objects have been made with the same intensity with which they make us. All social production is founded upon previously accumulated labour, and it comes to life in concrete and diverse operations. Marx reminds us of two fundamental aspects in his 1857 *Grundrisse*:

> Production thus not only creates an object for the subject, but also a subject for the object ... It is only consumption that consummates the act of production, since consumption completes the product as a product by dissolving it, by consuming its independent material form ... Consumption is therefore the concluding act which not only turns the product into a product, but also turns the producer into a producer.[4]

The pairing of *Marx-archaeology* is not intended to tame archaeological objects based on a certain theory or biased interpretation. It is well known that objects rebel against straitjacketed positivist or empiricist postulates and actively resist

---

3 Marx 2010, p. 190.
4 Marx 2010, pp. 30–1.

opportunistic interpretations. They eventually neutralise any dimension aiming to exhaust them by means of exclusive and fixed concepts.

From material to aesthetic, archaeological objects cover all social dimensions. They respond to precise requirements, be they economic, social, political or moral. They reveal the practices that attained them and the practices they helped to build. They empty or fill social life with *content*. Objects appear as conservative or revolutionary, but, above all, and to many archaeologists' despair, *they are honest*, and they systematically refuse to be taken in vain or replaced with ideas that attempt to supplant them (concepts that wish to take their place). In the end, they inexorably show the path to their reality, ruling out all biased perspectives of historical research. This is because, above all, objects *are true* and constitute the most solid reference to look at (and to *rely upon* in order to understand our existence). Objects are *effective*, composing the real otherness that makes us subjects and prevents us from taking the place of the patient objects that exist only in alienated minds.

Unlike words, objects reify facts; they *are the result of relationships*, regardless of whether words intervene therein. Objects force words into motion and get them to work. With words, anything can be said, even if in the end it is possible that all stays as it was before one spoke. Words are suited for everyone and everything; they are basically *affective* and, on their own, they do not change things *effectively*. They usually move metaphorically and conditionally. Words need to become body. That is why they are pronounced. However, material relationships mediate the body to which words aspire, and the name of such a relationship is written on the objects. A word needs to be shared in order to *show itself* and, at the same time, *say something* about the relationship that generates it; objects are there precisely to suggest that which the words that once surrounded them can no longer *say*.

Archaeological objects open the world and demand that we go beyond our current consciousness and language. In the face of these new realities, the archaeological discourses that remain stagnant cancel the world by perpetuating it without changes.

Things happened in a certain way. They may have passed through certain possibilities and met with accidents or unsuspected contingencies, but, in one way or another, their passing incorporated, avoided or rejected other things. Yet the fact remains that what happened did so in a certain manner. There are many more things to discover than those we have discovered up to the present that we share, and that is where our hope for change lies. It is possible that we have forgotten certain aspects of the social reality of the past that might help us to transform our own.[5]

---

5 Lull 2007, pp. 167–8.

2 Why Marx?

Why consult Marx on these matters? Because, for Marx, neither words nor things sufficed for themselves, and because he understood that the meaning of subjects and objects varied at the pace of human relations, integrated into the socio-historical process of every society. Furthermore, he understood that social materiality was the meeting point of the physical and metaphysical, between being and thought (in naked terms); social materiality is the beginning and the outcome, the real scope of the human world.

In reaction to the dissatisfaction created by the endless redundancy of self-involved thinking, and in opposition to the physical and unappealable mechanics of being at the mercy of the world in its unyielding process of free-falling, Marx adopts Feuerbach's materialist inversion. He removes from it every contemplative, lazy and cowardly mechanism, and he tells us of the *praxis* that makes up reason with the same strength and interest with which he vouches for praxis-ridden reasoning. The Marxian starting point, therefore, considers thought to be socially produced, and it is this genesis that we must address in the first place.

Life precedes thought. Life is objective. Although thinking *appears to be* a matter of subjects, the subject cannot construct itself. The subject *is built into consciousness* while its own *consciousness is constructed from the outside*.

> It is not consciousness that determines life, but life that determines consciousness.[6]

What makes the subject objective is not its will either, but that which precedes it: the objective conditions of social life that structurally contributed to construct the social being. This does not mean that we are a mere neutral vessel to be filled up, but rather that the vessel (I-We-All) that *comprises us* is also built from social matter.

For materialism, the world is made exclusively of sensitive objects integrated into material systems, albeit not necessarily tangibly so (concepts, propositions, categories and theories are not physical). All material systems are changing and, therefore, changeable. Every material object is involved in a process. Matter is dynamic – it is transformed by others or it transforms itself. Marx would agree that a theory is materialist when real and that material referents intervene in its genesis, constitution and implications, and seeks to transform

---

6 Marx and Engels 2010, p. 37.

them. For us archaeologists, this is a definitive anchor of which one should make the most. The matter of the past consists of the actors, audiences and theatre of real life, and of the representations of the latter that humans made in other times and places. As historians, we long to see and learn about that *play* thanks to archaeology. We see it with the expectation that such objects will not only speak of us in some way, as all human things do, but also guide us towards *the others*. The others being those who await in the form of objects, matter and images still hidden underground or imprisoned in frozen cabinets, hardly allowing us to guess what they went through, which body they comprised or what place they held in society. Those objects will even propose to us what they represented, and we will actually be forced to heed what they excite in us, which ranges from emotion to knowledge. We will probably be frightened when we fail to see ourselves behind that which they manifest, or when we discover how little they mention us, even though we are the only ones interrogating them; or perhaps we will rejoice when they suggest one of our senses or preserve something they share with us. That is an opportunity that we cannot miss.[7]

3   Whence Does Marx Derive?

The first and, for me, most important setting from which Marx emerges is the one upon which Hegel concluded. Marx stems from the tradition of German philosophical idealism in its Hegelian dialectical version and that of its neo-Hegelian critics, especially Feuerbach with his dialectical inversion and 'soft' materialism. The beginning of Marx's subversion is his proposal of a seemingly impossible three-way between German philosophy and two other apparently contradictory fields: French utopian socialism and British political economy.[8]

Marx uses the impulse of all these tendencies to question them, turn them around and accurately critique the three stances, precisely because they are *only* stances, elucubrations of thought which keep things the way they were or accept them as one believes them to be. Marx provides dialectics with a hitherto unknown dimension, furnishes it with a material body and applies a dynamic critique to all paths walked by the bourgeoisie, which go from becoming revolutionary at the end of the eighteenth century to becoming reactionary at the dawn of the new century. The legs Marx walks on combine dialectics and materialism in a fusion that transcends them as it moves forward.

---

7   Lull 2007, p. 169.
8   Lenin 1977, pp. 21–8.

His work is marked by a *being* whose existence precedes and demands all consciousness, a being that must deny itself in order to move forward and then deny that denial in order to be really mindful – not so as to restore the original social sense, but to revolutionise it.[9] The proletariat was best qualified as a social subject to change things and lead the revolution, because it represented the social majority and was the farthest from obtaining collective benefit. Even if it does not seem so, this is the same proletariat that, after improving its living conditions thanks to a tenacious struggle, halted its course towards *real freedom* as a result of unfounded and induced desires of *formal freedom*. That proletariat lost its substance, fell into precariousness/deprivation and slavery, and changed awareness for chimaeras. Perhaps this abyss of helplessness and oblivion demands a new stance that will retrieve the revolutionary role which Marx conferred to all the exploited.

4 Marxism Is More Than Marx

I would even argue that 'Marxism' is more than he himself would have presumed. It is more than a philosophy, since it entails the overcoming of speculative philosophy and foretells its end. Instead, Marx proposes a radical turn from speculative idealism to realistic materialism. However, he also suggests that it is more than a science, because in order to know reality, it *considers* the dialectics of matter in its particular historical unfolding. Although it can be compared with (realistic) science, because everything is the reality of a motion that must be accounted for, Marxism does not understand reality as naturalism, but rather as society building its own nature while originating from nature itself, one constantly warding off and surpassing the other. Marxism, therefore, presupposes an objective science because the place of the object is the place our own consciousness. Yet, it does not start off from reality in order to know it, but to transform it. Its aim is the development not of thinking, but of social living. Hereby science becomes politics.

Yet, it is also more than politics, as it derives from the material possibilities of knowledge in each historical moment. This is the reason that Marxism does not understand politics based on alleged human essences that operate by means of ethical prescriptions of what is fair, good and right – which are claimed, yet cannot be demonstrated but in praxis. Marxism represents a form

---

9 It is worthwhile to bear in mind the following maxim: 'The philosophers have only interpreted the world, in various ways; the point, however, is to *change* it'. Marx and Engels 2010 [1845–47], p. 5.

of politics originating in social praxis to envision, if necessary, and propose, whenever it is possible, solutions by means of a revolutionary action capable of transforming the world.

Every Marxism sees itself as part of that motion of social reality. It is both the real awareness of that unfolding and the unfolding itself. Marxism aims at *everything* and, consequently, it cannot be reduced to a philosophy of praxis that will result again in philosophy, politics, ethics or science, which make up only aspects of a yet unknown social reality. Marxism seeks to address the shifting reality that tells of itself and puts concepts in its place, ahead of the very elements and places or settings that produce concepts. Marxism places social life at the roots of its reflection and seeks to distinguish all that is speculative while striving to account for the genealogy of the material sense of the sentences that words compose.

5 What Can We Historians and Archaeologists Learn from Marxism?

History always overcomes situations without overlooking them completely. History is not a criterion or concept of development that inexorably walks over human beings and responds to who-knows-what causalities or coincidences, ideas or spirits. History is closer and more specific; we are ourselves history in the making, as we make one another, produce one another, and produce social life by incorporating therein everything that we come across.

For many historians and archaeologists, Marx simply facilitates a theory of the path of history, a sort of 'general route' which, being idealist by definition like every model, sometimes gets thrown into the bin of mandatory roadmaps. What Marx provides is not a theory of the path, but rather a method capable of accounting for how and why we produce ourselves socially at each moment, and for how our ways of fulfilling, differentiating and shaping ourselves differ at each historical time.

Marx and Engels already warned in *The German Ideology* that the premises from which they departed were not arbitrary ones, nor dogmas, but real entities:

> They are the real individuals, their activity and the material conditions under which they live, both those which they find already existing and those produced by their activity.[10]

---

10   Marx and Engels 2010, p. 31.

It is we humans who produce our realities, '[b]y producing their means of subsistence men are indirectly producing their material life'.[11] History, in all its outcomes, is formed by:

> ... the different generations of individuals entering into relation with one another ... that the physical existence of the later generations is determined by that of their predecessors ... [and] inherit the productive forces and forms of intercourse accumulated by their predecessors, their own mutual relations being determined thereby.[12]

History produces us while reproducing with and through us, although we are also renewed productive forces, original means of production and objects of mutual work which social life previously lacked. Therefore, on this new journey of our history, we experience different ways of responding to the new demands and needs that our present entails, which we inevitably encounter. As a society, we incorporate other ways of producing in order to survive together, and through them we try to overcome previous material contradictions. As these contradictions unfold, we gradually come to understand that comprehension itself follows the same process and complies with the same breaks and vibrations as any other production of social reality:

> The production of ideas, of conceptions, of consciousness, is at first directly interwoven with the material activity and the material intercourse of men – the language of real life.[13]

History is produced by the objective conditions accumulated and expressed by those who preceded us; by the needs that they engendered and satisfied; and by the production of other solutions and relations that we generate in that same changing, tangible, real and thinkable universe that we inhabit – one that we strive to comprehend in order to make sense of our own existence.

Over time, accumulated work, real relationships and ideologies, desires, illusions or disappointments pile up, whereas the production of history itself moves firmly and persistently on the concreteness of its realisation.

---

11   Ibid.
12   Marx and Engels 2010, p. 438. In this text, Marx still uses 'forms of intercourse' as a synonym for the category of social relations of production, which was later preferred.
13   Marx and Engels 2010, p. 36.

6   Marxian Categories

For idealists, human beings transition from honesty to thievery, and from workers to owners, as easily as they transition from childhood to adulthood or from sadness to laughter. Human beings are all this contained expression and are capable of *everything that will manifest*, and even if that manifestation does not materialise, idealism *foresees* it. Idealists are *occupied* with the idea that a child *will become* an adult more than they are *preoccupied* with whether it actually comes to be one. Equating lived experience with thought, they tend to ignore with the same precision that the child *can* die. Idealists have convinced us of the *power of the idea* to escape the inevitability of death, and when we acknowledge the proposal of infinite ideas, we fall into the abyss of eternity, the ineffable and the key concepts of the 'conclave' of absolutist categories. Marx warns us of this.

Marxian categories are dynamic. They make sense and express themselves in reality and activity; they are not based on a defining and definitive formal structure. Social activity itself establishes the *occupation* assumed by objects and social *subjects* in each moment and place in which they are *realised* – as *objects of labour, labour power, means of labour* or *products*. Marxian categories try *to show* those moments and places of production without prejudging a determined order or responding to a *given name*. The *name* is a snapshot that sets reality *for us* in a given *position* and *situation* (*standpoint and disposition*), which is insufficient to capture the movement and the dynamics of the thing.

Marx did not use *categories* in the executive sense of things that are *exclusively ours*, which we bring to the world and which ultimately become confused with the *tangible and sensitive things*, which categories try to make understandable. For him, *naming* categories did not mean establishing meanings *categorically*, and neither did establishing meanings consist in *giving* them a positive and static content. Marxian categories try to give authority to reality and are not subdued by the power of the idea. We must be alert, since categories can make us confuse the static perspective of their condition with the activities they refer to – activities which make sense in the *production* of objects and subjects and in the social relations involved in that production. Things manifest themselves *categorically* in their active development. Production allocates a place and activity to social objects and subjects, providing content to Marxian categories.

Thus, the *object of labour* is not that of the 'absolute' that physiocrats proposed for the *earth being* or the *human being*. Clay is the *object of labour* for the potter, as ore is for the metalworker, but both raw materials are in turn a *product* for the quarryman. He extracts these resources from the ground or the bedrock, which acts as an *object of labour* and a *means of production* for the farmer as well as (paradoxically) for the landowner. Women are a *means of production* in patriarchal hands, as are slaves in the hands of the master; at the same time, but at a different stage, both are transformed into *objects of labour* for the dominant male or the capitalist. It is not only tools that are *means of production*, but also revenue and capital for the capitalist bourgeois.

The same thing can feature in all categories. Land is an *object of labour* for the farmer and their main *means of production*, but land is also *labour power*, like water or rain if we *value* them as such at some point in history. Moreover, land is always a *product* of itself in its perpetual renewal. As human beings, we are a *social product*, physically and emotionally, and constitute the indispensable *labour power* of every human society. At other times we could be *means of production* for the businessperson or *objects of labour* for slavers. A knife, which is traditionally a *means of labour*, takes the place of an *object of labour* when we revive its edges in a maintenance operation necessary for it to continue *being* a knife. Furthermore, a knife is a *product* by definition and its edges can be used to measure the state of the *labour power*.

Marxian categories do not compose the solipsism *everything refers to everything, because everything remains contained in the conscious subject*. Therein, the referred whole never entirely concerns the referring whole, since between them no intention occurs. There is, however, an active and passive relationship that transforms, dilutes and transcends them. These are categories acquired by the different dimensions of the real. They seek to be said by *showing* the various moments that subjects and objects provide and assume in the unfolding of their productive activities, at the same time affected by the unfolding itself and decisive for the outcome.

Marx did not intend to elaborate a new representation of the world, nor did he want to offer static categories that placed philosophy before history. Marxian categories are always historical categories; they *are* insofar as they *manifest* historically. They themselves undergo modifications of that adjustment with the real.

Marx's interest lay in deducing from the concrete real those social categories that accurately showed their material unfolding, implied history and referred thereto. Thus, *mode of production, socio-economic formation, social relations of production, forms of property* or *productive forces* constitute dynamic vessels that history fills according to its unfolding along with the outcome of the gnoseological process. The questions that he intended to ask and to answer were very specific: How do human beings operate in social life? Under what conditions and needs do we live? How do we produce our material life? What tasks connect us effectively and specifically? From where do our ideas and symbols emerge? What activities treasure aesthetic developments? What conditions can we overcome, and under what forces? What is the place of politics at each moment? Marxian categories appeal to the concreteness to which they allude, not to the formal logic that cloaks them.

As we will immediately see, even throughout Marx's work Marxian categories vary in their designation, character or both. Because his goal was to understand the real content of history while keeping aloof from any ethical or aesthetic assessments, his concepts are intended to follow the pace that history requires. Therefore, one must forsake all speculative presumption of the *must be*. It is history itself that *pronounces* its categories. However, Marx occasionally confuses us, for instance when he uses as rhetorical resources certain concepts that are yet to reach the accuracy and specificity of later works. In any case, this is an irrelevant problem if compared with the *categorial* or *categoric* debates of Marxism from the mid-twentieth century through the present.[14]

6.1 Labour and Production

A quick look at these categories illustrates what I have just outlined. Up until 1844, Marx considered labour, insofar as it is an *essential* vital activity of 'man', the key concept of *the human*. Gradually, with the tempering naturalism and humanism latent in the *Paris Manuscripts*, the concept takes refuge in production. With *The German Ideology* (1845–6), *producing* becomes the real social sphere that covers specific labour, with the latter losing its essentialist load and expressing, under the shelter of production, an effective and concrete social activity. From 1857 onwards, with the 'Introduction to a Contribution to the Critique of Political Economy' and the *Grundrisse* (1857–8), *production* was certainly more real and social than was *labour* essential or generic in 1844. *Production* also emphasises society as the protagonist of its real and effective production; this is opposed to the essentialism of our species represented by Feuerbach's *generic human being*.

Labour, understood as vital human essence, refers to all activities carried out by men or women, individually or socially; in other words, any human activity

---

14   After Marx, his categories undertook unexpected routes, inaugurated by Engels himself after his friend's death and covered by the *avant-garde* of the Soviet Revolution or by *philosophers* of the Central-Western European critique. Confusion definitively took hold of Marxism when its categories gave in to the requirements of several ideologies that sought to underpin (based on reason and its forms) the *must be of revolutionary thinking* or its *rebellious* counterpoints. They all provided the confusion, slogans, precepts and discipline required to alter the original revolutionary alternative.

could be understood as a synonym for labour. By contrast, if labour is involved and explained in the universe of social production, we must conclude that it is production itself that gives a social meaning to labour, not the other way around. That is why Marx saw fit to modify the noun 'labour' from that moment onwards ('social labour', 'socially necessary labour'; he even coined 'productive labour', an apparent but not true redundancy). The defining and generic role of *labour* as *that which is human* relies on *production* in order to obtain the social and historical character of its realisation.

6.2   Alienation and Exploitation

The transference of the concept of *labour* to that of *production* is no less subtle than the one Marx applied to the categories of *alienation* and *exploitation*. For Marx in 1841, Epicurus was 'the first to grasp appearance as appearance, that is, as alienation of the essence, activating itself in its reality as such an alienation'.[15] Later, he experiences the influence of Feuerbach, for whom man alienates himself when he takes for granted that which is his own construction: *man creates his ghosts and then submits to them.*[16] By contrast, Hegel assumes that reality is explained by its own internal movement of alienation. Hegelian alienation is neither appearance nor illusion, but rather the *mediation* or process by which the being becomes an object. It is a realisation and it is becoming a thing – an essential step in order to truly become and be self-controlled, once the split between being only the subject and being only the object has been separated.[17] Alienation is the second stage of dialectics, the movement of Being towards Nothing, its questioning and denial. It is the necessary mediation, the way into going out of oneself in order to be realised and recover to the point of reaching self-consciousness.

By contrast, far from the previous abstract places ('being out of oneself'), be they psychological ('in transition to') or anthropological ('submission to recreated symbolic principles'), and starting with the *The Paris Manuscripts* in 1844, Marx understands alienation as a *double real appropriation* undergone by the producer under capitalism: *alienation of the thing* or *alienation of the worker* from their product, and *self-alienation* as a real loss of meaning of their own activity (wage worker). However, he will continue using the term *alienation* until *Capital*, reshaping it with the content of *exploitation*. *Exploitation* points directly and starkly to the process of practical usurpation of people's means

---

15   Marx and Engels 2010, p. 64.
16   Fernández Buey 1998, p. 51.
17   Sacristán 1983, p. 285.

of livelihood, in specific historical conditions, by a specific class of individuals. In this way, Marx breaks definitively the metaphysical thread of his Hegelian dependence.

6.3 Forms of Property / Modes of Production

The third pairing, which exemplifies even better the Marxian landing on the concrete reality of material life and the last farewell to terms embellished with immutable and volitional connotations, is formed by the immediate passage of *forms of property* to *modes of production*. Both categories are used by Marx to distinguish concrete stages of the unfolding of history. However, the second of these conveys meaning to the first, although the first is unfortunately used to name the object of study. In 1845, he termed *forms of property*[18] the different states and stages of the division of labour,[19] which, in turn, depend on society's means of production.[20]

Ten years later, the *Grundrisse* clarified the suggested pre-capitalist forms by changing the term 'tribal' to 'community', revising it as a form of appropriation and collectivist land use. This use would have a second expression in the Asiatic forms, characterised, on this occasion, by a sovereign or exclusive proprietor emblematically situated above small communities, in the fashion of a supreme unit entitled to the whole surplus product of social work. It is a property which paradoxically is characterised by a *legal* absence of property.

The second form of property also presupposes the community as its substratum. However, communal property is here separated from private property, and its foundation lies not in the countryside but in the city; the countryside is presented as territory belonging to the city. It is a warrior community of owners

---

18 'The first form of property is the tribal [a reference to Greece and Rome] ... The second form is the ancient communal and state property ... The third form is feudal or estate property'. Marx and Engels 2010, pp. 32–4.

19 'The various stages of development in the division of labour are just so many different forms of property, i.e., the existing stage in the division of labour determines also the relations of individuals to one another with reference to the material, instrument and product of labour'. Marx and Engels 2010, p. 32.

20 'This mode of production must not be considered simply as being the reproduction of the physical existence of the individuals. Rather it is a definite form of activity of these individuals, a definite form of expressing their life, a definite mode of life on their part. As individuals express their life, so they are. What they are, therefore, coincides with their production, both with what they produce and with how they produce. Hence what individuals are depends on the material conditions of their production'. Marx and Engels 2010, pp. 31–2.

with urban predominance. It is polymorphic and presents many local variants, although most Marxian assertions are based on Greece and Rome.

The third form of property corresponds to what is known to us as feudal and contains specific processes, wherein the countryside becomes again the starting point. Community is meeting, not unity. Within it, public property is only a complement to individual property. The property of the individual is not mediated by the community. Rather, the community exists as a relation of independent subjects.

Throughout the Marxian proposal, the *modes of production* become the foundation of the forms of property, even if the latter are used to refer to them. The *forms of property* have the defect of emphasising the politico-legal dimension of societies as definitive and defining, while *modes of production* give prominence to the socio-economic sphere from which they emerge.

6.4 How Does the Course of History Take Place?

Can we talk about the logic of history? From the Marxian perspective, history is due to something (specific conditions) and procures something (effect thereof), and therefore requires empiricism to observe and theory to explain.

Historical events unfold (develop) an internal logic that is not *foreseen* but consequential. Seen from this perspective, facts do not occur randomly, nor do they appear by means of circumstantial and equally fortuitous concatenations; rather, they are the product of material conditions and specific situations in which they express their own development. Like any product, history consumes an object of demand and necessity. Whether they *are produced* or *produce themselves*, historical events respond to a social demand that is alien to the volitions of individuals.

If history were a mere succession of events, it would require only an empirical study limited to a chronicle, thereby rendering the method unnecessary. For Marxism, the unfolding of events is what manifests a logic; it is not logic that forces the course of history. The process of history works with certain conditions, which also create effects, and so forth, sequentially, in part bound by specific determining factors that take it in various directions. Any stage of history is, therefore, a necessary product of the previous one, which contained the factors that made its overcoming necessary.

History is a general process with particular stages and moments that depend on the operating ways of the objective material and subjective conditions derived from society. For Marxism, the main factor is the *mode of operation itself* or the *mode of production* which ultimately determines specific social solutions. History does not follow *one* single process, even though there are determining factors in any social change whose intervention requires following certain itineraries; for Marx, history is fundamentally the history of class struggles.

Among the modes of production, the formation of capitalism is probably the easiest to explain. That is because it is a mode of production that emerges out of contradictory feudal conditions and relations which gradually gained autonomy and relevance as a result of the different flows of the *productive forces* hoarded by an emerging bourgeoisie. This was the world that Marx researched for much of his life, culminating in *Capital*.

In short, the outline of the formation of capital can be summarised by mentioning a change in the material conditions of production (transformations in the *productive forces*), which combined poorly with certain pre-existing and exhausted *social relations of production*. Capital vindicated the end of feudal privilege and, moreover, demanded participation in the unequal access to, and concentration of, wealth, until eventually the objective conditions of material life were capitalised in other hands – *its* hands. The bourgeoisie thus acquired the capacity to demand wage labour and assault political power in hitherto non-existent conditions. In this way, as a specific mode of production, capitalism shows that the first changes occurred in the infrastructure of the social (the material base); and on the short and medium term, they caused substantial changes in philosophical, moral and political ideas – the necessary hotbed for an effective assault on power.

This analysis of reality derives from certain premises that Marx took from Hegel's *Philosophy of History*, before they were evaluated and critiqued. For Hegel, history is a '*knowing*, self-mediated becoming'.[21] The historian contemplates the factual unfolding in order to reflect upon and reason about the process of this endless succession of events, states, situations, groups and individuals, which vary or change at the pace of their destruction and construction. History is, therefore, dialectical; it remains while seeking its own development. However, it is also teleological, as it points towards the freedom of the spirit that takes shape in the aspiration of human beings to *feel* free.

In Hegel, the aspiration for freedom is diluted in the *freedom to think*. The alluded freedom[22] hardly means *freedom to choose* life or to claim the mater-

---

21 Hegel 2018, p. 320. Emphasis added.
22 Since Kant and according to all subsequent idealism, freedom to think is *the* condition for freedom to act. Hegel conveys it as such and inaugurates the political optimism according to which ideas, *realised* in words, can change things. The thread is recklessly stretched with his neo-Hegelian successors. It is then frayed, and with no regard to objectives, integrated into postmodern interpretations and the current 'capitalist realism' – Fisher's (2009) fortunate label with which to define the capitalist stage of our time.

ial conditions with which to live it. Perhaps Hegel thought that, in moments of maximum rationality, once selfishness and passions had been relocated to the realm of the means of production of freedoms, human beings would neither obtain individual benefits nor enjoy the exploitation and suffering of others. For Hegel, history is a process that unfolds itself; it is the process of the being as a spirit that returns to itself after its realisation (achieving awareness of reality). Its realisation lies in the mediation[23] (in that which *is not*) that becomes necessary for such a return. Thus, history is the real process through which the spirit will gain self-consciousness. If we undertake the Hegelian inversion, as Marx did following Feuerbach, and replace the subject of Hegelian history – the spirit – with the Marxian real subject – human beings (as they *produce* their life)[24] – then it is easy to see that, although the analytical perspective has changed radically, the Hegelian dialectical framework remains a structure of the Marxian proposal without undermining Marx's original standpoint, even vis-à-vis Feuerbach.

Marx embraces dialectics because reality is dialectics itself, and exercising dialectics is the only way of knowing it. Reality is dynamic and, consequently, so are the categories of thought. Thought is linked to reality and both move dia-

---

23   That is the Hegelian content of *Entfremdung* [alienation].
24   Little is said about the Fichtean influence on Marx and, when mentioned, it refers almost exclusively to matters of state and society. However, Fichte had, since 1794, suggested that social relations were dialectical relations between individuals, as well as between them and *what is* collective, somehow instituted as such (in groups, nations or states). Fichte understood social acts as being relationships of experiences, beliefs and knowledge, being *transpersonal* and characteristic of everything that is social and moral. He was the first to propose the reality of the social and draw attention to the collective aspect of social acts, in opposition to the individualistic conceptions of Rousseau and Kant. He was also the first to propose the intervention of the *we*, the *groups* and the *nations* as collective subjects of history, knowledge and morality. Although Fichte always alludes to social reality and the moral ideal as a whole, the integrating category is social, because 'society is a goal in itself. Thanks to it there is an improvement of the species'. The creating activity of humanity/society manifests in the fact-act, a form of social *participation* that precedes and ensures consciousness. *Participation* in the *transpersonal* is the characteristic of everything that is social and moral, and it cannot be reduced to a separation or identification between the self, the other and us (see Gurvitch 1965, pp. 63–73). Idealism had dealt with human activity abstractly, while bourgeois materialism was basically interested in the sensitive aspect that captures the object. Marx, by contrast, grants social activity the character hinted at by Fichte (*participation in the transpersonal*, consciousness based on action), but went further by isolating its subjectivity and by understanding *praxis* as a primary objective activity (that which is produced and manifested therein, we being inside of it). The first contribution in that direction can be traced in the abovementioned Fichtean *participation*. Although diluted among considerations of volitional and

lectically. Reality self-reproduces in the social sphere based on its production. Production determines social relations with the same intensity with which social relations reproduce production and address specific natural conditions. These conditions (which produce and are produced) are nourished by the different ways in which the task is faced and changed along with it. Although the *ways* of producing *set* the course, the *ways* of thinking have much to *say* in the eternal dilemma of maintaining and questioning that course. They *walk hand in hand*; from head to toe they are engendered and nurtured on the same path.

The ways of thinking tend to *understand* first and afterwards justify the ways of producing that created them, especially if that production holds and realises us materially and subjectively. The ways in which a society is produced are what socialises the ways of thinking society. Society, as something real, and these ways of production, as forms of reality, support two forms of thoughts: that which affirms and that which denies production.

Kant argued that unsociable sociability[25] is the origin of the *Unavoidable State*, a provocative induction of *that is how we are*. Marx overcomes Kant and disregards such misguided intuition by considering that we have socially manufactured this so-called human nature, because we *make* ourselves in *every* possible way and, therefore, *that is how we stand* in every mode of production, but under no circumstances *is that how we are*.

7   The Concept of Social

Social criteria are built within us, as a community, at the pace of the production of social life. Social production brings about various forms of understanding and knowledge of the world, with the same possibilities and intensities involved in the construction of houses and things, knives and governments, politics and aesthetics. The whole of society is a conglomerate of social objects and subjects under construction, which produce and self-reproduce on a material substrate of *accumulated labour*. Social production is built upon

---

romantic *intentionality* and *aspiration*, they do not cease to surprise us as an early referent for Marxian *praxis*.

25   In 1784, Kant understands as *unsocial sociability* the antagonism of men and an *inclination* to form society tied to a constant resistance that continually threatens to break it up. This disposition lies in man's nature, whose inclination to live in society and be recognised by it clashes with his willingness to obtain everything as he pleases. He cannot do without the fellow beings that he can neither tolerate (Kant 1963, fourth thesis).

such previous labour, coming to concrete and diverse life in specific ways of operating, which incorporate their own updated possibilities. The unfolding of this concept is not independent of the unfolding of the agents of production and of its history. Rather, it is produced and materialised by accumulated labour and updated in the agents – with them and *for* them. In each moment of production, the concept *knows* what it *can know*. It is, therefore, consciousness reintegrated into real life, a life which precedes and fosters it. The notion engenders knowledge when it *knows* the history of the material process that placed it there. The notion is thus able to locate the place of the factors and conditions of social life.

8   Factors and Conditions of the Production of Social Life

Nature produces all sorts of things and situations. Individual or relational things in disintegrating, integrating or final circumstances. As factors in the production of social life, things and individuals, as well as their relations and situations, contribute (based on, with, against or because of these factors) to the creation of society, and at the same time they take shape and are *realised* in this process led by social activity.

These factors, once they are socially mediated, become social subjects and objects set up in the material conditions of the development of social life. Since a *condition* is a property of things, the latter, like socially mediated individuals, become social agents by *socialising* the relations of appropriation of nature and by *naturalising* that same relation of appropriation (Figure 8.1).

9   The Unfolding of Productive Forces

Social subjects and objects, being conditions as well as products of social life, exercise the characteristic *activity* of *productive forces*, assuming different roles in the production: *objects of labour, labour powers, means of labour* or *products*. Both social objects and subjects assume these dimensions interchangeably according to the specific historical unfolding of *productive forces*. *Productive forces* ensure production itself (they are what produces and what is produced) and acquire those dimensions at each stage of their manifestation.

Productive forces do not form a feedback circuit, but rather a dialectic system of overcoming in which Objects of Labour$_1$ + Labour Powers$_1$ + Means of Labour$_1$ = Products$_1$, which becomes new Objects of Labour$_1$, i.e. the starting point of another sequence of ramifications (Objects of Labour$_2$ + Labour

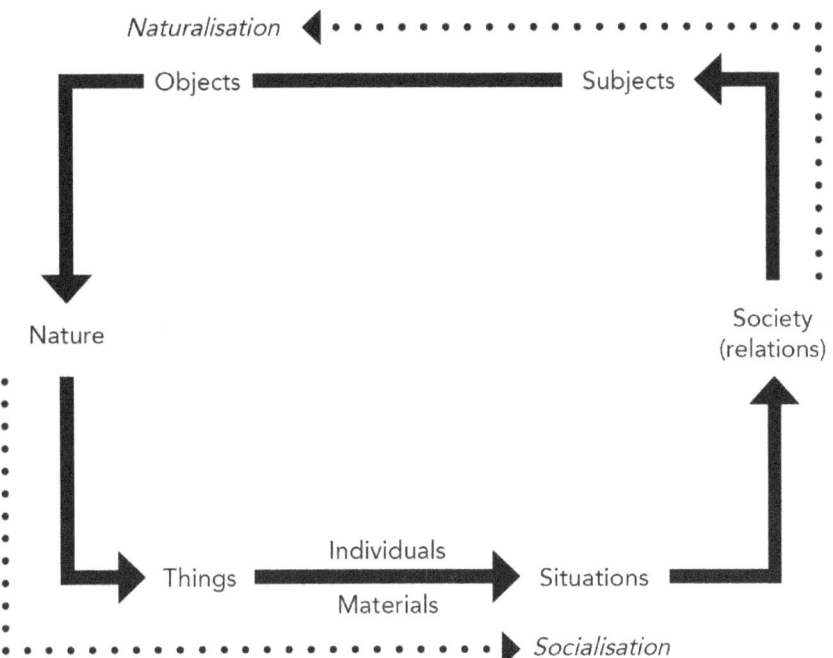

FIGURE 8.1   The constitution of society: socialisation and naturalisation

Powers $_2$ + Means of Labour$_2$ = Products$_2$), and so on in a permanently open but not necessarily progressive spiral motion (Figure 8.2).

It is no surprise that in the work of Marx the development of *productive forces* was central to social development and became the ultimate cause, determination or condition of social life. *Productive forces* express the determination and material possibility of the very existence of social subjects and objects, to the point where it becomes difficult to locate the specific role that they play in the production they sustain and ensure. In fact, every specific activity contributes to the general production of the *productive forces* that it permanently updates. Moreover, every activity is a productive force of production. Production itself is the main *productive force* of any community trying to set up reality and continue being.

From a neo-Marxist perspective, one might fall into the temptation of placing *social relations of production* at the same, or even higher, degree of relevance as the *productive forces* when it comes to the setting up of the modes of the production of societies. This would imply that both categories express, through dialectical self-implication, a particular mode of production in specific cases and moments of history.[26] Such perspective would see the *social*

---

26   It is often overlooked that the social relations that Marx first mentioned were referred to

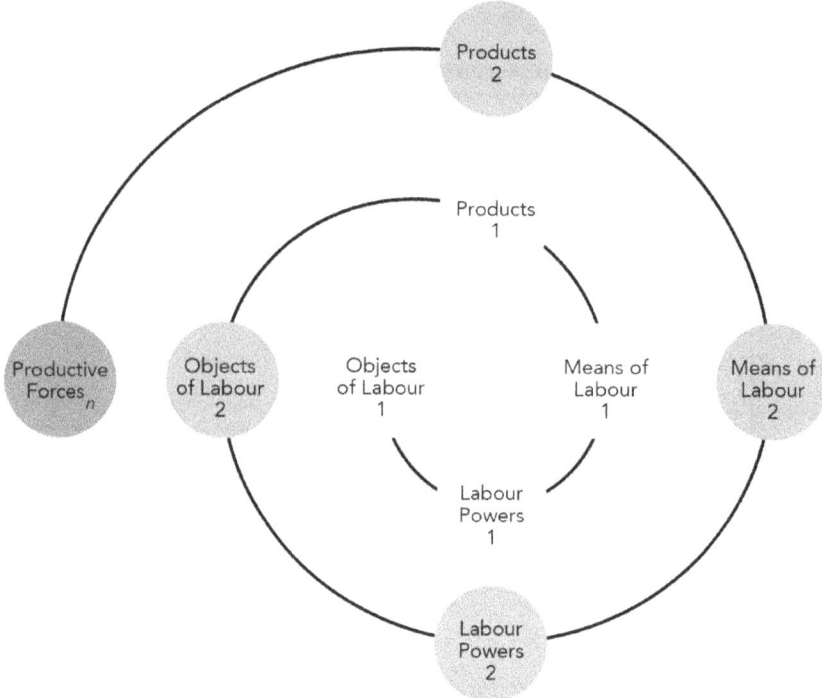

FIGURE 8.2   The development of productive forces

relations of production as characteristic of the relation between subjects (individuals/society) that sustains the *social organisation* of labour, all the while forgetting the actual social relations that labour activity itself generates and which precede and exceed mere *organisation*. The *productive forces* are considered characteristic of the relations between subjects and objects (society/nature). This interpretation reduces *productive forces* to technologies, as specific manifestations of the context of labour, as if technologies did not in turn express the relations between subjects which entail and *comprehend* the objects that attain said technologies – all the while establishing other non-technological relations that also function as *productive forces* of social life. In other words, the *social relations of production* and *productive forces* would converge in history from different fields of conception. Thus, the *social relations of production*

---

restrictedly as *intercourse* (e.g. *The Paris Manuscripts* and *The German Ideology*). It is only since his 1857 introduction, which was written as the foreword for *A Critique of Political Economy* (and did not see the light until the twentieth century), that he sees production relations as wide-ranging social relations.

(subject-subject relations) would be those that determine labour and coexistence outside of production itself, while *their productive forces* (subject-object relations) would entail material developments, overlooking the fact that the production of things is also a producer of social relations.

Perhaps these readings *overinterpret* some Marxian texts[27] and forget that the *social relations of production* are within the *productive forces* – they are *productive forces* themselves. They are a necessary yet insufficient condition[28] to account for the *productive forces*.[29] Because they contain social relations, the *productive forces* not only attain themes, but also notions, criteria, tales and fantasies geared towards the reproduction of social life. The *productive forces* are not to be confused with technologies, unless we want to reduce all social activity to labour activity.[30]

---

27 In several passages, Marx identifies the *productive forces* with the land and assimilates labour force with human beings. In this way, probably without intending it, he underlines the economistic aspect later assumed by this category. On occasion, he also relegates the impact of the social cooperation of production to the status of vague social relations that seem to derive from some place not specified before 1857. Something similar occurs with his unfortunate use of the term *property* to *designate* different *modes of production*, or the reference to *people* instead of society in some passages of his *Critique of Hegel's Philosophy of the State*.

28 As is the case with individuals regarding social relations. These are not realised at the instance of the will of individuals. Even if the individual is necessary for them to occur, their presence does not determine the type of relations produced. Relations are an external reality that includes the subject, although it may seem that such reality only comes from the subject. The individual is necessary for the relations to occur, but insufficient to accomplish them.

29 Only the relation entailed by the creation of individuals could claim the same degree of relevance as the *productive forces*, since the production of individuals, being an essential production, is possible within a specific biological social relation, at least for now.

30 I believe Marx is in part responsible for this misunderstanding, by taking the individual and its condition as a starting point, and by appealing to the liberation from that condition in order to achieve a free society. Perhaps it would have been more appropriate to invoke the initial social relations in order to achieve certain relational freedoms at the endpoint. The starting point of real society is not the individual, to whom Marx rhetorically grants social predominance, but the relation that includes the individual. He insists in many of his texts that he is not referring to the individual, but the *generic being* [*Mensch*]; yet, when he speaks about freedom, he again mentions the individual, as *illustrated*. This resembles Fichte's insistence on the *I-we* or the *transpersonal* and *trans-subjective* as a way of naming the socio-relational. The minimum unit of social expression is not the individual, but rather the relation between individuals. This is the true social field. Perhaps Marx insisted on the individual after he was appalled by the Hegelian proposal of 1820 (Hegel 1991), which to *him* seemed to place the individual at the bottom of an abstract entity (the state and its institutions); in Marx's eyes, this entity minimises or denies the real individual

The *social relations of production* are contained in the productive forces and have little to do with the randomness of individual decisions. These are specific *social relations of production* that reproduce society in the directions that the *productive forces* allow. The *productive forces* make up the real sphere in which the variable *social relations of production* comes into existence, as well as the medium in which they are expressed and the universe that exceeds them – because they *comprehend* and *facilitate* them.

10 Production

Production is the activity in which the *productive forces* manifest, and it is what consumes and feeds us. We live in permanent production. Production is expressed in the coordinates allowed by the *productive forces* as limits and possibilities of its reality. Production reintegrates *social productive forces* and transforms them into individual objects of consumption. Given that society is produced in every possible way, reducing production to an economic factor implies simplifying social reality and explaining its history based on what appear to be its individual elements, without noticing that the addition of individuals does not imply a relation and, therefore, does not constitute a social body.

Social life is not a product alienated from its production. Social life is its own production. Any social production is much more than the final product, which is an entity that cannot express itself clearly. Neither does the final product accurately reveal the specific production that procured it – that which can be found in a small proportion in all products, but in none entirely. I am referring to social production itself, which transcends the specific mechanics of materials and, by contrast, infects all social objects and subjects, stamping them with that particular way we have of living and relating to one another.

The production of our own individual life takes place relationally. As humans, we are conceived through a basic subject-subject social relationship, which will probably change when new subject-object relations provide alternative ways of biological reproduction. Furthermore, from its inception the social production of our life expresses unequal participation of the sexes. This is a starting biological difference which conveniently tends to be forgotten. All social production emerges around this production.

(which paradoxically is also abstract). Freedom of the individual is a political problem of the utmost importance, which usually corners or neglects relational freedom, the place whence the individual becomes aware and which places them before themselves.

The entire production of a society is carried out by means of various practices and specific social relations. These take the form of activities, work or specific tasks which contribute new subjects and objects (new *productive forces*) to a society that consumes them in order to obtain the necessary energy that enables it to restart a new productive cycle and continue its course. The entire production of a society is what sets forms, functions and things (situations, relationships and objects), allowing us to live, cohabit or be killed; it is what produces the apparent and the real; and it is what builds the materials, language, concepts and criteria, as well as the meanings and the sense of our life at every given moment in history.

As an effective relationship between objects and subjects, all production includes subjective and objective relations of production that manifest in the light of production itself. These relations will materialise in the forms, ways and possibilities that production allows. Finally, social production yields products of all sorts (things and concepts) with which it seeks to meet the needs of the individual consumption of its members – needs that have been recreated socially based on life's own minimum threshold of subsistence.

The first conclusion that we can draw from production is that it takes place in a social sphere of relations,[31] whose purpose is no other than to keep social subjects active by providing them with the consumptive means they require. Production is social because it is relational at first and individual at the end, i.e. in consumption. These two poles of production convey a sharp social/individual opposition that requires mediation to be overcome: distribution.

On this occasion, to illustrate how what is socially produced and what is individually consumed meet halfway, we will use archaeological information. Thanks to research in prehistory, we term game-drive hunting one of the first human activities aimed at gathering food, which is still practised in remote areas or else embellishes anachronistic hobbies. Thanks to the evidence collected, we can even imagine a small group collectively taking part in the task, which will provide the supplies for lost energy. A collectively invested effort will allow the capturing of prey in order to restore energy. Nearby, or in the place in which they finished their task, they will partake in the benefits of the product in the way dictated by the very production: jointly. Anyone who has participated in the social moment of production will hardly be excluded at the individual moment of consumption. Between these two moments, the shared feast will not require any distribution; the presence of the attendants will suffice. The *distribution* of food, subsumed in the *participation* of the activity, will accommodate the pace of that social reality (which is producer and produced). The

---

31   'My own existence is social activity'. Marx and Engels 1988, p. 105.

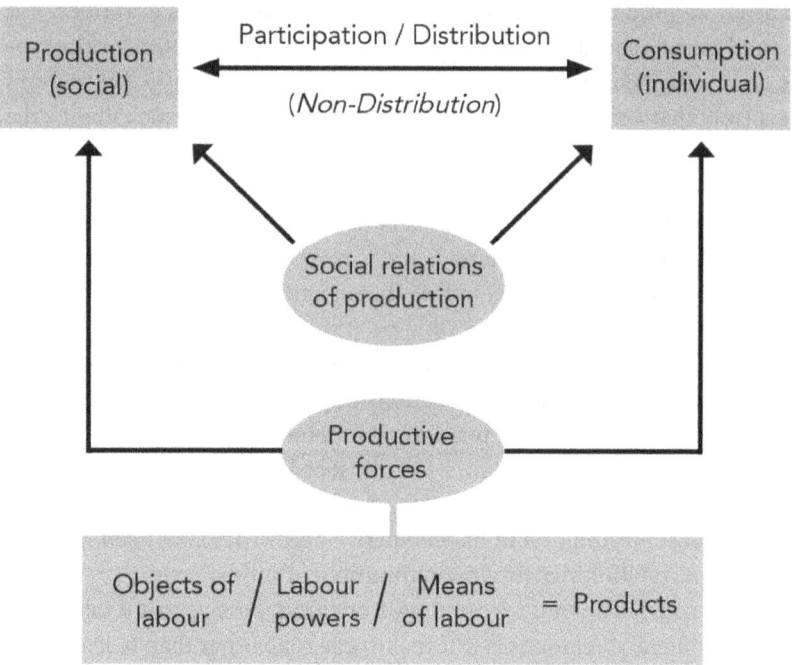

FIGURE 8.3 The unfolding of production

participation in production determines the *sharing*. Distribution does not exist as such; rather, it is some sort of opportunistic *non-distribution*. No one can be denied anything by anyone (Figure 8.3).

11   The Division of Tasks and Social Division of Labour

The participation of social subjects in different tasks is the first indication of the hitherto invisible division of the economic and social spheres. Within communal societies, the technical division of labour takes place according to several contingent factors. These are societies whose mechanisms of distribution correlate with the participation in production, such as the example given above. Given the turn in production, the resulting social formation does not change its usual practices, because the *community*, as accumulated *social labour*, may prevent asymmetry in the access to resources – asymmetry being more in line with the new times marked by the production of particular universes, which are *segmented* despite being part of the *same* community. The mechanisms of distribution will continue to be those that determined the undifferentiated allocation of the product (those which formed the community itself), even if the distance in social relations widens increasingly. The old social forms will remain if the community does not suffer a crisis caused by new economic forms, making them lose reality and meaning. The previous communal and cooperative life, built by communal *social relations of production*, collides with the new ways of producing, with protagonists in various particular fields within the same shared world. These new fields of production with their brand new particular spheres of relations and their diversified products demand the presence of distribution to reach all members of the community.

Thus, steps in the contradiction between total production, now segmented in particular universes of expression, and certain inherited relations of distribution, are loaded with egalitarian mechanisms increasingly afar from the specific ways in which production is *realised*. This imbalance will take social relations to places removed from the economic activities, at the same time reshaping the resulting extra-economic social relations as new specific *productive forces* in the construction of social life.

The division of tasks will not dismantle the social structure it comes from (it will not become a social division) until the contradiction is not materially manifested. While distribution remains anchored in the margins set by the production that makes up that society, which now is only social (formerly it was socio-economic), the collective can continue reproducing itself without overcoming the contradiction. And that *illusion* of future reality anchored in past reality will produce social and ideological mechanisms that will escape from the strictly economic sphere, even if they derive from it and from its needs. Thus, albeit produced segmentally in that sphere[32] by distancing itself from economy in a narrow sense, the social field tries to produce society with nourishment that will not suffice on its own to survive materially.

The division of tasks does not necessarily imply a social change aimed at the unequal access of individual consumption which differentiated activities demand, as long as the community appeals to its first constitution. The social relations of production, although now open to various activities, will continue to allot the same resources to individuals in the whole of society. The reality of the social subject in terms of its participation in the global product does not change in quantity, but it varies in quality; it is enriched and questioned (with a humble 'it is not so'). A progressive acceleration has been *produced* in the constitution of the social subject, who receives their part of a production that they cannot recognise as derived from their own work, but rather as from their community.

---

32   To make sense of these social relations within distribution, Marx saw relations of exchange in them (see n. 742); that is to say, he assumed that distribution was where the exchange of every social relation took place.

The new social subject benefits from two worlds. On the one hand, it benefits from the particular and subjective aspect of its concrete realisation, thanks to the task and relations in which it partake. On the other hand, they benefit from the abstract aspect of the activity of others, which they *know* to be concrete because of the alien products coming from activities in which they do not partake (which, *effectively*, they *do not know*).

With distribution, the individual assumes a subjective dimension of the social which widens their own universe of interests, to which they had hitherto been limited by their activity; the new relations attained by diversity (the different roles of agents in society and their relation to objects) facilitate this dimension. For the subject, this return of individual consumption to social production, mediated by social distribution, constitutes a first notion of the political sphere. The latter manifests as a debtor of the development of the social division of labour, a new field contributing differences in experience and thought (it engenders opposing ideologies, manifests different symbolisms of particular universes, incorporates new perceptions and values, and develops new forms of communication).

The return to social production with this new individual is now produced from a rather different situation than the traditional one, with a subject who now has a subjective and privative awareness of the social (*awareness of the difference*), and which, in contrast to *other awarenesses*, procures the advent of the strictly political sphere of society.

The distribution that emerges from the social division of labour generates the *place* of politics, ethics and ideologies (Figure 8.4). New stories have a place in it, since whatever happens to the community is no longer one thing, but many. Not all its members actively and collectively produce a community (*one community*); they rather produce a plural history with subjects living with people who do not work with them, and these subjects want to know about those people who live next to them but not with them. This *social* exchange of distribution will give rise to that first political relationship which, along with the production of individuals,[33] will lead to an association of communities while expanding relations and exchanges.

---

33 Marriage happens to be the first political institution, at least in an abstract sense. Marx insisted in 1844 on the social *naturalness* of that primal activity (between man and woman), specifically in the *Paris Manuscripts*, also called *Economic and Philosophic Manuscripts*. Moreover, Marx insisted that the essential result of the whole production process is the *existence* of mankind (Marx 2010, pp. 294ss.), which emerges from the material intensity and possibility of such a relationship.

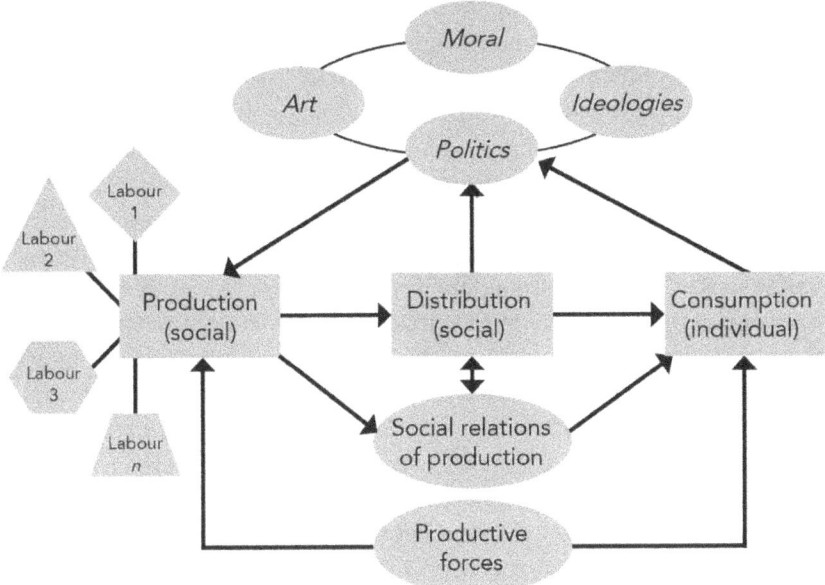

FIGURE 8.4 The mediating role of distribution in the processes of production

When social relations are separated from the labour activities that produce them, human communities open to new expressions and social experiences. Where social labour, i.e. production, has diversified in a context in which the social subjects and objects remain united in the distribution but divided in participation, the horizon of production broadens and the valuation of social things is reconducted towards unsuspected roads. When social mechanisms do not follow their production, distribution must deal for the first time with the *ought to*. With distribution and the new objective and subjective relationships that it engenders, opposing assessments and diverse opinions are incorporated into society and people even live in different ways. The new relations give way to cooperation or grievances. A plural history is born which addresses that manifestation of differences and can abolish the common universe on which it was built. The subjects, now political as well, try to manage how *social life ought to take place*, with manoeuvres that will implement strategies and further divide the different spheres of the production/consumption – strategies that will always fail if they do not consider the limits and possibilities defined by the *productive forces*.

This return of individual consumption to social production, now mediated by politics, may also take an ugly turn. The individual, aware of the role of others as well as its own in society, and aware of its own place, can contribute to joint social reproduction or, on the contrary, vouch for the present reality and highlight the contradiction characterised by inequalities in the contribution that the new production itself expresses. It is a step towards protesting, along with others in the same situation (the same particular universe of perceptions), who are harmed by a common good for which they believe to be collaborating most. The opposite explanation alternates with this possibility: it is likely that the divorce or shift in production – which we should perhaps call *production policy* – is probably due to social agents that benefit from the cooperative, egalitarian and collectivist distribution, when their work lost prominence in the reproduction of the group. Now (in fact since the Neolithic in certain places ...) these individuals (packed with weapons and free time) have enough objective conditions to make sense of their lives by claiming a previously unthinkable place. This is the *appropriation* by force of the social subjects and objects produced by others. Be that as it may, the specific paths of social production must be investigated in history and not determined by any social theory.

With the social division of labour began a one-way journey in the development of societies. The moment when the division finally reaches all areas of production, the doors of society open to various pathologies (from inequality to exploitation). For Marx, the social division of labour occurs when the division of tasks is entangled in a contradictory way with the pre-existing social relations, adapting them to the new times. Such contradictions, once they have been overcome, strengthen us; but when we cannot manage them, they claim many lives along the way. This is where the manifestations of the individual against society[34] and of property, surplus, exploitation and class division begin.

Acknowledgments

I would like to express my gratitude to my colleagues Rafael Micó, Cristina Rihuete Herrada, Roberto Risch and Miguel Valério for their fruitful criticisms and comments. I am also indebted to the latter and to Ana Martínez García-

---

34 In 1690, Locke (1985 [1690], p. 39) summarised the foundation of the praise of the individual in detriment of society, recognising the fruit of his work as an exclusive property and intentionally ignoring the weight of the accumulated labour by the effort of everyone. For him, the individual's starting point is a permanent social *tabula rasa*. This apology of (false) equal opportunities silences the fact that individuals have an unequal departure threshold sanctioned by inheritance, an institution which allots dissymmetric privileges in the initial material conditions.

Mauriño for their translation of the Spanish version of the paper into English. Finally, I am thankful to Ianir Milevski for his invitation to contribute to this volume and for his many suggestions. As usual, I remain solely responsible for any potential mistakes.

References

Fernández Buey, Francisco 1998, *Marx (sin ismos)*, Barcelona: El Viejo Topo.

Fisher, Mark 2009, *Capitalist Realism: Is There No Alternative?*, Winchester: Zero Books.

Gurvitch, Georges 1965, *Dialéctica y Sociología*, translated by Joaquín González, Caracas: Ediciones de la Biblioteca de la Universidad Central de Venezuela.

Hegel, G.W.F. 1991 [1820], *Elements of the Philosophy of Right*, translated by H.B. Nisbet, Cambridge: Cambridge University Press.

Hegel, G.W.F. 2018 [1807], *The Phenomenology of Spirit*, translated by Michael Inwood, Oxford: Oxford University Press.

Kant, Immanuel 1963 [1784], *Idea for a Universal History from a Cosmopolitan Point of View*, translated by Lewis White Beck, Indianapolis, IN: The Bobbs-Merrill Co.

Lenin, Vladimir I. 1977 [1913], 'The Three Sources and Three Component Parts of Marxism', in *Lenin Collected Works*, Volume 19, Moscow: Progress Publishers.

Locke, John 2018 [1690], *Two Treatises of Government: In the Former, The False Principles and Foundation of Sir Robert Filmer, and His Followers, Are Detected and Overthrown: The Latter, Is an Essay Concerning the Original, Extent, and End of Civil Government*, 7th ed., London: Penguin.

Lull, Vicente 2005, 'Marx, producción, sociedad y arqueología', *Trabajos de Prehistoria*, 62, 1: 7–26.

Lull, Vicente 2007, *Los objetos distinguidos: La arqueología como excusa*, Barcelona: Ediciones Bellaterra.

Marx, Karl 2010 [1844], *Economic and Philosophic Manuscripts of 1844*, in *Marx and Engels Collected Works*, Volume 3, *Karl Marx, March 1843 – August 1844*, translated by Martin Milligan and Dirk J. Struik, London: Lawrence & Wishart.

Marx, Karl 2010 [1857–8], *Economic Works*, in *Marx and Engels Collected Works*, Volume 28, *Marx 1857–61*, translated by Ernst Wangermann, London: Lawrence & Wishart.

Marx, Karl 2010 [1867], *Capital: A Critique of Political Economy*, Volume 1, in *Collected Works*, Volume 35, translated by Samuel Moore and Edward Aveling, London: Lawrence & Wishart.

Marx, Karl and Friedrich Engels 2010 [1840–1], *Notebooks on Epicurean Philosophy*, in *Marx and Engels Collected Works*, Volume 1, *Karl Marx: 1835–1843*, translated by Richard Dixon, London: Lawrence & Wishart.

Marx, Karl and Friedrich Engels 2010 [1845–7], *The German Ideology*, in *Marx and Engels Collected Works*, Volume 5, *Marx and Engels: 1845–1847*, translated by W. Lough, London: Lawrence & Wishart.

Sacristán, Manuel 1983, *Sobre Marx y marxismos*, Barcelona: Icaria.

CHAPTER 9

Politics and Social Ontology in Prehistory

Vicente Lull, Rafael Micó, Cristina Rihuete Herrada and Roberto Risch

1   Introduction

Few references are found in the writings of Karl Marx and Friedrich Engels that provide insight into their understanding of political practice and of its role throughout history.[1] Also, Vladimir I. Lenin,[2] Rosa Luxemburg[3] and other early 'Marxists' discussed the emergence of class society and the functioning of the state at length, but not the importance and meaning of 'politics' for social organisation in general. Consequently, it is no surprise that the classical definition by Max Weber,[4] according to which political action is the exercise of power and domination at a communal level, still prevails in the dominant readings of the past as well as the present. Politics is thus an arena of conflict, a more or less violent fight to impose certain types of behaviour, values and beliefs upon social groups and individuals. Such a conflict-driven definition practically excludes the possibility of political decision-making in societies and social realms lacking the personalisation or institutionalisation of power and domination, probably referring to most of human history.

Our aim will be to explain how an alternative understanding of political action can be derived from Marx's general economic thinking. As expressed in his introduction to the *Grundrisse*,[5] the fundamental contradiction in all human economies emerges between the 'moment' of the production of goods, as an inevitably collective enterprise, and the 'moment' of consumption, where each member of the community might have different needs, preferences and desires. The structural and temporal difference between production and consumption is bridged and resolved in each historical context through specific relations of distribution and exchange. Consequently, political praxis emerges from the need to establish the rights, rules and values that determine the relations between the members of a group or community with regard to production

---

1 Marx 1843; Engels 1972.
2 Lenin 1964.
3 Luxemburg 1971.
4 Weber 1921.
5 Marx 1973.

and consumption, and, hence, the limits of the social entity itself. Such an understanding of the political field does not necessarily assume a pervasive exercise of power, violence or domination, and provides a less state-centred perspective on the human past and present, when a-cephalic or poly-cephalic societies address political decision-making.

2   Conventional Understandings of 'Politics'

'Politics' is a term frequently used in multiple aspects of everyday life as well as research activity. Concerning the latter, it addresses an object of knowledge (past societies practiced *politics*, which archaeology wants to and can understand) and, according to post-processual critique, an inherent dimension of knowledgeable subjects, which shapes their unavoidable prejudices and, incidentally, eliminates any possibility of objective knowledge. We will not deal with the political conditionings of the archaeological task along these lines. Rather, we suggest a theoretical and, to a certain degree, a methodological framework which allows us to tackle the study on political relations from a historical-materialist perspective.[6]

Taking on this task whilst assuming that we share the same definition of 'politics' most likely means taking on disagreements from the start. This in turn will foster misunderstandings. In order to minimise this risk, we may start by considering the term's etymology. 'Politics' refers to the governance of the *polis*, the collective that inhabited a city state in ancient Greece. Beyond this historical singularity, a more wide-ranging use would focus on public affairs – the relations upheld in a social collective – as well as their government, steering and management. As can be seen, the Greek conception remains respected, according to which the collective is always the protagonist above individualities, being both subject and object of political action. This is because, as Aristotle stated and as is still admitted today, the human being is a *zoon politikon*.[7]

That said, *zoon politikon* (literally 'political animal') is usually understood and translated as 'social animal', allowing ambiguity to thrive.

– Are politics present in every human relation due to their social nature? If so, that would equate 'politics' and 'society'. The study of politics would reach the status of an anthropology or general sociology to become a leading science of human affairs.

---

6   The present text summarises and qualifies points previously expressed in other publications by our research team (Castro et al. 2001; Lull and Micó 2007, and 2011; Risch 2018).
7   Aristotle 1932.

- On the other hand, if we did not believe in subsuming society and history under politics, we would have to face the following question: are politics *only* present in a certain domain of social life? In that case, the question would be what that domain is and where it is placed. Philosophy and political thinking have come up with very different answers, depending on whether the focus lies on society or on the individual itself. Some suggest that politics issue from a shared ethical imperative, sprung from the willingness of every people in humankind to be recognised as such. Others, on the contrary, propose that it lies in the individual ability to lead or to reason and the resulting judgement of what is more convenient for oneself and, by extension, for others.

Asking and answering these questions assumes a topological metaphor, according to which politics takes up a 'space' in the social realm. When analysing any realm, the definition of one of its components ('what is politics?') must take into consideration its own features – its 'essential topography' – as well as its connection to other components of the same realm: its 'circumstantial topography'.

The spatial metaphor of human existence refers back to an ontology that details the layout of that realm, its elements, the relations that link them, and its limits. The location and definition of the political domain depends on the implicit or explicit social ontology, which will be the starting point of the learning process: what is so-called 'society', how does it work and why does it diversify and change?

3 Marxist Ontology and the Concept of 'Politics' in Prehistory

An account of social ontologies would involve a scholarly effort beyond our purposes here. Thus, we will focus on a Marxist approach, which we apply in our research on prehistoric archaeology.

The concept of 'production' plays a crucial role in this ontology. The production of material conditions that sustain any form of social life make up the first historic fact: anything social is created through diverse, dynamic and changing relations between subjects (men and women) and objects (natural resources, raw materials, artefacts). In the introduction to the *Grundrisse*, Marx[8] suggested that production can be understood as a unitary cycle that unfolds, dialectically, into three 'moments' revealed by analysis:

---

8   Marx, 1973, pp. 83–111.

(1) **Production** entails the active intervention of social subjects and means of production in order to obtain a product. The social subjects are formed in this 'moment' by participating in essentially collective tasks that require involvement with varying intensity and duration. The 'state of nature' featured by autonomous individuals has never come to be; it is a 'myth of origin' fuelled by liberalism.

(2) **Use-consumption** of what is produced – in the context of more or less intense, varied and extended practices – makes sense of the production. In the case of social subjects, consumption restores the working force. Thus the (re)productive cycle is closed and the conditions for the following one are laid out. Given that consumption provides individual satisfaction whilst production is always social, there is a permanent tension between both 'moments', which will be sorted out by distribution.

(3) **Distribution** implies the moving of products until they reach the places where they will be used and consumed. The way objects are allocated is and has been highly diverse throughout history, from reciprocity to tributes. The same broad variability applies to the allocation of subjects, expressed in multiple kinship rules and/or in migrations and abductions. During distribution, general production surpasses the strictly economic environment and becomes a social realm that will be crucial in order to define 'politics'.

These three moments can be distinguished analytically, even though in practice they are usually presented as a unit, especially production and use-consumption. Thus, the event of producing something specific (for example, a tool) implies the use of certain objects (for example, other tools) and the consumption of others (for example, fuel), as well as of the subjects themselves (workforce).

Given the holistic scope of this ontology, we may ask within which of these three moments politics is placed. Placing it within production or use-consumption would lead us to support an unconditioned idealism.

- If political relations arise from the moment of production, we would have to admit the priority of thinking over acting, as argued by the ontologies of culture and identity: human intervention regarding matter always depends on a preliminary and guiding idea. This perspective takes on the theological model and applies it to human activity. It subordinates the material world to the will of our almighty thinking.
- If we place politics *entirely* within the moment of use and consumption, both being realms developed on an individual scale, we would have to admit to an individualistic idealism. According to it, each person is free and undefined, being able to choose from what production has to offer.

In turn, the moment of distribution refers to a middle ground, subject to both production and use-consumption and, at the same time, capable of influencing them. This is where the meaning of 'management' lies, or where we find the meaning of 'government'. Thus, we suggest that politics is the social realm in which certain standards are shaped, which rule the effective distribution of objects and social subjects for their final and/or productive and reproductive use-consumption. Politics can condition production and consumption from a place of its own, found within distribution.

Do policies result from free, arbitrary will? The answer is no. Political criteria are built on experiences arisen from the realms of production and use-consumption, even though it is simultaneously able to influence future practices within those realms. Furthermore, political criteria are not fuelled by sovereign will. Rather, it is fuelled by physical, technological and, in general, by the economic conditions of the process of production, where the foundations of all social relations lie. Usually, political criteria focus on answering questions such as:

- Which products must be obtained and in what amount?
- Who will participate in which task? For how long and with what intensity and demand? (Who is expected to partake and in which conditions and timeframes and at what pace?)
- Are there too few, enough or too many people in relation to a given goal?
- What resources, raw materials and means of production are available in order to complete any given task? (What is counted on when doing something specific?) Are there too few, enough or too many of each?
- For whom are the produced goods and/or provided services intended? In what quantity or measure?
- What is the value of all things subject to exchange? What system of equivalence should be applied?

Everybody has something to say about these issues, a result of being involved in relations that shape individuals and groups. However, there are relational reasons that condition the answers beyond a hypothetical free will. We will analyse them, as well as the practical consequences of their differences, in the next section.

4   Politics, Production and History

We have suggested that politics emerges and occupies its own, intermediate spot in the moment of distribution. The more separated the moments of production and use-consumption are regarding time and space, the more relevant the forms of distribution – and therefore politics – become. That distance between production and use-consumption is historically diverse. Evaluating it in each case depends on the state of two factors.

(1) **Division of productive tasks** ('technical division of labour' or 'labour division' according to Marx), which has to do with the degree of fragmentation of productive procedures and the specialisation of certain groups in their accomplishment.

(2) **Social division of production**, an expression that refers to the degree of fragmentation or 'displacement' of the social community regarding its engagement with the moments of production in general (production distribution to use-consumption). That is to say, the degree of fragmentation of the groups engaged in the cyclic succession of these three moments (is it the same people that work together to produce something, that meet up to decide its distribution, and that use-consume what has been produced?).

The development of both, the productive and the social divides, involves the breaking up of the community into contexts in which individual experiences take place. In turn, individual experiences promote specific prospects on life, hence the emergence of diverse interests that are expressed in projects of coexistence or convenience as ideologies.

The spread of particular experiences sets an end to unanimity – if it ever existed – to conforming to a general spontaneous, direct and common interest. Inevitably, disagreements come up. They frequently demand immediate solutions as there are economic imperatives that are detached from the pace of political activity (for example, the sowing or the harvest cannot suffer delays due to the risk of jeopardising nourishment; the pressing need to obtain certain raw materials or artefacts under the risk of paralysing other productions and compromising subsistence; individual claims to live in certain places are called for by others, etc.). Through the fragmentation of the realms of the productive cycle, *politics emerges as a specialised, stable and lasting realm*. Now, as it is *institutionalised*, it acquires its own, distinctive visibility. And now that it is *equipped with its own spaces and objects*, it is easier to identify through archaeology. We are not limited to deducing its action when the productive cycle implied few social divisions and the distance between production and consumption was very short.

5   Politics in Motion

Politics arise from relation, move towards decision, create rights and obligations and peak in execution. Throughout this process, paths are taken and means are made use of. In short, the making and materialisation of decisions can result from two ways: *negotiation* and *coercion*.

– The way of *negotiation* uses dialogue and deliberation. Each involved party seeks to persuade and receive the consent of the other. In the end, consensus is reached (even though not all parties necessarily benefit equally).
– The way of *coercion* uses physical and psychological violence as a means against different or opposed standpoints. The goal is obedience and submission. The end is reached by imposition (which always benefits one party at the other's cost).

When a certain (political) standard regarding the distribution of subjects or objects is reiterated over time, it becomes a norm. From a legal point of view, it outlines a relation of property, in which rights and obligations are established. Strictly speaking, a group possesses something when it has its access and benefit guaranteed.

The term 'property', in its general sense of control and access by a group, may not include *exclusion* and *exploitation* of another or other groups. However, it often does. Settling whether one or another situation took place depends on empirical research. Therefore, it would be wrong to assume that in certain regions and times some specific human groups, either because of their sex, age or any other physical or subjective condition, were by default either owners or owned. If research discovers forms of property that involve exploitation, appropriation implies the withdrawal of *surplus value*, and therefore the identification of an alienated *surplus profit* or added value. Otherwise, we are dealing with economic *gains* meant for collective consumption and use rather than for private benefit.[9]

'Politics' and 'property' belong to the same group of concepts. Politics always strengthens or puts ownership into question. If policies are manifested materially and repeatedly, it is said that someone exerts 'power', and thus has 'sovereignty'. Relations of exploitation involve an unequal distribution of power and sovereignty (correlates of private property), which is now in the hands of the exploitative class. In these cases, coercion is the most frequently used way of

---

9   On the social and economic difference between *surplus gain* and *surplus profit*, see Risch 2016.

guaranteeing the efficiency of political decisions. For this reason, collectives specialised in executing forms of physical and psychological violence emerge: *civilisation* and its political organisation, the *state*, have arisen.[10]

6   Conclusion

Political practice does not directly produce subjects nor objects. Its primary goal is shaping bodies and social subjects. Politics brings them together in meetings, deliberations or ceremonies, claims them and eventually destroys them in armed conflicts. That is to say, politics uses and consumes objects and subjects produced in other places through other (socioeconomic) relations. However, by doing so it influences and even determines the production and use of materials without intervening in its development. That is why it seems that politics is nothing concrete in itself, because it always points towards or refers to something else.

From the perspective of an archaeological research of politics, we suggest a syntagmatic approach in which the meaning emerges from regarding objects in themselves and in the relations that are established with others. It is just as important to identify the material means used in political activity, their places and specific objects and subjects, as well as the materials linked to the moments of production and use-consumption, the distribution of which interests politics.

References

Aristotle 1932 [367–347 BC], *Politics*, translated by H. Rackham, Loeb Classical Library 264, Cambridge, MA: Harvard University Press.

Castro, Pedro v., Sylvia Gili, Vicente Lull, Rafael Micó, Cristina Rihuete Herrada, Roberto Risch and María Encaerna Sanahuja 2001, 'Teoría de la producción de la vida social. Un análisis de los mecanismos de explotación en el Sudeste ibérico (c. 3000–1550 cal ANE)', *Astigi Vetus*, 1: 13–54.

Engels, Friedrich 1972 [1884], *The Origins of the Family, Private Property and the State*, New York: Pathfinder Press.

Lenin, Vladimir I. 1964 [1917], 'The State and the Revolution', in *Lenin Collected Works*, Moscow: Progress Publishers.

---

10   Lull and Micó, 2011.

Lull, Vicente and Rafael Micó 2007, *Arqueología del origen del Estado: las teorías*, Barcelona: Bellaterra.

Lull, Vicente and Rafael Micó 2011, *Archaeology of the Origin of the State: The Theories*, Oxford: Oxford University Press.

Lull, Vicente and Roberto Risch 1996, 'El Estado Argárico', *Verdolay*, 7: 97–109.

Luxemburg, Rosa 1971, *Selected Political Writings*, London: Monthly Review.

Marx, Karl 1843, *Critique of Hegel's Philosophy of Right*, translated by Joseph O'Mallery, available at: https://www.marxists.org/archive/marx/works/1843/critique-hpr/.

Marx, Karl 1973 [1857–58], *Grundrisse: Introduction to the Critique of Political Economy*, Harmondsworth: Penguin.

Risch, Roberto 2016, 'How did wealth turn into surplus profit? From affluence to »scarcity« in prehistoric economies', in *Rich and Poor – Competing for Resources in Prehistoric Societies*, edited by Harald Meller, Hans Peter Hahn, Reinhard Jung and Roberto Risch, Halle (Saale): Landesmuseum für Vorgeschichte.

Weber, Max 1921 [1972], *Wirtschaft und Gesellschaft*, 5th ed., Tübingen: Mohr Siebeck.

CHAPTER 10

Vere Gordon Childe and Latin American Social Archaeology

Marcelo Vitores

1   Introduction

The Marxist archaeologist Vere Gordon Childe (Figure 10.1) was, without doubt, one of the most remarkable figures in the history of twentieth-century archaeology, as has already been recognised.[1] One issue relates to which aspects of his works were utilised or accepted by researchers, and what value was assigned to them. The so-called Arqueología Social Latinoamericana (Latin American Social Archaeology) was one of the first schools of thought to draw on his legacy in order to build a theoretical standpoint and the relationship between both perspectives is of interest. There are two points to be borne in mind; firstly, the present discussion of this theoretical perspective is mostly focused on its first decades, when a shift occurred in how Childe's work was applied, and secondly, today it is more acceptable to think more in terms of social archaeology in a broader geographical context than just Latin America.[2] Despite these qualifications, this review is based on the premise that a critical evaluation of Childe's work can still be beneficial for social archaeology.

We must highlight that Childe never expressly dealt with the archaeology of the Americas, with the exception of an isolated example[3] or the occasional use of ethnographic references.[4] So, how did his work become so relevant for Americanists? In the first place, it was embraced through his more generally applicable concepts, namely the Neolithic and urban revolutions.[5] They were a re-elaboration of previous classificatory and evolutionary schemes that prioritised historical change and its causes. Being recognised as valid and universal archaeological problems, they transcended far beyond Childe's original model,

---

1   Daniel 1958, and 1981, p. 284; Ravetz 1959; Brami 2019.
2   Compare Tantaleán and Aguilar 2012, p. 23; McGuire 2008, pp. 64–7.
3   Childe 1950a.
4   For example, Childe 1946, and 1951, pp. 43, 63–4.
5   Flannery 1994; Smith 2009; Trigger 1980, pp. 173–6.

FIGURE 10.1   Vere Gordon Childe (in centre wearing a tie) with workmen at Skara Brae, Britain (around 1930).
ADAPTED FROM TRIGGER 1980, FIGURE 14

allowing them to be applied to a wide array of empirical contexts and be reformulated for different perspectives.[6]

The emphasis on explanation of processes of change and economic and social analysis of cultures or human groups, made Childe one of the first 'modern' archaeologists. His production was prolific, broad in interests and very stimulating, placing him as a forerunner in different and even opposing theoretical frameworks.[7] Labelled as an empiricist, diffusionist or culture-historical advocate, Childe was recognised as the great synthesiser of European and Near-Eastern prehistory.[8] Alternately, by stressing his interest in social evolution and processes of change, as well as his attention to deducing laws of human behaviour, he was proposed as a predecessor of the *New Archaeology* and the sub-

---

6   Compare Manzanilla 1988; Wailes 1996; Flannery 1994.
7   Fuentes and Tureuna 2009, p. 47; Jiménez Villalba 1995; Trigger 1994.
8   Daniel 1981, p. 286.

sequent processual perspective.[9] He also advanced problems that concerned post-processual archaeology.[10] However, avoiding reading between the lines, his most outstanding position was an explicitly Marxist one.[11] Some authors have denied the Marxism of Childe, arguing that he did not focus on class struggle as a historical driving force.[12] However, Childe had a more subtle perspective, spotting the social contradictions in other levels and contexts. Indeed, his interpretation of history blended several concepts from historical materialism with archaeological units of analysis. He also advocated for a socially active role of social science.[13] In this way, Childe influenced a broad spectrum of Americanist researchers by fixing the object of inquiry and rationalising the role of the discipline in its own social context.

2 Background of Latin America Social Archaeology

In the 1970s, interests and concerns of some archaeologists 'south of Río Bravo' coalesced in what was later know as Latin American Social Archaeology (hereafter referred to as LASA).[14] Early in its development, this theoretical perspective fixed on a Marxist analysis, framed in, and aimed at, the practice of archaeology in Latin American societies.[15] Among the main motivations of its supporters was a perceived dissociation between academic endeavour and social and political concerns, which was paralleled by the divorce between models to explain both the past and the present.[16] This movement mainly developed in Mexico and Peru, but it had several antecedents and sources. One of them was 'indigenism', a social and political movement that idealised

9   For example, Champion et al. 1991, p. 274; Renfrew 1994; Sabloff 1996.
10 Fuentes and Tureuna 2009, p. 47; Trigger 1994.
11 Childe 1956, 1958a, and 1979.
12 Faulkner 2007.
13 Fuentes and Tureuna 2009; Harris 1994; McGuire 1993, 2002, and 2008; Patterson 2003; Trigger 1980, 1984, 1987, and 1993.
14 This short review is meant to bring a brief context to the present discussion. Those interested in a more comprehensive inquiry on LASA history and variations, can check the provided bibliography, which includes some concise syntheses (for example, Fuentes and Soto 2009; McGuire 2002, pp. 62–8, and 2008, pp. 64–8). Moreover, Tantaleán (2006) points to some critics, and there is a compilation with different perspectives on LASA (Tantaleán and Aguilar 2012). The most complete review about Childe's works was made by Bruce Trigger (1980).
15 Lorenzo et al. 1979.
16 Bate 1998; Lorenzo et al. 1979; Lumbreras 2005.

the aboriginal past, establishing a position contrary to economic and ideological colonialism. It was influential in Peruvian archaeology until the mid-twentieth century, while it persisted longer in Mexico. However, in both cases this school of thought initiated a deliberation on the social role of archaeology.[17] For some of its supporters, indigenism had a socialist orientation, but a populist tendency prevailed such that the socialist perspective did not attain any great influence in the discipline. North American archaeology had a more influential impact at that time. Notions of historical materialism were subsequently introduced into Latin America due, in part, to the stimulus of the political ambiance of the 1960s, when the Cuban Revolution had already occurred and many other countries had governments related to, or at least tolerant of, leftist positions. This background facilitated the engagement in Marxist viewpoints and some promotion of their supporters, a tendency later reversed following the decline and retraction suffered because of the political changes.[18]

LASA explored several reformulations of historical materialism, finally rejecting French structuralist Marxism and some of its dogmatic perspectives. Simultaneously, there was a return to the works of Marx and Engels in order to expound a conceptual framework aimed at the social objectives that originated the inquiry.[19] Among the strictly archaeological antecedents, we should note the impact of the book *Prehistoria de Cuba* (Prehistory of Cuba), published by Tabío and Rey in 1966,[20] which resembled contemporary works by scholars from the Soviet Union.[21] Even so, according to Lumbreras,[22] it did not formulate a model that was followed, with the possible exception of the research undertaken by Sanoja and Vargas.[23] However, from the beginning, the works of Childe were the most cited and explicitly used as a source of inspiration.

---

17   Compare with Lumbreras 1974, pp. 157–63; McGuire 1993, and 2002, p. 63; Tantaleán 2004, and 2006.
18   Bate 1998; Fuentes and Soto 2009; McGuire 1993, and 2002; Tantaleán 2004, and 2006.
19   Compare with Bate 1998, and 2007a; Lumbreras 2005.
20   Tabío and Rey 1966.
21   Bate 1998; Fuentes and Soto 2009.
22   Lumbreras 2005.
23   McGuire 2002, p. 66.

3 The Paths to the Americas

Initially, the ideas of the Australian archaeologist were mostly unknown outside Europe. In the United States they gained a little more attention in the post-war period.[24] In Latin America, it was not until the middle of the twentieth century that researchers began to disseminate them.

In Mexico, European schools of thought were more extensively known, as many anthropologists escaping from fascist persecution introduced them. That was the case of Pedro Bosch Gimpera, who maintained a scientific correspondence with Childe,[25] and Pedro Armillas, also from Spain, who taught the Childean hypotheses on the Neolithic and urban revolutions in his courses about Mesoamerica.[26] On the other hand, Mexican archaeologist José Luis Lorenzo carried out postgraduate studies at the London Institute of Archaeology while Childe was its director. Back in Mexico, José Luis Lorenzo would apply Childe's theoretical models, collect his works and stimulate their study.[27]

In Peru in the 1950s, John V. Murra applied some of the concepts relating to Neolithic and urban revolutions in his dissertation about the Andean area.[28] Meanwhile, an amateur archaeologist and plantation owner, Rafael Larco-Hoyle, adapted the idea of the Neolithic Revolution in his explanation of coastal Peruvian history, but he was biased towards a scheme of cultural evolution in stages that would later drift to perspectives such as cultural ecology.[29] However, the person who contributed the most to the diffusion in the Andes of the concept of the Neolithic and urban revolutions was Emilio Choy, a Marxist historian and son of Chinese migrants. In spite of not having a degree in archaeology, he was a major influence for generations of Peruvian archaeologists since the early 1960s, many of whom considered Choy a mentor and a forerunner in the development of social archaeology.[30]

---

24 Patterson 2003, p. 53.
25 Díaz-Andreu (2009) describes the academic networks and their political context for this period. Years later, Mexico continued hosting researchers that were forced to migrate because of political issues – for example, the Chileans Luis Felipe Bate and Julio Montané, active participants in LASA development (McGuire 1993, p. 108), and also the Argentinian José Pérez Gollán (Lumbreras 2005, p. 33).
26 Olivé Negrete 1988.
27 Olivé Negrete 1988; Pérez 1981.
28 Lumbreras 2005, p. 25.
29 McGuire 1993, p. 107, and 2002, p. 65. Following Patterson (2003, p. 53), it is worth noting that even though V.G. Childe was mostly omitted in North American anthropological works, J. Steward had formulated his theory inspired by Larco Hoyle's approach(!), who in turn used Childe's model.
30 Lumbreras 1974; Tantaleán 2006.

In addition, from the mid-1950s, Spanish translations of Childe's books began to appear.[31] Among the first was *Man Makes Himself*[32] in 1954, *What Happened in History*[33] and *Piecing Together the Past*[34] in 1956, and *The Prehistory of European Society* and *Society and Knowledge*[35] in 1958. And from the 1960s on, *Progress and Archaeology* (1960),[36] *Social Evolution* (1964),[37] *New Light on the Most Ancient East* (1968),[38] and *A Short Introduction to Archaeology and History* (1971).[39] Some of his papers were published in Spanish long afterwards in a compilation.[40] However, the diversity of books translated in those decades gives us an idea about how accessible his work was and allows us to assess the selection criteria that later authors made.

4 In the Name of Childe

Several Latin American scholars, sharing some knowledge of Childe's work and wishing to enhance their archaeological practices with socio-political concerns, began gathering in seminars and conference meetings in the 1970s. There, the impulse arose to formalise their proposal in a book: *La arqueología como ciencia social* [Archaeology as Social Science] by Luis Lumbreras.[41] Shortly afterwards (1975), a meeting was arranged with a programmatic aim. It was known as 'Reunión de Teotihuacán' and was summarised in a collective manifesto[42] entitled *Hacia una arqueología social* [Towards a Social Archae-

---

31   Compare with Gathercole et al. 2009; Pérez 1981, pp. 76–8. Spanish translations are omitted in the references in order to avoid inflating this section. The other texts, already quoted, cover most of the issue. As an aside, note that, very often, book titles are radically altered or changed in translation, as happens with movie titles distributed in Hispanic countries. For example, *Man Makes Himself*, which conveys the conclusion of the book in a concise metaphor on the dialectic relationship between humanity and its traditions, was changed to *Los orígenes de la civilización* ('The origins of civilisation') which reduces the original meaning to nothing.
32   Childe 1951.
33   Childe 1950b.
34   Childe 1956.
35   Childe 1957.
36   Childe 1944.
37   Childe 1947c.
38   Childe 1935b.
39   Childe 1947b.
40   i.e. Pérez 1981.
41   Lumbreras 1974.
42   At the meeting and involved in developing the manifesto were José Luis Lorenzo, Luis Lumbreras, Eduardo Matos Moctezuma, Mario Sanoja, Iraida Vargas, Antonio Pérez Elías,

ology].⁴³ This initiative appealed explicitly to the archaeological authority of Vere Gordon Childe, highlighting his 'rebellion' against the traditional theories and practices in mainstream archaeology as a way to open new theoretical and methodological paths.⁴⁴

In Felipe Bate's words, Childe's work incited 'the necessity to make way for alternative theories in interpretation of Precolumbian processes'.⁴⁵ The first step was to emulate his positioning of *archaeology as a social science*. Even this phrase mimicked the title of one of Childe's papers on the subject which was broadly circulated in the group. It summarised⁴⁶ several topics taken up by LASA. First, it postulated that archaeology has a contribution to make to the study of human institutions, and thus the 'Science of Man'⁴⁷ was acknowledged as a necessity. In this sense, even if unable to bring practical results at that moment, archaeology should gain awareness of the broader context in which it belongs in order to avoid degenerating into escapist entertainment.⁴⁸ The paper was a reflection on the concept of *culture* (then still equated with *society*), or *evolution* and *progress*, but also applied Marxist categories (*productive forces, mode of production*, etc.), and they revalidated the evolutionary scheme coined by Morgan and underwritten by Engels (*savagery, barbarism* and *civilisation*) as archaeologically useful. In the short text,⁴⁹ several concepts were redefined after a short review of their history in the discipline (even pointing to the ideological influences of a few), highlighting that sociological definitions must fit archaeologically observable conditions. At the beginning of LASA, this characterisation of the field would supposedly help develop the scientific theory that

---

Joaquín García Bárcena, Julio Montané and José Antonio Pérez Gollán. The last two, a Chilean and an Argentine, were in Mexico as political refugees. That is why the name of the last participant was deliberately omitted in the first publications, given the political situation in his country (see Lorenzo et al. 1979, p. 67; Lumbreras 2005, p. 33).

43   Lorenzo et al. 1979.
44   Lorenzo et al. 1979, pp. 82–3.
45   Bate 1998, p. 18. My translation.
46   Childe 1947a.
47   Certainly, the invocation of 'man' is gender biased, and nowadays clearly outdated, but it used to be a strong rhetorical figure attached to many connotations, as we can see in the title of Childe's book, *Man Makes Himself*.
48   Childe 1947a.
49   This short paper was published in 1947 in the *Third Annual Report* of the Institute of Archaeology of the University of London, and it summarises topics developed in many of his books (for example, Childe 1935b, and 1951) but suggests a very concise and synthetic program, which can explain why it was so widely and promptly disseminated among the proponents of the new school of thought. We can guess that its circulation was fostered by José Luis Lorenzo, given the fact that it has he who translated it (Pérez 1981, p. 80) and who could access it when he did his graduate studies in London.

would enable people to plan their future. It had the additional benefit of taking on the incorrect term of 'prehistory', which represents the most important part – or even the only one – of native history among colonised peoples.[50]

The above-mentioned book by Luis Guillermo Lumbreras (Figure 10.2) is suitable for analysing the adoption of several of Childe's ideas at this time. For instance, in the first part, when expounding the shift to historical materialism, Childe is introduced as the first archaeologist who adopted the notion of *social revolution*.[51] This is exemplified in the first publication where Childe outlined his scheme of cultural evolution in terms akin to Marxism,[52] however the concept of revolution was previously deployed.[53] In the second part, Lumbreras exemplifies *Neolithic* and *urban revolutions* in an Andean case study, almost transposing some hypotheses and historical situations from the Near Eastern model.[54] He describes a similar sequence of social, economic and environmental changes, including an ecological contraction at the origin of Neolithic period, and the search for raw materials as an incentive for civilisation expansion (which was not exactly the theoretical proposition in Childe's model but a particular circumstance of the cases analysed by him).

The same is true for the notions of *savagery*, *barbarism* and *civilisation* that were intentionally selected and applied after Childe – following also Engels and Morgan.[55] Lumbreras even spent a few pages discussing the opposition – and combination – of *evolution* and *diffusion*,[56] which in turn refers to another two popular texts by Childe.[57] He also criticised authors that used the concept of revolution in their explanations but in an empiricist way, ignoring its primal theoretical content. However, Lumbreras himself treated revolutions as radically fast events,[58] a superficial portrayal of the concept that was also criticised by detractors.[59] This is opposed to the original formulation, given by Childe,[60] who stated that 'the Neolithic Revolution was not a catastrophe, but a process' in the same way that urban revolution was.[61] Curiously, perhaps because

---

50   Lumbreras 1974, p. 30.
51   Lumbreras 1974, p. 105.
52   i.e. Childe 1951.
53   Trigger 1980.
54   See Childe 1944, and 1951.
55   Lumbreras 1974, pp. 177, 213.
56   Lumbreras 1974, pp. 110–12.
57   i.e. Childe 1935b, and 1951.
58   Lumbreras 1974, p. 182.
59   Olivé Negrete 1988, pp. 19–21.
60   Childe 1951, p. 83.
61   Childe 1950a.

FIGURE 10.2　Luis Guillermo Lumbreras at Lima, Peru (2018).
PHOTOGRAPHY BY MARCELA RÍOS

nobody can extract themselves from their socio-historical context, in Lumbreras's book the *contradictions* implicitly gave place to the *crises*,[62] the latter a concept that persists in works by subsequent authors.[63] The Lumbreras book and other texts also emphasised the reconstruction of daily life, arrangement of data in axes of space, chronology and chorology, and archaeological examples were stated in analytical terms of historical materialism (*mode of production, productive forces, instruments of labour*, etc.), as Childe did before.[64]

62　Very early on, Childe was criticised for not taking into account conflict in the way a Marxist approach should (Faulkner 2007; Ravetz 1959). But such an opinion was based on the reduction of conflict to class struggle, while Childe actually thought of it as contradictions (Trigger 1980, pp. 175–6). On the other hand, he also pointed out that a society's status quo could be sustained by ideological means, or means of another kind, avoiding the supposed inevitability of a *crisis* and the subsequent social change (Trigger 1994).
63　See Bate 1998, p. 86.
64　For example, Childe 1946, and 1958b.

FIGURE 10.3
Luis Felipe Bate at Ocozocoautla, Chiapas, México (2015).
PHOTOGRAPH BY GUILLERMO ACOSTA OCHOA

We can recognise, as was later admitted,[65] that the work of Vere Gordon Childe operated at first as a paradigm. Indeed, it offered not solely a theoretical perspective, but also a set of operative definitions and even hypotheses. Initially, LASA (presented here with Lumbreras's works, but also represented by those of Montané, Sanoja, Vargas and others) was criticised as merely mechanistic-economic in character. Since the 1980s, a shift in LASA followed this path, with a major role played by Luis Felipe Bate (Figure 10.3), Manuel Gándara and the 'Oaxtepec' and 'Evenflo' groups.[66]

---

65   Lumbreras 2005.
66   Fuentes and Soto 2009; McGuire 2002, p. 67.

5 Continuities, Divergences and Parallels

In the years of the second trend within LASA, Marxism seemed poorly fitted to analyse and explain non-capitalist societies. Marx and Engels investigated pre-capitalist societies mainly to understand the conditions for the emergence of capitalism, but they also paid attention in order to outline a general understanding of socioeconomic transformations and even human evolution.[67] They lacked information on prehistory and ancient history, fields that Childe later worked on. But the classificatory schemes proposed by Marx, Engels or Childe left many gaps, especially when approaching pre-class societies.[68] New discussions were dedicated to clarify the theoretical outline and to integrate it within a proper archaeological methodology. In order to do so, the LASA school returned to the work of Marx and Engels, looking for general foundations from which theory could be constructed.[69] This has a parallel with the shift previously made by Childe,[70] but in doing so, LASA was not inspired by him. This review resulted in the establishment of a theory of the 'social totality' where the concepts of *lifestyle* and *culture* acted as bridges between the observable reality for the archaeologist and the more abstract analytical categories.[71]

Primarily, it was Bate who coordinated the accord between concepts: starting with the definition of *tangible society*, the categories *mode of production*, *social formation* and *culture* coalesced as different layers of a society's existence, not as independent entities. That is 'a *tri-categorial* relationship between social formation, lifestyle and culture, in the framework of the *concrete analysis of a tangible society*'.[72]

Some authors continued to occasionally refer to Childe's definitions in order to develop their own variants.[73] Many topics were restated in other terms, which could invalidate any attempts to test or refute them.[74] So, the 'Neolithic Revolution' transmuted into '*tribal revolution*', which highlighted the transformation of social relations rather than the development of an economy of production; and the 'urban revolution' was merged into the complementary

---

67 See Engels 1975, and 2010; Hobsbawn 1965; and Marx 1965.
68 Bate 1998, p. 54; Lumbreras 2005, pp. 25–6.
69 Bate 1998; McGuire 2002.
70 Childe 1956; Trigger 1994.
71 For instance, unlike French structuralist Marxism, social formation is thought of as an abstraction. See Bate 1998; Fuentes and Soto 2009; McGuire 1993, and 2002; and Rolland Calvo 2005.
72 Fuentes and Soto 2009, p. 17. My translation.
73 For example, Lumbreras 1988.
74 Gándara 1988.

problems of the 'initial class society' and the origin of state.[75] Concerning the latter, some authors[76] examined the Childean hypotheses, but just as one more precedent for discussion among many others.

In this context, references to Childe were usually restricted to acknowledgments of him as a Marxist archaeologist and an inspiration for LASA, or the inclusion of some of his critical remarks, for example on the role played by evolutionism as an instrument against historical mythologies – being careful not to create another myth, one of a magical force of progress.[77] This also applies to the criticism of cultural relativism, conceived as empiricist and purely descriptive, against the paramount relevance of explanation.[78] In any case, they were isolated quotes on par with those of researchers from other, different trends.

As an illustrative case, the above-mentioned criticism of culturalism led to the problematisation of *culture* and its definition (or to the concept being discarded).[79] This is considered a current debate and has endured in different frameworks such as the New Archaeology, but it greatly interested Gordon Childe before that.[80] In fact, the re-definition of *archaeological culture* was one of his first contributions.[81] It is an operational concept that, by means of typology and association, intermediates between the archaeological finds and the societies from the past (i.e. the units relevant to advance a historical explanation). In all cases, a living and functional integration of cultural components (Childe's *functionalist concept of culture*) was highlighted, with culture used by the same people in the same place and time, and performing as both an environmental adaptation and a social tradition.[82] At that time, Childe saw a complete correspondence between archaeological culture, the whole culture and the society to which it belonged. Later, he would point to the incongruence between each dimension of culture (material and immaterial, comprehens-

---

75   See also Bate 2007c.
76   See Gándara 2008.
77   Bate 1998, p. 80.
78   Bate 1998, p. 70; Gándara 2008, pp. 87, 191; and Lumbreras 2005, p. 33.
79   In anthropology (which usually sets the framework of academic archaeology in the Americas), some have proposed that the central concept of culture should be abandoned, as its definition is so diverse (Neufeld 1998). In archaeology, the reaction against cultural history has led to some degree of abandonment of this concept as well. However, it still retains value. Moreover, from a social perspective in archaeology, and avoiding culturalism, considerations of local cultures are relevant to the discussion of cultural diversity in both the past and the present (Milevski 2017).
80   Lumbreras 2005, pp. 29–30.
81   Childe was not the first using the notion, but he discussed, reformulated and broadly applied it (1956).
82   Childe 1935a, 1949, and 1951.

ively defined by anthropology and restrictively defined by archaeology or in common sense) and how the archaeologist is forced to equate them. Moreover, he remarked on the partially subjective definition of each one, and on what we could call today subcultures,[83] and the idea that every individual belongs simultaneously to many societies in everyday life. However, for archaeological purposes, such detail would be almost imperceptible and, usually, irrelevant.[84]

In LASA, the concept of culture was also subject to debate. For example, Lumbreras[85] objected to the notion as an ideological construct of the bourgeoisie, and he barely referred to it for descriptive purposes (e.g. characterising an ensemble of material items that would differentiate both the stages in development of productive forces and ethnic groups). This concession aimed only to maintain a shared language and relied on Childe to make it compatible with historical materialism.[86] Years later, with the second movement within LASA, culture was reinstated as the *phenomenal* expression of *tangible society* and was articulated with the abstract entities of social reality (see above). This is not a vindication of culture as a study object[87] but a ratification of its role in the chain of interpretation. Bate referred to *archaeological contexts*,[88] defined as data-retrieving units, and linked *archaeological culture* to a *living culture*. In spite of acknowledging Childe's proposal and appealing to some of its key notions (*association*, *superposition* and *recurrence*), *archaeological culture* was reinstated as a comprehensive aggregate of contexts and materials produced by a particular society within a given time span.[89]

Lumbreras would remain reluctant to use the term, objecting that it confers ontological status to an arbitrary breakdown of unitary phenomena, a predicament that starts when taking material culture away from the whole culture.[90] Finally, he would create an intermediate category, the *socially significant archaeological unit*, 'in order to account for the transfer of information from the remains studied by archaeologists ... towards the identification of concrete social activities that the remains testify to'.[91] Here, observational theory is in some measure considered independent of *substantive theory* (i.e. theoretical constructions that explain human phenomena). Curiously, the immediate

---

83   Childe 1947c.
84   Childe 1957a.
85   Lumbreras 1974.
86   Lumbreras 2005, p. 29.
87   See Bate 2007b.
88   Bate 1998.
89   Bate 1998, pp. 121, 233, notes 96 and 103.
90   Lumbreras 2005, pp. 71–2.
91   Lumbreras 2005, p. 38. My translation.

empirical reference is the archaeological context, resembling the way in which Bate conceives it, whereas construction of the socially significant archaeological unit also rests on notions of association, superposition and recurrence as defined by Childe.[92]

Acknowledging how much the proposals really differ[93] is difficult, at least without exhaustive reference to case studies, which is a frequently criticised deficiency in LASA and a focus of current research.[94] However, there is some continuity with Childe in how the construction of archaeological data was treated (regarding correspondences between evidence categories and explanatory categories) and how the criteria were applied. The big picture, nonetheless, is one of a progressive abandonment of Childean proposals. This is not to claim a transcendental necessity to keep him as a referent for LASA, but a remark on the unspoken nature of that rejection: between the initial stimulus and the subsequent disregard, there is no justification based on a detailed and critical evaluation like that, for instance, by Trigger.[95]

6   The Third Revolution

The above-mentioned topics cannot cover the thoughts and perspectives of either Childe or LASA. They just exemplify the selective retrieval of the former by the latter, without deepening the comparison of their viewpoints. Nonetheless, we undertake another brief comparison on the topic of knowledge.

Following an early interest in philosophy, Childe led the scrutiny of a sociological approach to epistemology in his last decade, combining contributions from Durkheim and Marx.[96] Among other things, he highlighted the inherent relativism of archaeological research, i.e. using culture to study culture.[97] In his view, archaeology records the enrichment of thinking as it is materialised[98] in a socially sanctioned collective action. He even advanced the idea, not rare today, that artefacts are symbols, and added that by means of them, 'men long

---

92 It is worth noting that those notions were previously stated by Wheeler, but Childe is who they recognise.
93 Trigger (1993) claimed that Marxism never actually developed a theory of material culture, which is in concordance with the varying ways LASA faced the issue.
94 Tantaleán 2006; Tantaleán and Aguilar 2012.
95 Trigger 1980, 1994, and 2003.
96 Childe 1956.
97 Childe 1948, 1957a, and 1958b.
98 Knowledge is incorporated and passed on by society, being materialised to be communicated.

dead are communicating ideas to be fitted into our ideal reproduction of reality'.⁹⁹ However, the ultimate purpose of knowledge is not to reflect the world as captured by the senses, but also to act upon it. Based on this, knowledge is constructed and tested. Thereby, knowledge is conditioned (not limited) by the means a society has to act on the world. Moreover, Childe claimed that societies do not fit an environment just *as it is* but as it is perceived. This perception, however, must possess a sufficient resemblance to reality in order to make survival feasible.¹⁰⁰ These factors provide an anchor point for the otherwise extreme relativism and constitute for the archaeologist an entry point into those *worlds of knowledge*. We should note that this is a unitary approach to both sides of the problem: knowledge as a study object on past societies and as a critical issue about the researcher.

With respect to LASA, following the cited examples, knowledge is mainly, and carefully, considered with reference to the researcher's epistemology and the consequences of its application. Some researchers deepened philosophical grounds and developed their own proposals.¹⁰¹ Knowledge in past societies was also considered – for example, its use as an instrument of domination.¹⁰² But beyond this implementation, in LASA's classificatory schemes, knowledge seems to have been subsumed in social awareness.¹⁰³ Clearly, when treated, it is subordinated to the deployment of social relations¹⁰⁴ without any hierarchy as a study object. In this way, even by omission, there is an arbitrary breakdown between analyses of present and past knowledge (i.e. between those of the researchers on the one hand and past peoples on the other).

Taking into account that the catalyst for the emergence of LASA was the troubled disconnect between theoretical frameworks for explaining the past and those for understanding and acting in the present (see section *Background of Latin America Social Archaeology*), the split would constitute an unattended problem in this theoretical perspective. Its omission could have been a reaction against post-processual archaeology, akin to subjectivist and hermeneutical positioning. Even so, at least for some LASA exponents, explanation and interpretation would be compatible goals.¹⁰⁵ On the other hand, Childe's

---

99   Childe 1957, p. 104.
100 Childe 1935a, 1947a, and 1957a.
101 For example, the conceptualisation of 'theoretical position'; Bate 1998, and 2007a.
102 See Lumbreras 1974, 1988, and 2005.
103 Bate 1998.
104 Childe subordinated knowledge causality to social relations too. But he did not lessen its standing as a subject of inquiry, while in LASA it seems somehow to have been an accessory.
105 Gándara 2009.

view was not a relativist one and remained attached to a materialist framework. The omission cannot be ascribed to a lack of access to the texts where he discussed the topic, as Spanish editions were available quite early.[106] The choice may have derived from the main interests of each researcher. Indeed, LASA authors were primarily concerned with social relations, especially those of exploitation, and how they were configured from the past to the present. On the other hand, Childe was interested in knowledge as a valid problem in itself, not as a subsidiary issue. This interest was always present. Furthermore, he referred to *the revolution of human knowledge* on par with the Neolithic and urban revolutions.[107] Material culture served as the example of applied science since the earliest prehistory. This led him to embed archaeology in the history of science, a valuable contribution that, according to Trigger,[108] nobody else has continued. There are traces of this motivation and the way it unfolded in every discussion in which Childe engaged: in his notion of progress, his reinterpretation of diffusion, his vindication of culture as tradition, his attack on racism and his assertion of the contribution of every society to human culture as a whole. Most of these topics were formulated in words that now look quite outdated but could be usefully revised in light of his later writings.

7   Conclusion

The work of Vere Gordon Childe had a dynamic and fundamental role in the development of LASA. It was a departure point, a stimulus for the programme of an archaeology with a social perspective and links to Marxist theory to provide explanations. At its very beginning, Childe's work provided not only an approach but a whole set of operational instruments, hypotheses and models. Soon, many topics were abandoned (e.g. the debate diffusion versus evolution, and the evolutionary classification from Morgan), some were redefined or had their contents displaced (e.g. Neolithic and urban revolutions), while others continued to be discussed and detailed (e.g. Marxist definitions as articulated in archaeological research, and the concept of culture). Some of the issues addressed paralleled those faced by Childe – for instance, the persistent interest in a critical discussion of culture as a valid concept as well as its usefulness or limits. Similarly, both returned to the sources of historical materialism

---

106   It is not a suggestion that language can be a barrier. The existence of translations is a proxy for the availability of hardcopies in the regional book market.
107   Childe 1951.
108   Trigger 1980.

in order to achieve a new re-elaboration that could fit the requirements of the field. And again, both were concerned with the social reality that surrounds and influences archaeology, therefore historicising and contextualising ideas, which are key components of a critique. With regard to the opposite perspective – i.e. the social role of archaeology, or how archaeology impacts society – both Childe and LASA reaffirmed the persistence of the past in the present, and the dangers of misrepresenting the former. The position of Childe[109] against fascist ideologies such as Nazism is a relevant example of this. LASA's standpoint was against colonialism – in its varying forms – and the exploitation it implies. Simultaneously, LASA distrusted *science* per se, that is, science that fails to acknowledge its ends and beneficiaries.[110] On the contrary, Childe agreed that the ultimate use of knowledge is action, but not at the expense of pure science, whose unintended discoveries could be future advances.[111]

From this common ground the paths diverged. This paper does not intend to elucidate the subjective and complex problem of motivations and circumstances, given the disparity between personalities and historical contexts. However, I suggest there was a cleavage point in research interests. LASA was mainly oriented towards analysing conflict and social relations, as much for the object of study (past societies) as for the researcher, and this is denoted by the frequent expression '*arqueología para quién*' – archaeology for whom. Childe had a strong interest in the configuration of social fabric; nevertheless, he was criticised as lacking focus, for example, on class struggle as a motor of change. As already mentioned, knowledge was a persistent and increasingly discussed theme that we can trace throughout his body of work, that even influenced the way other topics were approached. Trigger pointed out that this has been an ignored aspect which deserves greater regard when assessing Childe's views.[112] In the same way, considering the intellectual links of social archaeology for Childe, we could expect the former to gain some advantage in critically evaluating his work. For instance, some issues actively researched by scholars outside LASA could be approached with resources from Childe, in a way that would be compatible with the theoretical position of the school of thought. One of these topics could be the historical role of knowledge, as discussed above. Childe's position was not inconsequential. He regarded it from the Marxist perspective, with knowledge not limited to interpret the world, but to change it. Moreover, Childe's standpoint was not dogmatic. Marxism was seen by him as an appro-

---

109   Childe 1933.
110   Lorenzo et al. 1979.
111   Childe 1957.
112   Trigger 1994, 1998, and 2003.

priate framework, but he also highlighted that reality is a creative process and, as much as the world changes, frameworks should as well in order to keep pace and render them useful.[113] A more in-depth discussion of these contributions could also help to avoid a merely militant position, and enhance praxis, meaning by this a more integrated relationship between acquiring knowledge, criticising and taking action in the world, which is a current interest for many archaeologists.[114]

Beyond this potential, a broader appreciation allows us to recognise Childe's didactic style and his impulse for synthesis.[115] The clarity of his writing and his interest in communication with a broader, public audience were more effective than any current declamation on the utility of the social sciences. He avoided political correctness as well as embellishments of discourses that condemn a text to death within the narrow circle of academy. The question 'archaeology, for whom?' was posed many times by LASA, but it was hardly answered. Regardless of how elevated a social ideal can be and how complex a philosophical argument, a closed academic style will always leave the outstanding question unanswered. Given the relevance of praxis for Marxist archaeology,[116] setting a common language and effective communication with the public is essential. Childe not only combined and summarised archaeological data available for Europe and the Near East in his time, but he also promoted his own perspective, trying to account for the diverse facets of human activity in a coherent way. He did this by coordinating and integrating them at multiple scales; from the individual who thinks and acts in a society through to the condition of humanity as a species that evolved over millennia. According to Manuel Gándara,[117] Marxism integrates seeming opposites (e.g. explanation versus interpretation), allocating them to different but tightly related explanatory levels. We can find the integrative effort of Childe useful not only for a social or Marxist archaeology, but for any theoretical position.

Frequently, different aspects of human reality are presented as opposed to or incompatible with each other, when in fact they are not exclusive or mutually reducible. For instance, this is usually the case concerning the false dichotomy between ideational and material realms.[118] Such sectarianism, together

---

113   Childe 1956.
114   See McGuire 2008; Tantaleán and Aguilar 2012.
115   In a similar way, Brami (2019, p. 318) asserts that 'Childe's great talent was to identify the right questions – those that mattered to people – a talent acquired from politics'.
116   i.e. a critically constructed and applied knowledge (McGuire 2008, and 2012).
117   Gándara 2009.
118   Trigger 1998, and 2003.

with the frantic pursuit to impose any new tendency, does not necessarily fit the demands made by the subject being researched, but rather exposes the context in which the discipline exists.[119] It is an environment of fierce competition, where even the most postmodernist approach performs as a Darwinian one.

Under these circumstances, when we are pushed to skew the reality we look at, Vere Gordon Childe not only remains a source of worthy proposals that should be re-evaluated, but also offers a body of valid assumptions with which to examine human history in a more integrative way.

Acknowledgments

This text was written almost ten years ago in the context of a seminar on history and theory of archaeology. It was recently adapted and translated for publication. In both instances, I thank Ianir Milevski for providing the space for learning more about Vere Gordon Childe in the seminar he organised and for the opportunity to participate in the present volume. I want to also thank Luis A. Orquera for kindly reading the manuscript and adding valuable remarks and corrections on data. I am also thankful to Marcela Ríos, Guillermo Acosta Ochoa and Patricia Pérez Martínez, who provided me with the pictures of Luis Lumbreras and Luis Bate. My full appreciation to Daniela Ávido and Liora Kolska Horwitz, who undertook the painful task of proofreading the first English versions. The work environment of the Universidad Nacional de Luján made this paper possible.

References

Bate, Luis Felipe 1998, *El proceso de investigación*, Barcelona: Crítica.
Bate, Luis Felipe 2007a, *Arqueología y Marxismo*, in *Luis Felipe Bate, contribuciones al pensamiento marxista en la reflexión arqueológica*, Santiago de Chile: Las Armas de la Crítica.
Bate, Luis Felipe 2007b, '¿Es la cultura el objeto de la Antropología?', in *Arqueología y Marxismo*, in *Luis Felipe Bate, contribuciones al pensamiento marxista en la reflexión arqueológica*, edited by Roberto Monares and Miguel Fuentes, Santiago de Chile: Las Armas de la Crítica.

---

119   This feature, of course, is not exclusive to archaeology (see Greenberg and Park 1994).

Bate, Luis Felipe 2007c, 'Teorías y métodos en Arqueología ¿Criticar o proponer?', in *Arqueología y Marxismo: Luis Felipe Bate, contribuciones al pensamiento marxista en la reflexión arqueológica*, edited by Roberto Monares and Miguel Fuentes, Santiago de Chile: Las Armas de la Crítica.

Brami, Maxime N. 2019, 'The Invention of Prehistory and the Rediscovery of Europe: Exploring the Intellectual Roots of Gordon Childe's "Neolithic Revolution" (1936)', *Journal of World Prehistory*, 32: 311–15.

Champion, Timothy, Clive Gamble, Stephen Shennan and Alasdair Whittle, 1991, *Prehistoria de Europa*, Barcelona: Crítica.

Childe, Vere Gordon 1933, 'Is Prehistory Practical?', *Antiquity*, 7: 410–8.

Childe, Vere Gordon 1935a, 'Changing methods and aims in prehistory: Presidential address for 1935', *Proceedings of the Prehistoric Society*, 1: 1–15.

Childe, Vere Gordon 1935b, *New Light on the Most Ancient East*, London: Routledge & Kegan Paul.

Childe, Vere Gordon 1944, *Progress and Archaeology*, London: Watts & Co.

Childe, Vere Gordon 1946, 'Archaeology and Anthropology', *Southwestern Journal of Anthropology*, 2: 243–51.

Childe, Vere Gordon 1947a, 'Archaeology as a Social Science', *Third Annual Report*: 49–60, London University Institute of Archaeology

Childe, Vere Gordon 1947b, *History*, London: Cobbert Press.

Childe, Vere Gordon 1947c, *Social Evolution*, London: Watts & Co.

Childe, Vere Gordon 1948, 'The Sociology of Knowledge', *The Modern Quarterly*, 4: 302–9.

Childe, Vere Gordon 1949, 'Social Worlds of Knowledge', *L.T. Hobhouse Memorial Trust Lecture 19*, London: Oxford University Press.

Childe, Vere Gordon 1950a, 'The Urban Revolution', *The Town Planning Review*, 21: 3–17.

Childe, Vere Gordon 1950b, *What Happened in History*, Harmondsworth: Penguin Books.

Childe, Vere Gordon 1951, *Man Makes Himself*, New York: New American Library.

Childe, Vere Gordon 1956, *Piecing Together the Past*, London: Routledge & Kegan Paul.

Childe, Vere Gordon 1957, *Society and Knowledge*, London: George Allen & Unwin.

Childe, Vere Gordon 1958a, 'Retrospect', *Antiquity*, 32: 69–74.

Childe, Vere Gordon 1958b, 'Valediction', *Bulletin of the London Institute of Archaeology*, 1: 1–8.

Childe, Vere Gordon 1979, 'Prehistory and Marxism', *Antiquity*, 53: 93–5.

Daniel, Glyn 1958, 'Editorial', *Antiquity*, 32: 65–8.

Daniel, Glyn 1981, *Historia de la Arqueología: De los Anticuarios a V. Gordon Childe*, Madrid: Alianza.

Díaz-Andreu, Margarita 2009, 'Childe and the International Congresses of Archaeology', *European Journal of Archaeology*, 12: 91–122.

Engels, Friedrich 1975, *The Part Played by Labour in the Transition from Ape to Man*, Peking: Foreign Languages Press.

Engels, Friedrich 2010, *The Origin of the Family, Private Property, and the State*, London and New York: Penguin Classics.

Faulkner, Neil 2007, 'Gordon Childe and Marxist Archaeology', *International Socialist: A Quarterly of Socialist Theory*, 116, available at: https://isj.org.uk/gordon-childe-and-marxist-archaeology/.

Flannery, Kent 1994, 'Childe the Evolutionist: A Perspective from Nuclear America', in *The Archaeology of V. Gordon Childe: Contemporary Perspectives*, edited by David R. Harris, Chicago, IL: University of Chicago.

Fuentes, Miguel and Marcelo Soto 2009, 'Un acercamiento a la Arqueología Social Latinoamericana', *Cuadernos de Historia Marxista*, 4: 1–36.

Fuentes, Miguel and Rosa Tureuna 2009, 'V.G. Childe, fundador de la Arqueología marxista', *Cuadernos de Historia Marxista*, 4: 37–49.

Gándara, Manuel 1988, 'Observaciones sobre el término teórico "Estado Arcaico"', in *Coloquio V. Gordon Childe: Estudio sobre las revoluciones neolítica y urbana*, edited by Linda Manzanilla, México D.F.: Universidad Nacional Autónoma de México.

Gándara, Manuel 2008, *El análisis teórico en ciencias sociales: Aplicación a una teoría del origen del Estado en Mesoamérica*, PhD Thesis, Escuela Nacional de Antropología e Historia INAH-SEP, México.

Gándara, Manuel 2009, 'El estudio del pasado: explicación, interpretación y divulgación del patrimonio', *Cuadernos de Antropología*, 5: 97–123.

Gathercole, Peter, Terry Irving and Margarita Díaz-Andreu 2009, 'A Childe Bibliography: A Hand-List of the Works of Vere Gordon Childe', *European Journal of Archaeology*, 12: 203–45.

Greenberg, James B. and Thomas K. Park 1994, 'Political Ecology', *Journal of Political Ecology*, 1: 1–12.

Harris, David R. 1994, 'Introduction', in *The Archaeology of V. Gordon Childe*, edited by David R. Harris, Chicago, IL: University of Chicago.

Jiménez Villalba, Félix 1995, 'La teoría de las revoluciones en Vere Gordon Childe', *Anales del Museo de América*, 3: 161–4.

Hobsbawn, Eric 1965, 'Introduction', *Pre-capitalist Economic Formations*, Karl Max, New York: International Publishers.

Lorenzo, José Luis et al. 1979, 'Hacia una arqueología social', *Nueva Antropología*, 3: 65–92.

Lumbreras, Luis Guillermo 1974, *La arqueología como ciencia social*, Lima: Histar.

Lumbreras, Luis Guillermo 1988, 'Childe y la tesis de la revolución urbana: La experiencia central andina', in *Coloquio V. Gordon Childe: Estudio sobre las revoluciones neolítica y urbana*, edited by Linda Manzanilla, México D.F.: Universidad Nacional Autónoma de México.

Lumbreras, Luis Guillermo 2005, *Arqueología y sociedad*, Lima: Instituto de Estudios Peruanos.

Manzanilla, Linda (ed.) 1988, *Coloquio V. Gordon Childe: Estudio sobre las revoluciones neolítica y urbana*, México D.F.: Universidad Nacional Autónoma de México.

Marx, Karl 1965, *Pre-capitalist Economic Formations*, New York: International Publishers.

McGuire, Randall H. 1993, 'Archaeology and Marxism', *Archaeological Method and Theory*, 5: 101–57.

McGuire, Randall H. 2002, *A Marxist Archaeology*, New York, NY: Percheron.

McGuire, Randall H. 2008, *Archaeology as Political Action*, Berkeley, CA: University of California Press.

McGuire, Randall H. 2012, 'Utilizar la arqueología para hacer hablar al perro', in *La Arqueologia Social Latinoamericana. De la teoría a la praxis*, edited by Henry Tantaleán and Miguel Aguilar, Bogotá: Universidad de Los Andes.

Milevski, Ianir 2017, 'Patrimonio cultural y diversidad cultural. El caso de la arqueología en Israel/Palestina: Un punto de vista socialista', *Claroscuro. Revista del Centro de Estudios sobre Diversidad Cultural*, 16: 1–24, available at: http://ppct.caicyt.gov.ar/index.php/claroscuro/issue/view/700.

Neufeld, María Rosa 1998. 'Crisis y vigencia de un concepto: la cultura en la óptica de la antropología', in *Antropología*, edited by Lischetti, Mirtha, Ciudad de Buenos Aires: Editorial Universitaria de Buenos Aires.

Olivé Negrete, Julio César 1988, 'Presencia de Vere Gordon Childe en la Arqueología mexicana', in *Coloquio V. Gordon Childe. Estudio sobre las revoluciones neolítica y urbana*, 15–23, Manzanilla, Linda, México D.F. Universidad Nacional Autónoma de México.

Patterson, Thomas C. 2003, *Marx's Ghost: Conversations with Archaeologists*, Oxford and New York: Berg.

Pérez, José Antonio (ed.) 1981, *Presencia de Vere Gordon Childe*, México D.F.: Instituto Nacional de Arqueología e Historia.

Ravetz, Alison 1959, 'Notes on the Work of V. Gordon Childe', *The New Reasoner*, 10: 56–66.

Renfrew, Colin 1994, 'Concluding Remarks: Childe and the Study of Culture Process', in *The Archaeology of V. Gordon Childe. Contemporary Perspectives*, edited by David R. Harris, Chicago: University of Chicago.

Rolland Calvo, Jorge 2005, '"Yo [tampoco] soy marxista": Reflexiones teóricas en torno a la relación entre marxismo y Arqueología', *Complutum*, 16: 7–32.

Sabloff, Jeremy 1996, 'The Continuing Interest in V. Gordon Childe', in *Craft Specialization and Social Evolution in Memory of V. Gordon Childe*, 229–32, edited by Bernard Wailes, Philadelphia, PA: The University of Pennsylvania Museum.

Smith, Michael E. 2009, 'V. Gordon Childe and the Urban Revolution: An Historical Perspective on a Revolution in Urban Studies', *The Town Planning Review*, 80: 3–29.

Tabío, Ernesto E. and Estrella Rey 1966, *Prehistoria de Cuba*, La Habana: Departamento de Antropología, Academia de Ciencias de Cuba.

Tantaleán, Henry 2004, 'L'arqueologia Social Peruana: ¿Mite O Realitat?', *Cota Zero*, 19: 90–100.

Tantaleán, Henry 2006, 'La Arqueología marxista en el Perú: Génesis, despliegue y futuro', *Arqueología y Sociedad*, 17: 33–47.

Tantaleán, Henry and Miguel Aguilar (eds.) 2012, *La Arqueologia Social Latinoamericana: De la teoría a la praxis*, Bogotá: Universidad de Los Andes.

Trigger, Bruce G. 1980, *Gordon Childe: Revolutions in Archaeology*, New York: Thames and Hudson.

Trigger, Bruce G. 1984, 'Childe and Soviet Archaeology', *Australian Archaeology*, 18: 1–16.

Trigger, Bruce G. 1987, 'Gordon Childe: A Marxist Archaeologist', in *Studies in the Neolithic and Urban Revolutions: The V. Gordon Childe Colloquium, Mexico, 1986*, BAR International Series 349, edited by Linda Manzanilla, Oxford: BAR.

Trigger, Bruce G. 1993, 'Marxism in Contemporary Western Archaeology', *Archaeological Method and Theory*, 5: 159–200.

Trigger, Bruce G. 1994, 'Childe's Relevance for the 1990s', in *The Archaeology of V. Gordon Childe*, edited by David R. Harris, Chicago: University of Chicago.

Trigger, Bruce G. 1998, 'Archaeology and Epistemology: Dialoguing across the Darwinian Chasm', *American Journal of Archaeology*, 102: 1–34.

Trigger, Bruce G. 2003, 'Archaeological Theory: The Big Picture', in *Grace Elizabeth Shallit Memorial Lecture Series 2003*, Provo: Department of Anthropology, Brigham Young University.

Wailes, Bernard (ed.) 1996, *Craft Specialization and Social Evolution in Memory of V. Gordon Childe*, Philadelphia, PA: University of Pennsylvania.

CHAPTER 11

Transitions: from Archaeology to Historical Materialism

Savas Michael-Matsas

1   Reclaiming History

Humanity stands at a most dramatic inflection point in history. The unprecedented global capitalist crisis that erupted in the 2008 financial crash was immensely intensified by the global pandemic shock[1] and an approaching climate catastrophe,[2] producing a life-threatening 'perfect storm'.[3] The initial triumphalism of world capitalism after the dissolution of the Soviet Union in 1991 and 'The End of History'[4] myth collapsed in disrepute long ago. But if 'The End of History' narrative is abandoned even by Francis Fukuyama,[5] historical disorientation prevails both in mainstream and radical discourses, as well as in mass social consciousness. Humanity seems to navigate in the current perfect storm without a compass. Declining global capitalism, spreading disasters in an on-going, multidimensional structural crisis – social, economic, political, geopolitical, cultural, health, environmental – becomes the major obstacle in the actual life process itself. On the opposite end of the spectrum, what had emerged in the early twentieth century as the socialist alternative appears to have resulted – in the last decade of the same century – in historical failure with the disintegration of the Soviet Union and of bureaucratised 'actually existing socialism'. Thirty years after this dramatic change, its effects still deeply affect both enemies and supporters of socialism.

Unstoppable turbulence, crises and convulsions during the last three decades, endless wars, social disasters, environmental destruction, unprecedented mass migration, but also social upheavals, popular rebellions and mass mobilisations both in the Global South and the Global North, have demonstrated

---

1   Wallace et al. 2020.
2   Foster and Suwandi 2020.
3   Michael-Matsas 2020.
4   Fukuyama 1989.
5   Fukuyama 2011.

that history neither met its end nor fallen into a kind of permanent stasis. Everything is feverishly moving, yet seemingly going nowhere. The problem is the lack of a credible alternative to the current disastrous world situation, an apparently frozen horizon of history, or, in other terms, a deadly 'impossibility of possibility' according to the Heideggerian expression reformulated by Maurice Blanchot in 1981.[6]

The dead end is actually not reached by the potential of history; it is reached by any *linear conception of history* based on the liberal concept of continuous progress (or continuous decline) and, particularly, by the fetishism of technological progress, including the actual untimely celebrations for a 'fourth industrial revolution', a 'post-industrial society' and a 'digital age' in a 'brave new world'.

Linear historicism, economism and technological determinism affected and distorted presentations of historical materialism from its early period until today, dominating the orientation of political leaderships within the workers movement for decades, as well as those of the intellectuals of the left. The most notorious example is that of 'orthodox Marxism' in the Second International or Stalinism's '*DiaMat*' and '*IstMat*'.[7] Revolutionary Marxism waged bitter struggles against these distortions of historical-materialist dialectics, starting with Marx himself attacking self-proclaimed 'Marxists' and Engels rejecting a reduction of Marxism to economism, up to well-known 'heterodox' Marxists such as Rosa Luxembourg, Vladimir Lenin, Leon Trotsky, José Carlos Marriátegui, Walter Benjamin, Ernst Bloch and others.

Today, it is even more vital to emancipate Marxism from the multiple layers of a disastrous legacy that condemns it to sterility, thus making it a part of the problem of anti-historical disorientation instead of its solution. In our times, any linear conception of evolution is paralyzed in front of an avalanche of non-stop upheavals. Old methods of rigid classification of rapidly changing conditions become a main source of confusion, a real epistemological obstacle in the path of cognition and of practical or critical activity.

Historical materialism has to revolutionise its own form, to rediscover – beyond any inherited dogmatism – its living content as a method of dialectical exploration of history's uncharted territories, to reveal Ariadne's thread in order to advance in the labyrinth of its own contradictions, complexities and multiple temporalities.

---

6 Blanchot 2012, p. 29.
7 Abbreviations in Russian of Dialectical Materialism [*DiaMat*] and Historical Materialism [*IstMat*], used during the Stalinist period.

In other words, the urgent task in front of us is to recapture the lost sense of history, to reinvent it as an active, contradictory, open process; to resist to the nihilist pressures of being petrified in front of a mythical Medusa's head, the mirage of an eternal return of the same.

As long as historical materialism remains condemned to a historical amnesia of the past, it cannot navigate in the currently unfolding historical process, in history as present, exploring its contradictory trends, discovering its possibilities and transitioning towards the future.

Benjamin notably and rightly insisted in Thesis XIV of his 'On the Concept of History' that the historical materialist has to perform

> ... the tiger's leap into the past. Only it takes place in an arena in which the ruling classes are in control. The same leap into the open sky of history is the dialectical one, as Marx conceptualized the revolution.[8]

The historical materialist, according to Benjamin, has to construct 'a constellation in which his own epoch comes into contact with that of an earlier one',[9] a 'constellation, full of tensions' between the 'here-and-now' [*Jetztzeit*] and the past:

> Materialist historiography is to be conceived as the reaction to a constellation of dangers [*Gefahrenkonstelation*], which threatens both the burden of tradition and those who receive it. It is this constellation of dangers which the materialist presentation of history comes to engage. This constellation's actuality is comprised against its threat; it must prove its presence of mind. Such a presentation of history has as a goal to pass, as Engels put it, 'beyond the sphere of thought'.[10]

The founders of historical materialism, Marx and Engels, performed constantly this 'tiger's leap into the past' during their entire intellectual trajectory. They both protested against any reduction of their theory to economism or 'eurocentrism',[11] or to 'the all-purpose formula of a general historico-philosophical theory whose supreme virtue consists of being supra-historical'.[12] Marx and Engels were sensitive to every new discovery in scientific research so as to

---

8   Benjamin 2005.
9   Benjamin 2005, Addendum A.
10   Benjamin 1999, p. 475.
11   Anderson 2010.
12   Marx 1989a, p. 201.

deepen and change their own theoretical research. They paid special attention to anthropology and archaeology, two sciences making their first steps in their time in the mid- to late nineteenth century. The profound impact of the publication of the pioneering *Ancient Society* by Lewis Henry Morgan on them is well known.[13] In the first part of the twentieth century, Gordon Childe's groundbreaking work had already established the relevance of historical materialism to archaeological research.[14] Yet, this is a reciprocal relationship: archaeology can – and should – open new horizons for historical-materialist dialectics, against any dogmatic, lethal fossilisation of it.

Anthropology and archaeology – especially archaeology as 'the past tense of cultural anthropology', according to Colin Renfrew and Paul Bahn[15] – have made important advances in the twentieth century, mostly during the last four decades. They should become of central interest for historical materialism, providing a vital impulse for a new, urgently needed 'tiger's leap in the open sky of history'.

2   Twilight Capitalism and the Dawn of History

In November of 2021, the common work of two renowned radical scholars, late anthropologist David Graeber and archaeologist David Wengrow,[16] was published; it was elaborated during the last decade of global capitalist crisis, on the basis of an impressive wealth of evidence and recent scholarship of anthropological and archaeological research. The title of the book is equally impressive, even provocative: *The Dawn of Everything: A New History of Humanity*. It is addressed to academics as well as to a broader, educated yet non-specialised public. It has already caused a wave of mixed public reactions among scholars and the press: non-stop debates, sharp controversy, a strong tide of articles full of sincere praise, undisguised hostility or even a combination of both – accrediting with admiration the extensive scholarship presented by the authors together with a rejection of their main radical argument.

The authors consider their book as 'a quest to discover the right questions',[17] and they make 'an appeal to ask better questions' on human history.[18] Their

---

13   Morgan 1964.
14   And see Trigger 1980.
15   Renfrew and Bahn 1991, pp. 9–11.
16   Graeber and Wengrow 2021.
17   Graeber and Wengrow 2021, p. 25.
18   Graeber and Wengrow 2021, p. 493.

appeal is gladly received. Their own questions are thought-provoking and seminal, although the answers given could be problematic. A comprehensive critical assessment of the book goes beyond the scope of the present chapter. But Graeber's and Wengrow's work cannot be ignored or overlooked here if the central question of breaking with all misconceptions about a linear evolution of history is to be addressed, making the necessary 'conceptual shift' and opening new horizons. Graeber and Wengrow say:

> To make that shift means retracing some of the initial steps that led to our modern notion of social evolution: the idea that human society could be arranged according to stages of development, each with their own characteristic technologies and forms of organization (hunter-gatherers, farmers, urban-industrial society, and so on).[19]

The authors make a frontal attack against well-entrenched views and attitudes in the social sciences of archaeology and anthropology, also widespread among Marxists. They emphasise the political implications and dangers deriving from the instrumentalisation of these views by the ruling elites for legitimating their regimes and preserving their rule, particularly in times of structural crisis.

American anthropologist Graeber (well known also for his participation as an activist in the movement 'Occupy Wall Street') and British archaeologist Wengrow mobilise their vast knowledge in their respective fields, along with the experience of their research, to deconstruct a narrative dominating modernity up until today – a narrative formed as a reaction, starting from the first contact of Europeans with the so-called 'New World', and what the authors call the problematic notion of 'indigenous critique' of Native Americans to modern European society during the seventeenth century:

> ... by the eighteenth century, the indigenous critique and the deep questions it posed about money, faith, hereditary power, women's rights and personal freedoms was having an enormous influence on leading figures of the French Enlightenment, but also resulted in a backlash among European thinkers which produced an evolutionary framework for human history that remains broadly intact today.[20]

---

19 Graeber and Wengrow 2021, p. 5.
20 Graeber and Wengrow 2021, p. 441.

This evolutionary framework, widely taken for granted, corresponds with what Noam Chomsky and Mary Waterstone – based on Antonio Gramsci – had recently described as 'the hegemonic common sense'.[21] In his reply to Kwame Anthony Appiah's criticisms in the *New York Review of Books*, Wengrow wrote:

> Rousseau's answer, in 1754, to the novel question '"What is the origin of inequality?"' was, we argue, a synthesis between ideals of human freedom – shaped by Native American critiques of European society – and the concept of history as stages of technological progress, which was then gaining ground through the writings of A.R.J. Turgot. The just-so story told by Rousseau gave us our modern concept of civilization, whereby each step toward cultural advancement – the invention of agriculture, metallurgy, writing, cities, and the arts, even philosophy itself – came with a loss of freedoms. It's a familiar and deeply ambivalent story. As we show in *The Dawn of Everything*, it is also at odds with the facts of modern archaeology and anthropology.[22]

Graeber's and Wengrow's project has openly declared emancipatory aims. Boldly, they call their book 'a book of freedom'. It constructs a 'constellation of dangers', in Benjaminian terms, between today's twilight capitalism of the post-2008 global crisis and the dawn of human history.

They trace the mainstream discourse and actual policies of governments and central banks to face the current global crisis, as well as fixed ways of thinking and living, back to the two main foundations of bourgeois modern political theory, Rousseau's *Discourse on the Origin and the Foundation of Inequality Among Mankind* (1754) and Hobbes' *Leviathan* (1651) on social violence, the mythical *bellum omnium contra omnes* and the origins of the state. And, while Hobbes's magnum opus is most often used in favour of openly right-wing conservative and even authoritarian politics, Rousseau's working hypothesis about a primitive egalitarian 'state of nature' and the origins of inequality can be presented as a more 'socially sensitive' political liberal framework. Graeber and Wengrow write:

> Since the financial crash of 2008 and the upheavals that followed, the question of inequality – and with it, the long term history of inequality – have become major topics of debate ... Pointing this out is in itself a chal-

---

21   Chomsky and Waterstone 2021, p. 25.
22   Wengrow 2022.

lenge to global power structures; at the same time, though, it frames the issue in a way that people who benefit from those structures can still find ultimately reassuring, since it implies no meaningful solution to the problem would ever be possible ... Today, there is a veritable boom of thinking about inequality: since 2011, 'global inequality' has regularly featured as a top item for debate in the World Economic Forum at Davos ... The ultimate effect of all those stories about an original state of innocence and equality, like the use of 'inequality' itself, is to make wistful pessimism about the human condition seem like common sense: the natural result of viewing ourselves through history's broad lens. Yes, living in a truly egalitarian society might be possible if you're a Pygmy or a Kalahari Bushman. But if you want to create a society of true equality today, you're going to have to figure out a way to go back to becoming tiny bands of foragers again with no significant personal property.[23]

The authors of *Dawn of Everything*, definitely anti-capitalist and influenced by the anarchist tradition, maintain a critical but more nuanced, rather ambivalent position towards Karl Marx himself.

First, they keep situating Marxism in a line of thinking following the tradition of Rousseau.[24] On another occasion, we had the opportunity to situate Marx *beyond* Rousseau,[25] criticising attempts by leading theoreticians of European communist parties to eliminate the deep contradiction between Rousseau's bourgeois republican legacy and Marx's revolutionary communist theory on inequality, the legal order and the state. The classical locus merging the two traditions remains Galvano Della Volpe's book *Rousseau e Marx*, published in 1957, serving the political purpose of legitimising the line of a 'peaceful road to Socialism'.[26] Graeber and Wengrow, although they keep supporting the prevailing view of wrongly associating Rousseau with Marx, approvingly underline Marx's thesis on historical praxis, counter-posing it to mechanical, environmental or technological determinism (which is supported by numerous self-proclaimed Marxists as well): 'Perhaps Marx put it best; we make our own history, but not under conditions of our own choosing'.[27] In the same way, although *The Dawn of Everything* opposes the notions of 'Neolithic revolu-

---

23 Graeber and Wengrow 2021, pp. 6–8.
24 Graeber and Wengrow 2021, p. 360.
25 Graeber and Wengrow 2021.
26 Michael-Matsas 2008a.
27 Graeber and Wengrow 2021, p. 206.

tion' and 'urban revolution', introduced in the 1930s by V. Gordon Childe,[28] its authors do not omit to reclaim the spirit of the great Australian pioneer Marxist archaeologist:

> As long ago as 1936, the prehistorian V. Gordon Childe wrote a book called *Man Makes Himself*. Apart from the sexist language, this is the spirit we wish to invoke. We are projects of collective self-creation.[29]

Gordon Childe was primarily an already convinced grassroots socialist activist in the Australian labour movement, deeply involved in anti-war and Labour Party politics, before becoming a dedicated Marxist.[30] He turned to historical materialism as an archaeologist to overcome the methodological deadlocks faced by archaeology of that time, which was under the long domination of positivism as well as of its idealist opposition, cultural historicism. As a Marxist, Gordon Childe opposed, indeed, technological determinism, as Bruce G. Trigger had rightly pointed out:

> … instead of seeing cultural change as the result of technological innovation, he already saw technological progress occurring within the context of broader economic and political patterns. This allowed him to explain how the same technological innovation could produce very different types of societies in Europe and the Near East … The primary context in terms of which change was to be understood was not technology but social organization.[31]

The dialectical approach of Gordon Childe often clashed with the Stalinist straitjacket imposed on Soviet archaeology in the 1930s. It clashed as well, during the same period, with attempts by the British historian George Thompson, who, following a similar dogmatic formalism, imposed a class struggle schema of interpretation in cases of pre-class or proto-class social formations in transition to class stratification, such as prehistoric Mesopotamia.

Graeber's and Wengrow's critique of mainstream conceptions of progress in *The Dawn of Everything* focuses distinctly on a critique of origins: origin of abolition of freedoms, of inequality, of the state, of private property, of origins of everything in human history. Despite all differences and divergences with

---

28 Childe 1936, 1946, and 1947.
29 Graeber and Wengrow 2021, pp. 8–9.
30 And see Irving 2020.
31 Trigger 1987, p. 3.

Marxism, it converges with the profound critique made by the non-dogmatic Marxist Walter Benjamin, particularly in his reflections developed in his unfinished magnum opus *Das Passagen-Werk* [*The Arcades Project*]:

> The concept of progress had to run counter to the critical theory of history from the moment it ceased to be applied as a criterion to specific historical developments and instead was required to measure the span between a legendary inception and a legendary end. In other words: as soon as it becomes the signature of historical process as a whole, the concept of progress bespeaks an uncritical hypostatization rather than a critical interrogation.[32]

The linear conception of history is precisely this 'uncritical hypostatization' of progress as a straight line of continuity in three successive parts: 1) an initial fixed point, 'a legendary inception'; 2) a fixed sequence of rigidly separated stages of social development; and finally 3) a teleological completion, a predetermined *telos*, 'a legendary end'. This historical continuum should be 'blown to pieces' by the dialectical materialist conception of history, according to Benjamin, and each one of the three parts of the metaphysical conception of progress should be thoroughly criticised and rejected.

3   For a Critique of Origins

Benjamin focuses on the problematic of 'origin' [*Urpsrung*] as a historical category in his *Ursprung des deutschen Trauerspiels* (1924–5), translated as *The Origin of German Tragic Drama*.[33] His insights were further developed with his reflections on *Urphänomenen* [archaic, original phenomena], based on his reading of Goethe, as expressions of an *Urgeschichte* [archaic, original history], especially in *Das Passagen-Werk*.

In his work on the German Baroque *Trauerspiel*, Benjamin distinguishes 'origin' as *Ursprung*, as the primeval source, from origin as *Entstehung*, emergence:

> Origin [*Ursprung*], although an entirely historical category, has, nevertheless, nothing to do with genesis [*Entstehung*]. The term origin is not intended to describe the process by which the existent came into being,

---

32   Benjamin 1999, p. 478.
33   Benjamin 1998.

but rather to describe that which emerges from the process of becoming and disappearance. Origin is an eddy in the stream of becoming, and in its current it swallows the material involved in the process of genesis.[34]

In the view of this essay's author, it is best for the term *Entstehung* to be translated as *emergence* rather than *genesis*. Anyway, the main point here is that Benjamin conceives 'origin' [*Ursprung*] as 'that which emerges from the process of becoming and disappearance'; in other words, from a *contradictory* process of arising [*Entstehen*] and passing away [*Vergehen*].[35] Origin is not a *static* point of departure of linear development, but a *dynamic* process, emerging from *a driving contradiction*. Its specific character, its quality, is 'mobility, boiling, springing and driving of a thing', to use Jacob Boehme's expression.[36] According to Boehme, the mystical *Philosophus Teutonicus* (1575–1624),[37] *Qual*, the 'torment of matter', becomes the spring, the source, *Quelle*, from which emerges quality, *Qualität*.[38] Despite its mystical language, it is well known to readers of *The Holy Family* that Karl Marx and Friedrich Engels much appreciated Jacob Boehme's qualitative dialectics of an impulsive matter in motion, in contrast to mechanical materialism.[39] Origin(s), emerging from a contradictory process, appears as *a dynamic field of conflicting forces, combining unevenly multiple variables*.

'Emergence, thus, is the entry on stage of forces', wrote Michel Foucault, 'it is their irruption, the leap by which they jump from the sides to the stage of theater, each with its own vigor, its own juvenility'.[40] From this perspective, exploring *Urphänomenen* [original phenomena] of human *Urgeschichte* [original history] – such as the origins of social stratification, inequality and exploitation, investigating the emergence of permanent settlement, domestication, agriculture, class divisions and the state – methodologically involves, first of all, the discovery of *a specific emerging field of conflicting forces* and the probing into of the underlying contradictory process.

The same methodological principle applies in studying, for example, the appearance of ritualism and religion in sites such as Göbekli Tepe or Çatal-

---

34 Benjamin 1998, p. 45.
35 Lenin 1961, p. 107.
36 Boehme 1992, p. 40.
37 Boehme 1992.
38 Michael-Matsas 2006, pp. 108–9.
39 Marx and Engels 1975, p. 128.
40 Foucault 2001, p. 1012.

höyük,[41] or the origins of Aegean ritual practice at the sanctuary in Keros,[42] or the emergence of complex forms of social organisation of the Ancestral Pueblo societies in the northern US Southwest.[43] A historical dialectical-materialist method of inquiry, searching the dynamic field of conflicting forces in a process of arising and passing away of social forms, can shed light on the vast variety, heterogeneity and constant metamorphosis presented to anthropologists by so-called 'primitive societies at the margins of history', as well as to archaeologists by prehistoric social formations, including the various pre-agricultural forms of social organisation mentioned in *The Dawn of Everything*.

4   For a Critique of the 'Theory of Stages'

Karl Marx, in the first draft of his letter to Vera Zasulich in 1881, warned against the abstract uniformity with which 'archaic or primitive' societies are misrepresented by bourgeois writers[44] (a warning that could also be extended to address non-Marxist 'Marxists' of his and our times). In the second draft, he makes a crucial remark, very relevant to our topic:

> The archaic or primary formation of our globe itself contains a series of differing ages, one superimposed on the other; in the same way, the archaic form of society reveals to us a series of different types, marking progressive epochs.[45]

The Marxian statement itself encapsulates a series of different layers of important insights: 1) on historical time; 2) on combined and uneven development; and 3) on epochs of development.

4.1   *Historical Time*

The 'archaic or primary form of society' already combines in itself a *multiplicity of temporalities*, 'marking progressive epochs'. From the dawn of humanity, *historical time is heterogeneous*.

This vital Marxian thesis was abandoned by his epigones, particularly in social democracy and Stalinism. Their linear 'theory' of successive, rigidly sep-

---

41   Hodder and Meskell 2010, pp. 32–72.
42   Renfrew et al. 2013, pp. 144–60.
43   Sinensky et al. 2021, pp. 1–19.
44   Marx 1989b, p. 359.
45   Marx 1989b, p. 363.

arated 'stages of development' presented history moving in 'its progression through a homogenous and empty time', as Benjamin aptly denounced in Theses XIII and XIV of his masterpiece 'On the Concept of History'[46] in 1940, through the darkest moments of human history during the twentieth century. 'History is a polyrhythmical formation', according to a splendid formulation by Ernst Bloch.[47] The heterogeneity of historical time was thoroughly examined by Bloch in his analysis of fascism, by elaborating on the *dialectic of combined contemporary and non-contemporary contradictions*,[48] during the tragic period of the rise of Nazism to power in Germany.

Today, in conditions of the loss of historical orientation, described at the beginning of this paper, to recover our Marxist compass means, first of all, to discover again '[h]istory as polyrhythmic formation' and historical time, not as homogeneous and empty, but in all its complex *heterogeneity*.

4.2 Combined and Uneven Development

The Marxian statement in the second draft of the letter to Zasulich is *one of the first* expositions of what Trotsky elaborated on later, namely *the historical law of uneven and combined development* (against Stalin's ludicrous claim in 1925 that 'the law of uneven development did not exist at the times of Marx and Engels, in the pre-imperialist epoch').[49] Trotsky made uneven and combined development the basis of the theory of permanent revolution. In his historic battle against the rising bureaucracy and the Menshevik 'theory of stages' revived by Stalinism, he wrote:

> Stalin does not understand to this day that the *skipping of stages* (or remaining too long at one stage) *is just what uneven development consists of* … One had to understand the historical unevenness in its whole dynamic concreteness … One stage or another of the historical process can prove to be inevitable under certain conditions, although theoretically not inevitable. And conversely, theoretically 'inevitable' stages can be compressed to zero by the dynamics of development, especially during revolutions, which have – not for nothing – been called the locomotives of history.[50]

---

46 Benjamin 2005.
47 Bloch 1970, p. 615.
48 Bloch 1985a.
49 Trotsky 1929.
50 Trotsky 1932. Emphasis in original.

Combined and uneven development is summarised in Trotsky's *History of the Russian Revolution* as follows:

> The laws of history have nothing in common with a pedantic schematism. Unevenness, the most general law of the historic process, reveals itself most sharply and complexly in the destiny of the backward countries. Under the whip of external necessity their backward culture is compelled to make leaps. From the universal law of unevenness thus derives another law which, for the lack of a better name, we may call the law of *combined development* – by which we mean a drawing together of the different stages of the journey, a combining of the separate steps, an amalgam of archaic with more contemporary forms.[51]

'Laws of historical development' are perceived *dialectically* by both Marx and Trotsky, not as metaphysical norms of a mechanical determinism but as *tendencies* in conflict with *counter-tendencies*. Rejection of mechanical determinism does not mean rejection of dialectical forms of restraints, causation or interconnection. In this way, Marx analyses, for example, the *tendency law* of the falling rate of profit in Volume III of *Das Kapital*.[52]

Trotsky as well, in *The Third International After Lenin*, views combined and uneven development, especially as it functions in modern capitalism, as a unity of conflicting, interacting and interpenetrating centrifugal and centripetal social forces and *tendencies* determining different epochs. 'Only the correlation of these two fundamental tendencies', Trotsky writes, 'explains to us the living texture of the historical process'.[53] Ernst Bloch rightly defines dialectical historical materialism as 'the dialectical science of tendencies'.[54]

4.3   Epochs of Development

The correspondence of Marx with Zasulich and other Russian populists, and statements like that quoted above, are often counterposed to the brief presentation of historical materialism and successive epochs of social development in the 1859 preface of Marx's *A Contribution to the Critique of Political Economy*.

To avoid hasty misreadings or entrenched views, the 1859 preface has to be properly situated within the context of the entire Marxian oeuvre, partic-

---

51   Trotsky 1932.
52   Marx 1959, pp. 153–86.
53   Trotsky 1929.
54   Bloch 1985, p. 326.

ularly as a moment in the long process of elaboration of his major work in progress, *Das Kapital*. The preface, criticised as schematic, was immediately preceded by a great breakthrough, the manuscript of 1857–8 mostly known as the *Grundrisse*, a vast dialectical-materialist laboratory 'turning Hegel on his feet' to reveal the logic of capital dominating the modern world. The 1859 preface is not a step back from this achievement, but, as Marx wrote, it briefly presents, 'summarised', 'the general conclusion' and 'the guiding principle' of his studies.[55]

The categories used by Marx – mode of production, productive forces and productive relations, their relations and their dialectic as basis of social revolution – are, as he wrote on the method of political economy in the *Grundrisse*, expressions of 'the forms of being [*Daseinsformen* in the German original], the characteristics of existence [*Existenzbestimmungen* in the German original, also translated as determinations of existence]'.[56] The *central* category of historical materialism is not economy but the social *Lebensprozess* – the process of life, the social metabolism of nature and human society in its historically developing forms, its modes of production:

> The mode of production of material life conditions the general process of social, political and intellectual life. It is not the consciousness of men that determines their existence, but their social existence that determines their consciousness.[57]

The definition of mode of production, given by the Stalinist textbooks, as a unity of productive forces identified with the means of production, technology and productive relations, reduced into their economic determinations, is wrong.

In *The German Ideology*, Marx and Engels had warned that 'abstractions in themselves, divorced from real history, have no value whatsoever', and they focus on 'the study of the actual life-process'.[58] On this historical-material basis, the category of the mode of production is determined:

> This mode of production must not be considered simply as being the reproduction of the physical existence of the individuals; it is rather a

---

55 Marx 1977b, p. 20.
56 Marx 1973, p. 106.
57 Marx 1977b, pp. 20–1.
58 Marx and Engels 1976, p. 37.

definite form of activity of these individuals, a definite form of expressing their life, a definite **mode of life** [*Lebensweise* in the German original] on their part.[59]

The necessary political revolutionary conclusion is that the

> ... 'material elements of a complete revolution' are on the one hand the existing productive forces, on the other the formation of a revolutionary mass, which revolts not only against separate conditions of the existing society, but against the existing 'production of life' itself, the 'total activity' on which it was based.[60]

From this revolutionary perspective, the following sentence from the 1859 preface (quoted by supporters and enemies of Marx as evidence of his supposed support to the 'theory of stages') has to be read: '**In broad line**, the Asiatic, ancient, feudal and modern bourgeois modes of production **may** be designated as epochs marking progress of society'.[61] This sentence, with all its reservations about its own generality, should be read with what immediately follows it, including its often-quoted but usually overlooked, intentionally unexpected ending:

> The bourgeois mode of production is the last antagonistic form of the social process of production – antagonistic not in the sense of individual antagonism, but of an antagonism that emanates from the individual's social conditions of existence – but the productive forces developing within bourgeois society create also the material conditions for a solution of this antagonism. The **prehistory** of human society accordingly closes with this social formation.[62]

First, it is noteworthy that Marx uses the term 'prehistory' so early, in a book published in *1859*, when the concept and the term of prehistory had just emerged in the newborn sciences of archaeology and anthropology. Definitely, these two sciences have to be added to the three sources of Marxism famously mentioned by Lenin, German classical philosophy, English political economy and French socialism.

---

59   Marx and Engels 1976, p. 31. The emphasis in the original.
60   Marx and Engels 1976, p. 54.
61   Marx 1977b, p. 21. Our emphasis.
62   Marx, 1977b, pp. 21–2. Emphasis in the original.

Second, Marx, after presenting 'in broad lines' a succession of modes of production, 'Asiatic, ancient, feudal and modern bourgeois modes of production' as '*epochs marking progress of society*', he includes *all of them without exception* into 'prehistory', independently from their own specific differences that distinguish them into epochs of development. There is no place here for 'inevitable', rigidly separated 'stages' to be completed before the next step of history. The all-inclusive prehistory excludes them from what human *history* would essentially be.

In that sense, Walter Benjamin refers to the *Urgeschichte* [original history] of the present.[63] History begins not at the dawn or the twilight of class society, but when 'the free development of each would be the condition for the free development of all'[64] in a fully emancipated classless society – 'the realm of freedom'. Its material conditions of possibility are indeed produced within global capitalism itself, the highest and 'last antagonistic form of class society'; but it is the overthrow and abolition of capitalism that will bring the end of prehistory. *The revolutionary transformation of the world performs the real divide between prehistory and history.*

Lastly, the actuality of this passage of the 1859 preface should be noted. Marx transformed the concept of 'archaeology' (both the concept and the science, newfound in his time) and, by connecting it to – the also newly born – historical materialism,[65] he situates on a radically other level the crucial question of the prehistory/history divide. He anticipates a subject hotly debated by archaeologists and anthropologists even today in the twenty-first century. Marxism should learn a lot from these debates.

5   The Prehistory/History Divide Challenged

It is well known that the predominant attitude in archaeology, from the middle of nineteenth century onwards, is to determine the prehistory/history divide according to the criterion of the nonexistence or existence of writing documents. This criterion, well established among the academics of the Global North and consequently internationally as a legacy of colonialism, is challenged to keep oppressed peoples – outside or within the 'West' – out of 'history', affecting, thus, the actual thinking and practice of archaeology.[66]

---

63   Benjamin 1999, p. 462.
64   Marx and Engels 1995, p. 37.
65   And see Palerm 2008, pp. 449–77; Patterson 2009; and Milevski, this volume.
66   Schmidt and Mrozowski 2013, p. 3.

The challenge of the prehistory concept and the prehistory/history divide started by archaeologists and anthropologists of the Global South and among the native communities, such as the school of Latin American Social Archaeology, and was extended by researchers of post-colonial archaeology at large, up to this day, among researchers in the Global North itself.

The death of prehistory is proclaimed emphatically in the title of a collective volume edited by Peter R. Schmidt and Stephen A. Mrozowski, published in 2013. The editors, in their preface titled 'Reforming the Past, Looking to the Future', express the 'common concern' of the volume's contributors:

> ... we bear witness to the harm the prehistory label visited upon the Other, vast numbers of indigenous peoples in the Americas, Africa and Asia who, today, are trying to reclaim histories erased or denied through the application of 'prehistory' ... Not surprisingly, prehistory as a trope for time before written history has had less deleterious impacts on identities in Europe ... Archaeological practice, if it is conceived as praxis, engages us in overturning some of the misrepresentations of peoples outside or encapsulated within the West, their pasts silenced or erased.[67]

Schmidt and Mrozowski note the linearity of historical time as the main epistemological problem:

> ... this linearity submerges other forms of time-punctuated time, ritually rhythmic time, that are ignored, and linear designs are privileged at the expense of many cultures that reckon and think about time in non-linear ways.[68]

John K. Papadopoulos, in his insightful article in *World Archaeology* on 'Greek Protohistories',[69] convincingly argues against the problematic use of the prehistory/history divide based on the criterion of the existence of writing and, consequently, on this basis, the use of terms such as 'prehistory', 'protohistory' or 'history' – the last one equated with the presence of written sources. The problem in the Greek area, for example, is the division between 'Greek history' and 'Aegean prehistory', with the problematic liminal period – the Early Iron Age – hovering uncomfortably between the two. Such a periodisation of the

---

67 Schmidt and Mrozowski 2013, pp. 1–2.
68 Schmidt and Mrozowski 2013, p. 17.
69 Papadopoulos 2019.

Greek past does not square with what have become our own modern categories of 'historical period = the existence of literary sources', 'protohistory = some written documents but no literary or narrative texts' and 'prehistory = no writing'.[70]

However, Papadopoulos rightly asks, *cum grano salis*, how we can categorise as 'prehistory' a '[p]rehistory with plenty of texts'.[71] He continues:

> We do not know the language of Cretan hieroglyphic, or Minoan Linear A, and both scripts remain undeciphered. Their date, however, is clear: Middle Minoan IIA, or ca. 1800–1700 BC IIB ... The later Mycenaean Linear B (beginning 1450–1375, and continuing to ca. 1200 BC, though most of the inscribed material dates to the fourteenth and thirteenth centuries) was shown to be an early syllabic form of Greek ... But where is the history? No one has seriously claimed that Greece at that time was 'historic' or 'protohistoric'; it is regarded as 'prehistoric', despite the fact that Minoan Creta, beginning in the Middle Bronze Age was probably the earliest complex society in Europe.[72]

Papadopoulos later notes that:

> ... the inhabitants of Greece – fully literate, at least the scribal class in the employ of the Minoan and Mycenaean administrations – regularly appear in the writings of other cultures, including the Egyptians and the Hittites, yet we still refer to this period as prehistoric, not protohistoric.[73]

In his conclusions, he criticises the way 'a systemic divide' has been erected as an 'iron curtain', separating the Aegean Bronze and the Early Iron Age:

> ... this liminal, in-between period does not readily belong, for reasons difficult to fathom, in the intellectual realm of the prehistorian nor, largely on account of the lack of contemporary literary sources, in that of the Classical archaeologist; it floats rather uncomfortably between the two ...

---

70   Papadopoulos 2019, p. 2.
71   Papadopoulos. 2019, p. 5.
72   Papadopoulos 2019, pp. 5–6.
73   Papadopoulos 2019, p. 13.

He concludes by tracing the problem to the method of linear evolutionism: 'In the end, terms as "prehistory" and "protohistory" are problematic because they anticipate change and along evolutionary trajectories.'[74]

The linearity of 'evolutionary trajectories' does not merely demonstrate its problematic limitations with the prehistory/history divide; it also manifests its inability to deal with a most – if not *the* most – crucial task in the study of historical processes of the past or the present: to reveal the historical texture, the driving contradictory forces and dynamics of an *epoch of transition*.

6 Transitions in Archaeology

Linear 'evolutionary trajectories' finish always at dead ends. They cannot grasp transitions because they fail to grasp the inner contradictory nature of development.

At the beginning of the First World War, confronting the collapse of the social democratic Second International in 1914, and probing this political bankruptcy to its most fundamental methodological level, Lenin turned to a fresh reading of Hegel and dialectics.[75] He noted on development:

> Development is the 'struggle' of opposites. The two basic (or two possible? or two historically observable?) conceptions of development (evolution) are: development as decrease and increase, as repetition, **and** development as a unity of opposites (the division of a unity into mutually exclusive opposites and their reciprocal relation).
>
> In the first conception of motion, **self**-movement, its **driving** force, its source, its motive, remains in the shade (or this source is made **external** – God, subject etc.). In the second conception, the chief attention is directed precisely to knowledge of the **source** of '**self**-movement'.
>
> The first conception is lifeless, pale and dry. The second is living. The second **alone** furnishes the key to the 'self-movement' of everything existing: it alone furnishes the key to the 'leaps', to the 'break in continuity', to the 'transformation into the opposite', to the destruction of the old and the emergence of the new.[76]

Uneven and combined social development is never linear; it is always driven by contradictory tendencies and counter-tendencies. Transition is contradiction

---

74 Papadopoulos 2019, pp. 12–13.
75 Lenin 1961. See also Michael-Matsas 2007.
76 Lenin 1961, p. 360. Emphasis in original.

and connection.⁷⁷ From this perspective, in archaeology – as in the previous example – the transition from Late Bronze Age to Early Iron Age, the destruction of the old and the emergence of the new, has to be studied, and the Early Iron Age itself has to be seen not as a 'problematic liminal period hovering uncomfortably between prehistory and the historic classic period of ancient Greece' but as a crucial *transitional epoch*.

Accordingly, we can study dialectically earlier transitions, deeper in the past. Ianir Milevski focused on the transition from the Chalcolithic to the Early Bronze Age of the Southern Levant⁷⁸ as changing social formations, stressing the *uneven* character of the process:

> Although the transition from the Chalcolithic to the EB I [= Early Bronze I] in the Southern Levant (ca. 3,800–3,600 BC) took multiple forms at different times, its main aspects involved collapse of settlements of the Ghassulian culture and substitution by a new type of community. It was an uneven process that occurred in different ways in different regions as may be seen in the distinctions between settlements in the Beersheva Valley, different parts of Negev, Galilee and the Golan, etc. In the northern regions of the Southern Levant the transition was more abrupt than in the central regions. In the south, it was so abrupt that no EB I settlements have been found in the Beersheva valley.⁷⁹

The most important change during this turbulent period of transition, according to Milevski, was 'a restructuring of the division of labor, a differently organized system of crafts and a revolution in the circulation of goods' due to the domestication of donkeys [*Equuus asinus*].⁸⁰

On the basis of the study of the discovered evidence, Milevski draws the conclusion:

> In the final analysis, understanding the transition is a question of transformation from one form of social and economic relations to another. The transition from the Chalcolithic to EB I should be understood as an abrupt changeover, taking into consideration these socio-economic differences and changes in locales of settlements that introduced political and cultural dramatic changes. While the elites of the Chalcolithic only

---

77   Lenin 1961, pp. 180, 196.
78   Milevski 2013, pp. 193–208.
79   Milevski 2013, p. 202.
80   Milevski 2013, p. 203.

controlled surpluses of agro-pastoral and crafts production of villages, EB elites eventually developed capabilities of controlling exchanges of commodities between sites and regions.[81]

These 'capabilities of controlling exchanges of commodities *connecting* sites and regions' gave the advantage to Early Bronze elites and determined the direction and outcome of the transition itself:

> What differentiates Chalcolithic from the EB is the fact that the village formation of the earlier period disappeared, while the EB I became a pre-urban system that evolved into urban formations of the EB II–III. In that sense, we have to see the first urbanization in the Southern Levant as the beginning of one of the multiple forms that the 'Asiatic mode of production' took in the Near East.[82]

It is worth noting the central role of *surplus*: of its nature, mass and of its *control* permitting an important extension of the scale of exchange for changes in social organisation during the transitional period.

The extension of exchange and, consequently, of *interconnection* is crucial. 'Connection is transition', as Lenin[83] pointed out. It is clearly seen if we examine, from a Mediterranean perspective, the extension of interconnection in the Early Iron Age, another critical transitional epoch. As Nota Kourou writes, '[t]he amount of PG [= Protogeometric] and SPG [= Sub-Protogeometric] Euboean pottery, found together with Phoenician and Cypriot wares all over the Mediterranean ... signposts the vigorous practice of sailing and transportation in which Euboea was deeply involved during the Early Iron Age. This process triggered the spread of population abroad, the transmission of ideas and cultural interaction all around the *mare nostrum*'.[84] Interconnection, interaction and interpenetration are moments of a transitional process of transformation. The destruction of the old and the emergence of the new depend on the social forces producing and controlling the *surplus*.

Transitional social formations are *hybrids* combining various social relations and multiple temporalities. In such hybrids, the absence or presence of the role of a force mediating further development is crucial for the movement of transition. Surplus plays a role similar to the 'trickster', the term used by Claude

---

81　Ibid.
82　Ibid.
83　Lenin 1961, p. 180.
84　Kourou 2020, p. 9.

Levi-Strauss[85] in relation to Northern Native American communities, and by Ian Hodder and Lyn Meskell in connection to the human figure in symbolism in Holocene societies of the Middle East: an intermediary between opposed poles that mediates 'between beast of prey and herbivorous animals, hunting and agriculture, death and life'.[86]

In Hegel's dialectical logic of transition, the 'trickster' is the 'vanishing mediator' [*das Vermittelende*],[87] the actual outcome of a first negation of the origin ('the destruction of the old') which includes the conditions, a potential necessary for a second negation, a negation of negation, performing an *Aufhebung*, superseding the old, terminating it and simultaneously preserving it, though transformed ('the emergence of the new').

The lack or delay of formation, or apparent neutralisation and paralysis, or any other form of crisis affecting the role of the 'vanishing mediator', leads to a 'crisis of transition' – a concept that we had worked upon in an entirely different, modern-historic context: the collapse of the Soviet Union in 1991.[88]

The specific *nature* of the 'mediating factor' in specific transitional processes is a matter of continuous debate. In symbolic or contextual archaeology, introduced by Hodder, drawing from his great achievements in researching Çatalhöyük,[89] a *symbolic system* as a whole (in a different sense than that given by structuralism) acts as the determining mediator in social forms of organisation.

Jacques Cauvin gave even a primacy or pre-eminence of the symbolic, in relation to the social economic, in transition and social change.[90] He suggested that the rise of ritual or religious practices in Late Palaeolithic Central Europe, or in Natufian culture villages in the Southern Levant, or in the monumental ritual site of hunters-gatherers in Göbekli Tepe (c. 8,500–9,000 BC), represents a 'symbolic revolution' acting as the *prelude* to permanent settlement, domestication and agriculture. Hodder expressed reservations for these views:

> ... it may be unhelpful to talk of changes in religion as a "necessary prelude" to settled agglomerations of people with complex social forms dependent on domesticated plants because so much depends on how the terms are defined (are we talking of genetic change to plants or just intensive collecting and cultivating?) ... Do symbolism and ritual sur-

---

85 Levi-Strauss 1963, p. 224.
86 Hodder and Meskell 2010, p. 61.
87 Hegel 1969, p. 834.
88 Michael-Matsas 1992.
89 Hodder 2010, pp. 1–31.
90 Cauvin 1997, pp. 168, 278.

rounding violence and death lead to new social forms? Perhaps, but a simple causal analysis is likely to be confounded by problems of definition, interpretation and interdependence.[91]

Evidence from the figurines discovered in Çatalhöyük, according to Hodder,

> ... suggests that these objects were not in a separate religious sphere. Rather, it was the process of their daily production – not their contemplation as religious symbols – that was important. They gave meaning to the everyday, low intensity level, to subjectivities and to the social world that they helped imagine.[92]

At that stage of social development 'religion and the secular cannot easily be distinguished, especially in non-complex societies'.[93]

In a relatively immature social organism where human beings, individually, as Marx writes, have 'not yet severed the umbilical cord'[94] that unites them as it does their community with nature, when 'the Form of social life-process i.e. of the material process of production'[95] 'does not strip off its mystical veil',[96] this religious mystical veil cannot be easily distinguished from the form of the social life process [*Gestalt der geselschaftlichen Lebensprozesses, Lebensweise*]. This is similar to the point made by Hodder.[97]

However, not being easily distinguished does not mean that the religious 'veil' is *identical* to the actual life process itself, or that it is *primary* or *simultaneous* with social change in early societies by introducing *a symbolic revolution*, as Cauvin claims.

The social anthropologist and sociologist Alain Testart, in his essays on religions in the Neolithic, although finding Cauvin's introduction of 'symbolic revolution' in the 1990s 'a redeeming reaction' to the dominant imprint of natural sciences on archaeology, sharply criticises the attempt to present the symbolic revolution as a primary cause, regarding the claim that 'this ideological mutation could give birth to agriculture'[98] as totally unacceptable.

---

91 Hodder 2010, p. 27.
92 Hodder 2010, pp. 15–16.
93 Hodder 2010, p. 14.
94 Marx 1977c, p. 173.
95 Marx 1972, p. 94. In the German original: '*Die Gestalt der gesellschaftlichen Lebensprozesses, d. h. des materiellen Produktionsprozesses*'.
96 Marx 1977c, p. 173.
97 And see above Hodder 2010.
98 Testart 2010, p. 34.

Based mainly on the work of Emile Durkheim (and, in another way, of Max Weber), Testart aims to replace the symbolic with the *social* as the fundamental relation and primary cause. In the same Durkheimian terms, the archaeologist Jean Guillaine criticises Cauvin, putting into question the claim that 'the symbolic could be the driving force of evolution' or that it could 'precede the social'.[99] For Guillaine, following Durkheim, the social as such is fundamental. It precedes the economic and all other relations: 'the social is the propulsive force for the economic'.[100] But what is the *social*? The definition given by Durkheim himself is well known: 'Le social c'est le social'.[101] A tautology is never helpful.

The pre-eminence or primacy of the symbolic or the social as such have a clearly admitted target: the supposed primacy of the economic factor in historical materialism – a misconception answered by its founders long ago but unfortunately still a part of the hegemonic common sense.

Symbolic activity perceived as the driving force of social evolution or the social as such preceding the *social relations of production of labour* are both separated from *the social life process*, the social metabolism of human society with nature. The centrality of the concept of social metabolism in Marx, as well as its current actuality, has been brought forward by István Mészáros,[102] as well as by Foster and Suwandi[103] in his work on climate crisis and catastrophe capitalism.

Symbolic activity's role in social development, of course, should not be bypassed or mechanically separated from social labour, and social relations should not be reduced into secondary effects of economic determinism.

Marx, analysing the labour process as metabolism [*Stoffwechsel*] with nature in *Das Kapital*, does not dismiss the role of imagination, purpose and reasoning in social productive activity. He insists on this point:

> But what distinguishes the worst architect from the best of bees is this, that the architect raises his structure in imagination before imagination before he erects it in reality. At the end of every labour-process, we get a result that already existed in the imagination of the labourer at its commencement. He not only effects a change of form in the material on which

---

99   Guilaine 2011, pp. 33–4.
100 Guilaine 2011, p. 31.
101 Durkheim 1982, quoted in Testart 2012, p. 510.
102 Mészáros 1995, pp. 39–42.
103 Foster and Suwandi 2020.

he works, but he also realizes a purpose of his own that gives the law to his modus operandi, and to which he must subordinate his will.[104]

It is worth mentioning that, in a note, he approvingly quotes Hegel from his shorter logic, the first part of the 'Encyclopaedia', precisely on the *mediating role* of the 'cunning of Reason':

> Reason is just as cunning as she is powerful. Her cunning principally consists of her mediating activity, which, by causing objects to act and re-act on each other in accordance with their own nature and without any direct interference in the process, thus carries out reason's intentions.[105]

Ernst Bloch reminds us that 'Marx defined productive power itself as that part of inner and outer nature which human beings know how to control'.[106] With this Marxian anti-economist definition as a guiding principle, Bloch stresses: 'First and foremost, work is for Marx the cradle of history – and it is not a fetishized and specialized condition with an *abstract homo economicus*'.[107] Bloch develops further this notion by integrating what he names and analyses as the 'utopian function'[108] into the social labour process, both in productive and cultural activity – which were initially not separated – before further development of the division of labour and the emergence of class divisions. Following this line of inquiry emerging from the concept of the utopian function of social labor, we could see that *homo* could not become *homo sapiens* without becoming, at the same time, *homo poeticus*.[109]

7 Conclusions (in Transition)

The last thirty years, especially after the irruption of the global crisis and the pandemic shock, there is a prevailing feeling that we live in a period that is both transitional and interminable. Any linear/evolutionist conception of history disintegrates in such conditions, resulting in the loss of any sense of history itself.

---

104 Marx 1977c, p. 284.
105 Marx 1977c, p. 285.
106 Bloch 1988, p. 24.
107 Bloch 1988, p. 25.
108 Bloch 1988, pp. 103–41.
109 Michael-Matsas 2006, pp. 21–35.

It's become common these days, as Chomsky said in a lecture on February 14, 2019,

> ... to quote Gramsci's observation that the old order is collapsing but a new one has not yet risen, and 'in the interregnum a great variety of morbid symptoms appear'. And encouraging ones as well.[110]

At the same period over the last decades, archaeology made important advances, shedding light particularly on epochs of transition, when a 'skipping of stages' (or remaining too long at one stage) – as Trotsky[111] pointed out is – is manifested.

This research and these discoveries and debates can – and should – open new horizons for historical-materialist dialectics, liberating it from sterile fixation to anti-Marxist dogmas presented as 'Marxism'. Historical materialism, as Bloch[112] has rightly defined it, is 'a dialectical science of tendencies', hence of *transitions*.

Transition is *uneven and combined development*. Transition is *contradiction, connection* and *mediation* between the opposed poles of a transformation. Mediation is not a 'reconciliation' of opposites, a restoration of the old order after its dissolution, as in the Hegelian pseudo-negation of negation – 'a negation of pseudo-essence', as accurately criticised by Marx.[113] A real mediation, according to Marx – and Hölderlin as well – a mediation where the 'vanishing mediator' emerges, should include a *break of continuity*, a 'qualitative rupture', a 'caesura', an 'infinite separation'. As Hölderlin writes in his *Remarks on Oedipus and Antigone*, 'it is a revolutionary upturn *Umkehr*'.[114]

It is only such a 'revolutionary upturn' that can lead, through the interpenetration of opposites, to their mutual qualitative transformation – not into a restoration of the old, but into the revolutionary change of the original dynamic source of the specific dialectical movement, creating the new.

Historical materialism as a dialectical science of tendencies, contradictions, transitions and mediations develops into what Ernst Bloch, again, has called 'the new science of the mediated future', completing his previous definition.[115]

---

110   Chomsky and Waterstone 2021, p. 254.
111   Trotsky 1931.
112   Bloch 1985b, p. 326.
113   Marx 1977a, p. 149.
114   Hölderlin 1965, pp. 82–3. And see Michael-Matsas 2008b, p. 176.
115   Bloch 1985b, p. 326.

Schmidt and Mrozowski,[116] as we saw, gave the title 'Reforming the Past, Looking to the Future' to their preface of *The Death of Prehistory*. We could paraphrase it with a call for *reclaiming the historical past, preparing for the future*.

Drawing knowledge and inspiration from archaeology and following the advice of the American Marxist philosopher Bertell Ollman to 'study history backwards' from the present, we could discover not only the past, but the tendencies to the future as well:

> ... the future is an essential moment in the present. It is not only what the present becomes, but whatever happens in the future exists in the present, within all present forms, as potential.[117]

Being in history is history 'δυνάμει [*dynamei*]'[118] and 'κατά το δυνατόν [*kata to dynaton*]'. Being in possibility and according to possibility, in the Marxist meaning that Bloch gave to the Aristotelian terms, is re-elaborating the great insights of the medieval Arab-Jewish philosophy, especially of ibn Sina/Avicenna, ibn Rushd/Averroes and Avicebron/Shlomo ibn Gabirol.[119] Emancipatory theory and praxis need to reclaim history and its lost sense *now, in dürftiger Zeit, at the time of dearth*.[120]

The future is both necessary and open.

Acknowledgments

I would like to thank Ianir Milevski and Sebastian Budgen for their invitation to participate in the collective work on Marxist archaeology. It was an honour as well as a great inspiration for me to confront the challenges of our times. I sincerely thank Nota Kourou, Professor Emerita of Archaeology at the University of Athens, for her continuous help and constant encouragement during this work. I would like to thank for his comradeship and advice *in dürftiger Zeit*, Osvaldo Coggiola, Professor of History at the University of São Paulo, Brazil.

My full gratitude to my dear friend, comrade, co-thinker, teacher and mentor, Professor Bertell Ollman of New York University. I would also like to thank Anna

---

116 Schmidt and Mrozowski 2013.
117 Ollman 1993, p. 140.
118 Pascucci 2006, p. 83.
119 Bloch 2018; Moir 2019.
120 Hölderlin 1961, p. 111.

Marka Bonissel, scholar of English literature and great performance artist, for her important help to edit the English draft of my paper.

Last but not at all least, all my affection, devotion and gratitude to my lifelong companion, comrade and wife Katerina Matsa.

References

Anderson, Kevin 2016, *Marx at Margins: On Nationalism, Ethnicity, and Non Western Societies*, Chicago, IL: University of Chicago Press.

Benjamin, Walter 1998, *The Origin of the German Tragic Drama*, translated by J. Osborne, London: Verso.

Benjamin, Walter 1999, *The Arcades Project [Das Passagen-Werk]*, translated by H. Eiland and K. McLaughlin, Cambridge, MA: Harvard University Press.

Benjamin, Walter 2005 [1940], 'On the Concept of History', available at https://www.marxists.org/reference/archive/benjamin/1940/history.htm.

Blanchot, Maurice 2012, *Correspondance (1953–2002)*, Paris: Gallimard.

Bloch, Ernst 1970, *Philosophische Aufsätze*, Frankfurt am Main: Suhrkamp.

Bloch, Ernst 1985a [1935], *Erbschaft dieser Zeit*, Frankfurt am Main: Suhrkamp.

Bloch, Ernst 1985b, *Das Prinzip Hoffnung*, Frankfurt am Main: Suhrkamp.

Bloch Ernst 1988, *The Utopian Function of Art and Literature*, Boston, MA: MIT Press.

Bloch, Ernst 2018, *Avicenna and the Aristotelian Left*, translated by L. Goldmann and P. Thompson, New York: Columbia University Press.

Boehme, Jacob 1992 [ca. 1612–9], *The Aurora: That Is, The Day-Spring*, Sequim, WA: Holmes.

Cauvin, Jacques 1997, *Naissance des divinités, Naissance de l'agriculture*, Paris: CNRS Editions.

Childe, Vere Gordon 1936, *Man Makes Himself*, London: Watts & Co.

Childe, Vere Gordon 1946, *What Happened in History*, London: Penguin Books.

Childe, Vere Gordon 1947, *History*, London: Cobbet Press.

Chomsky, Noam and Marv Waterstone 2021, *Consequences of Capitalism: Manufacturing Discontent and Resistance*, London: Hamish Hamilton.

Durkheim Emile 1982 [1895], *The Rules of Sociological Method: And selected texts on sociology and its method*, edited and introduced by S. Lukes, translated by W.D. Halls, New York: The Free Press.

Foster, John Bellamy and Intan Suwandi 2020, 'Covid 19 and Catastrophe Capitalism. Commodity Chains and Ecological-Epidemiological-Crisis', *Monthly Review*, 72, 2, available at: https://monthlyreview.org/2020/06/01/covid-19-and-catastrophe-capitalism/.

Foucault, Michel 2001 [1971], *Dits et écrits (1954–1975)*, Volume 1, Paris: Quarto Gallimard.

Fukuyama, Francis 1989, 'The End of History?', *The National Interest* 16: 3–18.
Fukuyama Francis 2011, 'The "End of History" 20 Years Later', *New Perspectives Quarterly*, 30, 4: 31–9.
Graeber, David and David Wengrow 2021, *The Dawn of Everything: A New History of Humanity*, London: Allen Lane.
Guilaine, Jean 2011, *Caïn, Abel, Ötzi: L'héritage néolithique*, Paris: Gallimard.
Hegel, Georg W.F. 1969 [1812], *Science of Logic*, translated by A.V. Miller, London: George Allen & Unwin.
Hodder, Ian 2010, 'Probing Religion at Çatalhöyük', in *Religion in the Emergence of Civilization – Çatalhöyük as a Case Study*, edited by Ian Hodder, Cambridge: Cambridge University Press.
Hodder, Ian, and Lynn Meskell 2010, 'The Symbolism of Çatalhöyük in it Regional Context', in *Religion in the Emergence of Civilization – Çatalhöyük as a Case Study*, edited by Ian Hodder, Cambridge: Cambridge University Press.
Hölderlin, Friedrich 1961, *Selected Poems and Fragments*, translated by M. Hamburger, London: Penguin.
Hölderlin, Friedrich 1965, *Remarques sur Oedipe: Remarques sur Antigone*, Paris: Éditions 10/18.
Irving, Terry 2020, *The Fatal Lure of Politics: The Life and Thought of Vere Gordon Childe*, Melbourne: Monash University Publishing.
Kourou, Nota 2020, 'Euboean Pottery in a Mediterranean Perspective', in *Euboica II: Pithekoussai and Euboea between East and West*, edited by Teresa E. Cinquataquattro and Matteo d'Acunto, Napoli: Università Degli Studi di Napoli 'L'orientale'.
Lenin, Vladimir I. 1961 [1895–1916], *Collected Works* 38: *Philosophical Notebooks*, Moscow: Progress Publishers.
Levi-Strauss, Claude 1963, *Structural Anthropology*, New York: Basic Books.
Marx, Karl 1972 [1867], *Das Kapital: Kritik der politischen Ökonomie*, Volume I, Berlin: Dietz Verlag.
Marx, Karl 1959 [1863–83], *Capital: A Critique of Political Economy*, Volume III, edited and completed by F. Engels, Moscow: Institute of Marxism-Leninism, USSR.
Marx, Karl 1977a [1844], *Economic and Philosophic Manuscripts of 1844*, Moscow: Progress Publishers.
Marx, Karl 1977b [1859], *A Contribution to the Critique of Political Economy*, Moscow: Progress Publishers.
Marx, Karl 1977c [1867], *Capital: A Critique of Political Economy*, Volume I, introduced be E. Mandel, translated by B. Fowkes, New York: Vintage Books.
Marx, Karl 1973 [1857–8], *Grundrisse: Foundations of Political Economy (Rough Draft)*, translated with a foreword by M. Nicolaus, London and New York: Penguin Classics.
Marx, Karl 1989a [1877], 'Letter to Otechestvennyie Zapiski', in *Marx-Engels Collected Works*, Volume 24, Moscow: Progress Publishers.

Marx, Karl 1989b [1881], 'Drafts of the Letter to Vera Zasulich', in *Marx-Engels Collected Works*, Volume 24, Moscow: Progress Publishers.

Marx, Karl and Frierich Engels 1975 [1844], *The Holy Family*, in *Marx-Engels Collected Works*, Volume 4, Moscow: Progress Publishers.

Marx, Karl and Friedrich Engels 1976 [1845–6], *The German Ideology*, in *Marx-Engels Collected Works*, Volume 5, Moscow: Progress Publishers.

Marx, Karl and Frierich Engels 1995 [1948], *Le Manifeste du Parti Communiste*, translated by L. Lafargue, Paris: Le Temps des Cerises.

Michael-Matsas, Savas 1992, 'On the Concept of the Crisis of Transition', in *Restoration or Revolution?*, Athens: 'Leon' Publications [Greek].

Michael-Matsas, Savas 2006, *Homo Poeticus*, Athens: Agra Publications [Greek].

Michael-Matsas, Savas 2007, 'Lenin and the Path of Dialectics', in *Lenin Reloaded: Toward a Politics of Truth*, edited by Sebastian Budgen, Stathis Kouvelakis and Slavoj Zizek, Durham: Duke University Press.

Michael-Matsas, Savas 2008a, 'Marx beyond Rousseau', *Theseis*, 102 [Greek], available at http://www.theseis.com/index.php?option=com_content&task=view&id=1006&Itemid=29.

Michael-Matsas, Savas 2008b, 'Dialectics and Revolution Now', in *Dialectics for the New Century*, edited by Bertell Ollman and Tony Smith, New York: Palgrave Macmillan.

Michael-Matsas, Savas 2020, 'Pandemic and Crisis: The Perfect Storm 1', *Política Obrera*, 26, available at: https://politicaobrera.com/internacionales/2613-pandemic-and-crisis-the-perfect-storm-1.

Mészáros, István 1995, *Beyond Capital: Towards a Theory of Transition*, London: Merlin Press.

Milevski, Ianir 2013, 'The Transition from the Chalcolithic to the Early Bronze Age of the Southern Levant in Socioeconomic Context', *Paléorient*, 39, 1: 193–208.

Moir, Cat 2019, *Ernst Bloch's Speculative Materialism*, Historical Materialism Books Series, Leiden: Brill.

Morgan, Lewis H. 1964 [1877], *Ancient Society*, edited by Leslie A. White, Cambridge, MA: Harvard University Press.

Ollman, Bertell 1993, *Dialectical Investigations*, New York: Routledge.

Palerm, Ángel 2008, *Antropología y Marxismo*, Clásicos y Contemporáneos en Antropología 4, México D.F. Centro de Investigaciones y Estudios Superiores en Antropología Social, Universidad Autónoma Metropolitana.

Papadopoulos, John K. 2019, 'Greek Protohistories', *World Archaeology*, 50, 5: 690–705.

Pascucci, Margherita 2006, *La potenza della povertá, Marx legge Spinoza*, Verona: Ombre Corte.

Patterson, Thomas C. 2009, *Karl Marx, Anthropologist*, Oxford & New York: Berg.

Renfrew, Colin and Paul Bahn 1991, *Archaeology: Theories, Methods and Practices*, London: Thames and Hudson.

Renfrew, Colin, Olga Philaniotou, Neil Brodie, Giorgos Cavalas and Michale J. Boyd (eds.) 2013, *The Settlement at Dhaskalio*, Cambridge: McDonald Institute for Archaeological Research, Cambridge University.

Schmidt, Peter R. and Stephen A. Mrozowski (eds.) 2013, *The Death of Prehistory*, Oxford: Oxford University Press.

Sinensky, R.J., Gregson Shachner, Richard H. Wilshusen and Brian N. Damiata 2021, 'Volcanic Climate Forcing, Extreme Cold and the Neolithic Transition in the Northern US Southwest', *Antiquity*, 93, 384: 1–19.

Testart, Alain 2010, *La déesse et le grain: Trois essais sur les religions néolithiques*, Paris: Editions Errance.

Testart, Alain 2012, *Avant l'histoire: L'évolution des sociétés de Lascaux à Carnac*, Paris: Gallimard.

Trigger, Bruce G. 1987, 'Gordon Childe: A Marxist Archaeologist', in *Studies in the Neolithic and Urban Revolutions: The V. Gordon Childe Colloquium, Mexico, 1986*, BAR International Series 349, edited by Linda Manzanilla, Oxford: BAR.

Trigger, Bruce G. 1980, *Gordon Childe: Revolutions in Archaeology*, London: Thames and Hudson.

Trotsky, Leon 1929 [1928], *The Third International After Lenin*, translated by M. Schachtman, New York: The Militant, available at https://www.marxists.org/archive/trotsky/1928/3rd/index.htm.

Trotsky, Leon 1932 [1930], *The History of the Russian Revolution*, translated by M. Eastman, New York: The Militant, available at https://www.marxists.org/archive/trotsky/1930/hrr/.

Trotsky, Leon 1931 [1930], *The Permanent Revolution*, translated by J.G. Wright, New York: The Militant, available at: https://www.marxists.org/archive/trotsky/1931/tpr/index.htm.

Wallace, Rob, Alex Liebman, Luis Fernando Chaves and Rodnik Wallace, 'Covid 19 and Circuits of Capital', *Monthly Review*, 72, 1, available at: https://monthlyreview.org/2020/05/01/covid-19-and-circuits-of-capital/.

Wengrow, David 2022, 'The Roots of Inequality: An Exchange', *The New York Review of Books*, 69, 1, available at: https://www.nybooks.com/articles/2022/01/13/the-roots-of-inequality-an-exchange/.

Index

Note on the Index
This *index* contains the main themes, places and authors cited in the different chapters of the volume. The numbers that follow each item indicate the page numbers. Although the words 'Marx', 'Engels', 'Marxism', 'Dialectical Materialism' and 'Historical Materialism' appear throughout the entire volume, the *index* indicates all relevant pages where the themes and the names are specifically noted in the text and the bibliographical references. For the term "Archaeology", however, there is no reference in the index, but items related to archaeological theory, methods and schools within the different chapters. Authors cited (including authors of the chapters of this volume) appear in the index when mentioned in the text and in the bibliography, but not in works by others that discuss or comment on those authors. Items of the *index* included in the bibliographical references are only authors. Number of pages of all the other subjects of the *index* only refer to occurrences in the text and notes. The reader can go from there to the bibliographical references in each of these subjects.

Abu el-Haj, Nadia   8, 25, 27
Acosta Ochoa, Guillermo   41, 49, 52–54, 69–71, 74
Activity-area analyses   40–46, 51, 53, 56–63, 67
Adams, Robert M.   114–115, 131
Adams, William H.   207, 224
Aegean (see Mediterranean)
Africa (Africans)   10, 23, 173, 175, 211, 299, 309
Aguilar, Miguel   40, 74, 270, 272, 283, 287, 292
Agriculture, agriculturists, farmers (see also Botanic remains)   52, 76, 82, 85–87, 91, 93–96, 115, 118–120, 125–126, 158–160, 187–188, 192, 203, 212–217, 240, 298, 302–303, 314–315
Aimi, Antonio   148–149, 163
Albritton, Robert   218, 224
Allen, Mark   138, 163
Allen, Tyler D.   222, 224
Allen, William   213, 224
Alon, David   91, 98
Althusser, Louis   16–17, 27, 108–109, 113, 119, 121, 123–124, 131
Alva, Walter   143, 149, 153, 163, 169
Álvarez, Myrian   66, 71, 73
Americas   10, 23, 107–111, 114, 126, 129–130, 270, 274, 281, 297, 309
   North   25, 115, 201–228, 273–274, 303
   Central (see also Latin America)   39–75, 107–136

   South (see also Latin America)   23–24, 144, 270–292
Amnesty International (Aminstía Internacional)   137, 163
Anatolia   302, 314
Anderson, Kevin B.   110, 131, 295, 320
Anderson, Perry   81, 98
Anderson, Walfred A.   213, 225
Anfinset, Niels   88, 98
Angus, Ian   179, 195
Anievas, Alexander   108, 131
Aoyama, Kazuo   119–120, 127, 131, 133
Archaeological theory and methods   3–5, 10–12, 17, 21, 25, 39–41, 45, 82, 114, 172, 205–206, 232, 262, 272, 274, 276–277, 280, 282–285, 288
Argentina (Argentinians)   24, 274, 276
Aristotle   173, 179, 262, 268
Arkush, Elizabeth   138, 140, 163
Army and warfare (see also Violence)   22, 25, 174, 176–177, 183, 185–187, 190–191, 194, 210, 216, 243–244, 274, 293, 300, 313
Aron, Cindy S.   210, 224
Asia (see also Near East, Anatolia, Levant, Palestine)   10, 23, 76, 108, 112–116, 121, 126, 129–130, 309
Asiatic mode of production   76, 81, 97, 181, 243, 307–308, 313
Atchison, Jennifer   45, 71
Aubert, Jean-Jacques   177, 195
Australia (see Oceania)

Bača, Martin 7, 30
Bahn, Paul 296, 322
Bajema, Marcus 6, 27, 117, 125, 129, 131, 207
Banaji, Jairus 191, 192, 196
Banks, Leonard 158, 169
Banning, Edward B. 79, 98
Bar-Adon, Pessah 89, 98
Barker, Alex W. 23, 30
Bar-Yosef, Ofer 10, 27
Barrett, Jason W. 120, 131
Barzilai, Omry 94, 103
Bate, Luis F. 6, 19, 27, 40–41, 43, 46–48, 70–71, 272–274, 276, 278–281, 283–284, 288–289
Baviera, Mara 220, 225
Bawden, Garth 146, 157, 162–163
Beard, Mary 173, 190, 196
Becker, Jeffrey 188, 196
Bekels, Corrie 174, 196
Bello, Walden 218, 225
Ben-Shlomo, David 87, 100
Benjamin, Walter 214, 218, 225, 294–295, 298, 301–302, 304, 308, 320
Di Bennardis, Cristina 82, 98
Berlin, Isaiah 140, 163
Bernbeck, Reinhard 10–11, 27
Bernier, Hélène 159, 163, 165–166
Berón, Mónica 137, 166
Bettinger, Robert L. 47, 71
Bhaskar, Roy 204, 225
Billman, Brian 154, 158–159, 163–164
Binford, Lewis 48, 50–51, 71
Blackmore, Chelsea 123, 131
Blanchot, Maurice 294, 320
Blanton, Robert E. 115, 128, 131–132
Blee, Alisa 45, 71
Bloch, Ernst 294, 304–305, 317–320, 322
Bloch, Maurice 5, 13, 28, 100
Boaretto, Elisabetta 94, 104
Bodu, Pierre 45, 74
Boehme, Jacob 302, 320
Bolger, Diane 81, 98, 105
Bonani, Giorgio 87, 102
Bonavia, Duccio 155, 164
Boness, Doron 92, 98
Bonnassie, Pierre 191, 196
Botanic remains (see also Wood) 53–54, 59, 70
Bourget, Steve 144, 150, 152–153, 164, 170

Bourke, Stephen J. 77, 87, 94, 98
Bowers, Peter M. 208, 224
Boza, María Fernanda 158, 164
Braidwood, Robert J. 114, 132
Braswell, Geoffrey E. 129, 132
Braun, Eliot 83, 87, 98, 104
Bradley, Keith 187, 190, 196
Brami, Maxime N. 270, 287, 289
Breton, André 22, 27
Briceño, Jesús 159, 166, 169
Brighton, Stephen A. 208, 225
van den Brink, Edwin C.M. 83, 98
Britain 173–176, 192, 217, 271
Briz i Godino, Iván 45, 71, 73
Bronze Ages 10, 76–77, 79, 81–87, 94–97, 114, 310, 312–313
Brown, Dona 210, 225
Brown, Peter 174, 196
Buck-Morss, Susan 218, 225
Buonasera, Tammy 45, 71
Burial practices 16, 85, 91–93, 95, 126, 144, 148–150, 153–154, 159
Burton, Margie M. 78, 95–96, 99

Callinicos, Alex 180, 186, 196
Cameron, Dorothy O. 89, 99
Campagno, Marcelo 82, 99
Campbell, Kendall 158, 164
Canziani, José 158, 164
Capitalism (capital, capitalistic, see also Pre-capitalistic) 3, 6, 8–10, 12, 17–20, 23–26, 85, 108, 109–111, 184, 186, 201–228, 240, 242, 245, 280, 293, 296, 298–299, 305–306, 308, 316
Carandini, Andrea 187–188, 196
Carballo, David M. 128, 132–133
Carlson, Carolyn 213, 225
Carneiro, Robert 139, 165
Cartledge, Paul 187, 196
Castillo, Luis Jaime 141, 144, 146, 148–150, 154, 159, 164–166, 169
Castro, Pedro V. 262, 268
Cauvin, Jacques 314–316, 320
Chalcolithic period (Southern Levant) 16, 76–98, 312–313
Champion, Timothy 272, 289
Chamussy, Vincent 154, 165
Chapdelaine, Claude 159, 165
Chapman, Robert 83, 99

INDEX 327

Chernykh, Evgeny N.   129, 134
Chero, Luis   144, 149, 153, 163
Childe, Vere Gordon   4–5, 16, 19–20, 22, 24, 27, 79–80, 82, 88, 99, 113–114, 119, 132, 209, 270–292, 296, 300, 320
Chile (Chileans)   143, 274, 276
Chomsky, Noam   298, 318, 320
Cicero, Marcus Tullius   81, 99
Claridge, Amanda   176, 196
Clark, John E.   127, 132
Classical Antiquity (ancient/classical mode of production, see also Slavery)   17, 82, 172–200, 236, 243, 262, 307–308, 312
Coal (extraction, production)   43, 210–223
Coalwood (Cleveland Cliffs Iron Company)   220–223
Cocks, Catherine   210–211, 225
Cohen-Weinberger, Cohen   92, 104–105
Communism (Communist)   9, 48, 77, 111, 218–219, 299
Cooke, Richard G.   69, 71
Correal, Gonzalo   69, 71
Costambeys, Marios   192, 196
Costin, Cathy L.   88, 99
Cotler, Julio   138, 165
Courty, Marie-Anne   88, 104
Craftmanship (craft specialisation)   69, 87–89, 114, 120, 123, 128, 146, 149, 157–160, 271–272
Crabtree, John   137, 165
Croucher, Sarah K.   208, 225
Cruz, Jorge Ezra   69, 71
Cucina, Andrea   129, 136
Cuenca, Ricardo   138, 165
Cultural history   281, 300
Curtoni, Rafael Pedro   24, 33

Daniel, Glyn   270–271, 289
Darmangeat, Christophe   13, 28
Darwin, Charles (Darwinism)   12–13, 28, 77, 288
Demarest, Arthur A.   119, 132
Dessel, Jack P.   78, 83, 87, 95, 99, 101
Diakonnoff, Igor   84, 99
Dialectical materialism (see also Historical materialism, Marxism)   3–38, 81–82, 92, 180, 294
Diamond, Jared   112–113, 132

Díaz-Andreu, Margarita   275, 289–290
Digital Collection of Niagara Falls Guidebooks, USA   210, 211, 225
Dillehay, Thomas   50, 72, 154–155, 158, 165
Donnan, Christopher B.   144, 146, 148–151, 155, 159, 163–165
Dudden, Faye   211, 225
Duke, Philip   209–210, 225
Durand, Francisco   137, 165
Durkheim, Emile   283, 316, 320
Durocher, Matthew   222, 225

Eagleton, Terry   141, 165, 203, 208, 225
Earle, Timothy   10, 12, 28, 76, 82, 99
Economics (and see Political economy)   13–17, 19, 21–23, 39, 41, 47–49, 53, 68–69, 76–77, 80–85, 92–96, 111, 114, 116–121, 127–129, 137–143, 157, 161, 175
Engels, Friederich   4–5, 7, 10, 12–15, 28, 31, 76–77, 82, 99, 102, 109–110, 115–116, 130, 141, 167, 185, 203, 205–206, 219, 226, 234–235, 237–238, 241–243, 253, 259–261, 268, 273, 277, 280, 290, 294–295, 302, 306–308, 321
Ensor, Brian E.   118, 128, 132
Epstein, Claire   87, 99
Escoriza Mateu, Trinidad   150, 165
Estrada-Belli, Fernando   119, 122, 124–125, 132–133
Ethnography (anthropology)   12–13, 17, 24, 45, 47, 52, 55, 76, 79–80, 121–123, 138–140, 144–145, 148, 161, 201, 201–202, 242, 262, 270, 272–274, 281–282, 296–298, 303, 307–309, 315
Eudave, Itzel   53, 72
Europe   6, 9–10, 15, 23–24, 77, 107–110, 112–116, 121, 126, 129–131, 173–175, 183, 187, 206, 216–217, 241, 271, 274–275, 285, 297–300, 310, 314
Evans, Cliford   144, 149, 169
Evans, Susan T.   117, 133

Faith, Rosamond   192, 196
von Falkenhausen, Lotar   6, 8, 28
Faulkner, Neil   24, 28, 185–186, 196, 272, 278, 290
Faunas (animal husbandry)   41, 45, 53–56, 65, 67–68, 77, 80, 85, 87, 90, 96, 110, 112, 114, 116, 122, 129–130, 194, 314

Fawcett, Clare   30, 34, 99, 209, 226
Fentress, Elizabeth   188, 196
Fernández Buey, Francisco   242, 259
Ferreira Bicho, Nuno   45, 73
Feudalism   109, 181, 191–195, 243–245, 307–308
Field, Judith   45, 72
Finkelstein, Israel   79, 86, 99
Fisher, Mark   245, 259
Flannery, Kent V.   40, 72, 270–271, 290
Foote, Nelson   169, 225
Foster, John Bellamy   293, 316, 320
Foucault, Michel   302, 320
Fracchia, Adam   208, 225
France (French)   9, 14, 19, 76, 173, 216–217, 235, 273, 280, 297, 307
Franco, Régulo   144, 149, 152, 157, 165, 167
Fraresso, Carole   159, 165
Fried, Morton H.   79–80, 99
Friedman, Jonathan   12, 28
Fuentes, Miguel   145, 169, 271–273, 279–280, 288–290
Fukuyama Francis   293, 321
Fullagar, Richard   45, 71–72
Funari, Pedro Pablo A.   144, 146, 165, 228

Gaido, Daniel   85, 100
Gal, Zvi   90, 100
Gamboa, Jorge   157–158, 165–166
Gándara, Manuel   40, 54, 72, 279–281, 284, 287, 290
Gandulla, Bernardo   8, 21, 32, 88, 90, 100, 103, 105
García-Bárcena, Joaquín   51, 72
García-Piquer, Albert   83, 100
Gardner, Andrew   29, 176, 197
Garfinkel, Yosef   78, 87, 96, 100
Garnsey, Peter   187, 197
Gathercole, Peter   275, 290
Gayoso, Luis   158o–159, 166
Germany   24, 173–175, 216, 304
Getzov, Nimrod   87, 95, 104
Ghassulian culture (see Chalcolithic period)
Ghezzi, Iván   139–140, 166
Gibaja, Juan F.   45, 73
Giersz, Miłosz   154, 158, 166
Gilead, Isaac   77–79, 83, 86–87, 89, 91, 94, 98, 100, 101, 105–106
Gilman, Antonio   13, 28

Godelier, Maurice   5, 13, 28, 76–77, 81, 100
von Goethe, Johann W.   21, 28, 301
Golani, Amir   96, 100
Golden, Jonathan   77, 86, 88, 100, 105
Golding-Meir, Nissim   92, 100
González Arratia, Leticia   49, 72
Gophna, Ram   86, 99, 101
Goren, Yuval   88, 98, 101
Goring-Morris. Nigel   92, 101
Gošić, Milena   79, 101
Graeber, David   20, 296–300, 321
Gramsci, Antonio   11, 28, 298, 318
Greece (Greeks)   116, 173, 179–182, 183, 186, 243–244, 262, 310, 312
Greene, Kevin   177–178, 197
Green, Sally   24, 28
Greenberg, James B.   288, 290
Greenberg, Raphael   25–26, 29
Grigson, Caroline   87, 94, 95, 101
Guilaine, Jean   316, 321
Gumerman, George   159, 166
Gurvitch, Georges   246, 259

Haldon, John   192–193, 197
Hamilakis, Yannis   23, 25–26, 29, 209, 225
Hansen, Richard D.   15, 133
Harman, Chris   208, 223, 225
Harmon, Austin M.   130, 133
Harper, Kyle   191, 197
Harris, David R.   272, 290–292
Harvey, David   202–203, 225
Haslam, Michael   45, 72
Headrick, Annabeth   122, 133
Hedrick, Ulysses   213, 225
Hegel, George W.F.   14, 29, 82, 101, 179–180, 235, 242–243, 245–247, 251, 259, 306, 311, 314, 317–318, 321
Heller, Agnes   53, 72–73
Hendon, Julia A.   120, 133
Hernández de Lara, Odlanyer   116, 138
Hester, Thomas R.   69, 120, 133
Hindess, Barry   76, 101
Hingley, Richard   173–174, 197
Hirth, Kenneth G.   128, 132, 133
Hirst, Paul Q.   76, 101
Historical materialism (see also Dialectical Materialism, Marxism)   3, 7, 19–20, 41, 138, 141, 172, 180, 214, 272–273, 277–298, 282, 285, 293–323

INDEX

Hobsbawm, Eric   12, 29, 76, 80–81, 101, 141, 167, 197
Hocquenghem, Anne Marie   140, 166
Hodder, Ian   12, 29, 105, 303, 314–315, 321
Holder, Thomas   211, 225
Hölderlin, Friedrich   318–318, 321
Holloway, John   204, 219, 222–223, 226
Hopkins, Keith   174, 197
Horden, Peregrine   182, 197
Horwitz, Liora Kolska   25, 30, 95, 103
Houston, Stephen D.   121, 123–125, 127–129, 133
Howe, Aaron   221, 233
Hunt, Peter   189–191, 197
Hunter-gatherers (hunting)   15, 39–75, 119, 158, 222, 253, 297, 314

Iacono, Francesco   4, 29
Iannone, Gyles   117, 133
Idealism (see also Hegel)   11, 180, 235–236, 239, 245–246, 264
Iconography (art)   16, 22, 54, 77, 79, 85, 87, 89–92, 95, 116–118, 121, 122, 124–125, 128, 145–146, 148, 155
Ilan, David   91, 101
Ingold, Tim   48, 72–73
Inomata, Takeshi   118, 123–124, 127–128, 131, 133
Iron Age   112, 114, 187, 310–313
Iron (production)   112, 187, 220–221
Irving, Terry   24, 29, 275, 290, 300, 321
Isendahl, Christian   126, 134
Iserlis, Mark   92, 100
Israel (see also Levant, Palestine)   23, 25–26, 76–106, 312–313
Italia (Italian)   109, 173–174, 183, 187–188

Jacobsen, Geraldine E.   87, 102
Jacomet, Stefanie   174, 196
James, Edward   174, 197
Jaruf, Pablo   88, 100, 103
Jiménez Villalba, Félix   271, 290
Joffe, Alexander   78, 83, 91, 95, 101
Joshel, Sandra   173, 197
Jung, Reinhard   10, 29, 269

Kamminga, Johan   45, 67, 73
Kant, Immnauel   245–247, 259
Karlin, Claudine   45, 74

Katzman, David M.   211, 226
Keinan, Adi   25, 29
Keller, Angela H.   120, 134
Kelley, Donald   12, 29
Keeley, Lawrence H.   138, 166
Kersel, Morag   23, 30
Khalidi, Walid   25, 29
Kim, Minkoo   8, 30
Kimura, Brigitta   45, 73
King, Eleanor M.   119–121, 123, 134
Kingship and royal palaces   10, 81, 96, 107, 117–118, 124–128, 145, 159
Klaren, Peter   139, 166
Kletter, Raz   25, 30
Klejn, Leo S.   6–7, 30
Koeppel, Robert   91, 102
Kohl, Philip L.   10, 30, 209, 226
Kohler, Timothy A.   115–116, 129, 134
Kolata, Alan   154, 158, 165
Koons, Michele   146, 159, 168
Kossinna, Gustav   26, 30
Kourou, Nota   313, 321
Krader, Lawrence   111, 134
Krekovič, Eduard   7, 30
Kriiska, Aivar   7, 30
Kuijt, Ian   92, 101
Kuperman, Tali   96, 100

Labour (see Production)
Labriola, Antonio   13, 30
Ladiray, Daniel   90, 104
Landa, Carlos   116, 138
Landlords (see also Feudalism)   182, 186, 192
Lapi, Bárbara   150, 165
Larkin, Karin   210, 226
Latin America (see also Central and South America)   5, 19, 39, 131, 137–138, 270–292, 309
Lau, George   155, 166
Launaro, Alessandro   188, 197
Laurence, Ray   176, 197
Laws of motion (of capitalism)   17, 201–228
Lazrus, Paula K.   23, 30
Lee, Hyeong Woo   8, 30
Lekas, Padelis   179, 181, 184–185, 197
Lenin, Vladimir I.   8–9, 19, 21, 30, 77, 235, 259, 261, 268, 294, 302, 307, 311–313, 321
Leone, Mark P.   11, 30, 225, 227

Levant (see also Palestine) 77, 79, 82–83, 87–88, 92, 95, 97, 313
Lévi-Strauss, Claude 13, 30
Levy, Janet 96, 101
Levy, Thomas E. 77, 79–80, 91, 94–96, 98–99, 102
Lewis, Juan 190, 197
Lewis, Quentin 208, 224
Liangren, Zhang 7, 30
Lilley, Ian 23, 31
Liphschitz, Nili 87, 102
Liran, Roy 88, 104
Lithics (chert, flint, obsidian, stone tools) 45, 56, 89, 94, 119–122, 125, 127–128, 159
Lofgren, Orvar 210, 226
Lombard, Marlize 45, 73
López, M. Juana 150, 170
López Mazz, José 138, 166
Lorenzo, José Luis 272, 274–276, 286, 292
Love, John 181, 197
Lovell, Jaimie L. 86–87, 98–100, 102
Lozny, Ludomir R. 6, 31–33
Lukács, György 11, 31, 202, 226
Lull, Vicente 10, 31, 83, 102, 139, 141–143, 160, 167, 231, 233, 235, 259, 262, 268–269
Lumbreras, Luis G. 6, 19, 31, 146, 167, 272–282, 284, 290–291
Lund, Mellisa 171, 199
Lupu, Ronit 92, 104
Luxemburg, Rosa 111, 134, 261, 269

Mackintosh, Will 210, 226
MacNeish, Richard S. 51, 73
Maguiña, Adriana 157–159, 169
Maguire, Louis C. 81, 98, 105
Malainey, Mary 45, 73
Mallon, Alexis 91, 102
Mandel, Ernest 31, 81, 102, 321
Mann, Michael 175, 198
Manrique, Nelson 138, 167
Mansur-Franchomme, María Estela 45, 73
Manzanilla, Linda 271, 290–292, 323
Mao Tse Tung 202, 226
Marciniak, Arkadiusz 23, 31, 87, 102
Marder, Ofer 6, 31
Mariátegui, José C. 129, 134
Marreiros, Joan Manuel 45, 73
Marx, Karl 4–5, 9–14, 17–19, 25, 31, 41–43, 47, 73, 76–77, 80–82, 93, 102, 108, 110–112, 130, 134, 138, 141, 167, 174–175, 178–181, 183–185, 198, 201–206, 208, 218–219, 223–224, 226, 231–232, 234–247, 249–251, 253, 255–256, 258–261, 263, 266, 269, 273, 280, 283, 291, 294–295, 299, 302–308, 315–318, 321–322
Marxism (see Dialectical Materialism and Historical Materialism) 3–26, 39–41, 47, 67–68, 83, 108, 113, 119, 130, 138, 172–174, 177–178, 180–182, 190–191, 195, 237, 244, 263, 270, 272, 276, 286–287, 294, 303–304
Marzano, Annalisa 188, 198
Matos Moctezuma, Eduardo 275–276
Matsuda, Akira 11, 31, 34
Matthews, Christopher N. 208, 226
Mattingly, David 175–176, 195, 198
Mauss, Marcel 140, 167
Maya (state) 16, 107–136
Mazar, Amihai 87, 102
McAnany, Patricia A. 118, 122–123, 127–128, 133–135
McGuire, Randall 3–6, 9, 11–12, 15–17, 25, 27, 31–32, 76–77, 102, 172, 180, 198, 202–203, 206–207, 209–210, 226, 270, 272–274, 279–280, 287, 291
McNally, David 208, 214, 224, 226
McVey, Judy 24, 32
Meadows, John 87, 102
Mediterranean 10, 23, 86, 115, 182, 188, 303, 309–310, 313
Meek, Ronald L. 108, 135
Meillassoux, Claude 13, 32
Memory 40, 44–45, 108
Meskell, Lynn 303, 314, 321
Mészáros, István 316, 322
Metallurgy ('metal revolution') 80, 88–90, 110, 112, 114–116, 119, 129, 154, 158–160, 298
Mexico 15, 39–75, 107–136, 272–274, 276, 279
Michael-Matsas, Savas 14, 22, 32, 311, 314, 317–318, 322
Micó, Rafael 10, 31–32, 83, 102, 139, 167, 262, 268–269
Milevski, Ianir 21, 23, 32, 79, 81, 84–85, 87, 90–92, 94–96, 98, 103–105, 308, 312, 319, 322

Milisauskas, Sarunas   6, 32
Millaire, Jean-François   148, 152, 157, 164, 167
Mining (quarrying)   43, 50, 182, 186, 187–189, 220, 239–240
de Miroschedji, Pierre   94, 96, 104
Mizrachi, Yoni   26, 29
Mohanty, B.B.   217, 226
Moche (social group, state)   17, 137–171
Monaghan, John D.   122, 135
Money   25, 109, 111, 123, 204, 217, 297
Montaigne, Michel   107–108, 111, 130, 135
Montané, Julio   274–276
Montelius, Oscar G.   8, 32
Moore, Henrietta L.   12, 32
Moore, Jason W.   202, 227
Morfino, Vittorio   109, 135
Morgan, Lewis H.   5, 12–13, 32, 73, 109–112, 116, 130, 135, 276–277, 285, 296, 322
Moriconi, Marcelo   138, 169
Morris, Ian   112–113, 135
Mouritsen, Henrik   174, 198
Mrozowski, Stephen A.   308–309, 319, 323
Mujica, Elías   149, 154, 163–165, 166–167, 169
Murra, John   140, 167–168, 274

Namdar, Dvory   87, 95, 104
National Archives and Records Administration, USA   215, 227
Navarro Ortega, Ana   150, 165
Near East   15, 76–99, 271, 300, 302, 314
Nelson, Scott   217, 227
Nesbitt, Jason   158, 166
Neufeld, María Rosa   281, 291
Neuville, René   91, 102
Newman, Margaret   144, 153, 164
Nielsen, Axel   138, 168
Nisancioglu, Kerem   108, 131
Novack, George E.   5, 21, 32, 77, 84, 104, 131, 135

Oceania (Australia)   10, 19, 23, 217, 274, 300
O'Donovan, Maria   11, 32, 206, 226, 228
Okamura, Katuyuki   11, 31, 34
Olivé Negrete, Julio César   274, 277, 291
Olives (Olive oil)   86–87, 94–95, 183
Ollman, Bertell   201–205, 218–219, 224, 227, 319, 322
Ontology   54, 261–269
Owen, Linda R.   45, 73

Palerm, Ángel   5, 9, 32, 308, 322
Palestine   16, 23, 25–26, 76–106, 312–313
Papadopoulos, John   309–311, 322
Pardo, Cecilia   155, 166, 168, 170
Park, Thomas K.   288, 290
Parkins, Helen   177, 198
Pascucci, Margherita   319, 322
Pasieka, Paul   195, 198
Patel, Raj   218, 227
Patterson, Thomas C.   4–5, 9, 12–13, 33, 73, 201–202, 209, 227, 272, 274, 291, 308, 322
Paynter, Robert   209, 227
Paz, Yitzhak   84, 104
Peacock, David   176, 198
Peasants and farmers   181, 186–188, 190, 193–195, 213–218
Pelegrin, Jacques   45, 73
Pellini, José Roberto   33, 123
Pérez, José Antonio   276, 291
Pérez Elías, Antonio   275–276
Pérez Gollán, José Antonio   275–276
Pérez Martínez, Patricia   66, 70–71, 73–74, 207
Perrot, Jean   90, 104
Petersen, Lauren   173, 197
Peterson, Frederik A.   51, 73
Perry, Linda   45, 74
Peru   17, 107, 110–111, 130, 137–171, 272–274, 278
Pezzarossi, Guido   208, 227
Pitts, Martin   176, 198
Plekhanov, Georgi   5, 13–14, 33
Plunket, Patricia   128, 136
Polanyi, Karl   140, 168
Politics (political action)   7, 9–12, 14, 16–17, 20, 21, 25, 76, 79, 81, 83–84, 89, 113–114, 121, 128–131, 137–144, 161, 163, 172, 174–176, 178, 185–186, 191, 202, 206–207, 210, 217, 233, 236–237, 241, 244–245, 247, 250, 252, 256–257, 261–269, 272–273, 275–276, 287, 293–294, 297–300, 306–307, 311–312
Political economy   10–12, 111, 130, 179–180, 219, 241, 250, 305–306
Politis, Gustavo   24, 33, 56, 74
Porath, Yosef   86, 90, 104, 106
Porr, Marín   45, 73
Portugali, Juval   86, 101

Post-processualism 11–12, 25, 40, 206, 262, 272, 284
Pottery vessels 84, 87–88, 92, 94, 121, 125, 148, 152–154, 157–160, 176, 313
Pozorski, Shelia 139, 158, 168, 171
Pre-capitalistic (modes of production) 7, 10, 76, 109–110, 174, 177–178, 181–195, 236, 243–245, 307–308
Precious metals (gold, silver) 111, 119, 187
Prehistory 16, 19–20, 39–75, 76–106, 113–114, 174, 181, 186, 261–269, 271, 273, 275, 277, 280, 285, 300, 303, 307–312, 319
Preucel, Robert 12, 28
Production (forces of, means of, modes of) 4, 11, 13, 15–18, 20, 41–42, 47–48, 68, 76–77, 81, 97, 109, 111–113, 126, 141, 174, 180–183, 186–187, 191–192, 207, 240, 243–245, 247, 249, 276, 278, 280, 306–307, 313
Processualism 10, 12, 39, 272
Property 12, 16, 18, 44, 77, 81, 93, 97, 110–111, 130, 181, 206, 217, 240, 243–244, 248, 251, 258, 267, 299–300
Proulx, Donald 154, 158, 168
Prządka, Patrycja 158, 166
Psychology 183, 217, 242, 267–268
Public archaeology 11, 22, 162
Pucci, Guiseppe 188, 198
Purcell, Nicholas 182, 197

Quilter, Jeffrey 142, 146, 152, 159, 164, 168–169

Ramseyer, Denis 45, 74
Ranger, Terence 173, 197
Rathbone, Dominic 187–188, 198
Ravetz, Alison 270, 278, 291
Regev, Joana 94, 104
Religion (cult, temples) 21, 79, 81, 90–96, 113, 118–119, 123, 128, 137–140, 142, 145, 156, 159, 174, 187, 302, 314–315
Remy, María Isabel 139, 168
Renfrew, Colin 30, 129, 272, 291, 296, 303, 322–323
Rey, Estrella 273, 292
Riba, Naama 23, 33
Risch, Roberto 10, 19, 33, 97, 104, 167, 262, 267–269
Rivera, Diego 22, 27

Rivera Irán, Irais 53, 69, 71, 74
Roads and transportation 41, 96, 116, 175–177, 183, 212–213, 313
Robin, Cynthia 123, 131, 134–136
Rogers, Guy 181, 198
Rolland Calvo, Jorge 280, 291
Roller, Michael P. 208, 227
Roman empire 172–200
Rosales, Teresa 158, 170
Rosas, Marco 146, 148, 154–155, 159, 168
Rose, Peter 188, 198
Rosen, Steven A. 24, 33, 89, 91, 104
Rosengarden, Frank 11, 33
Rosenswig Robert M. 81, 104, 113, 133, 135–136
Roskams, Steve 194, 198, 207
Rostworowski, María 146, 168–169
Roth, Ulrike 188, 190, 198–199
Rots, Veerle 45, 74
Rousseau, Jacob 108, 246, 298–299
Roux, Valentine 88, 104
Rowan, Yorke M. 77, 86, 91, 98, 99–101, 104–105
Rowlands, Michael 12, 28
Rowley, Michael 12, 28
Rucabado, Julio 155, 165–166, 168, 170
Ruiz Rejón, Manuel 13, 33
Russell, Glenn 158, 169
Ryding, James N. 12, 33

Sabloff, Jeremy 272, 299
Sacristán, Manuel 242, 260
Sahlins, Marshall 48, 74, 76, 105
Saitta, Dean J. 12, 33, 210, 227
Salvioli, Giuseppe 85, 105
San Francisco, Alexander 143, 169
Sanoja, Mario 40, 74, 273, 275–276, 279
Santamaría, Diana 51, 72
Saturno, William A. 124, 135
Saunders, Tom 193–194, 198–199
Saunders, Nicholas J. 129, 135
de Saussure, Ferdinand 13, 33
Sayer, Derek 202–203, 227
Scheidel, Walter 190, 199
Schmidt, Peter R. 209, 227, 308–309, 319, 323
Schortman, Edward 11, 34
Seaton, Peta 91, 105
Secondary products revolution 16, 50, 80, 87, 94

Semenov, Sergei Aristarkhovich   44–45, 74
Sepúlveda, Jairo   143, 169
Service, Elman   48, 74, 76, 79–80, 105
Sève, Lucien   13, 33
Shafer, Harry J.   120, 131, 133
Shalem, Dina   88, 90, 92, 100, 105
Shalev, Omer   97, 105
Shalev, Sariel   88–89, 105
Shanks, Michael   12, 25, 33
Sharer, Robert J.   117, 120, 133–135
Shelach (-Lavi)   3, 37
Sherratt, Andrew G.   80, 87, 105
Shimada, Izumi   146, 149, 151, 153, 157–159, 162, 169
Shiva, Vandana   217, 227
Sijpesteijn, Petra   191, 199
Silver, Morris   85, 105
Sinclair, M. Thea   210, 228
Sinensky, R.J.   303, 323
Slavery   7, 110, 174, 177–178, 182–193, 195, 236
Smith, Adam   111, 130, 136, 180
Smith, Michael E.   128, 136, 270, 291
Smithline, Howard   90, 110
Snodgrass, Anthony   176, 199
Social classes (consciousness, contradictions, exploitation, labour)   6, 8, 10–11, 13, 18–20, 22, 25–26, 82–83, 94, 97, 113, 115–116, 118, 120, 123, 129–130, 145, 153, 160–161, 180, 182, 187–188, 192, 194, 202, 204, 206–212, 214, 219, 224, 245, 258, 261, 267, 272, 278, 280–281, 286, 295, 300, 302, 308, 310, 317
Socialism   9, 21, 24, 26, 110, 195, 222, 235, 247–248, 273, 293, 299–300, 307
Solís, Juan   138, 169
Soto, Marcelo   272–273, 279–280, 290
Soviet Union   6–9, 19, 24, 115, 241, 273, 293, 300, 314
Stark, Barbara L.   129, 132, 136
Spriggs, Mattew   3, 5, 10, 28, 34
Stalin, Joseph (Stalinism)   6–7, 9, 19, 24, 34, 76–77, 294, 300, 303–304, 306
(The) State   6–7, 10–11, 16, 19, 24, 26, 80–83, 110–111, 113–115, 117–118, 120–122, 124, 126–128, 139, 146, 159–160, 173–177, 180–183, 185, 191–194, 217, 243, 246–247, 251, 261–262, 264, 268, 281, 298–300, 302

Stanish, Charles   146, 169
de Ste. Croix, Geoffrey   17, 34, 179–182, 192, 194, 199
Stothert, Karen   69, 74
Strong, William   144, 149, 169
Su Bingqi   7, 27, 33–34
Surplus   83, 87, 97, 111, 113–116, 177, 180, 182–185, 190–195, 204, 208, 212, 219, 243, 258, 267, 313
Suret-Canale, Jean   93, 105
Suwandi, Intan   293, 316, 320
Svoray, Tal   86, 105
Swenson, Edward   146, 154, 158–159, 165, 170

Tabío, Ernesto E.   19, 34, 273, 292
Tantaleán, Henry   74, 160, 170, 207, 270, 272–274, 283, 287, 291–292
Tate, Carolyn E.   122, 136
Taube, Karl A.   121, 133
Terrenato, Nicola   188, 196
Testart, Alain   48, 74, 315–316, 323
Textiles   43, 94, 127, 155, 158–159, 187–188
Thomas, Nicholas   5, 34
Tiesler, Vera   129, 136
Tilley, Christopher   12, 25, 33–34
Toh, Yu-ho   8, 34
de la Torre, Juan Carlos   150, 170
Topic, John   140, 170
Topic. Teresa   140, 170
Toyne, Marla   144, 153, 170–171
Traceology (use wear analysis)   44–45
Trade and exchange   41–42, 44, 77, 84–85, 88, 93–94, 96, 107, 111–112, 116, 118, 120–121, 127–129, 176–177, 193, 204, 217, 255–256, 261, 265, 313
Traxler, Loa P.   117, 120, 133–136
Trigger, Bruce   4–6, 8–10, 12, 22–23, 25–26, 34, 113–115, 130, 136, 176, 199, 209, 228, 270–272, 277–278, 280, 283, 285–287, 292, 296, 300, 323
Trotsky, Leon D.   6, 9, 14, 17, 20–21, 34, 130, 136, 172, 192, 199, 294, 304–305, 318, 323
Tufinio, Moisés   150, 157, 170–171
Tureuna, Rosa   271–272, 290

Uceda, Ricardo   144, 150–151, 153, 163–166, 169–171
Urban, Patricia A.   11, 34

Urbanisation (Urban revolution) 4, 16, 79–80, 82, 85–86, 88, 94, 96, 107–136, 159, 177, 181, 186, 189, 244, 270, 274, 277, 280, 285, 297, 300, 313
Urry, John 210, 228
Urunuela, Gabriela 128, 136.S
Ussishkin, David 24, 34, 91, 105

Value (theory of) 15, 41–44, 84, 111, 204, 208, 212, 216, 219, 240, 265, 267
Vargas-Arenas, Iraida 40, 74, 273, 275–276, 279
Vázquez, Víctor 158, 170
Vega, María del Carmen 144, 171
Veloz Maggiolo, Marcio 40, 74
Verano, John 144, 148–150, 152, 170–171
Verhoeven, Marc 80, 105
Vila-Mitjà, Assumpió 83, 100
Villages 16, 26, 85, 92–94, 96, 113, 117–118, 159, 192–193, 313
Violence 10, 17, 83, 97, 137–171, 185, 262, 267–268, 298, 315

Wacher, John 174, 199
Wailes, Bernard 271, 291–292
Walker, Phillip 138, 171
Walker, Susan 181, 199
Walker, William 138, 168
Wallace, Rob 293, 323
Walter McKain Mills, Robin 213, 225
Wang, Tao 6–9, 34
Waterstone, Marv 298, 318, 320
Weber, Max 175, 181, 261, 269, 316
Weedman, Kathryn J. 45, 74
Wengrow, David 20, 296–300, 321, 323
Weingarten, Debbie 217, 228

Weiss, Lindsay 208, 225
Whittow, Mark 191, 199
Wickham, Chris 175, 183, 187, 191–193, 199
Wikander, Örjan 178, 199
Whittaker, Charles Richard 177, 199
Willey, Gordon R. 114, 132, 154, 158, 171
Williams, David 136, 176, 198
Williamson, Bonny S. 45, 74
Wilson, Andrew 187, 199
Wilson, David 139, 154–155, 158, 171
Winckelmann, Johann Joachim 16, 35, 116
Winter-Livneh, Rona 86, 105–106
Withey, Lynne 210, 228
Wittfogel, Karl 77, 106
Wolf, Eric 4, 35, 81, 106, 113
Wood (woodland) 43, 55, 66–67, 150, 153, 189, 194, 221
Wood, Ellen 180–181, 186–187, 199–200, 203, 228
Wood, Margaret C. 210, 228
Woodburn, James 48, 75
Workers (see also Craftmanship) 6, 8, 21, 25–26, 42, 88, 114, 128, 210–212, 220–222, 239, 242, 294
Wurst, LouAnn 11, 25, 32, 203, 205–210, 212, 214, 224, 226, 228
Wyatt, Andrew R. 120, 135–136

Yamada, Shoh 45, 75
Yannai, Eli 90, 96, 100, 106
Yalouri, Eleana 25–26, 29
Yekutieli, Yuval 23, 35, 95, 106

Zarankin, Andrés 144, 146, 165, 228
Zohary, Daniel 87, 95, 106
Zasulich, Vera 5, 31, 77, 104, 303–305, 322.

www.ingramcontent.com/pod-product-compliance
Lightning Source LLC
Chambersburg PA
CBHW070610030426
42337CB00020B/3733